YOUR PERSONAL
HOROSCOPE
2017

JOSEPH POLANSKY

YOUR PERSONAL HOROSCOPE 2017

Month-by-month
forecast for every sign

Thorsons

The author is grateful to the people of STAR ★ DATA, who truly fathered this book and without whom it could not have been written.

Contents

Introduction

Welcome to the fascinating and intricate world of astrology!

For thousands of years the movements of the planets and other heavenly bodies have intrigued the best minds of every generation. Life holds no greater challenge or joy than this: knowledge of ourselves and the universe we live in. Astrology is one of the keys to this knowledge.

Your Personal Horoscope 2017 gives you the fruits of astrological wisdom. In addition to general guidance on your character and the basic trends of your life, it shows you how to take advantage of planetary influences so you can make the most of the year ahead.

The section on each sign includes a Personality Profile, a look at general trends for 2017, and in-depth month-by-month forecasts. The Glossary (*page 5*) explains some of the astrological terms you may be unfamiliar with.

One of the many helpful features of this book is the 'Best' and 'Most Stressful' days listed at the beginning of each monthly forecast. Read these sections to learn which days in each month will be good overall, good for money, and good for love. Mark them on your calendar – these will be your best days. Similarly, make a note of the days that will be most stressful for you. It is best to avoid booking important meetings or taking major decisions on these days, as well as on those days when important planets in your horoscope are retrograde (moving backwards through the zodiac).

The Major Trends section for your sign lists those days when your vitality is strong or weak, or when relationships with your co-workers or loved ones may need a bit more effort on your part. If you are going through a difficult time, take a look at the colour, metal, gem and scent listed in the 'At a Glance' section of your Personality Profile. Wearing a piece of jewellery that contains your metal and/or gem will strengthen your vitality, just as wearing clothes or decorating your room or office in the colour ruled by your sign, drinking teas made from the herbs ruled by your sign or wearing the scents associated with your sign will sustain you.

Another important virtue of this book is that it will help you to know not only yourself but those around you: your friends, co-workers, partners and/or children. Reading the Personality Profile and forecasts for their signs will provide you with an insight into their behaviour that you won't get anywhere else. You will know when to be more tolerant of them and when they are liable to be difficult or irritable.

In this edition we have included foot reflexology charts as part of the health section. So many health problems could perhaps be avoided or alleviated if we understood which organs were most vulnerable and what we could do to protect them. Though there are many natural and drug-free ways to strengthen vulnerable organs, these charts show a valid way to proceed. The vulnerable organs for the year ahead are clearly marked in the charts. It's very good to massage the whole foot on a regular basis, as the feet contain reflexes to the entire body. Try to pay special attention to the specific areas marked in the charts. If this is done diligently, health problems can be avoided. And even if they can't be completely avoided, their impact can be softened considerably.

I consider you – the reader – my personal client. By studying your Solar Horoscope I gain an awareness of what is going on in your life – what you are feeling and striving for and the challenges you face. I then do my best to address these concerns. Consider this book the next best thing to having your own personal astrologer!

It is my sincere hope that *Your Personal Horoscope 2017* will enhance the quality of your life, make things easier, illuminate the way forward, banish obscurities and make you more aware of your personal connection to the universe. Understood properly and used wisely, astrology is a great guide to knowing yourself, the people around you and the events in your life – but remember that what you do with these insights – the final result – is up to you.

A Note on the 'New Zodiac'

Recently an article was published that postulated two things: the discovery of a new constellation – Ophiuchus – making a thirteenth constellation in the heavens and thus a thirteenth sign, and the statement that because the Earth has shifted relative to the constellations in the past few thousand years, all the signs have shifted backwards by one sign. This has caused much consternation, and I have received a stream of letters, emails and phone calls from people saying things like: 'I don't want to be a Taurus, I'm happy being a Gemini', 'What's my real sign?' or 'Now that I finally understand myself, I'm not who I think I am!'

All of this is 'much ado about nothing'. The article has some partial truth to it. Yes, in two thousand years the planets have shifted relative to the constellations in the heavens. This is old news. We know this and Hindu astrologers take this into account when casting charts. This shift doesn't affect Western astrologers in North America and Europe. We use what is called a 'tropical' zodiac. This zodiac has nothing to do with the constellations in the heavens. They have the same names, but that's about it. The tropical zodiac is based on the Earth's revolution around the Sun. Imagine the circle that this orbit makes, then divide this circle by twelve and you have our zodiac. The Spring Equinox is always 0 degrees Aries, and the Autumn Equinox is always 0 degrees Libra (180 degrees). At one time a few thousand years ago, these tropical signs coincided with the actual constellations; they were pretty much interchangeable, and it didn't matter what zodiac you used. But in the course of thousands of years the planets have shifted relative to these constellations. Here in the West it doesn't affect our practice one iota. You are still the sign you always were.

In North America and Europe there is a clear distinction between an astrological sign and a constellation in the heavens. This issue is more of a problem for Hindu astrologers. Their zodiac is based on the actual constellations – this is called the 'sidereal' zodiac. And Hindu astrologers have been accounting for this shift all the time. They keep close tabs on it. In two thousand years there is a shift of 23 degrees, and they subtract this from the Western calculations. So in their system many a Gemini would be a Taurus and this is true for all the signs. This is nothing new – it is all known and accounted for, so there is no bombshell here.

The so-called thirteenth constellation, Ophiuchus, is also not a problem for the Western astrologer. As we mentioned, our zodiac has nothing to do with the constellations. It could be more of a problem for the Hindus, but my feeling is that it's not a problem for them either. What these astronomers are calling a new constellation was probably considered a part of one of the existing constellations. I don't know this as a fact, but I presume it is so intuitively. I'm sure we will soon be getting articles by Hindu astrologers explaining this.

Glossary of Astrological Terms

Ascendant

We experience day and night because the Earth rotates on its axis once every 24 hours. It is because of this rotation that the Sun, Moon and planets seem to rise and set. The zodiac is a fixed belt (imaginary, but very real in spiritual terms) around the Earth. As the Earth rotates, the different signs of the zodiac seem to the observer to rise on the horizon. During a 24-hour period every sign of the zodiac will pass this horizon point at some time or another. The sign that is at the horizon point at any given time is called the Ascendant, or rising sign. The Ascendant is the sign denoting a person's self-image, body and self-concept – the personal ego, as opposed to the spiritual ego indicated by a person's Sun sign.

Aspects

Aspects are the angular relationships between planets, the way in which one planet stimulates or influences another. If a planet makes a harmonious aspect (connection) to another, it tends to stimulate that planet in a positive and helpful way. If, however, it makes a stressful aspect to another planet, this disrupts that planet's normal influence.

Astrological Qualities

There are three astrological qualities: *cardinal, fixed* and *mutable*. Each of the 12 signs of the zodiac falls into one of these three categories.

Cardinal Signs
Aries, Cancer, Libra and Capricorn
The cardinal quality is the active, initiating principle. Those born under these four signs are good at starting new projects.

Fixed Signs
Taurus, Leo, Scorpio and Aquarius
Fixed qualities include stability, persistence, endurance and perfectionism. People born under these four signs are good at seeing things through.

Mutable Signs
Gemini, Virgo, Sagittarius and Pisces
Mutable qualities are adaptability, changeability and balance. Those born under these four signs are creative, if not always practical.

Direct Motion

When the planets move forward through the zodiac – as they normally do – they are said to be going 'direct'.

Grand Square

A Grand Square differs from a normal Square (usually two planets separated by 90 degrees) in that four or more planets are involved. When you look at the pattern in a chart you will see a whole and complete square. This, though stressful, usually denotes a new manifestation in the life. There is much work and balancing involved in the manifestation.

Grand Trine

A Grand Trine differs from a normal Trine (where two planets are 120 degrees apart) in that three or more planets are involved. When you look at this pattern in a chart, it takes the form of a complete triangle – a Grand Trine. Usually (but not always) it occurs in one of the four elements: Fire, Earth, Air or Water. Thus the particular element in which it occurs will be highlighted. A Grand Trine in Water is not the same as a Grand Trine in Air or Fire, etc. This is a very fortunate and happy aspect, and quite rare.

Houses

There are 12 signs of the zodiac and 12 houses of experience. The 12 signs are personality types and ways in which a given planet expresses itself; the 12 houses show 'where' in your life this expression takes place. Each house has a different area of interest. A house can become potent and important – a house of power – in different ways: if it contains the Sun, the Moon or the 'ruler' of your chart; if it contains more than one planet; or if the ruler of that house is receiving unusual stimulation from other planets.

1st House
Personal Image and Sensual Delights

2nd House
Money/Finance

3rd House
Communication and Intellectual Interests

4th House
Home and Family

5th House
Children, Fun, Games, Creativity, Speculations and Love Affairs

6th House
Health and Work

7th House
Love, Marriage and Social Activities

8th House
Transformation and Regeneration

9th House
Religion, Foreign Travel, Higher Education and Philosophy

10th House
Career

11th House
Friends, Group Activities and Fondest Wishes

12th House
Spirituality

Karma

Karma is the law of cause and effect which governs all phenomena. We are all where we find ourselves because of karma – because of actions we have performed in the past. The universe is such a balanced instrument that any act immediately sets corrective forces into motion – karma.

Long-term Planets

The planets that take a long time to move through a sign show the long-term trends in a given area of life. They are important for forecasting the prolonged view of things. Because these planets stay in one sign for so long, there are periods in the year when the faster-moving (short-term) planets will join them, further activating and enhancing the importance of a given house.

Jupiter
stays in a sign for about 1 year

Saturn
2½ years

Uranus
7 years

Neptune
14 years

Pluto
15 to 30 years

Lunar

Relating to the Moon. See also 'Phases of the Moon', below.

Natal

Literally means 'birth'. In astrology this term is used to distinguish between planetary positions that occurred at the time of a person's birth (natal) and those that are current (transiting). For example, Natal Sun refers to where the Sun was when you were born; transiting Sun refers to where the Sun's position is currently at any given moment – which usually doesn't coincide with your birth, or Natal, Sun.

Out of Bounds

The planets move through the zodiac at various angles relative to the celestial equator (if you were to draw an imaginary extension of the Earth's equator out into the universe, you would have an illustration of this celestial equator). The Sun – being the most dominant and powerful influence in the Solar system – is the measure astrologers use as a standard. The Sun never goes more than approximately 23 degrees north or south of the celestial equator. At the winter solstice the Sun reaches its maximum southern angle of orbit (declination); at the summer solstice it reaches its maximum northern angle. Any time a planet exceeds this Solar boundary – and occasionally planets do – it is said to be 'out of bounds'. This means that the planet exceeds or tres-passes into strange territory – beyond the limits allowed by the Sun, the ruler of the Solar system. The planet in this condition becomes more emphasized and exceeds its authority, becoming an important influence in the forecast.

Phases of the Moon

After the full Moon, the Moon seems to shrink in size (as perceived from the Earth), gradually growing smaller until it is virtually invisible to the naked eye – at the time of the next new Moon. This is called the waning Moon phase, or the waning Moon.

After the new Moon, the Moon gradually gets bigger in size (as perceived from the Earth) until it reaches its maximum size at the time of the full Moon. This period is called the waxing Moon phase, or waxing Moon.

Retrogrades

The planets move around the Sun at different speeds. Mercury and Venus move much faster than the Earth, while Mars, Jupiter, Saturn, Uranus, Neptune and Pluto move more slowly. Thus there are times when, relative to the Earth, the planets appear to be going backwards. In reality they are always going forward, but relative to our vantage point on Earth they seem to go backwards through the zodiac for a period of time. This is called 'retrograde' motion and tends to weaken the normal influence of a given planet.

Short-term Planets

The fast-moving planets move so quickly through a sign that their effects are generally of a short-term nature. They reflect the immediate, day-to-day trends in a horoscope.

Moon
stays in a sign for only 2½ days

Mercury
20 to 30 days

Sun
30 days

Venus
approximately 1 month

Mars
approximately 2 months

T-square

A T-square differs from a Grand Square (see above) in that it is not a complete square. If you look at the pattern in a chart it appears as 'half a complete square', resembling the T-square tools used by architects and designers. If you cut a complete square in half, diagonally, you have a T-square. Many astrologers consider this more stressful than a Grand Square, as it creates tension that is difficult to resolve. T-squares bring learning experiences.

Transits

This term refers to the movements or motions of the planets at any given time. Astrologers use the word 'transit' to make the distinction between a birth, or Natal, planet (see 'Natal', above) and the planet's current movement in the heavens. For example, if at your birth Saturn was in the sign of Cancer in your 8th house, but is now moving through your 3rd house, it is said to be 'transiting' your 3rd house. Transits are one of the main tools with which astrologers forecast trends.

Aries

THE RAM

Birthdays from
21st March to
20th April

Personality Profile

ARIES AT A GLANCE

Element – Fire

Ruling Planet – Mars
   Career Planet – Saturn
   Love Planet – Venus
   Money Planet – Venus
   Planet of Fun, Entertainment, Creativity and Speculations – Sun
   Planet of Health and Work – Mercury
   Planet of Home and Family Life – Moon
   Planet of Spirituality – Neptune
   Planet of Travel, Education, Religion and Philosophy – Jupiter

Colours – carmine, red, scarlet

Colours that promote love, romance and social harmony – green, jade green

Colour that promotes earning power – green

Gem – amethyst

Metals – iron, steel

Scent – honeysuckle

Quality – cardinal (= activity)

Quality most needed for balance – caution

Strongest virtues – abundant physical energy, courage, honesty, independence, self-reliance

Deepest need – action

Characteristics to avoid – haste, impetuousness, over-aggression, rashness

Signs of greatest overall compatibility – Leo, Sagittarius

Signs of greatest overall incompatibility – Cancer, Libra, Capricorn

Sign most helpful to career – Capricorn

Sign most helpful for emotional support – Cancer

Sign most helpful financially – Taurus

Sign best for marriage and/or partnerships – Libra

Sign most helpful for creative projects – Leo

Best Sign to have fun with – Leo

Signs most helpful in spiritual matters – Sagittarius, Pisces

Best day of the week – Tuesday

Understanding an Aries

Aries is the activist *par excellence* of the zodiac. The Aries need for action is almost an addiction, and those who do not really understand the Aries personality would probably use this hard word to describe it. In reality 'action' is the essence of the Aries psychology – the more direct, blunt and to-the-point the action, the better. When you think about it, this is the ideal psychological makeup for the warrior, the pioneer, the athlete or the manager.

Aries likes to get things done, and in their passion and zeal often lose sight of the consequences for themselves and others. Yes, they often try to be diplomatic and tactful, but it is hard for them. When they do so they feel that they are being dishonest and phoney. It is hard for them even to understand the mindset of the diplomat, the consensus builder, the front office executive. These people are involved in endless meetings, discussions, talks and negotiations – all of which seem a great waste of time when there is so much work to be done, so many real achievements to be gained. An Aries can understand, once it is explained, that talk and negotiations – the social graces – lead ultimately to better, more effective actions. The interesting thing is that an Aries is rarely malicious or spiteful – even when waging war. Aries people fight without hate for their opponents. To them it is all good-natured fun, a grand adventure, a game.

When confronted with a problem many people will say, 'Well, let's think about it, let's analyse the situation.' But not an Aries. An Aries will think, 'Something must be done. Let's get on with it.' Of course neither response is the total answer. Sometimes action is called for, sometimes cool thought. But an Aries tends to err on the side of action.

Action and thought are radically different principles. Physical activity is the use of brute force. Thinking and deliberating require one not to use force – to be still. It is not good for the athlete to be deliberating the next move; this will only slow down his or her reaction time. The athlete must act instinctively and instantly. This is how Aries people tend to behave in life. They are quick, instinctive decision-makers and their decisions tend to be translated into action almost immediately. When their intuition is sharp and well tuned, their actions are powerful and successful. When their intuition is off, their actions can be disastrous.

Do not think this will scare an Aries. Just as a good warrior knows that in the course of combat he or she might acquire a few wounds, so too does an Aries realize – somewhere deep down – that in the course of being true to yourself you might get embroiled in a disaster or two. It is all part of the game. An Aries feels strong enough to weather any storm.

There are many Aries people who are intellectual. They make powerful and creative thinkers. But even in this realm they tend to be pioneers – outspoken and blunt. These types of Aries tend to elevate (or sublimate) their desire for physical combat in favour of intellectual, mental combat. And they are indeed powerful.

In general, Aries people have a faith in themselves that others could learn from. This basic, rock-solid faith carries them through the most tumultuous situations of life. Their courage and self-confidence make them natural leaders. Their leadership is more by way of example than by actually controlling others.

Finance

Aries people often excel as builders or estate agents. Money in and of itself is not as important as are other things – action, adventure, sport, etc. They are motivated by the need to support and be well-thought-of by their partners. Money as a way of attaining pleasure is another important motivation. Aries function best in their own businesses or as managers of their own departments within a large business or corporation. The fewer orders they have to take from higher up, the better. They also function better out in the field rather than behind a desk.

Aries people are hard workers with a lot of endurance; they can earn large sums of money due to the strength of their sheer physical energy.

Venus is their money planet, which means that Aries need to develop more of the social graces in order to realize their full earning potential. Just getting the job done – which is what an Aries excels at – is not enough to create financial success. The co-operation of others needs to be attained. Customers, clients and co-workers need to be made to feel comfortable; many people need to be treated properly in order for success to happen. When Aries people develop these abilities – or hire someone to do this for them – their financial potential is unlimited.

Career and Public Image

One would think that a pioneering type would want to break with the social and political conventions of society. But this is not so with the Aries-born. They are pioneers within conventional limits, in the sense that they like to start their own businesses within an established industry.

Capricorn is on the 10th house of career cusp of Aries' solar horoscope. Saturn is the planet that rules their life's work and professional aspirations. This tells us some interesting things about the Aries character. First off, it shows that, in order for Aries people to reach their full career potential, they need to develop some qualities that are a bit alien to their basic nature: they need to become better administrators and organizers; they need to be able to handle details better and to take a long-range view of their projects and their careers in general. No one can beat an Aries when it comes to achieving short-range objectives, but a career is long term, built over time. You cannot take a 'quickie' approach to it.

Some Aries people find it difficult to stick with a project until the end. Since they get bored quickly and are in constant pursuit of new adventures, they prefer to pass an old project or task on to somebody else in order to start something new. Those Aries who learn how to put off the search for something new until the old is completed will achieve great success in their careers and professional lives.

In general, Aries people like society to judge them on their own merits, on their real and actual achievements. A reputation acquired by 'hype' feels false to them.

Love and Relationships

In marriage and partnerships Aries like those who are more passive, gentle, tactful and diplomatic – people who have the social grace and skills they sometimes lack. Our partners always represent a hidden part of ourselves – a self that we cannot express personally.

An Aries tends to go after what he or she likes aggressively. The tendency is to jump into relationships and marriages. This is especially true if Venus is in Aries as well as the Sun. If an Aries likes you, he or she will have a hard time taking no for an answer; many attempts will be made to sweep you off your feet.

Though Aries can be exasperating in relationships – especially if they are not understood by their partners – they are never consciously or wilfully cruel or malicious. It is just that they are so independent and sure of themselves that they find it almost impossible to see somebody else's viewpoint or position. This is why an Aries needs as a partner someone with lots of social graces.

On the plus side, an Aries is honest, someone you can lean on, someone with whom you will always know where you stand. What he or she lacks in diplomacy is made up for in integrity.

Home and Domestic Life

An Aries is of course the ruler at home – the Boss. The male will tend to delegate domestic matters to the female. The female Aries will want to rule the roost. Both tend to be handy round the house. Both like large families and both believe in the sanctity and importance of the family. An Aries is a good family person, although he or she does not especially like being at home a lot, preferring instead to be roaming about.

Considering that they are by nature so combative and wilful, Aries people can be surprisingly soft, gentle and even vulnerable with their children and partners. The sign of Cancer, ruled by the Moon, is on the cusp of their solar 4th house of home and family. When the Moon is well aspected – under favourable influences – in the birth chart, an Aries will be tender towards the family and will want a family life that is nurturing and supportive. Aries likes to come home after a hard day on the battlefield of life to the understanding arms of their partner and the unconditional love and support of their family. An Aries feels that there is enough 'war' out in the world – and he or she enjoys participating in that. But when Aries comes home, comfort and nurturing are what's needed.

Horoscope for 2017

Major Trends

Electric Uranus has been in your sign for many years now, and he will still be there in the year ahead. In the past six or so years your life – the conditions and circumstances of your life – has been radically altered. The old saying, 'life can change at any moment' is certainly true for you. You've been living it. The cosmos has been setting you free from old restrictive conditions. And, sometimes it had to do it in dramatic, even explosive, ways. Your body and image have been a continuous work-in-progress. Every time you think you have it 'just right' a new idea or look comes to you and you start to change again. The good part of all this is a sense of personal freedom that many of you have never known. It's a heady feeling. By now most of you have learned the lessons of Uranus, but there's still another year to go. You should handle it with ease.

Jupiter moved into your 7th house of love in September 2016. He will be there for most of the year ahead – until October 10. This is one of the main headlines of the year ahead. It's a strong and happy social year. Many of you are ready to 'settle down' these days – especially after so many years of being footloose and fancy free. Serious relationships, both romantic and in business, are happening this year. More on this later on.

Jupiter will move into your 8th house on October 11. This will bring prosperity to your spouse, partner or current love. Often it indicates inheritance, though no one needs necessarily to die – you can be named in someone's will or be appointed to some administrative position in an estate. Also it favours projects involving personal transformation, weight loss and detox regimes.

Saturn spends most of the year in harmonious alignment with you. This is a good health signal. But towards the end of the year he moves into Capricorn and into a stressful aspect (this begins on December 21). Health will need more attention from that point on, well into 2018 and 2019. Saturn in your 9th house most of the year shows a happy and expanding career. Most likely there is more career-related travel. But when Saturn moves into your 10th house (on December 21) career becomes more serious. You have to perform. Bosses are strict and demanding.

Pluto has been in your 10th house for many, many years and will be there in the year ahead. As we have written in previous years, a cosmic detox is happening in your career. This involves your whole approach and strategy and the people involved in it. Many are having 'near-death' kinds of experiences or surgery. Your industry is changing. The rules of the game are changing.

Your areas of greatest interest this year are the body and image (a long-term interest); love, romance and social activities (until October 10); personal transformation, reinvention, sex and occult studies (from October 11 onwards); religion, higher education and travel (until December 21); career (another long-term focus); and spirituality (also a long-term focus).

Your areas of greatest fulfilment this year are love, romance and social activities (until October 10); personal transformation and reinvention, sex and occult studies (from October 11 onwards); health and work (until April 29); children, fun and creativity (from April 29 onwards).

Health

(Please note that this is an astrological perspective on health and not a medical one. In days of yore there was no difference, both of these perspectives were identical. But now there could be quite a difference. For a medical perspective, please consult your doctor or health practitioner.)

Health needs more attention this year. Three long-term planets are in stressful alignment with you for most of the year. Jupiter moves away from this stressful aspect on October 11, but Saturn will come into stressful alignment on December 21.

The problem this year is that your 6th house of health is empty for the most part; only short-term planets will move through there. Your tendency would thus be to ignore health issues – and if not to totally ignore them, not to give health the attention that is needed. You will have to force yourself to pay more attention here.

Our regular readers know that there is much that can be done to enhance the health and prevent problems from developing (or getting worse). Give more attention to the following vulnerable areas (the reflex points are shown on the chart below):

- The heart. The heart has become important in recent years, and will become even more important after December 21 when Saturn moves into a stressful alignment with you. Spiritual healers seem to agree that heart problems are caused by undue worry and anxiety. So more faith and confidence is needed.
- The lungs, arms, shoulders and respiratory system. These are always important for you, Aries. Mercury, the ruler of these areas is your health planet. Regular arm and shoulder massage is a powerful therapy. Give the wrists and elbows more support when exercising.
- The head, face and scalp. These too are always important for you. Incorporate regular scalp and face massage into your health regime. This will not only strengthen these immediate areas but the entire body as well. Reflexes in the scalp and face affect every

Important foot reflexology points for the year ahead

Try to massage all of the foot on a regular basis – the top of the foot as well as the bottom – but pay extra attention to the points highlighted on the chart. When you massage, be aware of 'sore spots' as these need special attention. It's also a good idea to massage the ankles and below them.

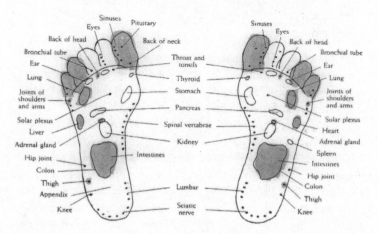

organ and system of the body. Craniosacral therapy is, in general, a good therapy for Aries – the plates in the skull are moveable and need to be kept in right alignment.

- The adrenals are another important area for you. The important thing here is to avoid anger and fear, the two emotions that stress the adrenals.
- The musculature. For you, Aries, more than most, good health means physical fitness (and not just 'no symptoms'). A weak muscle can knock the spine and skeleton out of alignment and this will cause all kinds of other problems. So regular physical exercise is important for you. A health tonic. A day at the gym will, in many cases, do you more good than a visit to the doctor.

After all these years our regular readers surely know that Mercury, your health planet, is very fast moving. Only the Moon moves faster than him. In a given year he will move through all the signs and houses of your Horoscope. So there are many short-term health trends and remedies that are best discussed in the monthly reports.

Mercury will travel backwards four times this year, which is highly unusual. Generally he is only retrograde three times. (This was the case last year too). It is not advisable to make dramatic changes to the diet or health regime during these periods: January 1–8, April 9 to May 3, August 11 to September 5 and December 3–23.

Home and Family

Your 4th house of home and family is not a house of power this year. Nor was it last year. I read this as a good thing. You seem basically content with things as they are and have no pressing need to make major, dramatic changes. This tends to the status quo.

Of course every year brings its share of crises and drama. Generally there are two Lunar eclipses every year, and these impact on the home and family. (The eclipsed planet, the Moon, is your home and family planet.) This year is no different. This year the eclipses occur on February 11 and August 7. The good news is that they reveal what in the physical home needs fixing. Perhaps there were problems (and sometime these are serious) that you weren't aware of. Left to themselves, they can bring major damage. But the eclipse reveals them to you so that you can make repairs. The eclipses also bring emotional dramas with family members, and especially with a parent or parent figure. There is a need for more patience with them over these periods and it's advisable for them to take things easy and stay out of harm's way.

Pluto has been in your 10th house for many years now. This indicates problems with one of the parents or parent figures in your life. Physical death could have happened in many cases, but generally it shows surgery or near-death kinds of experiences. This trend continues in the year ahead. This parent or parent figure has been more spiritual the past two years; there is much internal growth going on here. On December 21, as Saturn crosses the Mid-heaven, this person seems more serious, more exacting, more of a disciplinarian. He or she should be successful in detox or weight loss regimes this year.

Your family planet, the Moon, moves very fast. She is the fastest of all the planets. Every month she will move through your entire chart, so there are many short-term family trends that are best discussed in the monthly reports. In general, family issues tend to be short-term issues for you.

Siblings or sibling figures in your life are prospering, but having a more or less stable family year. If they are of childbearing age, they seem more fertile. A parent figure could move in the coming year. There is good fortune in the purchase or sale of a home. Children or children figures in your life are likely to move after October 11. Grandchildren (if you have them) have been taking more responsibility over the past two years and seem prosperous. A move could happen for them after October 11.

If you're redecorating or otherwise beautifying your home – in a cosmetic kind of way – June 21 to July 22 and July 31 to August 26 are good times. If you're planning renovations or major repairs June 4 to July 22 is good.

Finance and Career

Your money house is not powerful this year Aries, not a major focus of attention. Generally this is a good thing. It shows a basic contentment with the status quo and thus tends to the status quo. Of course, there will be periods in the year – as the short-term, fast-moving planets move through your money house – where finances become important and active, but these are short-term trends, not trends for the year.

In spite of this, the year ahead looks prosperous. Venus, your financial planet, spends a lot of time – triple her usual time – in your sign. She will be there from February 3 to April 4 and then again from April 29 to June 6. This shows some important financial development happening, something with many twists and turns, something that goes forward for a while and then back-tracks – mirroring Venus's motion. It also indicates other things. Venus will bring you financial windfalls. She will see to it that financial opportunity seeks you out rather than you having to run after it. She will bring a lucrative partnership or joint venture opportunity too. But be patient here. There are many wrinkles to be ironed out.

Venus is a fast-moving planet. In any given year she will move through your entire chart, spending time in each of the houses of your Horoscope. Thus earnings and opportunities for earnings will come to you in many ways and through many different circumstances and people – all depending on where Venus is at any given time. (The aspects she receives will also play an important role.) These short-term trends are best dealt with in the monthly reports.

Your career – your life work, your professional status and standing – is much more important than mere money this year. It will become even more important towards the end of the year and into 2018 and 2019. You're in a preparatory stage this year. Towards the end of the year, as Saturn, your career planet, crosses your Mid-heaven and enters your 10th career house, you're going to be asked to take on more responsibility. You need to be ready for this. So it won't hurt to take on extra responsibility now – in preparation. Get used to it.

Your career planet spends most of the year in Sagittarius, your 9th house. This shows career-related travel happening. Your willingness to travel will boost the career. It also indicates – and this will depend on your age and stage in life – a need to either mentor others or to educate yourself in areas that boost the career. By all means attend (or give) business-related seminars and lectures.

Pluto, as we have mentioned, has been at the top of your chart for many years now. This gives him great prominence and power. Thus, bosses and authority figures are having (and have been having) surgery and near-death kinds of experiences. In some cases there has been actual, literal, death. Your company or industry has been having near-death kinds of experiences too. And, in many cases, your actual career has 'died and been born again' – resurrected. By the time Pluto is finished with you (you've got many more years to go) you will be fearless in career matters. You will also have your 'dream' career – your ideal.

Love and Social Life

As we have mentioned, this is the real headline of the year ahead. This is one of the best and happiest love and social life years you've had in a very long time – perhaps in the last 12 or so years.

Benevolent Jupiter is established in your 7th house of love until October 10. Combine this with Venus's three-month sojourn in your sign and you have a signature for romance, marriage or serious relationship. It all seems very happy.

For many years now marriage – committed relationship – hasn't been advisable. Uranus in your own sign was denying it. Your self will, your passion for personal freedom and independence – though good in itself – was not good for serious long-term relationships. But Uranus is almost finished with you. In a year or two he will be out of your sign. You're ready for some stability in your life. For those of you born early in the sign of Aries (March 20 to April 5), Uranus is already finished with you. Marriage, or relationships that are 'like' marriage, are advisable. If you were born between April 6 and April 19, it still might be advisable to wait. Enjoy romance for what it is but there's no need to rush into anything.

Jupiter in your 7th house shows someone of good education and refinement coming into your life. Perhaps he or she is a foreigner. Perhaps you meet him or her in a foreign land. This is a person you can look up to and respect. Jupiter in your 7th house is an aspect for someone who falls in love with the minister or professor. There is an allure for 'mentor' type people.

From February 3 to June 6 Venus, your love planet, will either be in, or hovering near, your sign. This shows that love pursues you. There's nothing special that you need to do to find it – it will find you.

Love and money go hand-in-hand in your chart: Venus is both your love and financial planet. So when one is going well so is the other. When love is happy, so are finances. When finances go well, so does love. Wealth in a partner is certainly an added allure, but refinement, education and philosophical compatibility are just as important – and perhaps even more so this year.

As we have said, you don't need to do much to find love this year. But educational and religious-type settings are good. People you worship with are playing cupid.

Venus moves through your entire horoscope in a given year. So every month the love venues can change depending on where she is at any given time. These short-term trends are best discussed in the monthly reports.

Those of you working towards a second marriage still need patience. Marriage is not advisable this year. Those working on the third marriage have a very nice opportunity. There is someone of high status interested in you.

Self-Improvement

A planet at the top of the chart indicates much more than a person's career. It shows that the affairs governed by the planet are of the highest priority; that you will be involved in these issues. So, Pluto's position on your Mid-heaven for many years now shows that issues of death, surgery (a form of near-death experience), wills and estates and in some cases debt and taxes have been paramount in your life for many years. Dealing with these issues has been a high priority – and perhaps part of your current mission in life. This can sound scary, but this is not the cosmic agenda here. Through these experiences you're confronting death and gaining a deeper understanding of it. This is happening both on the material and spiritual levels. Very few people understand the intricacies of wills or probate law until they have undergone the experience. So the purely material understanding is expanded. But spiritual understanding of this is also happening. You're learning what physical death is all about – why it is not to be feared, but understood. When death is understood spiritually, we will live better and more effectively. Many of our cherished hopes and wishes are blocked because of the fear of death. Once you get through this, new vistas of life open up.

Pluto in the 10th house also indicates success in projects involving personal transformation and reinvention. Spiritually speaking this is your real mission these days. You are being called to give birth to your own ideal of self.

Spirituality has been important for some years now – ever since Neptune moved into Pisces in 2011. For the past two years – and for most of this year – Saturn has been testing your spirituality. In some cases, there was a conflict between the worldly career and your spiritual values – a classic conflict. In some cases, the forces of tradition (parents, elders or authority figures in your life) attacked your spirituality – your practice and ideals. You're being forced to integrate the two urges: to have a viable spiritual life and a worldly career; to be practical in the world without losing your spiritual ideas. It's not so easy to do. You still have this challenge this year, but it will soon be over. By December 21, as Saturn moves into Capricorn, this issue should be resolved. Perhaps it will help some of you to understand that spirituality is always eminently practical. It seems unworldly, but it has great worldly effects. Spirituality only shows a 'different approach' to practicality. A better approach. Your intuition has been tested these past few years – and this continues in the year ahead. This is ultimately good. No reliable tool gets forged without testing.

Saturn's move into your 10th house at the end of the year will bring strong career demands. You have to succeed by sheer merit, by being the best in what you do. Often this aspect brings a stern, demanding boss who overworks you and expects 'the impossible', who seems never satisfied, who is sparing in praise, but quick to criticize. This isn't pleasant, but it will stretch you if you handle it properly. Don't resist the demands. Do your utmost to fulfil them. You'll be amazed as you start achieving things that you believed were impossible. These things are not really burdens but spiritual gifts – as you will see in hindsight.

Month-by-month Forecasts

January

> Best Days Overall: 5, 6, 13, 14, 22, 23, 24
> Most Stressful Days Overall: 11, 12, 17, 18, 19, 25, 26
> Best Days for Love: 2, 12, 17, 18, 19, 20, 21, 31
> Best Days for Money: 1, 2, 7, 8, 10, 12, 18, 19, 20, 21, 28, 29,
>   31
> Best Days for Career: 5, 6, 13, 14, 23, 24, 25, 26

You begin your year with 90 per cent of the planets in the upper half of your chart. Not only that, your 10th house of career is ultra-powerful. You're in a yearly career peak and this is where the focus should be. Home and family issues can be downplayed for now. Emotional wellness will come with outer success. The best thing you can do for your family and friends is to succeed outwardly.

Health needs watching this month – especially until the 19th. The career is demanding (and interesting) but try to schedule more rest periods. Your health planet Mercury spends most of the month in conservative Capricorn, so you're conservative in health matters. Back and knee massage will enhance your health. Watch your posture. Bad posture habits could be throwing the spine out of alignment. Avoid making major health regime changes until after the 8th, when Mercury starts to go forward.

Last month the planetary power shifted from the West to the East and this will be the situation for the next five or so months. Time to exercise more independence and create the conditions you want in life. The planetary power is now moving towards you and away from others. Thus, your way is the best way these days. Others are more likely to adapt to you rather than vice versa.

Personal independence will grow even stronger (if that's possible) from the 28th onwards as Mars crosses your Ascendant and enters your 1st house. When a person is under the influence of Mars, it's as if he or she has taken amphetamines. Everything is speeded up. There is more energy, but also more impatience. With some people it's like taking an 'anger' pill. Things that they would normally let pass can now make them erupt. These are the main dangers of a Mars' transit. Impatience and temper can lead to conflicts, accidents and injury.

Venus, your love and money planet, has her solstice at the end of the month (the 29th to the 31st). (The Sun's solstice happened last month.) So, it is good to pause in love and finance. There will be a brief lull and probably a change of direction.

February

Best Days Overall: 1, 2, 9, 10, 19, 20, 28
Most Stressful Days Overall: 7, 8, 14, 15, 21, 22
Best Days for Love: 9, 10, 14, 15, 19, 20, 28
Best Days for Money: 3, 4, 5, 6, 9, 10, 14, 15, 19, 20, 24, 25, 28
Best Days for Career: 1, 2, 9, 10, 19, 20, 21, 22, 28

Mars spends the month in your 1st house and 80 per cent of the planets are still in the Eastern sector. This is basically good, but with you, Aries, there can be a tendency to overdo the independence thing. It is good to be independent, this is your nature, but try not to run rough shod over others. Review our discussion of Mars last month. Mars in your 1st house has some very positive things to offer too. The aspect gives energy and charisma. You will excel in sports and exercise regimes. Things get done quickly. Life is fast paced – just as you like it. (This is even more than usual – 90 per cent of the planets are moving forward from the 6th onwards. And before the 6th *all* the planets are moving forward.) Progress happens swiftly this month.

The main headline are the two eclipses that happen this month. This guarantees change and volatility. The Lunar Eclipse of February 11 (in America it occurs on the 10th) takes place in your 5th house, affecting the children and children figures in your life. There are dramas and life-changing events happening. Keep them (as much as possible) out of harm's way over this period, a few days before and after the eclipse. Every Lunar Eclipse impacts on the home and family and on parents or parent figures. Be more patient with them. Passions run high in the family. Often repairs are needed in the home.

The Solar Eclipse of the 26th occurs in your spiritual 12th house and is a pretty direct hit on Neptune, your spiritual planet. Thus it indicates important changes in your spiritual life. This can take many forms. Sometimes people change teachers and teachings, or change their practice. If you belong to a spiritual-type organization there are shake-ups happening there. Guru figures have dramas in their lives.

Every Solar Eclipse affects children and children figures. So we have a continuation of the previous eclipse. Again keep them out of harm's way as much as possible. The finances of a parent or parent figure are affected and he or she is making very dramatic changes. If a parent or parent figure is ailing this eclipse can bring a near-death kind of experience.

The dream life will be hyperactive during this Solar Eclipse period, and even before it actually happens. But these dreams are not significant. Don't be overly concerned. The psychic world is being churned up.

March

Best Days Overall: 1, 9, 10, 18, 19, 28
Most Stressful Days Overall: 6, 7, 13, 14, 21, 22
Best Days for Love: 1, 9, 13, 14, 18, 27
Best Days for Money: 1, 2, 3, 5, 6, 9, 13, 14, 18, 23, 24, 27, 30
Best Days for Career: 1, 10, 19, 20, 21, 22, 28

Venus entered your sign on February 3 and she will be here for the rest of the month ahead. Thus love and money have been pursuing you. The love and social life has been good this year and is even better since February 3. The only fly in the ointment is Venus's retrograde from the 4th onwards. Perhaps a relationship seems to be going backwards instead of forwards. The beloved is still very devoted to you, but less sure than usual. Love is under review until April 15. Avoid important decisions one way or the other. The retrograde of Venus slows down the social life (Jupiter in your 7th house of love is also retrograde) but doesn't stop it. This is just a 'pause that refreshes'.

The same thing is happening financially. Financial expansion and earnings are still happening but more slowly than before. It is very important that you don't make matters worse by being careless. Make sure cheques are signed and dated properly. Read the fine print on your purchases. If you're buying big ticket items (although it's best to avoid doing so at this time) make sure you have all your receipts and that there is a good returns policy. A little care in the beginning can save much heartache later on. The good news here is that you're very focused on finance now. Mars, the Lord of your Horoscope, enters your money house on the 10th. This extra attention should pay off.

Normally with 80 per cent of the planets moving forward, this would be a good month – from your birthday onwards – for starting new projects or launching new products. But the retrograde of Venus suggests waiting a while. April might be a better time for these things.

Basically though March is a happy month. Your 1st house is chock-full of planets from the 20th onwards. You have energy, charisma and sparkle. You look good and dress well. You are (from the 20th onwards) at the maximum of your personal power and independence. If there are conditions that are less than comfortable for you in your life, this is the time to make the necessary changes. Later on in the year (in a month or so) it will be more difficult to do. You're having life on your terms these days. The world caters to you rather than vice versa.

Students have to work harder at their studies (those at college level). Foreign travel is best being rescheduled.

April

Best Days Overall: 5, 6, 14, 15, 16, 24, 25
Most Stressful Days Overall: 3, 4, 10, 11, 17, 18, 30
Best Days for Love: 4, 10, 11, 12, 13, 23
Best Days for Money: 1, 4, 10, 11, 12, 13, 19, 20, 21, 23, 26, 27, 28, 29
Best Days for Career: 5, 6, 15, 16, 17, 18, 24, 25

A happy month ahead Aries, enjoy. Many nice things are happening both in love and finance, but perhaps in roundabout kinds of ways. Something good, an opportunity, might seem to leave you, but it will return.

Health looks good this period. You have energy and magnetism. You're still getting your way in life, which is always nice, though wrong choices can have consequences later on down the road. You're still in a period of maximum personal power and independence. If there are still conditions that irk you, make changes now.

Venus spends most of the month in your 12th house of spirituality. Thus love is very idealistic now. In many cases the idealism is so strong that anything less just won't do. On the other hand, you have the ability to experience nuances in love that few ever experience. Your capacity to give and receive love is greatly enlarged. Love opportunities happen in spiritual settings this month – at charity events, spiritual seminars or lectures, and prayer meetings. Follow your highest ideals and love will find you there. On the 28th Venus crosses your Ascendant again and enters your 1st house. This indicates that love is pursuing you; there's nothing much you need to do, it will find you.

This is a good month (the entire month) to buy clothing and personal accessories. Your sense of style is excellent and the purchases will be good.

The month ahead is prosperous too. Venus starts to move forward on the 15th, relieving many financial log-jams. There is financial clarity now. On the 19th the Sun enters your money house and you begin a yearly financial peak – a period of peak earnings. When Venus enters your sign on the 28th there will be financial windfalls and opportunities – these too come to you with little or no effort on your part. (The effort will most likely come later on.)

Last month, on the 20th, the planetary power shifted from the upper to the lower half of your Horoscope, and will remain there for many more months. Your career planet, Saturn, goes retrograde on the 6th. So career is de-emphasized now. It's time to get more involved with the family and your emotional well-being.

May

Best Days Overall: 2, 3, 12, 13, 21, 22, 29, 30
Most Stressful Days Overall: 1, 7, 8, 14, 15, 27, 28
Best Days for Love: 2, 3, 7, 8, 12, 13, 21, 22
Best Days for Money: 2, 3, 7, 8, 12, 13, 17, 18, 21, 22, 23, 24, 25, 26
Best Days for Career: 3, 13, 14, 15, 22, 30

Prosperity continues to be strong this month. Your financial planet spends the month in your 1st house. You are a 'financial magnet' drawing both money and financial opportunity to you. You look rich. People see you as prosperous – you project this kind of image. Moreover, your money house is still very powerful this month, until the 20th. This shows great focus. By the spiritual law, we get what we focus on.

Students are having a much better month than last month. Mercury was retrograde most of April (from the 9th onwards) and this slows down learning and information retention. But this month Mercury begins to move forward again, on the 3rd. Your ruling planet, Mars, will be in your 3rd house all month. On the 20th the Sun also enters the 3rd house of communication and intellectual interests. The mind is sharper and clearer. There is a hunger for information and knowledge. There is strong motivation to study. Teachers, writers, journalists and marketing people are also having a better month – communication skills are stronger than usual.

Mars makes beautiful aspects to Jupiter from the 10th to the 14th. This brings financial expansion and travel opportunities. Students applying to colleges should hear good news (best case scenarios). If you are involved in legal issues, this period brings some good news too.

Health is still good. Any doubts about it get resolved after the 3rd. You can enhance it further through scalp and face massage, craniosacral therapy (until the 16th) and neck massage after the 16th.

Love is very happy this month. Jupiter is still in your 7th house of love and your love planet is in your own sign. Love still pursues you ardently, and you are popular socially in general. You radiate grace to others – it's as if you took a 'love pill'. People respond to it though you might not be projecting it consciously.

Retrograde activity increased last month – 40 per cent of the planets were in retrograde motion. This lessens a bit this month after the 3rd, when only 30 per cent will be retrograde. While it is best to start new projects when the planetary momentum is more forward, this might still be a good time to start a new project or launch a new product. From the New Moon of the 25th onwards would be best. Although there was less retrograde activity in March and April than now, the planet that was retrograde, Venus, is an ultra-important one for you. So, this month seems better.

June

Best Days Overall: 8, 9, 18, 19, 26, 27
Most Stressful Days Overall: 3, 4, 10, 11, 12, 24, 25, 30
Best Days for Love: 3, 4, 10, 11, 20, 21, 28, 29, 30
Best Days for Money: 3, 4, 10, 11, 13, 14, 20, 21, 22, 23, 28, 29, 30
Best Days for Career: 9, 10, 11, 12, 19, 27

Mars, the ruler of your Horoscope – a very important planet – spends almost the entire month 'out of bounds' – from the 1st to the 29th. This shows that you're moving outside your normal sphere. You're 'out of your usual boundaries'.

Mercury will also spend a good deal of the month 'out of bounds'. Thus you're outside your usual sphere intellectually and in health matters. You're thinking 'outside the box' – in unorthodox kinds of ways.

In a way this is good. Health becomes more delicate after the 21st and you do need 'new and different' solutions and you seem willing to try them. The most important thing, as we have mentioned many times, is a high energy level. Don't let yourself get overtired. Make sure you get enough sleep. Enhance your health through neck massage until the 6th. From the 6th to the 21st you will respond well to arm and shoulder massage. Breathing exercises will be good – plain old fresh air is good. After the 21st the diet becomes more important. This should be checked with a professional. Watch your mood and emotions during this period and do your best to keep them positive and constructive.

Finances still seem good. On the 6th Venus moves into her own sign and house – your money house – and stays there for the rest of the month. Venus is stronger when she is in her own sign (Taurus) and house, so earning power is stronger than usual. Social connections are always important for you financially, but more so this month. A partnership or joint venture is likely.

The current love seems financially supportive. The current love's financial planet went retrograde on April 20 and is still retrograde this month. So he or she needs to be more cautious in financial dealings.

Your beloved is experiencing a slowdown in their financial affairs, so they might as well be helpful to you. Curiously, this focus on you brings more prosperity to him or her (but there are delays involved).

The Sun makes beautiful aspects to Jupiter from the 2nd to the 5th, which brings luck in speculations and 'happy money' - money that is earned in happy ways. Children and children figures prosper in this period too.

The love planet's move into your money house shows a shift in your love attitudes. Now, wealth and material gifts are romantic turn-ons. Singles are very much attracted by these. For singles love opportunities come as you pursue your normal financial goals and with people involved in your finances. A visit to the accountant or financial planner could become much more than that.

July

Best Days Overall: 5, 6, 15, 16, 23, 24
Most Stressful Days Overall: 1, 8, 9, 21, 22, 28, 29
Best Days for Love: 1, 10, 19, 20, 28, 29
Best Days for Money: 1, 10, 11, 17, 18, 19, 20, 28, 29
Best Days for Career: 5, 6, 8, 9, 15, 16, 23, 24

Your 4th house of home and family was very strong last month and is still strong in the month ahead - until the 22nd. The planetary power, figuratively speaking, is furthest away from your career and outer activities. Thus these activities are less important for the moment. (Your career planet is still retrograde all month.) This will change in coming months, but this is the case now. The cosmos impels you to 'cater to your base' - the home, your family and your emotional life. The cosmos has its own way of arranging these things. You become more nostalgic. You remember - vividly - old, seemingly obscure events. The dream life becomes more active and you feel a need to ponder your dreams' meanings. The urge to probe the unconscious and emotional side of life - the interior life - is stronger than the pulls of the outer world. The universe is not denying you a career or career progress - on the contrary, it is forcing you to become emotionally healthier and more stable so that future career progress can happen.

Every now and then we have to go backwards in order to go forward. This is one of those times.

There are other good reasons to focus more on the emotional life. Health is not what it should be and still needs watching. Overall your energy is not what it should be. Interior activity requires less energy than outer activity.

Continue to enhance the health by resting more, spending quiet times at home, scheduling in more massages and natural treatments. Diet is still important, until the 6th. After that, give more attention to the heart. Regular chest massage will be beneficial. Schedule more leisure activities with the children and family. Laugh more. Joy itself is a powerful healing therapy these days.

Your health will start to improve dramatically after the 20th. Perhaps some pill, herb or therapist will get the credit for this, or some miracle diet or supplement. But the truth of the matter is that the planetary power shifted in your favour. The other things were just the side effects of this shift.

Finance is becoming less important this month. On the 5th Venus leaves the money house and it is basically empty during July (only the Moon will move through there on the 19th and 20th). Financial goals – the short-term ones anyway – are more or less achieved and your focus is elsewhere. Venus will make nice aspects to Jupiter on the 18th and 19th. This brings a nice payday and happy romantic meetings for singles.

August

Best Days Overall: 1, 2, 3, 11, 12, 20, 21, 29, 30
Most Stressful Days Overall: 4, 5, 18, 24, 25, 31
Best Days for Love: 9, 10, 18, 19, 24, 25, 28, 29
Best Days for Money: 6, 7, 9, 10, 13, 14, 16, 18, 19, 24, 25, 28, 29
Best Days for Career: 2, 3, 4, 5, 11, 12, 20, 21, 29, 30, 31

The month ahead is basically happy and healthy, but two eclipses will create excitement and change. You're basically in a party period now. Your 5th house of fun and creativity became powerful on July 22 and is still powerful until the 22nd of this month. The eclipses might interrupt the party but they won't stop it.

The Lunar Eclipse of the 7th is the stronger of the two – as far as you're concerned. It affects Mars, the ruler of your Horoscope. So take it easy that period and avoid stressful situations. This eclipse occurs in your 11th house and affects family and friends. There are life-changing kinds of dramas happening with them. Repairs could be needed in the home. Its impact on Mars shows a need to redefine yourself and your image – the way you think about yourself and the way you want to be seen by others. This is generally a good thing. We are always changing and growing and every now and then we need a redefinition. But this seems to happen in a forced way. Events force the issue, and this can make it stressful or unwelcome. The marriage and social lives of children and children figures get tested. There is a crisis here.

The Solar Eclipse of the 21st occurs right on the cusp of your 5th and 6th houses – thus it impacts on the affairs of both these houses. This eclipse is strongest on children and children figures in your life. They have personal life-changing dramas. Most of the time these are normal things – sexual awakening, leaving school and going off to college, marriage or divorce etc. But sometimes, especially if they haven't been careful in dietary matters, the eclipse can bring a detox of the body. The body throws off its effete material. Often this gets diagnosed as disease, but astrologically speaking it isn't. The children are redefining themselves now (especially the oldest) and this will manifest as a new look – a new image – a new presentation to the world. This will be a six-month process. They will also be forced to make important financial changes. You can have job changes and changes in your health regime.

Overall your health is good. The eclipse can produce a scare, but most likely it will not be more than that.

September

Best Days Overall: 7, 8, 16, 17, 25, 26
Most Stressful Days Overall: 1, 14, 15, 20, 21, 28, 29
Best Days for Love: 7, 8, 16, 17, 20, 21, 28
Best Days for Money: 3, 4, 7, 8, 10, 12, 13, 16, 17, 20, 21, 28, 30
Best Days for Career: 1, 7, 8, 16, 17, 26, 27, 28, 29

Last month's Solar Eclipse of August 21 could have brought job changes. These often occur within the same company or situation, possibly with another one. If this is the case for you, the job changes seem very fortunate. Your 6th house of health and work is very powerful all month, but especially until the 22nd. Job seekers have no problem whatsoever. There are all kinds of job opportunities for you. You can pick and choose. The New Moon of the 29th will further clarify this situation. All the information you need for a right decision will come to you, right up to the next New Moon in October.

Health is good, yet there is a focus on health. Hopefully this indicates preventive regimes and diet. Often when the health is good and the 6th house is this strong there can be an over-emphasis on this area: trying to fix things that are not really broken. Or magnifying little things into big things.

Finances seem happy. Venus is in your 5th house until the 20th – this shows happy money – money that is earned in pleasurable ways. There is a joy in the act of money-making. Sometimes this shows that financial opportunities or important contacts happen as you're having fun – at a resort or park or the theatre. You spend money on fun kinds of things but can earn from them as well. Often something that starts out as an enjoyable hobby can become a business enterprise. You're always a financial risk-taker, but until the 20th you are even more so than usual. The problem with this aspect – though it is a happy one – is a tendency to overspend, to be overly optimistic about financial matters. Sometimes this is not realistic. After the 20th, as Venus moves into Virgo, financial judgement is more rational, more conservative. You will spend, but you won't overspend. You'll get value for your money.

The love life is also enjoyable this month – especially until the 20th. Those in relationships are having fun with the beloved. You're doing fun kinds of things together. Singles will find love opportunities as they do the things that they enjoy doing. Your joy will not only create wealth but attract love as well. When your love planet enters Virgo on the 20th she starts to travel with Mars. So a romantic meeting is close at hand (it can happen next month too). The workplace, health spa, gym or doctor's surgery can be a venue for romance during this period. You're attracted to health professionals and to people involved in your health.

October

Best Days Overall: 5, 6, 13, 14, 22, 23, 24
Most Stressful Days Overall: 11, 12, 18, 19, 25, 26
Best Days for Love: 7, 8, 17, 18, 19, 27, 28
Best Days for Money: 1, 7, 8, 10, 11, 17, 18, 20, 27, 28, 30
Best Days for Career: 5, 6, 13, 14, 23, 24, 25, 26

The planetary power is now at its maximum Western, social position. Even the ruler of your Horoscope, Mars, will move into your 7th house on the 22nd. It's as if you are far away from yourself, in a foreign country. Your needs and interests don't matter much. It's all about other people – their needs, their interests, what they want to do. For an independent Aries this is challenging, but you seem to be handling it properly. It's also therapeutic. It's healthy every now and then to take a vacation from oneself. Many psychological and spiritual pathologies emanate from too much self-concern; it skews one's perspective on life.

Your way is not the best way this period. Let others have their way so long as it isn't destructive. This attitude enhances your social popularity, which is strong and active this month.

The love life is the main headline this month. Your 7th house of love is chock-full of planets – and beneficent ones. The social life has been good all year, but now you're in a yearly peak. It is the culmination of the year. In many cases it's a lifetime peak, in other cases it's 'one of the lifetime peaks' – much depends on your age. Romance is in the air.

Those of you already in a relationship are experiencing more happiness within the relationship. All of you are attending more parties, weddings and gatherings. Even children or children figures in your life are experiencing romance or meeting new and important friends (much depends on their age). The 26th and 27th seems especially good for that.

You get on with all sorts of people these days – religious types, academics, money people, athletes and intellectuals. There is a broad base to your social life. This is a good month for planning a wedding. Business partnerships or joint ventures are also likely this period. Venus, your financial planet, enters the 7th house too on the 14th.

The other major headline of the month is Jupiter's move out of your 7th house into the 8th house on the 11th. This indicates prosperity for the current love interest or spouse. Their prosperity will go on well into next year.

Health needs more attention. There are many planets in stressful alignment with you. As always make sure you get enough rest. Physical exercise and scalp massage are especially beneficial until the 22nd (these are always good for you). The hips and kidneys could do with more attention. Massage the hips regularly (and the buttocks too). After the 17th sexual moderation is important – you seem more sexually active that period anyway. Enjoy it, but don't overdo it.

November

Best Days Overall: 1, 2, 9, 10, 19, 20, 29, 30
Most Stressful Days Overall: 7, 8, 14, 15, 21, 22
Best Days for Love: 6, 7, 14, 15, 16, 17, 26, 27
Best Days for Money: 3, 4, 6, 7, 8, 16, 17, 26, 27
Best Days for Career: 2, 10, 20, 21, 22, 30

Your 8th house became powerful on October 23 and remains very powerful until the 23rd of this month. The 8th house is going to be a major interest for the next 12 or so months.

The 8th house is about getting rid of things, not adding more things. It's about reducing the clutter in our lives – tidying up. This applies to the physical body, the mental and emotional life and to our physical circumstances. In the 8th house we expand and grow through contraction – through getting rid of what doesn't belong in our lives. It sounds counter-intuitive to talk about expansion through contraction, but it is easier to understand if you think of your breathing. The more complete the out-breath, the deeper will be the next in-breath. The more you get rid of what doesn't belong in your life, the greater will be the inflow of what's really important.

Marie Kondo's *The Life Changing Magic of Tidying Up* is a very 8th-house kind of book. You should read it now – and next year too. Her test for what belongs in your life is the 'joy test'. You pile up your possessions and go through them one by one, asking yourself: 'Does this thing give me a feeling of Joy?' If the answer is yes, you keep it. If the answer is no, you get rid of it. This is one way to do it. The other way, which I prefer, is to ask the question 'do I use this thing? Do I really need it?' If the answer is yes, keep it. If the answer is no, get rid of it. As you do this, you'll be amazed at how much 'lighter' you feel. You've made room for the new and the better to come into your life.

With your 8th house so strong this month (your financial planet moves in there on the 7th) it is a good time to pay off debts, to consolidate your bills, if possible, and to refinance or restructure your debts to more manageable levels. Sometimes it is necessary to borrow money, and this is a good month for this too. You have very good access to outside capital. If you have good business or product ideas, there are outside investors available to help you.

Health is much improved over last month. Self-esteem and self-confidence are perhaps less – there is less bravado and bragging these days! But overall energy is much better. You can enhance the health further through colon cleanses, practising safe sex and sexual moderation until the 6th. Physical detox regimes are beneficial all month. After the 6th thigh massage is powerful. An herbal liver cleanse might be in order if you feel under the weather.

The social life is still very active, but much less so than last month. Continue to put others first and to cultivate your social skills.

December

Best Days Overall: 7, 8, 16, 17, 26, 27
Most Stressful Days Overall: 5, 6, 11, 12, 18, 19, 20
Best Days for Love: 7, 8, 11, 12, 16, 17, 28
Best Days for Money: 1, 2, 5, 6, 7, 8, 14, 15, 16, 17, 24, 25, 28, 29
Best Days for Career: 8, 17, 18, 19, 20, 28

In October the planetary power began to shift to the upper half of your Horoscope. This month, from the 21st onwards, the shift is even more pronounced. From the 12th to the 26th almost all of the planets (90 per cent) are above the horizon. The other times it is 80 per cent. So your career and outer ambitions are important now. Your 4th house of home and family is empty this month (only the Moon moves through there on the 5th and 6th). Your 10th house of career, in contrast, is ultra-powerful – especially from the 21st onwards. Career is the main headline this month. This is where the focus should be. The month ahead should be successful.

Saturn makes a major move (it only happens every two to two-and-a-half years) into your 10th house on the 21st. The Sun will move in on the 21st and Venus on the 25th.

Saturn's move is very significant. It indicates more career responsibilities. Yes, these can be burdensome, but it's generally a sign of success. The people who take more responsibility are the people who get promoted. The career will be demanding, for sure. But if you take up the burdens – don't try to evade them – you will find unexpected help. Also you'll be setting the stage for long-term – enduring – success.

Bosses are likely to be over-demanding, exacting, over-controlling and on your case. This is generally not pleasant. The best way to handle this is to give your boss more than is demanded. There is a spiritual law involved here.

Health is good until the 21st but afterwards (and for the next two years) will need watching. There are many planets in stressful alignment with you. You won't be able to escape the demands of the career, but you can handle them in more energy efficient ways. Delegate wherever possible. Take short breaks when you feel tired. Spend more of your free time at a health spa or schedule more massages or other natural therapies. Keep the focus on the really important things in your life and let go of the trivia. (Marie Kondo's advice about possessions applies to the thought process as well.) Your health planet spends the month in Sagittarius, your 9th house. Health can be enhanced through thigh massage (which will also strengthen the lower back) and liver care.

The month ahead is prosperous, with Venus in lucky Sagittarius (and the lucky 9th house) until the 25th. Earnings increase. You spend more (perhaps overspend) but you also earn more. You have a happy-go-lucky, optimistic attitude to finance. Perhaps you are too optimistic. After the 25th, as Venus moves into Capricorn, the financial judgement is more realistic, more conservative. Pay rises (official or unofficial) are likely.

Taurus

THE BULL

Birthdays from
21st April to
20th May

Personality Profile

TAURUS AT A GLANCE

Element – Earth

Ruling Planet – Venus
  Career Planet – Uranus
  Love Planet – Pluto
  Money Planet – Mercury
  Planet of Health and Work – Venus
  Planet of Home and Family Life – Sun
  Planet of Spirituality – Mars
  Planet of Travel, Education, Religion and Philosophy – Saturn

Colours – earth tones, green, orange, yellow

Colours that promote love, romance and social harmony – red-violet, violet

Colours that promote earning power – yellow, yellow-orange

Gems – coral, emerald

Metal – copper

Scents – bitter almond, rose, vanilla, violet

Quality – fixed (= stability)

Quality most needed for balance – flexibility

Strongest virtues – endurance, loyalty, patience, stability,
   a harmonious disposition

Deepest needs – comfort, material ease, wealth

Characteristics to avoid – rigidity, stubbornness, tendency to be overly
   possessive and materialistic

Signs of greatest overall compatibility – Virgo, Capricorn

Signs of greatest overall incompatibility – Leo, Scorpio, Aquarius

Sign most helpful to career – Aquarius

Sign most helpful for emotional support – Leo

Sign most helpful financially – Gemini

Sign best for marriage and/or partnerships – Scorpio

Sign most helpful for creative projects – Virgo

Best Sign to have fun with – Virgo

Signs most helpful in spiritual matters – Aries, Capricorn

Best day of the week – Friday

Understanding a Taurus

Taurus is the most earthy of all the Earth signs. If you understand that Earth is more than just a physical element, that it is a psychological attitude as well, you will get a better understanding of the Taurus personality.

A Taurus has all the power of action that an Aries has. But Taurus is not satisfied with action for its own sake. Their actions must be productive, practical and wealth-producing. If Taurus cannot see a practical value in an action they will not bother taking it.

Taurus's forte lies in their power to make real their own or other people's ideas. They are generally not very inventive but they can take another's invention and perfect it, making it more practical and useful. The same is true for all projects. Taurus is not especially keen on starting new projects, but once they get involved they bring things to completion. Taurus carries everything through. They are finishers and will go the distance, so long as no unavoidable calamity intervenes.

Many people find Taurus too stubborn, conservative, fixed and immovable. This is understandable, because Taurus dislikes change – in the environment or in their routine. They even dislike changing their minds! On the other hand, this is their virtue. It is not good for a wheel's axle to waver. The axle must be fixed, stable and unmovable. Taurus is the axle of society and the heavens. Without their stability and so-called stubbornness, the wheels of the world (and especially the wheels of commerce) would not turn.

Taurus loves routine. A routine, if it is good, has many virtues. It is a fixed – and, ideally, perfect – way of taking care of things. Mistakes can happen when spontaneity comes into the equation, and mistakes cause discomfort and uneasiness – something almost unacceptable to a Taurus. Meddling with Taurus's comfort and security is a sure way to irritate and anger them.

While an Aries loves speed, a Taurus likes things slow. They are slow thinkers – but do not make the mistake of assuming they lack intelligence. On the contrary, Taurus people are very intelligent. It is just that they like to chew on ideas, to deliberate and weigh them up.

Only after due deliberation is an idea accepted or a decision taken. Taurus is slow to anger – but once aroused, take care!

Finance

Taurus is very money-conscious. Wealth is more important to them than to many other signs. Wealth to a Taurus means comfort and security. Wealth means stability. Where some zodiac signs feel that they are spiritually rich if they have ideas, talents or skills, Taurus only feels wealth when they can see and touch it. Taurus's way of thinking is, 'What good is a talent if it has not been translated into a home, furniture, car and holidays?'

These are all reasons why Taurus excels in estate agency and agricultural industries. Usually a Taurus will end up owning land. They love to feel their connection to the Earth. Material wealth began with agriculture, the tilling of the soil. Owning a piece of land was humanity's earliest form of wealth: Taurus still feels that primeval connection.

It is in the pursuit of wealth that Taurus develops intellectual and communication ability. Also, in this pursuit Taurus is forced to develop some flexibility. It is in the quest for wealth that they learn the practical value of the intellect and come to admire it. If it were not for the search for wealth and material things, Taurus people might not try to reach a higher intellect.

Some Taurus people are 'born lucky' – the type who win any gamble or speculation. This luck is due to other factors in their horoscope; it is not part of their essential nature. By nature they are not gamblers. They are hard workers and like to earn what they get. Taurus's innate conservatism makes them abhor unnecessary risks in finance and in other areas of their lives.

Career and Public Image

Being essentially down-to-earth people, simple and uncomplicated, Taurus tends to look up to those who are original, unconventional and inventive. Taurus people like their bosses to be creative and original – since they themselves are content to perfect their superiors' brainwaves. They admire people who have a wider social or political consciousness and they feel that someday (when they have all the comfort and security they need) they too would like to be involved in these big issues.

In business affairs Taurus can be very shrewd – and that makes them valuable to their employers. They are never lazy; they enjoy working and getting good results. Taurus does not like taking unnecessary risks and they do well in positions of authority, which makes them good managers and supervisors. Their managerial skills are reinforced by their natural talents for organization and handling details, their patience and thoroughness. As mentioned, through their connection with the earth, Taurus people also do well in farming and agriculture.

In general a Taurus will choose money and earning power over public esteem and prestige. A position that pays more – though it has less prestige – is preferred to a position with a lot of prestige but lower earnings. Many other signs do not feel this way, but a Taurus does, especially if there is nothing in his or her personal birth chart that modifies this. Taurus will pursue glory and prestige only if it can be shown that these things have a direct and immediate impact on their wallet.

Love and Relationships

In love, the Taurus-born likes to have and to hold. They are the marrying kind. They like commitment and they like the terms of a relationship to be clearly defined. More importantly, Taurus likes to be faithful to one lover, and they expect that lover to reciprocate this fidelity. When this doesn't happen, their whole world comes crashing down. When they are in love Taurus people are loyal, but they are also very possessive. They are capable of great fits of jealousy if they are hurt in love.

Taurus is satisfied with the simple things in a relationship. If you are involved romantically with a Taurus there is no need for lavish entertainments and constant courtship. Give them enough love, food and comfortable shelter and they will be quite content to stay home and enjoy your company. They will be loyal to you for life. Make a Taurus feel comfortable and – above all – secure in the relationship, and you will rarely have a problem.

In love, Taurus can sometimes make the mistake of trying to control their partners, which can cause great pain on both sides. The reasoning behind their actions is basically simple: Taurus people feel a sense of ownership over their partners and will want to make changes that will increase their own general comfort and security. This attitude is OK when it comes to inanimate, material things – but is dangerous when applied to people. Taurus needs to be careful and attentive to this possible trait within themselves.

Home and Domestic Life

Home and family are vitally important to Taurus. They like children. They also like a comfortable and perhaps glamorous home – something they can show off. They tend to buy heavy, ponderous furniture – usually of the best quality. This is because Taurus likes a feeling of substance in their environment. Their house is not only their home but their place of creativity and entertainment. The Taurus' home tends to be truly their castle. If they could choose, Taurus people would prefer living in the countryside to being city-dwellers. If they cannot do so during their working lives, many Taurus individuals like to holiday in or even retire to the country, away from the city and closer to the land.

At home a Taurus is like a country squire – lord (or lady) of the manor. They love to entertain lavishly, to make others feel secure in their home and to encourage others to derive the same sense of satisfaction as they do from it. If you are invited for dinner at the home of a Taurus you can expect the best food and best entertainment. Be prepared for a tour of the house and expect to see your Taurus friend exhibit a lot of pride and satisfaction in his or her possessions.

Taurus people like children but they are usually strict with them. The reason for this is they tend to treat their children – as they do most things in life – as their possessions. The positive side to this is that their children will be well cared for and well supervised. They will get every material thing they need to grow up properly. On the down side, Taurus can get too repressive with their children. If a child dares to upset the daily routine – which Taurus loves to follow – he or she will have a problem with a Taurus parent.

Horoscope for 2017

Major Trends

Uranus has been in your spiritual 12th house for many years now. This is creating change – and much experimenting – in your spiritual life and practice. Many of you have changed teachers, teachings and practices over the years and the trend is continuing.

Since Uranus is also your career planet, this transit indicates a growing idealism about your career and life work. Just being successful and prominent in your profession is not enough for you. It leaves you vaguely dissatisfied. You need to be involved in things that really matter, that truly benefit others and the whole planet.

In a year or two Uranus will enter your sign and will stay there for many years, bringing dramatic and sudden change into your life. Taurus folk are not very comfortable with change. They love the status quo and routine – it's predictable and stable. But very soon now you'll have to learn to be comfortable with change. We'll discuss this further in 2018.

Jupiter has been in your 6th house of health and work since September last year and will be here for most of the year ahead – until October 10. This is a good health message. If there have been any pre-existing conditions you should hear good news about them. This also indicates that dream job opportunities are coming to you. If you hire others you're expanding the workforce. Children and children figures in your life are prospering.

Jupiter will enter your 7th house of love on October 11. For singles this indicates love and serious relationships – perhaps even marriage. For those already attached it brings new friends and an expanded – more active – social life.

Your religious beliefs have had a real testing over the past two years, and this continues in the year ahead. This is usually not pleasant, but it is good. It forces you to rethink and re-evaluate these beliefs; in many cases they get modified or even discarded. This will be complete by the end of the year.

Saturn's move into your 9th house at the end of the year (on December 21) affects mostly college-level students. They have to work harder at their studies. They need more discipline. They have to succeed in school by sheer merit, without any 'gamesmanship'.

Your areas of greatest interest this year are health and work (until October 10); love and romance (from October 11 onwards); personal transformation, personal reinvention, sex and occult studies (until December 21); religion, higher education, foreign travel; groups, group activities, the online world; and spirituality.

Your paths of greatest fulfilment this year are children, fun and creativity (until April 29), home, family and emotional wellness (from April 29 onwards); health and work (until October 10); love and romance (from October 11 onwards).

Health

(Please note that this is an astrological perspective on health and not a medical one. In days of yore there was no difference, both of these perspectives were identical. Now there could be quite a difference. For a medical perspective, please consult your doctor or health practitioner.)

Health looks excellent this year. Until October 10 there are no long-term planets in stressful aspect to you. And even after October 11, only Jupiter will be in stressful alignment, and he is not a maleficent kind of planet. In addition, your health house is very strong until October 10. So your attention is focused here. You're on the case. In fact, if anything, you might be too much on the case – more than is necessary. Often this leads to a tendency to magnify trifling problems into big ones.

As we mentioned earlier, pre-existing conditions should be much improved this year. Your health is basically good, but there will be periods in the year when your health and energy are less good. These things come from planetary transits; they are temporary things and not trends for the year. When the challenging transits pass, normal health and energy return.

Good though your health is, it can be made even better. Pay attention to the following (the reflex points are shown in the following chart):

- The neck and throat. These are always important for a Taurus. Regular neck massages will be a potent 'pick me up' and a preventive for future problems. Craniosacral therapy is also good for the neck.
- The kidneys and hips. These are also always important for a Taurus. Venus, the ruler of these areas, is your health planet. Regular hip massage (and the buttocks too) should be incorporated into the health regime. A herbal kidney cleanse might be a good idea if you feel under the weather.
- The liver and thighs. These only became important since September 2016, but they remain so for most of the year ahead – until October 10. Regular thigh massage will be good. A herbal liver cleanse would also help.

Since these are the most vulnerable health areas in your chart this year, problems, if they happened (God forbid) would most likely begin here. Thus keeping them healthy and fit is sound preventive medicine.

Important foot reflexology points for the year ahead

Try to massage all of the foot on a regular basis – the top of the foot as well as the bottom – but pay extra attention to the points highlighted on the chart. When you massage, be aware of 'sore spots' as these need special attention. It's also a good idea to massage the ankles and below them.

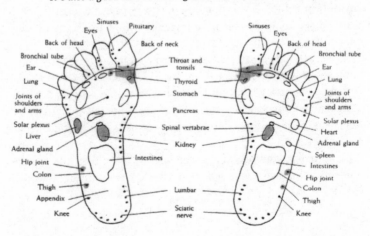

As Venus is such a fast-moving planet – she will move through every area of your chart in a given year – there are many short-term health trends that depend on where Venus is at any given time and the aspects she receives. This is best covered in the monthly reports.

Since Venus is *both* the ruler of your Horoscope and your health planet – she serves double duty in your chart – there is a strong connection between health and personal appearance. Your state of health instantly reflects itself in your personal appearance. Good health will do more for your looks than hosts of cosmetics, perfumes and powders.

Jupiter is the ruler of your 8th house of transformation. Thus his position in your house of health gives a tendency towards surgery. This is often seen as the 'quick fix' to a problem. Sometimes it is, sometimes not. Detox regimes should be explored first – you can get good results with these.

Home and Family

Your 4th house of home and family wasn't strong last year and is not strong in the year ahead either. This can be seen as a kind of contentment with things as they are. It tends to the status quo. You have no pressing need to make dramatic changes here.

Of course, there are going to be periods of excitement and family drama. Every year there are at least two Solar Eclipses and this year is no different. There is a Solar Eclipse on February 26 and on August 21. Since the Sun is your family planet, these eclipses produce important changes. Perhaps there is some hidden problem in the home, perhaps a family member has some hidden problem or grievance. The eclipse will force these things to the surface so that you can deal with them. This year, you're also affected by a Lunar Eclipse (February 11) that occurs in your 4th house. This will bring more of what we mentioned above. But these are temporary things that soon pass. And when they do, it's back to the status quo. We will cover the effect of the eclipses in more detail in the monthly reports.

Siblings and sibling figures in your life are likely to move this year. The move seems happy (it could be job related). A parent or parent figure is also likely to move – after October 11. Children or children figures are not advised to move, however, though they might want to.

They seem more depressed this year. Counselling therapies or medita-tion will be a big help to them, but a move will not do much for their psychological state. Grandchildren (if you have them) have been moving around a lot in recent years, and could do so this year too. They seem emotionally restless. Even if they don't actually move they will renovate their existing home or spend much time in other places. It will be 'as if' they have moved.

If you're planning to redecorate or beautify the home in cosmetic kinds of ways – i.e. to repaint, or change the curtains, or buy objets d'art for the home – July 22 to September 20 is a good time. If you're planning major repairs – construction projects – July 20 to September 5 is a good time.

The health of a parent or parent figure is much improved over previ-ous years. He or she could benefit from detox regimes. He or she has a tendency to surgery. Children and children figures will benefit from vigorous exercise, head, face and scalp massage. Siblings and sibling figures need a disciplined daily regime – more attention to the liver, thighs, spine, knees, teeth and bones will be very helpful.

Finance and Career

Your money house hasn't been prominent for many years now. You are always focused on money, but of late, less so than usual, Taurus. This too I read as a good thing. It shows contentment with things as they are. There are no pressing needs to make dramatic changes. You sort of take prosperity for granted – which is as it should be. However, if financial problems arise, lack of attention (taking your eyes off the ball) is a likely cause. You'll have to force yourself to focus more.

In spite of the empty money house I expect your year to be prosper-ous. There are no major financial impediments. You have a lot of financial freedom. Taurus is free to be Taurus – prosperous. We mentioned earlier that there are lucrative job opportunities this year. Also, those of you running a business will be hiring more people. This is not a message of poverty.

After October 11, when Jupiter enters your 7th house, there is pros-perity for the current love, spouse or partner. He or she will have substantial financial windfalls and many happy opportunities. You will socialize more with 'money people' - rich people. If you have good ideas, it seems easy to attract investors.

Mercury, your financial planet, is a very fast-moving planet, as our regular readers know. Only the Moon moves faster than him. In a given year he will move through every sector of your horoscope. This shows that earnings and earnings opportunities can come to you in many ways and through many different kinds of people - depending on where Mercury is at any given time. These short-term trends are best dealt with in the monthly reports.

Mercury will be retrograde four times this year (as he was last year too). This is unusual. Normally he travels backwards only three times a year. So, this year more homework, more reviews of your financial goals, strategy and investments are necessary. More so than usual. When Mercury is in retrograde motion the financial thinking is not what it should be, thus the most important thing is to gain mental clarity and resolve your doubts. When this happens, you'll be able to make good moves when Mercury starts to move forward again. This year Mercury's retrograde periods are January 1-8; April 9 to May 3; August 11 to September 5 and December 3-23. We will discuss this further in the monthly reports.

Your 10th house of career is also empty this year, indicating that career is not a major focus. Again this should be read in a good way. You seem content with things as they are and have no pressing need for change. Changes will definitely happen - Uranus, your career planet, is the planet of change - but they are likely to be happy. As has been the case for many years now, it is good to enhance your career by being involved in charitable and altruistic causes. These are good for their own sakes, but will also cement your professional image. Important career contacts will also be made. Your technological skills and online activities in general will enhance the career too.

Siblings and sibling figures will have a stable financial year, although the eclipses (as mentioned above) will force changes in their financial thinking and strategy. The spouse, partner or current love interest will prosper, as we have mentioned. He or she has excellent financial intuition until October 11. Parents and parent figures also have a stable financial year. Children and children figures are prospering. Grandchildren (if you have them) seem content with things.

Love and Social Life

Both 2015 (the latter part) and 2016 were good love years. Many of you have married or entered into serious kinds of relationships. Socially things have been quiet since last September, with no major developments one way or another. This too is a good signal. There is basic contentment here. This is the case until October 10. But after that Jupiter enters into your 7th house of love and marriage – heating up and expanding the love life.

Those of you involved in an existing relationship might decide to take it a step further and tie the knot. Those of you still unattached will start meeting 'marriage material' – people you would consider marrying. There will be many opportunities for serious relationships. The love life will bloom well into next year too.

Pluto, the generic ruler of sex, is your love planet. Jupiter, the actual ruler of sex in your chart will be in your 7th house. Need we have a clearer message? The sexual magnetism seems the most important thing to you. This is the primary allurement. Wealth doesn't hurt, but seems secondary to that. Good sex will cover many sins in a relationship or marriage, and problems here could threaten the relationship. If problems arise in the marriage or relationship, this area is what will need fixing.

Good sex alone, no matter how good, is not enough to make a marriage work. Even the best of sexual chemistries will have a life span of about a year. Then they start to get a bit jaded. Other compatibilities need to be there.

Pluto, your love planet, is in your 9th house of religion and philosophy and Jupiter (the occupant of your 7th house) is the generic ruler of these things. So, the Horoscope is saying that you need a good philosophical compatibility. It doesn't mean that you have to agree on every point, but it's important that you share a similar outlook on life, the same religious values, the same feelings of what life is all about – its meaning and purpose.

There is an old saying: 'people who pray together, stay together'. This is certainly true in your case. Problems in a relationship can be worked through in this way. It would also be good to take foreign trips together or take classes together as a couple. The philosophical harmony – the harmony of the Higher Mental bodies – needs to be strengthened.

This strong 9th-house connection in love shows other things too. Foreign countries are likely venues for romantic meetings. So is your place of worship or college. Religious or educational functions and gatherings bring romantic opportunity. People in your place of worship seem eager to make introductions.

Often with these kinds of aspects one falls in love with the pastor, minister or professor. There is an attraction for highly educated people – mentor types. You like people you can learn from.

If you are working on your first or second marriage there is love this year and marriage opportunity. If you are working on your third marriage, your prospects improve after December 21. Next year – 2018 – will bring marriage opportunities.

Self-Improvement

The spiritual life – especially the abstract variety – is generally not that important to a Taurus. Taurus is down to earth and practical. Taurus sees life on earth – even the mundane things – to be spiritual. (You're probably right too!) You feel close to the Divine when you are physically comfortable and at ease. But over the past six or seven years this has begun to change. The spiritual life has not only been important but active and full of dynamic change. Very experimental. Very interesting. Uranus, ensconced in your 12th house has seen to that. Your career is partly responsible for this. In order to get to where you want to go, your spiritual understanding must increase. And, in many cases, people involved in your career are on a spiritual path and this has enhanced your interest. No matter, the Divine knows exactly what will attract you.

With Mars as your spiritual planet you like the path of action. You like to express your spiritual ideals in positive actions. Silent meditation is generally not for you. You like to be doing something – building an orphanage, hospital or church. Feeding hungry people. Doing practical acts of charity. Being there for someone in hospital. This tendency is even more pronounced these days and it's very good. But along with this the Horoscope is indicating some scientific, intellectual background too. Uranus is the planet of science. A scientific approach to the spiritual life will not diminish your actions, but enhance them. You will know why you're doing what you're doing. Your faith will be buttressed by knowledge.

Uranus rules astrology. Astrology has a very strong spiritual basis to it. We call it esoteric astrology. It is a philosophy of the stars. Thus this is a valid spiritual path these days. Jnana yoga, hermetic science and kabbala would also be interesting. These are rational scientific approaches.

Uranus in your 12th house shows 'spiritual experimentalism'. This has its good and bad points. On the positive side, you learn what path, what approach works for you through trial, error and observation – the scientific method. On the negative side it can make a person a 'spiritual faddist', running after the latest fads and trends, jumping from one to another. Spiritual progress takes persistence. If you jump around too quickly you only delay yourself.

The main challenge this year is integrating spirituality with a worldly career. Everyone finds their own personal solution to this. Some people opt for a spiritual-type career. They work for a charity or start a non-profit organization and work at it full time. Some people pursue a worldly career and start a non-profit business on the side. Some people get involved in charitable works while involved in a worldly career. You will find your solution for yourself. There are no rules about this.

Month-by-month Forecasts

January

Best Days Overall: 7, 8, 15, 16, 25, 26
Most Stressful Days Overall: 1, 7, 8, 13, 14, 20, 21, 27, 28
Best Days for Love: 2, 7, 8, 12, 15, 16, 20, 21, 25, 26, 31
Best Days for Money: 1, 6, 9, 10, 15, 18, 19, 25, 26, 28, 29
Best Days for Career: 1, 5, 6, 13, 14, 23, 24, 27, 28

It looks like a happy and successful month ahead, Taurus, enjoy. Your 9th house – a happy-go-lucky kind of house – is strong until the 19th so there are happy travel opportunities occurring. You might not actually travel, but the opportunity is there. Life is expansive. The horizons are widened. Students at college level should do well.

Your financial planet Mercury will spend most of the month in your 9th house – a good financial signal. It indicates expanded earnings. The only issue is that Mercury will be retrograde until the 8th so there might be delays and glitches involved in this expansion. Take more care in your financial dealings until the 8th. Read the fine print in all contracts very carefully – and it would be better not to sign them over that period. Avoid major purchases or investment decisions then. By the 13th, as Mercury re-enters your 9th house – this time in forward motion – most financial perplexities will be resolved. And earnings will happen faster.

On the 19th the Sun will cross your Mid-heaven and enter your 10th house of career. You enter a yearly career peak and much progress will be made. You have good support from the family, and the status of the family as a whole seems raised.

The Sun's solstice happened last month. This month Mars and Venus have their solstices, around the same time. With Mars it is from the 27th to the 31st, with Venus is from the 29th to the 31st. This suggests a pause – a personal pause and a pause in your spiritual and charitable life – and then a change of direction. These pauses are healthy. Nothing seems to get done outwardly, but inwardly the ground is being prepared for the future.

The bottom half of your chart is almost totally empty. Only one long-term planet is there. So the upper half is very dominant. The focus will be – and should be – on the career and outer objectives. Home and family issues can be downplayed right now.

We see the same situation with the Eastern and Western sectors of the chart. There is only one long-term planet in the Western sector. The Eastern half is overwhelmingly dominant. Thus you're in a period of personal independence. It is a time to have your way in life, a time for creating your own happiness. You have the power to create your destiny now, to be pro-active. If some condition irks you, make the necessary changes. Others will go along with you eventually.

February

Best Days Overall: 3, 4, 12, 13, 21, 22
Most Stressful Days Overall: 9, 10, 16, 17, 18, 24, 25
Best Days for Love: 3, 4, 9, 10, 12, 13, 16, 17, 18, 19, 20, 21, 22, 28
Best Days for Money: 3, 4, 5, 6, 14, 15, 24, 25, 26
Best Days for Career: 1, 2, 9, 10, 19, 20, 24, 25, 28

Health and energy have been less robust than usual since January 19. And this is the situation until the 18th of the month ahead. Your overall health is very good this year, as we have mentioned, but this particular period is less good, so get more rest when possible.

You're still very much in a yearly career peak and much progress is being made. When Mercury crosses your Mid-heaven on the 7th, pay rises can happen (official or unofficial ones). The authority figures in your life are favourably disposed to your financial goals.

Mercury's speedy motion this month indicates good financial confidence. You cover a lot of territory. Financial progress seems swift. In general the pace of events is swifter than usual. All the planets are moving forward until the 6th, with 90 per cent of them in forward motion after that.

The main headline this month are two eclipses. This is guaranteed to shake things up and create some excitement. The Lunar Eclipse of the 11th (in America it's on the 10th) occurs in your 4th house of home and family. This tends to bring personal – often life-changing – events and dramas to family members, parents or parent figures. It can bring a need for sudden repairs in the home. Cars and communication equipment get tested and might need replacement or repair. Siblings and neighbours are also affected here, so be patient with them this period. This eclipse affects you strongly (it's in stressful alignment with the Sun), so reduce your schedule and avoid high-stress activities now.

The Solar Eclipse of the 26th will also impact on the home and family – every Solar Eclipse does. So there is a reinforcement of the previous eclipse. Important changes need to be made in the home and family relationships. You know what they are; the eclipse will force the issue. This eclipse affects Neptune, the ruler of your 11th house. So your high-tech gadgets – smart phones, computers, laptops and software – can play up. Repairs or replacements might be needed. Make sure important files are backed up.

There can be dramas in the lives of friends. The marriages (and social life in general) of children or children figures get tested. Bosses and parents or parent figures are forced to make important financial changes. This eclipse seems less stressful on you personally than the previous one, but it won't hurt to take things a little easier anyway.

The month ahead is very spiritual too. Venus, the ruler of your Horoscope, enters your 12th house on the 3rd and spends the rest of the month there. Mars and Uranus are already in your spiritual house, so it is powerful this month. A good month to study spiritual literature, attend classes, seminars or workshops and spend more time on your spiritual practice.

March

Best Days Overall: 2, 3, 11, 12, 21, 22, 30
Most Stressful Days Overall: 9, 10, 16, 17, 23, 24
Best Days for Love: 1, 2, 3, 9, 11, 12, 16, 17, 18, 21, 22, 27, 31
Best Days for Money: 4, 5, 6, 7, 8, 13, 14, 18, 19, 23, 24, 28, 29
Best Days for Career: 1, 10, 19, 20, 23, 24, 28

One of the main headlines this month is the retrograde of Venus. This begins on the 4th and continues until April 15. Since she is the ruler of your Horoscope, this can make you feel less confident. There is a lack of direction. It is interesting that this occurs during a period of strong independence and personal power. You have the energy and power you need for personal happiness, for having things your way, but you're not sure what 'your way' is. Mars moves into your sign on the 10th and this increases your independence even further. You could be tempted to rush into changes that you're not sure about – and this will cause headaches down the road. What good is achieving things if you only have to undo them later on? Take the time to get clear on personal goals – how you want your body to be, what kind of look do you want to present to the world, what kind of regime you want to undertake, etc. Take your time. When clarity comes – and it will – you'll be in a good position to put your ideas into action.

Since Venus is also your health planet, don't rush into miracle diets or miracle therapies just yet. Study things further. Job seekers should study prospective offers more carefully too – and this applies to those of you who hire others. Get the facts. Get mentally clear. Resolve all doubts.

Health is excellent this month, but should you feel under the weather head, face and scalp massage will be excellent remedies. You respond well to spiritual-type therapies too. If you feel under the weather see a spiritual healer.

The month ahead is a spiritual month. Not only is your 12th house the strongest in your chart, but the ruler of your 12th house – Mars – will be in your 1st house (a prominent position) from the 10th onwards. Spiritual interests – meditation, contemplation, journaling, the study of sacred scripture – come naturally these days. Those of you already on a spiritual path will make great progress. Those of you who are not will just feel more idealistic for no apparent reason.

The financial planet will move into your 12th house on the 13th and spend the rest of the month there. The financial intuition will be excellent. Mercury's conjunction with Neptune on the 4th and 5th also brings good financial intuition. When such intuition happens it rarely seems 'rational' at the time – it is only later that we see how rational it was.

Mercury will conjunct Uranus on the 26th and 27th. This brings sudden, unexpected financial good. It can happen via the career or through parents or parent figures.

Mars in your sign from the 10th onwards makes you more physically active. You will want to exercise more, spend more time at the gym, indulge in sports, etc. Exercise is good, but the chart favours the more spiritual kinds – yoga, tai chi and so on. A more refined kind of exercise seems best.

Green is always a good colour for you; it is the colour of your sign. This month you might want to add more red – especially from the 10th onwards. Wearing the colours of the stars puts you more in tune with them and helps on the subtle levels of energy.

Love is a bit problematic this month. Venus is retrograde and Pluto, your love planet, receives stressful aspects. Hang in there, these are short-term problems.

April

Best Days Overall: 7, 8, 17, 18, 26, 27
Most Stressful Days Overall: 5, 6, 12, 13, 19, 20, 21
Best Days for Love: 4, 7, 8, 12, 13, 17, 18, 23, 26, 27
Best Days for Money: 1, 7, 8, 10, 11, 18, 19, 20, 21, 24, 25, 28, 29
Best Days for Career: 5, 6, 15, 16, 19, 20, 21, 24, 25

Continue to gain clarity on your goals until the 15th. This is the most important thing. When Venus moves forward on the 15th you will be entering your period of maximum personal power. It was worth the wait. The changes you make now will be good ones. And you have plenty of power to create conditions as you want them to be.

Continue your spiritual interests until the 19th. Spiritual break-throughs will be seen outwardly after that date.

This is a happy month ahead. The Sun moves into your sign on the 19th. Family seems very devoted to you and there is good family support. You have energy and star quality this period. Your personal appearance shines. Health is excellent. If you feel under the weather, spiritual-type therapies are still powerful.

Finances are good this month, though more complicated than usual. Mercury in your sign brings windfalls and financial opportunity and the money people in your life are supportive. But Mercury will go into retrograde motion on the 9th, indicating that your financial thinking could be unrealistic. As always, avoid making major financial decisions – major purchases or investments – from the 9th onwards. Don't stop your life over a Mercury retrograde, but avoid major expenditures.

The money people in your life can change their mind during Mercury's retrograde or delay certain actions. Use the delays to gain clarity and set goals for the future.

On the 21st Mars will move into your money house. (Mercury will move backwards into Aries on the 20th.) Financial intuition becomes important – except it needs verification during this period. Financial guidance will come in dreams or through other spiritual sources – ministers, gurus, spiritual channels, astrologers, tarot readers, etc. But you should confirm your insights with several of these sources before making any decisions. Mars in your money house will incline you to make quick financial decisions, but you should resist the urge until Mercury starts moving forward again early next month.

There is career success on the 13th and 14th – and the family as a whole seems successful too. But career is starting to wind down. The planetary power is beginning to shift to the lower half of the chart. The shift will be stronger next month, but you start to feel it from the 19th onwards.

May

Best Days Overall: 4, 5, 14, 15, 23, 24, 29, 30
Most Stressful Days Overall: 2, 3, 9, 10, 17, 18
Best Days for Love: 2, 3, 4, 5, 9, 10, 12, 13, 14, 15, 21, 22, 23, 24
Best Days for Money: 2, 3, 7, 8, 13, 16, 17, 18, 23, 24, 25, 26
Best Days for Career: 3, 13, 17, 18, 22, 30

The month ahead is Taurus heaven. It is a month of prosperity. The cosmos impels you to do what you most love to do – focus on finances.

There are many nice financial developments happening this month. Your financial planet starts moving forward on the 3rd, so your financial intuition is much more reliable now. From the 1st to the 11th Mercury and Uranus are travelling together. This brings sudden financial windfalls. Parents and bosses seem supportive. On the 16th Mercury will cross your Ascendant and enter your 1st house, bringing financial windfalls and opportunities to you. The money people in your life are supportive. You look rich and feel rich. People see you as a 'money person'. Mars will be in your money house all month. This again shows strong financial intuition (the period from the 10th to the 14th is exceptionally good). You are fearless in financial matters these days. The Sun will enter the money house on the 20th, further energizing it. He brings good family support. You begin a yearly financial peak. Wealth and earnings will increase.

Health is still excellent all month. There are no planets in stressful alignment to you (only the Moon, occasionally, will make stressful aspects, but these are short-term things). You have plenty of energy and with energy comes increased possibilities. However, if you feel under the weather at times you still respond well to spiritual-type therapies. Physical exercise and scalp/face massage are also still powerful therapies.

Love is bittersweet this month. Venus and Pluto are not in good aspect. Thus you and the current love are in disagreement. You have to work harder on your relationship. The love life should improve next month.

Retrograde activity is still strong this month. Until the 3rd 40 per cent of the planets are retrograde; after the 3rd it's 30 per cent. When starting new projects or ventures it is always best to have as many planets moving forward as possible. But if you must launch a new venture or product, this may be the time to do it – from your birthday onwards. This will give you a waxing (growing) personal solar cycle along with a waxing universal solar cycle. The 3rd to the 10th and then from the 25th onwards are the best times for new starts this month.

June

Best Days Overall: 1, 2, 10, 11, 12, 20, 21, 28, 29
Most Stressful Days Overall: 5, 6, 7, 13, 14, 26, 27
Best Days for Love: 1, 2, 5, 6, 7, 10, 11, 20, 21, 28, 29
Best Days for Money: 1, 2, 3, 4, 13, 14, 22, 23, 24, 30
Best Days for Career: 9, 13, 14, 19, 27

The planetary power is still mostly in the Eastern sector this month, although this will start to change next month. So if there are conditions that need changing in your life, this is the time to do it. Later on it will be more difficult.

Health is still excellent. No long- or short-term planet is stressing you out (only the Moon will do so occasionally). You have all the energy you need to achieve whatever you want to do. If you happen to feel under the weather, continue using spiritual techniques until the 6th. After that, neck and throat massage will be powerful therapies.

Venus's move into your sign on the 6th is fortunate. She brings happy job opportunities for the job seeker. If there are vitamins, supplements or other health items that you need – they come to you naturally and normally without any special effort. Venus's move into your sign is like taking a 'grace' pill. She confers social grace, sweetness of disposition, charm and beauty. You get on better with others. The love life will improve. Disagreements with the current love seem resolved after the 6th. The only issue in love right now is Pluto's retrograde movement (since April 20). There's no need to rush into important love decisions one way or another. Let love take its course.

You are still in a strong prosperity period until the 21st. The money house is still powerful. Family support is still good (and you are probably spending more on the home and family). Family connections are important in finance. On the 6th Mercury enters your money house – another good sign. He will be in his own sign and house and thus more powerful on your behalf. Earnings should increase. Whatever business you're involved with, good sales, marketing, PR and advertising are important. This is so all month. People need to know about your product or service. Mercury in your money house also brings good wealth ideas.

By the 21st your short-term financial goals should be achieved. The money house empties and your focus shifts to other things – to intellectual interests and communication. This is as it should be. Money is only a means to an end. It is not the purpose of life. It buys freedom and time, so that a person can grow mentally and spiritually. This is a period to grow mentally.

By the 6th the planetary shift from the upper half of your chart to the lower half will be complete. For the next few months the lower half of your Horoscope will be more dominant than the upper half. Career can be downplayed. Now it is time to focus more on your home base and your emotional well-being.

July

Best Days Overall: 8, 9, 17, 18, 23, 24
Most Stressful Days Overall: 3, 4, 10, 11, 23, 24, 30, 31
Best Days for Love: 3, 4, 8, 9, 10, 17, 18, 19, 20, 25, 26, 28, 29, 30, 31
Best Days for Money: 1, 4, 10, 11, 16, 19, 20, 25, 26, 28, 29
Best Days for Career: 6, 10, 11, 16, 24

Your financial planet, Mercury, has been 'out of bounds' since June 18. It is still 'out of bounds' on the 1st but is moving back into its normal boundary. So, in your financial life, you've been moving out of your normal orbit into uncharted territory. After the 1st you're back in your normal sphere. The month ahead is prosperous. Venus (a very important planet in your Horoscope) moves into the money house on the 5th and spends the rest of the month there. This indicates great focus on the finances – which is 90 per cent of the battle. We get what we focus on. You spend on yourself and adopt an image of wealth. Personal appearance seems ultra-important in earnings. Be careful not to let the ego get too involved in finance though – anything that distorts the judgement is a problem.

Mercury has been in your 3rd house of communication since June 21, and remains there until the 6th. So, many of the financial trends we discussed last month are in effect until this date. Good marketing, advertising and PR are very important. On the 6th Mercury moves into your 4th house, indicating the importance of family and family connections. Family support should be good. You'll probably be spending more on the home and family too. The financial planet in the sign of Leo makes you more of a risk-taker in financial matters – more speculative. This is not normal for you. On the other hand, sometimes we need to take a risk – we need to overcome fear. On the 26th Mercury moves into Virgo, your 5th house. You're still speculating, but the financial judgement is better. After the 26th we get a feeling of 'happy' money. The act of money-making is more enjoyable than usual. You spend on fun kinds of things too.

Your 4th house becomes very powerful from the 20th onwards, when Mars moves into it, followed by the Sun on the 22nd. So the focus is on home, family and your emotional well-being. Interestingly, these interests help the career – in a direct kind of way. Next month the focus will be even stronger. The powers that be seem to approve of a good family and domestic life.

When the 4th house is strong, emotional wellness and harmony is the dominant factor in life. If that is happening everything else will fall into place. But if there is discord, nothing much will work out.

This is a good period – after the 20th – to do renovations in the home. However, the health becomes more delicate. Make sure to get enough rest.

August

Best Days Overall: 4, 5, 13, 14, 22, 23, 31
Most Stressful Days Overall: 6, 7, 8, 20, 21, 26, 27
Best Days for Love: 4, 5, 9, 10, 13, 14, 18, 19, 22, 23, 26, 27, 28, 29, 31
Best Days for Money: 4, 5, 6, 7, 13, 14, 16, 22, 23, 24, 25, 31
Best Days for Career: 2, 3, 6, 7, 8, 11, 12, 20, 21, 29, 30

Your 4th house remains very powerful this month. Continue to work on your emotional wellness and the harmony of the domestic sphere. In the philosophy of astrology, when we handle the 4th house properly, we enter a joyful, holiday kind of period. The 5th house of fun and creativity follows the 4th house – it doesn't precede it. Fun happens after emotional harmony is established, not before.

We have two eclipses this month. Both seem to affect you strongly so have a more relaxed schedule over those periods.

The Lunar Eclipse of the 7th occurs in your 10th house of career, so there are shake-ups happening in your company or industry. This will most likely require a course correction on your part. Often there are dramas in the lives of bosses, parents and parent figures. Sometimes the government changes its rules. The marriage of a parent or parent figure (and perhaps a boss as well) gets tested now. Cars and communication equipment get tested. It will be a good idea to drive more carefully.

The Solar Eclipse of the 21st occurs in your 4th house but very close to the cusp of the 5th house. Thus both houses are affected. Every Solar Eclipse affects the home and family anyway, and family members will have dramas in their lives (children too). Sometimes repairs (possibly extensive ones) to the home are necessary. When an eclipse happens in the 4th house any hidden problems in the home are revealed. Perhaps there are mice or other rodents lurking around. Perhaps mould has collected in the interior plasterboard. Perhaps there is a hidden leak in the pipework. Now you find out about these things – they show themselves – and action has to be taken. This is inconvenient to be sure, but it is good that the problem is no longer hidden and can be dealt with.

Retrograde activity is very strong this month. From the 13th to the 25th half of the planets are travelling backwards. This further compounds the problems caused by the eclipses. An eclipse demands immediate attention, but planetary retrogrades create delays. Your financial planet starts to go backwards on the 13th too. Therefore (as you know by now), you should avoid major purchases or important financial decisions until he starts going forward again on September 5.

September

Best Days Overall: 1, 10, 18, 19, 28, 29
Most Stressful Days Overall: 3, 4, 16, 17, 23, 24, 30
Best Days for Love: 1, 7, 8, 10, 16, 17, 18, 19, 23, 24, 28, 29
Best Days for Money: 3, 4, 8, 9, 12, 13, 18, 19, 20, 21, 28, 29, 30
Best Days for Career: 3, 4, 8, 17, 27, 30

Health and energy are much improved over last month. Problems were created last month (perhaps we should say 'revealed' – they existed before last month's eclipses happened) but now you have all the energy you need to handle them. Your health can be further enhanced by giving more attention to the heart until the 20th, and to the small intestine after then. Giving yourself permission to have fun – to enjoy life – will also enhance your health.

Your 5th house became powerful last month and remains so this month too. So, handle your issues and responsibilities but make sure you have some fun too. You can do both. Sometimes the best way to deal with an insurmountable problem is to let it go. Do something else. Get creative. Have fun. When you come back to the problem, you discover the solution comes to you easily. Your obsessive focus was blocking things. Often the solution is hilariously simple.

This is a month to get more involved with the children and children figures in your life. You relate very well to them. To be sure, you're a bit of a child yourself. Personal creativity is very strong now too. It is good to express some of this. Your sense of fun – your lightness of heart – will help the financial picture too. Mercury retrograded back into your 4th house last month; on the 10th he re-enters the 5th house. As we have already mentioned, this indicates happy money. You earn or have earnings opportunities while you're having fun – perhaps at the movies or theatre. Perhaps at a resort or party.

The love life is much improved this month. Pluto, the love planet, is still retrograde, but he is receiving very good aspects. So the social life is happy. There are many love and social opportunities happening. Only don't be in a rush. Enjoy things for what they are.

The love life of children or children figures is a bit stressed this month. If they are married or in a serious relationship, they need more patience. The problems seem more about the partner's issues than their own.

Mars makes beautiful aspects to the career planet Uranus from the 1st to the 3rd. Being involved in charities or good causes helps the career.

October

Best Days Overall: 7, 8, 15, 16, 25, 26
Most Stressful Days Overall: 1, 13, 14, 20, 21, 27, 28, 29
Best Days for Love: 7, 8, 15, 16, 17, 18, 20, 21, 25, 26, 27, 28
Best Days for Money: 1, 9, 10, 11, 20, 30
Best Days for Career: 1, 6, 14, 23, 24, 27, 28, 29

Jupiter has been in your 6th house of work all year and will be there until the 10th of this month. Your 6th house became powerful on September 22nd and remains so in the month ahead – 60 per cent of the planets are either there or moving through there. This is a lot of power. It is a wonderful time for job seekers; there are multiple opportunities happening now. (The whole past year has been good for this, but now it's even better.) Some of you could be working two or three jobs now. Others are merely having multiple employment opportunities. Power in this house also shows a great focus on health. But as we mentioned earlier, this focus can be too much. You don't need to magnify little things into big things.

On the 11th Jupiter moves into your 7th house of love and will be there well into next year. Mercury follows on the 17th and the Sun on the 23rd. Thus love is the main headline from the 23rd onwards. You will be in a yearly love and social peak. Singles are going to date more, and they will attract meaningful kinds of relationships. Many a marriage will happen in the next 12 months. Those already attached will be attending more weddings and gatherings. They will make new and significant friendships. A business partnership or joint venture might manifest.

Jupiter's move into the 7th house brings financial windfalls and general prosperity for the spouse, partner or current love interest. (Prosperity will get even stronger in 2018.)

There's more good news on the love front. Pluto (your love planet) started moving forward on September 28. So, all systems are go when it comes to love. There is opportunity and mental clarity – good social judgement. Enjoy.

The Sun will have his solstice on December 21. But this month Venus and Mars will have their solstice. They 'pause' in the heavens and then change direction. In the case of Venus (which is the more important one for you) this happens from the 16th to the 19th. So, this calls for a pause in your affairs and then a change of direction. It is a pause that refreshes. It might feel like a 'stoppage' but it's not.

Mars, your spiritual planet, has his solstice from the 23rd to the 30th. This suggests a change of spiritual direction – perhaps a change of direction in the charities or causes that you support.

November

Best Days Overall: 3, 4, 12, 13, 21, 22
Most Stressful Days Overall: 9, 10, 16, 17, 24, 25
Best Days for Love: 3, 4, 6, 7, 12, 13, 16, 17, 21, 22, 26, 27
Best Days for Money: 5, 6, 7, 8, 9, 16, 17, 19, 20, 26, 27, 29, 30
Best Days for Career: 2, 10, 20, 24, 25, 30

Health became more delicate last month on the 23rd and remains so until the 22nd of this month. This is nothing serious, just less than usual energy. Try to get enough rest and sleep. This is a short-term issue. After the 22nd your health and energy will rebound. Enhance the health in the ways mentioned in the yearly report until the 7th. After the 7th give more attention to the colon, bladder and sexual organs. Love is active and happy, but there's no need to overdo the sex thing. Your body will tell you when enough is enough. A herbal colonic might be a good idea if you feel under the weather.

The love life is still the main headline this month, with your 7th house still very powerful. Indeed, on the 7th Venus moves in and makes it even more powerful. You are socially popular and socially active. The 12th and 13th seem especially good on the romantic front (and bring a nice payday too). New friends come into the picture on the 16th, 17th, 29th and 30th. (This can happen online or via more regular ways.) Many of you will be more involved with astrology or have your personal horoscopes done.

Finances will be good this month (always important for you, Taurus). Until the 6th your social connections are important in this: your likeability is important. After the 6th, as Mercury enters your 8th house, you prosper by 'cutting back' – by eliminating waste and duplications, by cutting needless expense, by paying down or refinancing debt. It will be a very good period in which to get rid of old possessions that you don't need or use. Function should be your guide. Things that you use, keep. Things that don't get used should be sold or given to charity or otherwise disposed of. The financial planet in the 8th house suggests a need to make others rich. The financial interest of others (especially your partner or spouse) should come before your own. As you put others first, your own prosperity will happen naturally. Tax issues should be considered in financial decision-making. Those of you of appropriate age should consider wills and estate planning – it's a good period for this. It's also a good month to purchase insurance or annuities, if you need them.

December

Best Days Overall: 1, 2, 9, 10, 18, 19, 20
Most Stressful Days Overall: 7, 8, 14, 15, 21, 22
Best Days for Love: 1, 2, 7, 8, 9, 10, 14, 15, 16, 17, 19, 20, 28, 29
Best Days for Money: 3, 4, 5, 6, 7, 8, 14, 15, 16, 17, 24, 25, 26, 27, 30, 31
Best Days for Career: 8, 17, 18, 21, 22, 27

The planetary power began to shift to the upper half of your Horoscope in October, and during this month the shift becomes much more pronounced. Mars moves to the upper part of your chart on the 9th. Thus *all* the planets (with the exception of the Moon) will be in the upper half of your chart – and between the 14th to the 27th, even the Moon will be in the upper half. The career and outer goals are most prominent now. Emotional wellness will happen as a side effect of outward success. Focus on the career now. Great progress is being made here this month – and it's still not your peak career period (this will happen in January and February 2018).

Mars's move into your 7th house indicates spiritual-type friends these days. Love is more spiritual. Singles have romantic opportunities in spiritual settings – at charity events, spiritual seminars, lectures etc. If you can avoid power struggles in your relationship (one of the problems with Mars in the 7th house), love should be happy. The two rulers of libido – Mars, the generic ruler, and Jupiter the ruler of your 8th house – are both in your 7th house of love.* The sexual attraction and sexual magnetism is the most important thing. It's not everything to be sure, but will cover many problems in a relationship. You can't build

---

* *Pluto, a generic ruler of libido (along with Mars) is your love planet as well.*

a long-term relationship only on that, but this is still the primary attraction.

Mercury, your financial planet, spends most of the month retrograde – from the 3rd to the 23rd. This complicates holiday shopping. If possible do it early, before the 3rd. If this is not possible, just do more homework and make sure the stores have a good returns policy. With your financial planet in Sagittarius all month, the tendency could be to overspend.

Health is good this month. There are two planets in stressful alignment with you – Mars and Jupiter – but that's it. The other planets are supporting you or leaving you alone. You can enhance health further (if you feel under the weather) through detox regimes (until the 25th) and thigh massage. A herbal liver cleanse would also be helpful. After the 25th enhance the health through back and knee massage.

Gemini

Ⅱ

THE TWINS

Birthdays from
21st May to
20th June

Personality Profile

GEMINI AT A GLANCE

Element – Air

Ruling Planet – Mercury
  Career Planet – Neptune
  Love Planet – Jupiter
  Money Planet – Moon
  Planet of Health and Work – Pluto
  Planet of Home and Family Life – Mercury

Colours – blue, yellow, yellow-orange

Colour that promotes love, romance and social harmony – sky blue

Colours that promote earning power – grey, silver

Gems – agate, aquamarine

Metal – quicksilver

Scents – lavender, lilac, lily of the valley, storax

Quality – mutable (= flexibility)

Quality most needed for balance – thought that is deep rather than superficial

Strongest virtues – great communication skills, quickness and agility of thought, ability to learn quickly

Deepest need – communication

Characteristics to avoid – gossiping, hurting others with harsh speech, superficiality, using words to mislead or misinform

Signs of greatest overall compatibility – Libra, Aquarius

Signs of greatest overall incompatibility – Virgo, Sagittarius, Pisces

Sign most helpful to career – Pisces

Sign most helpful for emotional support – Virgo

Sign most helpful financially – Cancer

Sign best for marriage and/or partnerships – Sagittarius

Sign most helpful for creative projects – Libra

Best Sign to have fun with – Libra

Signs most helpful in spiritual matters – Taurus, Aquarius

Best day of the week – Wednesday

Understanding a Gemini

Gemini is to society what the nervous system is to the body. It does not introduce any new information but is a vital transmitter of impulses from the senses to the brain and vice versa. The nervous system does not judge or weigh these impulses – it only conveys information. And it does so perfectly.

This analogy should give you an indication of a Gemini's role in society. Geminis are the communicators and conveyors of information. To Geminis the truth or falsehood of information is irrelevant, they only transmit what they see, hear or read about. Thus they are capable of spreading the most outrageous rumours as well as conveying truth and light. Geminis sometimes tend to be unscrupulous in their communications and can do both great good or great evil with their power. This is why the sign of Gemini is symbolized by twins: Geminis have a dual nature.

Their ability to convey a message – to communicate with such ease – makes Geminis ideal teachers, writers and media and marketing people. This is helped by the fact that Mercury, the ruling planet of Gemini, also rules these activities.

Geminis have the gift of the gab. And what a gift this is! They can make conversation about anything, anywhere, at any time. There is almost nothing that is more fun to Geminis than a good conversation – especially if they can learn something new as well. They love to learn and they love to teach. To deprive a Gemini of conversation, or of books and magazines, is cruel and unusual punishment.

Geminis are almost always excellent students and take well to education. Their minds are generally stocked with all kinds of information, trivia, anecdotes, stories, news items, rarities, facts and statistics. Thus they can support any intellectual position that they care to take. They are awesome debaters and, if involved in politics, make good orators. Geminis are so verbally smooth that even if they do not know what they are talking about, they can make you think that they do. They will always dazzle you with their brilliance.

Finance

Geminis tend to be more concerned with the wealth of learning and ideas than with actual material wealth. As mentioned, they excel in professions that involve writing, teaching, sales and journalism – and not all of these professions pay very well. But to sacrifice intellectual needs merely for money is unthinkable to a Gemini. Geminis strive to combine the two. Cancer is on Gemini's solar 2nd house of money cusp, which indicates that Geminis can earn extra income (in a harmonious and natural way) from investments in residential property, restaurants and hotels. Given their verbal skills, Geminis love to bargain and negotiate in any situation, and especially when it has to do with money.

The Moon rules Gemini's 2nd solar house. The Moon is not only the fastest-moving planet in the zodiac but actually moves through every sign and house every 28 days. No other heavenly body matches the Moon for swiftness or the ability to change quickly. An analysis of the Moon – and lunar phenomena in general – describes Gemini's financial attitudes very well. Geminis are financially versatile and flexible; they can earn money in many different ways. Their financial attitudes and needs seem to change daily. Their feelings about money change also: sometimes they are very enthusiastic about it, at other times they could not care less.

For a Gemini, financial goals and money are often seen only as means of supporting a family; these things have little meaning otherwise.

The Moon, as Gemini's money planet, has another important message for Gemini financially: in order for Geminis to realize their financial potential they need to develop more of an understanding of the emotional side of life. They need to combine their awesome powers of logic with an understanding of human psychology. Feelings have their own logic; Geminis need to learn this and apply it to financial matters.

Career and Public Image

Geminis know that they have been given the gift of communication for a reason, that it is a power that can achieve great good or cause unthinkable distress. They long to put this power at the service of the highest and most transcendental truths. This is their primary goal, to communicate the eternal verities and prove them logically. They look up to people who can transcend the intellect – to poets, artists, musicians and mystics. They may be awed by stories of religious saints and martyrs. A Gemini's highest achievement is to teach the truth, whether it is scientific, inspirational or historical. Those who can transcend the intellect are Gemini's natural superiors – and a Gemini realizes this.

The sign of Pisces is in Gemini's solar 10th house of career. Neptune, the planet of spirituality and altruism, is Gemini's career planet. If Geminis are to realize their highest career potential they need to develop their transcendental – their spiritual and altruistic – side. They need to understand the larger cosmic picture, the vast flow of human evolution – where it came from and where it is heading. Only then can a Gemini's intellectual powers take their true position and he or she can become the 'messenger of the gods'. Geminis need to cultivate a facility for 'inspiration', which is something that does not originate in the intellect but which comes through the intellect. This will further enrich and empower a Gemini's mind.

Love and Relationships

Geminis bring their natural garrulousness and brilliance into their love life and social life as well. A good talk or a verbal joust is an interesting prelude to romance. Their only problem in love is that their intellect is too cool and passionless to incite ardour in others. Emotions sometimes disturb them, and their partners tend to complain about this. If you are in love with a Gemini you must understand why this is so. Geminis avoid deep passions because these would interfere with their ability to think and communicate. If they are cool towards you, understand that this is their nature.

Nevertheless, Geminis must understand that it is one thing to talk about love and another actually to love – to feel it and radiate it. Talking about love glibly will get them nowhere. They need to feel it and act on it. Love is not of the intellect but of the heart. If you want to know how a Gemini feels about love you should not listen to what he or she says, but rather, observe what he or she does. Geminis can be quite generous to those they love.

Geminis like their partners to be refined, well educated and well travelled. If their partners are more wealthy than they, that is all the better. If you are in love with a Gemini you had better be a good listener as well.

The ideal relationship for the Gemini is a relationship of the mind. They enjoy the physical and emotional aspects, of course, but if the intellectual communion is not there they will suffer.

Home and Domestic Life

At home the Gemini can be uncharacteristically neat and meticulous. They tend to want their children and partner to live up to their idealistic standards. When these standards are not met they moan and criticize. However, Geminis are good family people and like to serve their families in practical and useful ways.

The Gemini home is comfortable and pleasant. They like to invite people over and they make great hosts. Geminis are also good at repairs and improvements around the house – all fuelled by their need to stay active and occupied with something they like to do. Geminis have many hobbies and interests that keep them busy when they are home alone.

Geminis understand and get along well with their children, mainly because they are very youthful people themselves. As great communicators, Geminis know how to explain things to children; in this way they gain their children's love and respect. Geminis also encourage children to be creative and talkative, just like they are.

Horoscope for 2017

Major Trends

Though you still need to watch your energy this year, many nice things are happening. Jupiter is established in your 5th house of fun, creativity and children and will be there until October 10 – most of the year ahead. Thus, it is a fun kind of year. A creative year. A year for exploring leisure and fun. Geminis of childbearing age are more fertile than usual.

On October 11 Jupiter will enter your 6th house of health and work and stay there for the rest of the year. This will bring happy job opportunities – good ones. It will also impact on the romantic life as it makes the workplace a venue for romance. More on this later.

Saturn has been in your 7th house of love for the past two years and will be there until December 21 – almost all year. This has been testing relationships – marriages or other types of committed relationships. They have been getting stress tested. Many did not survive – the good ones did. This testing continues in the year ahead. By the end of the year, as Saturn moves out of your 7th house, the testing eases up. The lessons have been learned. The love life should improve. More details on this later.

Pluto has been in your 8th house for many years now and will be there for many more. So there is more dealing with death and death issues. Your understanding is deepening.

Neptune, your career planet and the most spiritual of the planets, still sits at the top of your chart – near the Mid-heaven. Thus spirituality is an important interest. Spiritual or idealistic careers attract you.

Serious love is being tested, but friendships are going well. The overall social life is good but unstable.

Finance doesn't seem a big issue this year.

Your most important interests this year are children, fun and creativity (until October 10); health and work (from October 11 onwards); love, romance and social activities (until December 21); personal transformation, personal reinvention, sex, occult studies; career; and friends, groups, group activities and online activities.

Your areas of greatest fulfilment are home, family and emotional wellness (until April 29); communication and intellectual interests (from April 29 onwards); children, fun and creativity (until October 10); and health and work (from October 11 onwards).

Health

(Please note that this is an astrological perspective on health and not a medical one. In days of yore there was no difference, both of these perspectives were identical. But now there could be quite a difference. For a medical perspective, please consult your doctor or health practitioner.)

Health and energy are improved over last year, but still need attention. Saturn will spend most of the year in stressful alignment with you, and Neptune has been in stressful alignment since 2012. The good news is that health will get better by the end of the year when Saturn moves away from his stressful aspect.

Your 6th house of health will become a house of power from October 11 onwards. This is a good thing. You will be more focused here and your partners, spouse or friends will also be too.

There is much, as our regular readers know, that can be done to improve the health. Give more attention to the following areas – the vulnerable areas of your Horoscope (the reflexes are shown in the chart opposite):

- The lungs, arms, shoulders and respiratory system. These are always important for Geminis, and regular arm and shoulder massage should be part of your daily health regime. The wrists and hands should also be massaged. Hand reflexology – see Mildred Carter's book, *Hand Reflexology* – is especially beneficial for you.
- The colon, bladder and sexual organs. Colonics or herbal colon cleanses are good if your feel under the weather. Safe sex and sexual moderation are always important for you.
- The spine, knees, teeth, bones, skin and overall skeletal alignment. These have become more important in recent years – ever since your health planet Pluto moved into Capricorn in 2008. Regular back and knee massage is good, as are regular visits to a chiropractor or osteopath. The vertebrae and skeleton need to be in right alignment. Therapies such as Rolfing, Feldenkrais and Alexander Technique would be helpful. Watch your posture as you

sit or get up from a chair – you could be unconsciously throwing
your spine out of alignment. Give the knees more support when
exercising, and if you're out in the Sun use a good sun screen.
Regular dental check-ups are a good idea too.

• The liver and thighs. These become important after October 11 as
Jupiter – the ruler of these areas – moves into your 6th house of
health. Regular thigh massage will not only strengthen the thighs
and liver, but the lower back as well. It will also send energy to the
colon. A herbal liver cleanse might also be helpful if you feel under
the weather.

Since these are the most vulnerable areas this year, problems, if they
happened (God forbid) would most likely begin here. Keeping them
healthy and fit is sound preventive medicine. Most of the time problems can be prevented, but even if they can't be totally avoided (due to
strong karmic momentum) they can be softened to a great degree. They
need not be devastating.

Important foot reflexology points for the year ahead

Try to massage all of the foot on a regular basis – the top of the foot as well as
the bottom – but pay extra attention to the points highlighted on the chart.
When you massage, be aware of 'sore spots' as these need special attention.
It's also a good idea to massage the ankles, and below them particularly.

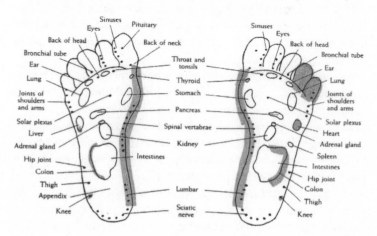

We've mentioned before that you have a tendency towards surgery, but detoxing methods should also be explored. These will often have the same result, but do tend to take longer.

Home and Family

Technically speaking, your 4th house of home and family is not a house of power this year. However, the Moon's North Node (which is not a planet but an abstract point) will be there until April 29. This indicates more involvement with the family, and there is a sense of fulfilment in this area. It is a happy aspect.

The North Node indicates feelings of excess. In the 4th house it would show more involvement with the family than is actually needed – but no matter, you enjoy it. It would also show an 'excess' of emotion – positive or negative. Make sure to keep it positive. It also indicates success in therapy – for those of you involved in this. Psychological breakthroughs are happening for you.

Family support will be 'more than is needed' – but more is better than less. And if you move during this period – until April 29 – the new home is likely to be 'bigger' than necessary.

We mentioned earlier that Geminis of childbearing age are more fertile than usual. Thus there can be multiple births (twins or more).

Moves can happen – there's nothing in your chart against it – but probably won't. You seem happy with the status quo and don't seem to have a need to move. (A move or renovation was likely to have happened in the past two years and this is another reason for satisfaction with the status quo.)

Parents or parent figures in your life (whoever plays this role for you) are prospering this year but a move is not advisable here. They are better off making the present home more pleasurable. Siblings or sibling figures in your life are likely to move or renovate their homes after October 11. Sometimes people don't literally move – sometimes they acquire another home or buy expensive items for the home. The effect is 'as if' they are in a new home. Children or children figures are more likely to renovate their house than to move. It looks like big repair jobs will be going on. Grandchildren (if you have them) are having a stable home and family year.

If you're planning to redecorate – to paint, change furniture, buy objets d'art or otherwise beautify the home – August 22 to October 14 is a good period. If you're planning major repairs or renovations, September 5 to October 27 will be good.

The health of parents or parent figures seems reasonable this year. Sure, there will be periods where their health is less easy than usual, but these seem like short-term trends – not trends for the year ahead. One of the parent figures will start feeling a lot better after December 21. This person seems very affected by the Solar Eclipse of February 26. It brings life-changing kinds of dramas to him or her, together with a redefinition of the personality and image. Children and children figures will also feel better after December 21. They respond well to spiritual healing techniques. Siblings or sibling figures can be having surgery (although it could have already happened).

Finance and Career

Finance, as we mentioned, doesn't seem a big issue this year. Your money house is basically empty. Only fast-moving, short-term planets will move through there this year. So, you're not paying that much attention to money. I consider this a positive. It shows satisfaction with things as they are. You have no pressing need to focus here, which tends to the status quo. Earnings will more or less be like last year. If financial problems arise, lack of attention is probably at the root of them. You'll have to force yourself to give the area more focus.

Though finances are not a big issue, the career is very important and a major focus. Prestige and status seem more important than mere money. You would take a high prestige assignment or position even if the pay was mediocre. Status trumps earnings. Many people don't think this way, but you do. And, you could be right. Career advancement – career status – often leads to more money down the road.

Geminis are flexible people, and this is so in finance too. The Moon, your financial planet, is perhaps the most flexible and changeable of all the planets. She will move through every sector of your chart in any given month. She will make aspects with every planet, every month. Thus money and earnings opportunities can come to you from many places and people in any given month. These short-term trends are best dealt with in the monthly reports.

In general, the New and Full Moons tend to be financially strong days. Moreover, your earning power is stronger when the Moon is waxing or growing larger rather than when it is getting smaller or waning. When the Moon is waxing it is good to make investments where you want 'growth' to happen. When the Moon is waning it is good to use any spare cash to pay off debts or other obligations. These are things that you want to reduce and you get cosmic help here.

Your prosperity should be stronger later in the year, from October 11 onwards. There are lucrative job opportunities coming and they will probably pay well.

Two Lunar Eclipses this year – one on February 11 and the other on August 7 – will shake up the financial life. This happens every year, so it is nothing to fear. You've gone through this many times. The eclipses force financial 'course corrections'. Twice a year – every year – you get a chance to make any necessary changes to the financial life.

Career is good this year, but will also get a lot better from October 11 onwards. On that date, Jupiter will start to make beautiful aspects to your career planet, Neptune. On December 21, Saturn will move away from his stressful aspect to Neptune and this will further improve things. In the meantime you just have to work a little harder.

A Solar Eclipse on February 26 will directly hit your career planet, and it occurs in your 10th house of career. So this will bring shake-ups in your company or industry. Course corrections will be needed in your career. And you will make them.

As we mentioned, you need an idealistic, meaningful career. Just being 'worldly successful' is not enough. Many of you will gravitate to non-profit organizations or charitable or spiritual-type organizations. The fine arts will also appeal to many of you. You don't need to be an actual artist or performer, but can be involved in the business, administrative side of things.

Love and Social Life

Saturn, as we have mentioned, has been in your 7th house of love for two years now, and he will remain there for almost the whole year ahead. Existing relationships are getting severely tested. There has been many a divorce or break up these past two years and even now, flawed relationships are in danger. None of this should be considered punishment (though it can be stressful and feel like punishment). The cosmos wants the best for you, and if a current relationship doesn't meet the standard, it will go.

For singles the past two years have been a bit different. The social life – dating and parties – has contracted. You haven't been going out as much as usual. This too is not punishment. The cosmos wants you to focus more on quality rather than quantity. Quality dates, quality relationships, quality gatherings – though fewer – are preferable to hosts of mediocre things.

The love life started to change last year, in September, as Jupiter, your love planet, moved into your 5th house. You got into a more romantic mood. You increased the dating and party going, but you most likely didn't marry. This is the case for the year ahead too. You'll indulge in fun relationships, but marriage doesn't seem on the cards. Marriage prospects will improve in 2018 and 2019 though – you're just getting prepared for it now.

In love you seem of two minds. One part is very sober, serious and traditional. You want stability and security, and favour older, more settled types of people. This is shown by Saturn in your 7th house. The other part of you just wants fun – pleasure. This part is not at all concerned with stability or security, just enjoyment. The feeling of love (even if it's illusionary) is preferable to dull, steady routine. This part is spontaneous and will fall in love quickly. The other part, the conservative part, will take its time to see whether it's 'safe' to fall in love. It is difficult to satisfy both parts of your nature – they often argue. A person that satisfies one part might be abhorrent to the other, and vice versa. The best relationship will be with someone who satisfies both parts of your nature – but these people are hard to find. Be patient.

On October 11, as your love planet moves into your 6th house, your love attitudes and needs also shift. Fun becomes less important and you are attracted to the person who serves your practical interests. This is how you feel loved and this is how you show it.

The workplace becomes a venue for romance. Job opportunities are coming, as we mentioned, but it is the social atmosphere and social opportunity that will determine which job you take. There can be office romances with co-workers. You're also attracted to health professionals or people involved in your health. A routine doctor's visit can wind up being much more than that.

Saturn in your 7th house shows someone older in your life. Not an old person, but someone older and more settled than you. There seems to be a good sexual magnetism, but he or she also appears overly controlling.

Self-Improvement

Your 12th house of spirituality hasn't been strong for many years, yet, because Neptune is the highest planet in your chart (and has been since 2012), spirituality is prominent. In general you gravitate to the path of love and devotion. Love, love, love and everything will work out. And Neptune on the Mid-heaven reinforces this. You're someone who, if anything, has an excess of logic and rationality. So there is a need to develop the love and devotional side – the irrational or arational side. Mantra chanting, singing and drumming ceremonies are all excellent for you. Too much rationality can produce tendencies to depression. There are so many things in life that can't be 'reasoned' away. We must rise above thought and this path will do the trick. If you feel depressed, half an hour of mantra chanting will take you right out of it. In fact, it will make you feel 'high' without having taken a drink or drug. One feels a sense of euphoria. And in this state, the Higher Energies can come through.

In a year or two Uranus will move into your 12th house and stay there for many years; spirituality will become even more prominent than it is now. This move will inject more science and rationality into the spiritual life. You will start to understand the science behind all this apparent 'voodoo'. Right now it doesn't seem to matter much, but when you understand the rationality behind the mystical practices, you'll be able to write and teach about it.

Since Uranus is your planet of religion and philosophy, there will be revelation about the mundane and mystical practices of your own native religion.

The Mid-heaven and 10th house show more than just a person's career. This is just the worldly reading of it. On a deeper level it shows a person's mission in life – the spiritual purpose for the incarnation. You were sent down to do something special, something no one else can do. You took vows on inner levels to achieve this. Since 2012 it has been time for you to learn what this is and to start doing it. Until you do there will be this subtle sense of dissatisfaction, regardless of how successful you are. It won't go away until you start to do your real mission. This doesn't mean that you have to give up your worldly career. Definitely not – not right away. But gradually you start to give more attention to your mission, and the worldly career gets put into its proper perspective.

How do I find out what I'm supposed to do? This is the question we always hear – it's a good question. Prayer is a good beginning. Ask the Divine to show you what it is. Gurus, ministers, spiritual channels, psychics and astrologers have information on this subject, and it might be advisable to consult them. Also, pay attention to your dreams. They are revelatory these days and there will be many dreams that lead you to your mission, once you penetrate 'dream language'. Write your dreams down.

Usually a person is called to do great and mighty things. Much more than they believe is possible for them. Things that seem beyond their powers and abilities. This is generally the main reason they get ignored – the human mind can't accept such greatness. But as you begin, according to your present abilities, you will find that the 'impossible' is very doable. We grow into our mission gradually.

Month-by-month Forecasts

January

Best Days Overall: 1, 9, 10, 17, 18, 19, 27, 28
Most Stressful Days Overall: 2, 3, 15, 16, 22, 23, 24, 30, 31
Best Days for Love: 1, 2, 10, 12, 18, 19, 20, 21, 22, 23, 24, 28, 29, 31
Best Days for Money: 1, 7, 8, 10, 11, 12, 16, 18, 19, 27, 28, 29
Best Days for Career: 1, 2, 11, 20, 27, 28, 30

You begin your year with a focus on the outer life – the career and outer goals. The great majority – sometimes 90 per cent – of the planets are in the upper half of your chart this month. Your 10th house of career is very powerful, while your 4th house of home and family is basically empty (only the Moon moves through there on the 15th and 16th). The planet that rules the home, Mercury, is retrograde until the 8th. So we have a very clear cosmic directive – focus on the career now and let home and family issues go for a while. Emotional wellness is always important, but the chart is showing that this will happen as a side effect of career success.

The planetary power is mostly in the Western sector now, though this will change in coming months. So your focus is on others, your social life and getting things done by consensus rather than by direct action. Personal independence is not very strong now, so if there are conditions that irk you, make a note of them but don't do anything yet. The time to make changes will happen soon.

Finance is not a big issue this month. You're strongest financial days are shown above. Earning power will be strongest from the 1st to the 12th and from the 28th onwards – the waxing (growing) moon periods. The 10th seems like an exceptionally strong financial day. Not only are the aspects good, but the Moon will be at her perigee (her closest distance to the Earth).

Saturn in your 7th house is still testing the love life. The good news is that you're trying hard. Mercury is in your 7th house from the 5th to the 13th, indicating that you're giving more focus here – and this is what is needed. The love life improves after the 19th as the Sun starts making nice aspects to the love planet. Your naturally good gift of the gab is a big help. There is good communication with the beloved then. You connect well on the intellectual level.

Your 8th house of regeneration is powerful until the 19th. It's time to go through your possessions and get rid of what you don't need or use. Detox regimes are good for the health but also for other areas of life.

Health is excellent this month, and gets even better from the 19th onwards.

February

Best Days Overall: 5, 6, 14, 15, 24, 25
Most Stressful Days Overall: 12, 13, 19, 20, 26, 27
Best Days for Love: 5, 6, 9, 10, 14, 15, 19, 20, 24, 25, 28
Best Days for Money: 5, 6, 7, 8, 14, 15, 24, 25, 26, 27
Best Days for Career: 7, 8, 16, 17, 26, 27

Continue to focus on the career. The upper half of your Horoscope is easily the most dominant and your 10th house of career is even stronger than last month. There is much success happening. Along with this there are changes here as well. A Solar Eclipse on the 26th occurs in this house. Not only that but it affects your career planet, Neptune. So success is happening but with shake-ups and disruptions. This Solar Eclipse affects you strongly, so make sure to reduce your schedule and rearrange stressful activities. My feeling about this eclipse is that the changes and disruptions that it brings will open doors for you.

Health is good on an overall level, but temporarily more delicate from the 18th onwards. Overall energy is not up to its usual standard so make sure you get enough sleep and rest. Enhance the health in the ways mentioned in the yearly report.

Career is much more important than finance this month. You prefer status to money – and you have a good point. Increased status – in your company or profession – generally leads to more money down the road. You are strongest financially on the days mentioned above, and also from the 1st to the 11th and from the 26th onwards – the Moon's waxing periods. Though the aspects are not so great on the 6th it should be a good financial day – the Moon will be at her perigee, closest to Earth. Money should come but with more work involved.

There is a Lunar Eclipse on the 11th that occurs in your 3rd house of communication. This one is not as strong as the Solar Eclipse but it won't hurt to take it easier anyway. (Others in your circle or environment can be affected.) This eclipse brings financial changes. It is a time for financial 'course corrections' – your strategy and thinking need to be upgraded. Events will happen that will force the issue. Cars and communication equipment can behave erratically over this period, and often repairs or replacements prove necessary. There are dramas in the lives of siblings, sibling figures and neighbours. Students can change schools or experience some upheaval at school.

March

Best Days Overall: 4, 5, 13, 14, 23, 24
Most Stressful Days Overall: 11, 12, 18, 19, 25, 26
Best Days for Love: 1, 5, 6, 9, 13, 14, 18, 19, 23, 24, 27
Best Days for Money: 5, 6, 7, 13, 14, 16, 23, 24, 27, 28
Best Days for Career: 6, 7, 15, 16, 25, 26

Late last month, on the 25th, the planetary power shifted from the West to the East. For the next five or six months, the Eastern sector of the self will be dominant. The planetary power now moves towards you, and thus personal independence and power increase day by day. Mercury is moving forward too, so you have confidence and clarity. Make the changes in your life that need to be made. Take responsibility for your own happiness.

When the Sun enters Aries on the 20th you have the added benefit of powerful 'starting energy'. This would be a good period (especially from the 28th onwards) to start a new business or project, or to launch a new product; 80 per cent of the planets are moving forward as well.

Career is still a major focus until the 20th, and you are in a yearly career peak. Your 10th house is strong, while your 4th house of home and family is empty (only the Moon moves through here, on the 11th and 12th). You seem very successful these days. (Last month was also successful.) The 1st to the 5th seems an especially strong career period – though the aspects are not especially great. You seem at the top of your game. You seem close to the people in power.

Finance is still not a major issue; career and friendships seem much more important. If there are financial problems it is probably because you're not paying enough attention to this area. Earnings should be strongest on the days mentioned above, but also from the 1st to the 12th – as the Moon waxes. The 12th and 28th – the Full Moon and New Moon – are also good earnings days, as are the 3rd and 30th (though you might have to work harder) as the Moon is at perigee then.

Health needs some attention until the 20th. So, as always, get enough rest. This is 90 per cent of the battle. Enhance the health in the ways discussed in the yearly report. Health is much improved after the 20th.

Love seems more challenging from the 13th onwards. You and the beloved seem distant from each other. You need to work harder to bridge your differences. You're seeing things from opposite perspectives. Part of the issue is that the beloved seems stressed out. The problems are probably not your fault.

April

Best Days Overall: 1, 10, 11, 19, 20, 21, 28, 29
Most Stressful Days Overall: 7, 8, 14, 15, 16, 22, 23
Best Days for Love: 1, 4, 10, 11, 12, 13, 14, 15, 16, 19, 20, 21, 23, 28, 29
Best Days for Money: 1, 3, 4, 5, 6, 10, 11, 15, 16, 19, 20, 21, 24, 25, 28, 29, 30
Best Days for Career: 3, 4, 12, 13, 22, 23, 30

Love is still very complicated. The two love planets in your chart, Venus (the generic love planet) and Jupiter (your actual one) are both retrograde. Venus has been retrograde since March 4, while Jupiter went into retrograde motion on February 6. Jupiter has also been receiving stressful aspect since March 13. So if love seems like it's going backwards, it is quite understandable. Try not to make matters worse than they need to be. Be more patient. Don't add to the negativity. Don't try to force things. Focus on the possible, not the impossible. Venus goes forward again on the 15th and that should improve things, and on the 19th the Sun moves away from this stressful alignment to Jupiter, which should further help. But love needs time and patience.

Your 11th house became strong on March 20th and remains very strong until the 19th. So this is a month for friendships and group activities – much more so than for romance. It is a month where fondest hopes and wishes come true. It is a month where you increase your technological prowess, your scientific and astrological knowledge. (It is a good period for having your full, personal horoscope done.)

Finance is still not a big issue. Generally this is good; it indicates someone who takes earnings for granted, someone who doesn't worry much about money. It shows contentment with things as they are. But, if problems arise, you need to pay more attention – though you don't feel like it. Earnings are strongest on the days mentioned above. Earning power also tends to be strong from the 1st to the 11th and from the 26th onwards – as the Moon waxes. The 15th is an exceptionally strong financial day – the aspects are good and the Moon is closest to Earth.

Health is good this month. Your energy level is high and you can achieve whatever you set your mind to. Mars moves into your sign on the 21st, boosting the energy even more. With Mars, sometimes the problem is that there is too much of a good thing. On the one hand there is more energy and zeal. You get things done quickly. You excel in sports and exercise. But Mars can make you impatient and in too much of rush, which can lead to accident or injury. Under the influence of Mars a person can come across as 'too sharp' – too biting – even though they don't intend it. Be careful here. Soften the voice tones. Avoid conflict and temper tantrums.

May

Best Days Overall: 7, 8, 17, 18, 25, 26
Most Stressful Days Overall: 4, 5, 12, 13, 19, 20
Best Days for Love: 2, 3, 7, 8, 12, 13, 17, 18, 21, 22, 25, 26
Best Days for Money: 1, 4, 5, 7, 8, 14, 15, 17, 18, 25, 26, 27, 28
Best Days for Career: 1, 9, 10, 19, 20, 27, 28

A very happy and productive month ahead, Gemini – enjoy. Your personal power and independence are at their maximum for the year right now. Mars will spend the month in your sign and on the 20th, the Sun will enter Gemini. This is the time to make those changes that you've been wanting to make (if you haven't already made them). The world conforms to you these days rather than vice versa. Your personal happiness is really up to you. You are less in need of others or their approval.

Friends seem very devoted to you and supportive. If you belong to trade or professional organizations, they seem supportive too. High-tech equipment is coming to you.

The love life is still being tested but there is much improvement over previous months. More improvement happens after the 6th as Mercury moves away from his stressful aspect to your love planet Jupiter. With Jupiter still retrograde, however, important love decisions shouldn't be made yet.

Health is excellent this month and gets even better after the 20th. Health is not your problem, instead hyper-activity – flitting from one activity to the next – seems to be the issue. If you feel the need, enhance the health in the ways mentioned in the yearly report. Your health planet, Pluto, is retrograde this month, so avoid making major changes to your health regime. Research things more.

The communication skills of Gemini are legendary, and on the 20th they get even stronger. The problem again can be too much of a good thing – too much talk, too much thinking. The mind is easily over-stimulated. Geminis are always good students, this month even more so than usual – especially after the 20th. There is success in studies and tests.

Finance – as we have seen since the beginning of the year – is not a major focus this month (this will change next month). Your good financial days are shown above. You have, in general, stronger earning power from the 1st to the 10th and from the 25th onwards – as the Moon waxes. This gives you more enthusiasm for financial activities. The 25th seems an unusually strong financial day. The overall aspects are good and the New Moon is a 'Super New Moon'. It occurs very near its perigee point, making it much more powerful than usual.

June

Best Days Overall: 3, 4, 13, 14, 22, 23, 30
Most Stressful Days Overall: 1, 2, 8, 9, 15, 16, 28, 29
Best Days for Love: 3, 4, 8, 9, 10, 11, 13, 14, 20, 21, 22, 23, 28, 29, 30
Best Days for Money: 3, 4, 13, 14, 22, 23, 24, 25, 30
Best Days for Career: 5, 6, 15, 16, 24, 25

Last month on the 20th you entered one of your yearly personal pleasure peaks. This continues until the 21st of this month. This is a period for some self-indulgence – for catering to the needs of the body and for sensual delights. It is also a good period for getting the body and image in shape. Your personal power and independence are still strong. If you direct this power wisely much will be accomplished. You have confidence too. People pick up on this.

Love is happy this month. Singles should not marry just yet, but you can enjoy romance for what it is 'in the moment'. The 13th and 14th seem especially good for love. There is a happy romantic meeting or opportunity. Those already attached have more harmony with the beloved. Happy social invitations and opportunities come.

Finance is the main headline this month. Mars enters your money house on the 4th and the Sun and Mercury enter it on the 21st. So the month ahead is a strong financial month. From the 21st onwards you are in a yearly financial peak – a period of peak earnings. There is great focus on finance and this tends to success. The best financial days are shown above. The New Moon of the 24th seems an especially strong financial day. It occurs in the money house and will clarify financial issues as the month progresses. But this New Moon – like that of last month – is stronger than usual as it occurs with the Moon near its perigee, its closest point to Earth. It is a Super New Moon.

You're spending on yourself and on your personal appearance from the 21st onwards. Writers, teachers and marketing people have a strong financial month – their skills are greater than usual and in demand. Most likely you're spending more on high-tech equipment, and this seems like a good investment. You can earn from this as well. You're creating an image of wealth and people see you as a 'money person'. This image of wealth will draw financial opportunities to you.

Mercury (the ruler of your Horoscope) spends a good time of the month 'out of bounds'. This shows that you're moving outside your normal sphere (especially in your financial life). You're 'thinking outside the box' – you're moving into uncharted waters. But it seems to pay off. Mercury is 'out of bounds' from the 18th onwards.

July

Best Days Overall: 1, 10, 11, 19, 20, 28, 29
Most Stressful Days Overall: 5, 6, 13, 14, 25, 26
Best Days for Love: 1, 5, 6, 10, 11, 19, 20, 28, 29
Best Days for Money: 1, 3, 4, 10, 11, 13, 14, 19, 20, 21, 22, 23, 24, 28, 29
Best Days for Career: 3, 4, 13, 14, 21, 22, 30, 31

Another happy and prosperous month Gemini.

Mercury, the ruler of your Horoscope, moves exceptionally fast this month – through three signs and houses of your chart. This indicates confidence, the ability to cover a lot of territory and quick progress. Health and energy are good; there is only one planet in stressful aspect with you – and he, Saturn, has been in this aspect all year. 'Give me health and a day,' says Emerson 'and I will make the pomp of emperors ridiculous.' He means that with good health the splendour is all around us, right where we are. And this is the case for you now.

Finances are still an important priority this month, until the 22nd. You're still in the midst of a yearly financial peak and you shine in the area of finances. Many of the financial trends discussed last month are still in effect. Your best financial days are listed above. But also keep in mind that you'll have more enthusiasm and greater financial power from the 1st to the 9th and from the 23rd onwards. The 21st looks like a particularly strong financial day as your financial planet, the Moon is at her perigee.

By the 22nd most short-term financial goals will have achieved and you can move on to your main interest in life – communication and intellectual interests. Many people erroneously seem to believe that finance is the be-all and end-all of life. But you know better. Finance is important, it is a means to an end – but not an end in itself. It buys us the freedom to do what we really enjoy and to grow intellectually and spiritually.

From the 22nd onwards (and you will begin to feel this even earlier) you're in Gemini heaven. The cosmos impels you to do what you most love doing – to focus on your area of greatest excellence: communication, reading and studying, teaching, writing, using your intellectual gifts. The only problem could be overdoing a good thing. You could be thinking and talking too much, more than is necessary. This can impact on your health (although not right away). It can cause insomnia and nerve problems. So use your intellectual skills, but don't abuse them.

Love looks happy this month. Marriage is not likely – nor is it advisable until Saturn leaves your 7th house in December – but the opportunities are here. Venus in your sign from the 5th onwards bestows beauty and grace to the image (and to the personality). Venus also makes nice aspects to Jupiter all month (especially on the 18th and 19th). You're attractive to the opposite sex. Do things that you enjoy – that you love to do – and love will find you there.

August

Best Days Overall: 6, 7, 8, 16, 24, 25
Most Stressful Days Overall: 1, 2, 3, 9, 10, 22, 23, 29, 30
Best Days for Love: 1, 2, 3, 6, 7, 9, 10, 16, 18, 19, 24, 25, 28, 29, 30
Best Days for Money: 1, 2, 3, 6, 7, 11, 12, 16, 18, 20, 21, 24, 25, 31
Best Days for Career: 9, 10, 18, 26, 27

We have two eclipses this month and planetary retrograde activity will be at its maximum for the year, but you seem relatively unscathed. Two planets that involve travel in your chart, Mercury and Uranus (Mercury rules short-term domestic travel, Uranus long-distance travel) go retrograde. Uranus goes retrograde on the 3rd and Mercury on the 13th. Travel should be rescheduled to avoid these periods if possible. If it's not possible – if you absolutely must travel – allow more time to get to your destination and make sure your tickets are insured. Protect yourself as best you can. (Happily Jupiter, the generic ruler of long-term travel, is moving forward – but his aspects are a bit stressful.)

The Lunar Eclipse of the 7th occurs in your 9th house of foreign travel (another signal to avoid long trips over that period). College students make important changes to their educational plans. Sometimes they change schools or courses – college applicants as well. Perhaps the school you thought you wanted doesn't accept you but an even better one does. Siblings of appropriate age are having their marriages or relationships tested. There are dramas in your place of worship. There will be a need to make more financial course corrections. Generally this happens due to some sudden expense but it can happen in other ways too.

The Solar Eclipse of the 21st occurs in your 3rd house and is a repeat of the previous Solar Eclipse of February 26. Cars and communication equipment will get tested and might need repairs or replacement. There are dramas in the lives of siblings, sibling figures and neighbours. Often there are disruptions in the neighbourhood (sometimes due to construction). Getting around your neighbourhood could be a problem, or the post office could change their rules in an inconvenient kind of way. Students who are not yet at college could change schools or educational plans. This eclipse is basically benign for you, but if you were born very early in the sign of Gemini (on May 20 or 21) you will feel its effects more strongly. This eclipse occurs very close to the cusp of your 4th house and thus impacts on the home and family too. Be more patient with family members over this period.

Finances are important this month as Venus will be in your money house until the 26th. Venus is considered beneficent, bringing prosperity and good fortune. The financial intuition is especially strong now and there is luck in speculation. Children and children figures in your life are supportive and seem important in the financial life. The 18th brings good fortune, as the Moon is at her perigee.

September

Best Days Overall: 3, 4, 12, 13, 20, 21, 30
Most Stressful Days Overall: 5, 6, 18, 19, 25, 26
Best Days for Love: 3, 4, 7, 8, 12, 13, 16, 17, 20, 21, 25, 26, 28, 30
Best Days for Money: 1, 3, 4, 10, 12, 13, 14, 15, 19, 20, 21, 30
Best Days for Career: 5, 6, 14, 15, 23, 24

The main headline this month is the planetary shift from the East to the West in your chart. The Western, social sector is dominant from the 5th onwards, and by the 20th, 80 per cent of the planets (including the Moon) will be in the Western half of your chart. The planetary power is moving away from you and towards other people. Personal independence and personal power are not factors in success now. Your social grace – your ability to get on with others – is. It is time to take a vacation from yourself and your self-interest and focus on the interests of others. Self-interest is not a sin – not by the philosophy of astrology. There's a time for this, but that time is not now.

Your 4th house of home and family is dominant this month, with half the planets either there or moving through there. The lower half of your Horoscope, in general, is stronger than the upper half. So we have a clear message. This is a time to get the home and domestic situation in right order; to set family relations in harmony. Career and outer goals are important, but less so this period. Now is the time to set the foundations for future career success, which will start happening at the end of the year – 90 per cent of life is preparation, actual events account for perhaps 10 per cent. It is the preparation that makes the event what it is.

Health became more delicate last month from the 22nd and remains so over the month ahead. Make sure to get enough sleep. Rest when tired. Focus on the important things in your life and let go of the trivia. Enhance your health in the ways discussed in the yearly report.

Finance isn't much of an issue this month, which I read as a good thing. You're basically satisfied here and have no need to give this special focus. The best days for finance are shown above. In general you'll have stronger earning power from the 1st to the 6th and from the 20th onwards. (The best money days that occur during these waxing Moon periods will be stronger than the ones in the waning Moon periods.) The 13th has good financial aspects and the Moon is at its perigee, but this occurs in a waning Moon period – it's not as strong as it could be. The Moon's apogee on the 27th (when she is most distant from the earth) will not be as weak as usual – it occurs during the waxing Moon. Finances are more or less stable.

October

Best Days Overall: 1, 9, 10, 18, 19, 27, 28, 29
Most Stressful Days Overall: 3, 4, 15, 16, 22, 23, 24, 30, 31
Best Days for Love: 1, 7, 8, 10, 11, 17, 18, 20, 22, 23, 24, 27, 28, 30
Best Days for Money: 1, 9, 10, 11, 12, 19, 20, 30
Best Days for Career: 3, 4, 11, 12, 20, 21, 30, 31

A happy month ahead, Gemini, enjoy!

Last month, on the 22nd, the Sun entered your 5th house of fun, creativity and children and will remain here until the 23rd of this month. In the meantime, other planets are also in this house – Mercury (until the 17th), Venus (from the 14th onwards) and Mars (from the 22nd onwards). Your 5th house is easily the strongest in the Horoscope this month with 60 per cent of the planets either there or moving through there. Each will deposit its gift of joy in your life.

This is a month for enjoying your life, for doing the things that make you happy. It is a month for exploring your creativity and getting involved in creative hobbies. Children and children figures in your life are important and you get on well with them. This fun-loving attitude helps the love life too. The 18th and 19th seem especially good days for love. Singles will have important romantic meetings. Happy social invitations and opportunities will happen. Life is good.

Health is much, much improved over last month. Last month's stresses seem like a distant dream. You're full of energy and vitality. Even after the 23rd, as the Sun enters your 6th house, the health is good. Your focus will most likely be on preventive kinds of measures. Sometimes when health is good, too much of a focus on it can lead to hypochondria.

Your love planet Jupiter makes a very important move on the 11th, out of Libra and into Scorpio – out of your 5th house and into your 6th. This indicates significant changes are happening in your love needs and attitudes. The romantic niceties are less important than they have been. Sex and sexual magnetism seems paramount now. You would now prefer practical service to the romantic niceties. A moonlight walk on the beach is nice, but someone who can cure your headache is nicer.

The social life at the workplace is going to improve too. The workplace is as much a venue for romance as a place of toil and endeavour.

Finance is stable this month. Earning power is strongest from the 1st to the 5th and from the 19th onwards. The good financial days in these periods will be stronger than the ones outside these periods. The Moon's perigee on the 9th is strong, but not as strong as it could be – the Moon is waning. However, her apogee on the 25th is not as weak as it would normally be either: she is waxing.

November

Best Days Overall: 5, 6, 14, 15, 24, 25
Most Stressful Days Overall: 12, 13, 19, 20, 26, 27
Best Days for Love: 6, 7, 8, 16, 17, 26, 27
Best Days for Money: 7, 8, 16, 17, 18, 26, 27, 28, 29
Best Days for Career: 7, 8, 16, 17, 26, 27

Jupiter's move into your 6th house has not only brought love changes, but job changes also seem in the works. And, these are happy job changes. Very happy opportunities are coming (and they could have already happened). These can be with your present company, or with another one. You have excellent job prospects for the rest of the year and well into next year.

Jupiter's move into your 6th house is bringing prosperity for the children or children figures in your life. They are in a year of peak earnings. Those of you who are creative (and many Geminis are) will find that their creations are more marketable now. Aunts and uncles are prospering (or living that kind of lifestyle).

As we have mentioned, the workplace has become your social centre. And, this is even more so after the 7th as Venus moves into your 6th house. A lot of your socializing seems work- and health-related. Parties at the gym, yoga studio, or health-related events seem happy and are venues for romance and friendship.

This is a good period (until the 22nd) to do those boring, menial tasks that need to get done – accounts, bookkeeping, filing, etc. You have the energy to do them and they should pass more painlessly.

On the 6th Mercury enters your 7th house of love. This tells us many things. You are very much there for others – for your friends and your beloved. Other people come first in your life (which is as it should be with so many planets in your Western sector). There is much personal popularity and you are proactive in love – you go after what you want. However, Saturn is still in your 7th house, slowing things down. Right now, I would say he is a positive influence. He prevents you from jumping too quickly into relationships and introduces some caution here. On the 22nd, the Sun also enters your 7th house and you begin a yearly love and social peak. Marriage is still not on the cards yet, but there is more (and happy) social activity.

Health needs more attention after the 22nd. There is nothing serious in store, just lower than usual energy. This can make you more vulnerable, so rest more and focus on the really important things. Enhance your health in the ways mentioned in the yearly report.

December

Best Days Overall: 3, 4, 11, 12, 21, 22, 30, 31
Most Stressful Days Overall: 9, 10, 16, 17, 24, 25
Best Days for Love: 5, 6, 7, 8, 14, 15, 16, 17, 24, 25, 28
Best Days for Money: 5, 6, 7, 8, 14, 15, 16, 17, 24, 25
Best Days for Career: 5, 6, 14, 15, 24, 25

The love life is getting better day by day. Mercury spends the whole month in your 7th house – review our discussion of this last month – and the Sun is there until the 21st and Venus is there until the 25th. Best of all, Saturn is finally leaving your house of love on the 21st. A major social and love burden is lifted off your shoulders. There is a new social freedom happening. Marriage is still not likely right away, but it is very likely next year – for those of you who are single.

You get on with all kinds of people this month – intellectuals, writers, teachers, artists, spiritual types and corporate types. The only problem in love is Mercury's retrograde in your 7th house. You don't seem sure about what you want. You change your mind too quickly; social confidence is not what it should be. Don't worry; this will improve by the end of the month.

Last month the planetary power shifted from the bottom half to the top half of your Horoscope. (If you cut the chart in half, you would see eight planets in the upper half and only two planets in the bottom.) Thus it is time to focus on your career and outer goals and let home and family issues go for a while. It is time to succeed in the world. You are beginning your yearly career push which will culminate in February and March of 2018.

Finances are not that important. (The love life is much more important these days.) Your best financial days are shown above. Earnings tend to be strongest while the Moon is waxing – from the 1st to the 4th and from the 18th onwards. A super Full Moon on the 4th will be an especially strong financial day. (The Full Moon occurs when the Moon is at her closest point to the earth.)

Health still needs watching until the 21st, although – health-wise – you're on the upswing. The lack of energy is only temporary. By the 21st you'll see very dramatic improvements.

Your 8th house of regeneration becomes ultra-powerful after the 21st. Your spouse, partner or current love interest is focused on finance, and perhaps feels stressed. This is a great period to shed the pounds (if you need to) and detox the body. It is also good for clearing the decks of excess possessions that you don't need or use.

Sexual activity should be in moderation. The tendency will be to overdo things.

Cancer

THE CRAB

Birthdays from
21st June to
20th July

Personality Profile

CANCER AT A GLANCE

Element – Water

Ruling Planet – Moon
  Career Planet – Mars
  Love Planet – Saturn
  Money Planet – Sun
  Planet of Fun and Games – Pluto
  Planet of Good Fortune – Neptune
  Planet of Health and Work – Jupiter
  Planet of Home and Family Life – Venus
  Planet of Spirituality – Mercury

Colours – blue, puce, silver

Colours that promote love, romance and social harmony – black, indigo

Colours that promote earning power – gold, orange

Gems – moonstone, pearl

Metal – silver

Scents – jasmine, sandalwood

Quality – cardinal (= activity)

Quality most needed for balance – mood control

Strongest virtues – emotional sensitivity, tenacity, the urge to nurture

Deepest need – a harmonious home and family life

Characteristics to avoid – over-sensitivity, negative moods

Signs of greatest overall compatibility – Scorpio, Pisces

Signs of greatest overall incompatibility – Aries, Libra, Capricorn

Sign most helpful to career – Aries

Sign most helpful for emotional support – Libra

Sign most helpful financially – Leo

Sign best for marriage and/or partnerships – Capricorn

Sign most helpful for creative projects – Scorpio

Best Sign to have fun with – Scorpio

Signs most helpful in spiritual matters – Gemini, Pisces

Best day of the week – Monday

Understanding a Cancer

In the sign of Cancer the heavens are developing the feeling side of things. This is what a true Cancerian is all about – feelings. Where Aries will tend to err on the side of action, Taurus on the side of inaction and Gemini on the side of thought, Cancer will tend to err on the side of feeling.

Cancerians tend to mistrust logic. Perhaps rightfully so. For them it is not enough for an argument or a project to be logical – it must feel right as well. If it does not feel right a Cancerian will reject it or chafe against it. The phrase 'follow your heart' could have been coined by a Cancerian, because it describes exactly the Cancerian attitude to life.

The power to feel is a more direct – more immediate – method of knowing than thinking is. Thinking is indirect. Thinking about a thing never touches the thing itself. Feeling is a faculty that touches directly the thing or issue in question. We actually experience it. Emotional feeling is almost like another sense which humans possess – a psychic sense. Since the realities that we come in contact with during our lifetime are often painful and even destructive, it is not surprising that the Cancerian chooses to erect barriers – a shell – to protect his or her vulnerable, sensitive nature. To a Cancerian this is only common sense.

If Cancerians are in the presence of people they do not know, or find themselves in a hostile environment, up goes the shell and they feel protected. Other people often complain about this, but one must question these people's motives. Why does this shell disturb them? Is it perhaps because they would like to sting, and feel frustrated that they cannot? If your intentions are honourable and you are patient, have no fear. The shell will open up and you will be accepted as part of the Cancerian's circle of family and friends.

Thought processes are generally analytic and dissociating. In order to think clearly we must make distinctions, comparisons and the like. But feeling is unifying and integrative.

To think clearly about something you have to distance yourself from it. To feel something you must get close to it. Once a Cancerian has accepted you as a friend he or she will hang on to you. You have to be really bad to lose the friendship of a Cancerian. If you are related to Cancerians they will never let you go no matter what you do. They will always try to maintain some kind of connection even in the most extreme circumstances.

Finance

The Cancer-born has a deep sense of what other people feel about things and why they feel as they do. This faculty is a great asset in the workplace and in the business world. Of course it is also indispensable in raising a family and building a home, but it has its uses in business. Cancerians often attain great wealth in a family business. Even if the business is not a family operation, they will treat it as one. If the Cancerian works for somebody else, then the boss is the parental figure and the co-workers are brothers and sisters. If a Cancerian is the boss, then all the workers are his or her children. Cancerians like the feeling of being providers for others. They enjoy knowing that others derive their sustenance because of what they do. It is another form of nurturing.

With Leo on their solar 2nd money house cusp, Cancerians are often lucky speculators, especially with residential property or hotels and restaurants. Resort hotels and nightclubs are also profitable for the Cancerian. Waterside properties attract them. Though they are basically conventional people, they sometimes like to earn their livelihood in glamorous ways.

The Sun, Cancer's money planet, represents an important financial message: in financial matters Cancerians need to be less moody, more stable and fixed. They cannot allow their moods – which are here today and gone tomorrow – to get in the way of their business lives. They need to develop their self-esteem and feelings of self-worth if they are to realize their greatest financial potential.

Career and Public Image

Aries rules the 10th solar career house cusp of Cancer, which indicates that Cancerians long to start their own business, to be more active publicly and politically and to be more independent. Family responsibilities and a fear of hurting other people's feelings – or getting hurt themselves – often inhibit them from attaining these goals. However, this is what they want and long to do.

Cancerians like their bosses and leaders to act freely and to be a bit self-willed. They can deal with that in a superior. They expect their leaders to be fierce on their behalf. When the Cancerian is in the position of boss or superior he or she behaves very much like a 'warlord'. Of course the wars they wage are not egocentric but in defence of those under their care. If they lack some of this fighting instinct – independence and pioneering spirit – Cancerians will have extreme difficulty in attaining their highest career goals. They will be hampered in their attempts to lead others.

Since they are so parental, Cancerians like to work with children and make great educators and teachers.

Love and Relationships

Like Taurus, Cancer likes committed relationships. Cancerians function best when the relationship is clearly defined and everyone knows his or her role. When they marry it is usually for life. They are extremely loyal to their beloved. But there is a deep little secret that most Cancerians will never admit to: commitment or partnership is really a chore and a duty to them. They enter into it because they know of no other way to create the family that they desire. Union is just a way – a means to an end – rather than an end in itself. The family is the ultimate end for them.

If you are in love with a Cancerian you must tread lightly on his or her feelings. It will take you a good deal of time to realize how deep and sensitive Cancerians can be. The smallest negativity upsets them. Your tone of voice, your irritation, a look in your eye or an expression on your face can cause great distress for the Cancerian. Your slightest gesture is registered by them and reacted to. This can be hard to get used to, but stick by your love – Cancerians make great partners once you learn how to deal with them. Your Cancerian lover will react not so much to what you say but to the way you are actually feeling at the moment.

Home and Domestic Life

This is where Cancerians really excel. The home environment and the family are their personal works of art. They strive to make things of beauty that will outlast them. Very often they succeed.

Cancerians feel very close to their family, their relatives and especially their mothers. These bonds last throughout their lives and mature as they grow older. They are very fond of those members of their family who become successful, and they are also quite attached to family heirlooms and mementos. Cancerians also love children and like to provide them with all the things they need and want. With their nurturing, feeling nature, Cancerians make very good parents – especially the Cancerian woman, who is the mother *par excellence* of the zodiac.

As a parent the Cancerian's attitude is 'my children right or wrong'. Unconditional devotion is the order of the day. No matter what a family member does, the Cancerian will eventually forgive him or her, because 'you are, after all, family'. The preservation of the institution – the tradition – of the family is one of the Cancerian's main reasons for living. They have many lessons to teach others about this.

Being so family-orientated, the Cancerian's home is always clean, orderly and comfortable. They like old-fashioned furnishings but they also like to have all the modern comforts. Cancerians love to have family and friends over, to organize parties and to entertain at home – they make great hosts.

Horoscope for 2017

Major Trends

Health needs attention this year, and overall energy could be a lot better, but in spite of this, many wonderful things are happening.

Jupiter in your 4th house of home and family for much of the year shows a focus here – even more than usual. It indicates great success in family issues and great pleasure from family members – a Cancerian paradise. More on this later.

There's even more fun ahead when Jupiter moves into your 5th house on October 11. You enter one of your lifetime personal pleasure peaks. Personal creativity soars. There is luck in speculations. There is both the urge and the wherewithal to do the things that you love to do.

The job situation is difficult this year, however. Perhaps it is constricting, and you're having to work hard. But the hidden blessing here is the social life that it brings. The job might be onerous but it has some good side benefits.

Pluto has been in your 7th house of love for many years now – since 2008 – and he will be there for many more years to come. Thus a major cosmic detox has been going on in your love and social life. Marriages and relationships have either 'died' or had near-death kinds of experiences. The whole social sphere is being transformed and reformed into a newer and better pattern, although while it's happening the process can be traumatic.

Neptune, your planet of religion and higher education, has been in stressful alignment with Saturn for two years. Students at college have had to work harder on their studies. Success has not come easily. It has to be earned the hard way – the old-fashioned way – through sheer merit. Your religious beliefs have also been tested these past few years. This trend continues in the year ahead. By the end of the year though, these issues will be a lot easier.

Uranus has been in your 10th house of career since March 2011, and will be here in the coming year too. This has brought sudden – and multiple – career changes to you. As far as the career is concerned – anything can happen at any time. Peace and smooth sailing are not permanent. Learning to deal with career insecurities has been one of the main lessons these past years. By now, the lessons have been learned and you handle these things much easier. Very soon – next year – Uranus will move into your 11th house and your career will start to become more stable. There's more on this later.

Your areas of greatest interest this year are home and family (especially until October 10); children, fun and creativity (from October 11 onwards); health and work (until December 21); love, romance and social activities; religion, metaphysics, higher education and foreign travel; career.

Your paths of greatest fulfilment this year are communication and intellectual interests (until April 29); finance (from April 29 onwards); home and family (until October 10); children, fun and creativity (from October 11 onwards).

Health

(Please note that this is an astrological perspective and not a medical one. In days of yore there was no difference, both of these perspectives were identical. But now there could be quite a difference. For a medical perspective, please consult your doctor or health practitioner.)

As we mentioned above, you need to pay attention to your health year. Three long-term planets – Jupiter, Pluto and Uranus – are in stressful aspect with you. This in itself is an issue, but when the short-term planets start moving into stressful alignment too, things get more serious. This happens between January 1 and January 19; March 21 and April 19; September 23 and October 23; and December 22 and December 31. These periods are especially delicate for health. Make sure to rest and relax more, to maintain high energy levels, and perhaps to spend more time at a health spa or book more massages. Since overall energy is not up to its usual standards, pre-existing conditions can flare up.

There is good news here too. Your 6th house of health is prominent this year, which indicates that you are paying attention and that you are focused here. The real danger would be if you ignored things.

There is more good news. There's much you can do to enhance the health and prevent problems from happening. And even if they can't be totally prevented, they can be softened to a great extent. Problems need not be devastating.

In your Horoscope the following are the areas that need more attention (the reflexes are shown in the chart opposite):

• The heart. This is usually not an issue with you, but in the past few years it has become one. It is good to develop a firm faith, a faith that out-powers worry and anxiety, the two emotions that stress the heart.

- The stomach (and the breasts, for women). This is always an important area for a Cancerian – diet is always an issue. As we have written for many years, *how* you eat is perhaps just as important as *what* you eat. The authorities are not in agreement as to what is healthy or unhealthy, so you need to find what's right for you. But the act of eating should be elevated to something sacred. Meals should be taken in a calm and relaxed way. If possible, soothing music should be playing in the background. Grace should be said (in your own words) before and after meals and food should be blessed (in your own words). This will elevate the energy vibrations of both the food and the digestive system.
- The liver and thighs are also always important for you. Jupiter, the planet that rules these areas, is your health planet. The thighs should be regularly massaged, which will not only strengthen the thighs and the liver but the lower back as well – and this is important this year. A herbal liver cleanse, periodically, would be good. Liver action seems more sluggish this year.

Important foot reflexology points for the year ahead

Try to massage all of the foot on a regular basis – the top of the foot as well as the bottom – but pay extra attention to the points highlighted on the chart. When you massage, be aware of 'sore spots' as these need special attention. It's also a good idea to massage the ankles and below them.

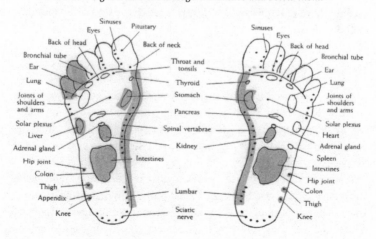

- The kidneys and hips. These have only recently become an issue. Regular hip massage should be part of your daily regime. If you feel under the weather a herbal kidney cleanse would be helpful.
- The spine, knees, teeth, bones, skin and overall skeletal alignment. These have become important in the past couple of years. Regular back and knee massage would be beneficial, as there are all kinds of reflex points along the spine that strengthen the whole body – including the stomach, liver and kidneys. Regular visits to a chiropractor or osteopath would be a good idea. The vertebrae and skeleton need to be kept in alignment. Give the knees more support when exercising. Regular dental check-ups are always recommended.
- The gall bladder.
- The colon, bladder and sexual organs. These will require some attention after October 11 as your health planet moves into Scorpio. Safe sex and sexual moderation will become important.

Your health planet Jupiter spends most of the year in Libra, your 4th house. This gives many messages. Libra is about love and relation-ships. Thus problems in the marriage or with friends could impact on your physical health. If problems arise, harmony needs to be restored as quickly as possible. Keep the peace. Keep the moods positive and constructive.

With these practices you should get through the year with minimum problems.

Home and Family

This is always an important area for you, Cancer, and this year even more so than usual. Jupiter has been in your 4th house of home and family since September 2016. Basically this is a happy aspect. If family problems arise (and they always do) you should receive best case scenarios.

Jupiter in your 4th house, as our regular readers know, indicates a move or the purchase of an additional home. It indicates an enlarge-ment, an expansion of the living space. Generally this shows a move to a larger, more spacious home, but not always. Sometimes the home is remodelled or renovated. Sometimes expensive items are purchased for the home that make it happier. The whole effect is 'as if' you had moved. There is good fortune in the purchase or sale of a home.

However, the most important thing this year is that your family circle expands. Generally this happens through birth or marriage. (Cancerians of childbearing age are much more fertile this year than usual. Pregnancy wouldn't be a surprise.) But often the family circle grows through meeting people who are 'like' family to you, people who play this role in your life.

Jupiter is your health planet (as we have already mentioned). His position in your 4th house shows that your personal health is very tied up with the health of the overall family. No doubt you are very involved with the health of family members (perhaps more so than with your own).

This position also indicates that you're working in a physical way to make the home healthier. If there is lead paint, asbestos, mould or other toxic materials present, you will spend to remove them. We can see you buying all kinds of health gadgets for the home and perhaps installing some gym equipment there. The home will be as much a health spa as a home.

On October 11, Jupiter moves into your 5th house. Thus the focus moves to the health of children or children figures in your life. Relations with children in your life will actually impact on your own personal health. Thus if (God forbid) health problems arise, restore the harmony with the children.

The children seem more prosperous this year – especially from October 11 onwards. Very happy financial opportunities come to them and they seem to be living the 'high life'. Their home life has been unstable for some years now and there could have been multiple moves or renovations over these past few years. It could happen in the year ahead too.

Parents and parent figures are also prospering this year – in fact the family as a whole seems more prosperous. A move is not indicated here, but renovations and major repairs are likely. Siblings and sibling figures are having a status quo family year. A move is not advisable. Grandchildren (if you have them) are also having a stable year.

You have good family support this year. It is mutual.

Finance and Career

Your money house is not powerful this year. It is basically empty – only short-term planets will move through there, giving short-term boosts to earnings, and then they'll be gone. Money is not a major focus, compared with other things. Some years are like that. Generally this indicates a stable kind of year, more or less similar to last year. You should understand that the empty money house is not showing financial disasters either, just lack of interest and attention. You sort of take earnings for granted.

However there will be some bumps on the road and necessary course corrections. Your financial planet, the Sun gets eclipsed twice this year. This you go through every year. Twice a year, the cosmos forces you to make needed changes in your financial thinking and strategy. But this year this force seems stronger than usual. Not only are there the normal two Solar Eclipses, but one of them – on August 21 – will also happen in your money house, greatly re-enforcing the financial drama. On February 11 there will be a Lunar Eclipse in the money house too, also bringing financial drama and change. So, this year you're affected by three eclipses rather than the usual two. (The other Solar Eclipse this year happens on February 26.)

While an empty money house indicates satisfaction and contentment – a good thing – it often shows the root cause behind financial problems, should they arise: lack of attention and lack of focus. Should problems arise (God forbid), start paying more attention.

The Sun is a fast-moving planet. In any given year he will move through all the signs and houses of your Horoscope. Thus money and earnings opportunities come to you in various ways and through various people, depending on where your money planet is at any given time and the kinds of aspects he receives. These short-term trends are best covered in the monthly reports.

Jupiter, your work planet, in your 4th house is a good financial signal for you and thus I feel there will be basic prosperity in the year ahead. Jupiter in the 4th house plays to your natural strengths – real estate, the food business, restaurants, house building and industries that cater to the home. It shows, as we have mentioned, the prosperity of the family as a whole and good family support.

Jupiter's move into your 5th house on October 11 indicates luck in speculations and money that is earned in happy ways. It shows someone who is enjoying their wealth – spending on fun kinds of activities.

Career has been unstable for many years now. Unstable, but exciting. There have been many career changes of late and more could happen this year too. It's as if you're searching for the perfect career, and every time you think you've found it a new idea or opportunity comes, and you change again. Uranus in your career house favours careers in media, technology, science, astrology and the online world. Whatever your actual career is, these activities play an important role.

As we mentioned earlier, your main lesson these past few years is learning to deal with career uncertainty and insecurity. Change – for good or ill – can happen at any moment. Nothing is set in stone. Career highs can be very high, but the lows can be ultra-low as well. It is like riding a bucking bronco.

Love and Social Life

Pluto, as we said earlier, has been in your 7th house of love for many years now, and will be there for many more to come. Thus a cosmic detoxing is going on in the love life (and the social life in general). This is seldom a pleasant experience. Anyone who has undergone a physical detox will tell you how shocked they are at the kind of crud that was lurking in the body. The same holds true socially. These negative habits, tendencies, impurities, false beliefs and concepts need to be purged in order for you to have the ideal marriage or love life. So it is best to cooperate with the process. All the love experiences that you've been having are purgative in nature. They bring up what doesn't belong there so it can be eliminated from the 'social body'. There are people in your social circle who also don't belong there. These too get purged.

Many a friendship or marriage has gone down the tubes in recent years. And even those that have survived have had many dramas – surgery or near-death kinds of experiences. In some cases it was not 'near death' but actual. Either a spouse or friend, or both. Often a friendship or marriage gets tested not because of the actual relationship, but because of the trials and tribulations the individuals are going through.

Pluto is the ruler of your 5th house of fun and creativity. So perhaps – especially in the case of singles – you haven't wanted anything too serious in the way of relationships. You only wanted love affairs – fun kinds of relationships. In the case of those of you who are married, infidelity could have been a major issue.

Your love planet, Saturn, has been in your 6th house of health and work for the past two years, and will remain here for almost all of the year ahead as well. Perhaps your job hasn't been the most pleasant, but there have been compensating benefits. It has helped your social life. In many cases there have been office romances with co-workers. In many cases you have made new friends there. A lot of your socializing has happened at the work place.

This alignment also indicates an attraction towards doctors and health professionals, or with people involved in your health. For singles, a visit to the therapist can become much more than that.

The love planet in the 6th house is not the best aspect for romance, however. It can give too critical an attitude. It gives a desire for perfection. There's nothing wrong with this, but you need to go about it in the right way. Don't be like the doctor searching for pathology, analysing every little nuance and imperfection. Keep your mind on the good things. If there are imperfections they will arise in due course – very naturally – and that will be the time to deal with them. Don't try to be too proactive about this. Your very analytical attitude is itself the obstruction to romance. Avoid destructive criticism like the plague. Nothing is quicker to destroy a relationship than this. Keep the criticism constructive – and even here watch the timing of it.

Saturn will change signs at the end of the year. He will move out of Sagittarius (where he's not very comfortable) into his own sign of Capricorn. This will improve the love life. Saturn is strong in his own sign. Your social magnetism will be stronger and there will be a desire for serious, long-term commitment. You will feel the effect of this more in 2018.

Self-Improvement

Uranus, as we have mentioned, has been in your 10th house of career for many years, which has created much career instability. But it has produced other things too. Since Uranus is the ruler of your 8th house of regeneration, he functions very much like Pluto – he shares many of Pluto's characteristics. On a worldly level it shows that you have been dealing with death and death issues and near-death experiences; with estate planning and surgery; with debt and tax issues. These affairs have been prominent for some years and will be in the year ahead too. Spiritually, the agenda here is to help you understand death better. It's as if you're forced by circumstances and events to get a better understanding and to lose your fear of death. When understood correctly, what we call 'fear of death' is only the body's 'love of life'. It wants to live and avoids anything that would interfere with that. Death is only an issue with the physical body. The soul and spirit are unmoved by it. They are immortal. An incarnation is only another 'incident' in a long, long history – and there will be many more of such incidents. Fear of death is perhaps the primary reason that people do not attain their dreams. When this fear goes, life will become happier and more fulfilled. So this cosmic agenda, though seemingly harsh, has a good purpose behind it.

The 10th house is much more than just a person's worldly career. It shows the spiritual mission for the life: the purpose of the incarnation. The spiritual part of you (your real self) wants to achieve something very specific in this incarnation. It is up to you to learn what this is and to do it. Uranus in your 10th house indicates that you're trying to do this. You're experimenting with this or that path. It also shows that the instabilities in your worldly career are leading you, little by little, to your true soul purpose. You're being 'set free' so to speak to follow your Divine Calling.

Neptune, the most spiritual of planets, has been in stressful alignment with Saturn for two years now, and this more or less continues in the year ahead (but less so than in previous years). Your religious beliefs – your world view – your personal philosophy of life – is being tested. It seems like this testing is from friends or the spouse, partner or current love interest. The testing is unpleasant to be sure, but it is healthy. Some of your beliefs will hold up, some will get modified, some will be replaced. Religion and philosophy are much more important than psychology (at which you're very good). These will shape the psychology. Change a person's religious beliefs and you immediately change their emotional reactions to events. Jupiter, the natural ruler of the 9th house of religion and philosophy, was considered the chief God among the ancients for this reason. He was causative to all the other Gods.

Month-by-month Forecasts

January

Best Days Overall: 2, 3, 11, 12, 20, 21, 30, 31
Most Stressful Days Overall: 5, 6, 17, 18, 19, 25, 26
Best Days for Love: 2, 5, 6, 12, 13, 14, 20, 21, 23, 24, 25, 26, 31
Best Days for Money: 1, 7, 8, 10, 13, 14, 16, 18, 19, 27, 28, 29
Best Days for Career: 3, 4, 5, 6, 11, 12, 20, 21

You begin your year with the upper half of your Horoscope dominant. Home, family and emotional wellness are always important to you, but these days it is good to focus on your career and outer ambitions. The Horoscope is not saying to ignore your family (and you wouldn't do that anyway), but to serve them by succeeding in the outer world. Making that new deal or getting that promotion will help the family in various ways. You're succeeding, not from a place of personal ambition, but for the sake of the family. Your career planet, Mars, has his solstice at the end of the month (from the 27th to the 31st). There will be a temporary pause then and, afterwards, a change of direction.

Health needs more attention being paid to it this month – especially until the 19th. The most important thing, as our regular readers know, is to get enough rest. Low energy is like hanging a neon sign up inviting opportunistic invaders in. Keep the aura strong and dynamic. Let go of inessential things. Focus only on what's really important in your life. Enhance the health in the ways mentioned in the yearly report.

Health will improve after the 19th, but it will still need watching.

Finances don't seem a major focus this month. Generally this is good; it shows contentment with the status quo. But sometime it indicates a lack of attention – a tendency to ignore the financial life – and this can lead to problems. Your financial planet, the Sun, is in your 7th house until the 19th, which indicates earnings coming through partnerships and joint ventures. Your social contacts and general 'likeability' are important. Who you know is more important than how much you have. You will probably be spending more on the social life too, but it seems like a good investment. The Sun in Capricorn also indicates sound financial judgement. You get value for money. It is an excellent period to set up long-term financial plans – savings, investment or retirement plans. On the 19th the Sun enters Aquarius, your 8th house. This is excellent for paying down or taking on debt (or refinancing existing debt) according to your need. Those of you of appropriate age will feel impelled to do estate planning. Tax planning is also beneficial now.

The financial planet in Aquarius is excellent for buying high-tech equipment and gadgets. These seem important in the financial life these days. You spend on this, but earn from it as well.

Love seems happy this month. You are in a yearly love and social peak until the 19th.

February

Best Days Overall: 7, 8, 16, 17, 18, 26, 27
Most Stressful Days Overall: 1, 2, 14, 15, 21, 22, 28
Best Days for Love: 1, 2, 9, 10, 19, 20, 21, 22, 28
Best Days for Money: 5, 6, 9, 10, 14, 15, 24, 25, 26, 27
Best Days for Career: 1, 2, 9, 10, 19, 20, 28

Health is much improved from the 6th onwards. On the 6th, the Moon, the ruler of your Horoscope, is at her closest distance to the Earth, her perigee. This brings confidence, self-esteem and energy. Personal appearance will shine too. On the 7th Mercury leaves his stressful aspect to you; on the 18th the Sun starts to make harmonious aspects to you; and on the 25th Mercury joins the party. So – health and overall energy are steadily improving.

Career is becoming ever more important. Uranus has been in your career house for many years now, and Mars – your career planet – joined him on January 28. This month, Venus enters on your 10th house on the 3rd. So career is busy, hectic and successful. There is a need for positive action here.

We have two eclipses this month and both are impacting on finance. Important changes need to be made and the eclipses will force the issue.

The Lunar Eclipse of the 11th (in America it happens on the 10th) occurs in your 2nd House. The eclipse in the money house shows that you need to make course corrections in your financial life. Events in foreign lands impact on your finances. A reduced schedule is advisable for this eclipse. Every Lunar Eclipse brings changes in your self-definition – your self-concept. It is a healthy thing to redefine yourself periodically. We are growing beings; we aren't the same now as we were six months ago. So this redefinition over the next six months will bring a change in the image – a change in the look – in the way you present yourself to the world. The spouse, partner or current love can have social dramas with friends. Parents or parent figures can have dramas at home and with family members. Family members can have career changes.

The Solar Eclipse of the 26th occurs in the 9th House and thus impacts on travel and educational plans. Since the Sun is your Financial Planet, finances are also impacted. Changes that weren't made during the previous eclipse happen now. Neptune, your travel planet, is affected here. Avoid foreign travel that period. College students (or those on the postgraduate level) are making important changes to their educational plans. There are upheavals in your place of worship.

March

Best Days Overall: 6, 7, 16, 17, 25, 26
Most Stressful Days Overall: 1, 13, 14, 21, 22, 28
Best Days for Love: 1, 9, 10, 18, 19, 20, 21, 22, 27, 28
Best Days for Money: 5, 6, 7, 9, 10, 13, 14, 16, 23, 24, 27, 28
Best Days for Career: 1, 10, 20, 21, 28, 30

Mars makes dynamic aspects with Uranus on the 1st – drive more carefully than usual and watch your temper. Parents and parent figures should take it easy that day too.

Career is the main headline in the month ahead. Over half of the planets are either in your 10th house or moving through there this month. This is a lot of power in the career house and it denotes focus – and focus brings success. There is not much you can do on the home front right now. Your home and family planet, Venus, goes into retrograde motion on the 4th, and Jupiter, the current occupant of your 4th house, started to go backwards on February 6. Only time will solve family dilemmas. Overt action is not called for. Focus on the career. That is where you are successful now.

Health is reasonable until the 20th, but after that it needs more attention. Keep in mind our discussion of this in the yearly report. Since the career is so hectic, so demanding and time consuming, it will be a challenge to maintain high energy levels. But you can do it. Let go of trivial matters and focus on what is essential. Get a better rhythm to your work. Take short breaks and schedule in regular massages. Avoid depression or negative feelings as much as possible (meditation is a help here).

Finances will be good this month. The changes you made last month are working out. Until the 20th you will have excellent financial intuition (and especially on the 1st and 2nd). You need to trust this intuition – it is the short cut to wealth and is always, when seen in hindsight, eminently logical and rational. The financial planet in the 9th house is always a positive aspect for earnings, as the 9th house is considered 'lucky'. On the 20th the Sun moves into your 10th house of career. This too is good. Earnings are high on your agenda and you aspire to wealth. There can be pay rises (official or unofficial) at work. You have the financial favour of the 'higher ups' in your life. Your good professional reputation leads to more earning opportunities. It will be good to invest in things that foster the career.

The love life is stressful until the 20th, but you will see dramatic improvement afterwards. With Venus retrograde from the 4th onwards go slow in love. The tendency for singles is to jump into relationships too quickly.

April

Best Days Overall: 3, 4, 12, 13, 22, 23, 30
Most Stressful Days Overall: 10, 11, 17, 18, 24, 25
Best Days for Love: 4, 5, 6, 12, 13, 15, 16, 17, 18, 23, 24, 25
Best Days for Money: 1, 5, 6, 10, 11, 15, 16, 19, 20, 21, 26, 27, 28, 29
Best Days for Career: 7, 8, 18, 24, 25, 28

Continue to pay close attention to your health. Last month, on the 20th, you entered one of the most vulnerable health periods of your year. Abnormal aches and pains are most likely to be happening because of lower than usual energy. Sometimes, pre-existing conditions seem to flare up more. The solution is to get enough rest and to enhance the health in the ways mentioned in the yearly report. Review our discussion of health last month too.

Career is still going strong. There is much outer success, but also more demands on your time and energy. This complicates health as well.

The Western, social sector of your chart has been dominant since the beginning of the year. This begins to change in the month ahead, from the 28th onwards, when the Eastern, personal sector starts to become more dominant. It won't totally dominate (there are four long-term planets in the West and they have been there for many years), but the Eastern sector will be stronger than it has been all year. The planetary power in the form of the short-term planets are moving towards you rather than away from you. They support you. The cosmos is concerned about the *all* but also about your personal interest. Your interest is no less important than any other's. Self-interest is not a sin – so long as you don't run roughshod over others (which you are unlikely to do). It is good now to evaluate your personal circumstances and see what irks you and what can be improved. Then, start to make the necessary changes. You have the power to make these changes now. Your personal independence and power are getting stronger day by day.

Your financial planet, the Sun, is in Aries until the 19th. On the one hand this indicates fast financial progress. It shows more financial independence than usual. There is a feeling of financial courage – of fearlessness – and a willingness to take risks. The only problem is that you might be too rash in your spending or investing. You seem more of an impulsive spender and investor these days. Take more time to evaluate things. Financial patience is needed. The lure of the quick buck can make you vulnerable to scams.

The good news is that pay rises can still happen. You still have the financial favour of the authority figures in your life. On the 19th the Sun moves into stable, conservative Taurus. This is a good financial signal. It indicates that the financial judgement is sound and your financial instincts are good. Taurus is all about money.

May

Best Days Overall: 1, 9, 10, 19, 20, 27, 28
Most Stressful Days Overall: 7, 8, 14, 15, 21, 22
Best Days for Love: 2, 3, 12, 13, 14, 15, 21, 22, 30
Best Days for Money: 2, 3, 4, 5, 7, 8, 14, 15, 17, 18, 25, 26, 29, 30
Best Days for Career: 7, 8, 17, 18, 21, 22, 25, 26

When the Sun moved into Taurus last month (on the 19th) your friends became more supportive financially. Social networking became a path to profits. You spent more on the latest technology and earned from this as well. This situation continues until the 20th.

Health improved after April 19, and further improves after the 6th of this month. Many mystery aches, pains and discomforts magically vanish. (They were caused by stressful planetary transits and when the stresses passed, so did they.) If you feel under the weather, enhance the health in the ways mentioned above in the yearly report.

In general, health and energy will be stronger (and personal appearance more radiant) when the Moon is waxing – from the 1st to the 10th and from the 25th onwards. You are particularly attractive on the 26th when the Moon is at perigee (her closest distance to Earth). Rest more on the 12th when the Moon is at her apogee (her furthest distance from Earth).

Career still seems successful, though it is not as active or demanding as in the past few months. Venus, a beneficent planet, spends the month in your 10th house. This shows the support of friends and family in the career. The family as a whole is elevated in status. Friends are succeeding and are providing career opportunities – opening doors for you. It is good to further your career by social means: attend and perhaps host the right kinds of parties and gatherings. With your career planet Mars in your spiritual 12th house all month it will be good to attend or host charity events. Being involved in charities in general seems helpful to the career.

Charity work will help the bottom line too – from the 20th onwards. This is a period for relying on your financial intuition and for going deeper into 'spiritual economics'. This is a time for 'miracle money'. Normal money will come, but the miracle money is much more interesting. The financial planet in Gemini from the 20th onwards indicates earning from your communication skills. It is a time for creative marketing, sales, PR and advertising. It is important to make good use of the media available to you.

Love is not a major interest this month, but nevertheless seems happy. It is not a time for major love decisions though – your love planet Saturn is retrograde.

June

Best Days Overall: 5, 6, 7, 15, 16, 24, 25
Most Stressful Days Overall: 3, 4, 10, 11, 12, 18, 19, 30
Best Days for Love: 9, 10, 11, 12, 19, 20, 21, 27, 28, 29
Best Days for Money: 3, 4, 13, 14, 22, 23, 24, 26, 27, 30
Best Days for Career: 4, 5, 15, 16, 18, 19, 24, 25

This month you enter your period of maximum personal independence and power (which will last well into next month too). So, take responsibility for your happiness. It's really up to you and not others. Make the changes that make you happy. It will be much easier to do this now (and next month). If you procrastinate until later, changes can still be made but with more difficulty.

Last month was a spiritual month and so is the month ahead – especially until the 21st. Your spiritual planet, Mercury, will spend much of the month 'out of bounds' and this seems the situation in your spiritual life. You're moving outside your usual sphere; perhaps you feel that the answers you seek cannot be found here and you look elsewhere. Often this indicates exploring alien or foreign teachings or teachers.

The financial intuition is still very important until the 21st. Continue to explore the spiritual dimensions of wealth – spiritual economics. There is much revelation happening in this area.

On the 21st, the Sun crosses your Ascendant and enters your 1st house. This is a wonderful financial transit. It brings physical money and also opportunity. You look and feel prosperous and others see you this way. You are a 'money person' to people around you. You dress more expensively and tend to flaunt your wealth (a temporary thing). Silver is always a beneficial colour for you, but after the 21st you might want to add some gold to the mix. It is good to wear gold jewellery as well. (This will further enhance your financial power.) You spend on yourself and invest in yourself after the 21st. Your personal appearance is important financially.

On the 4th Mars, your career planet, enters your 1st house bringing happy career opportunities to you. You look successful and people see you this way. Mars spends most of the month 'out of bounds'. This suggests that in your career pursuits you are outside your normal sphere. Perhaps you need to travel to exotic, out-of-the-way places. Perhaps people outside your usual sphere become important career-wise. There are many scenarios here.

Health is good all month. In general, it will be best when the Moon waxes – from the 1st to the 9th and from the 24th onwards. Health and personal appearance are especially good on the 8th when the Moon is at her perigee. Personal appearance will be strong from the 21st onwards.

July

Best Days Overall: 3, 4, 13, 14, 21, 22, 30, 31
Most Stressful Days Overall: 1, 8, 9, 15, 16, 28, 29
Best Days for Love: 5, 6, 8, 9, 10, 15, 16, 19, 20, 23, 24, 28, 29
Best Days for Money: 1, 3, 4, 10, 11, 13, 14, 19, 20, 23, 24, 28, 29
Best Days for Career: 3, 4, 13, 14, 15, 16, 23, 30, 31

You entered a cycle of prosperity last month on the 21st and it continues in the month ahead. The Sun, your financial planet, remains in
your 1st house until the 22nd, bringing financial windfalls and opportunity to you. Money and opportunity seek you out, rather than vice
versa. Just go about your daily business and prosperity will find you.
On the 22nd the Sun moves into your money house and you enter a
yearly financial peak – a period of peak earnings. The Sun in Leo indicates happy money. You earn your money in enjoyable, fun kinds of
ways. You have great financial confidence now. You might get a bit too
speculative during this period – but you seem lucky. Speculate according to your intuition, not automatically (and avoid speculations from
the 9th to the 11th).

Mars enters the money house on the 20th and spends the rest of the
month there. This adds to your speculative fervour. But this aspect also
indicates the favour of bosses, parents, parent figures and the authority figure in your life. They support your financial goals. Even the
government seems favourably disposed to you now and if you have
issues here it would be a good period to deal with them, from the 20th
onwards.

Mars entered your 1st house on June 4 and he is there until the 20th
of this month. This gives energy and charisma. You get things done in
a hurry but can be impatient. Rush is the main danger with this position. This can lead to conflicts, temper tantrums, injury or accident.
Avoid impatience.

Health is wonderful now. You look great. You are active and energetic and the muscles and physique are toned. In general health and
energy will be strongest when the Moon waxes – from 1st to the 9th
and from the 23rd onwards. Health and energy are good on the 21st
too, as the Moon is at her closest to Earth.

Your love planet Saturn is still retrograde all month, so love is still under review. You should see big improvements here from the 20th onwards however. Love happens as you pursue your work and financial goals – or with people involved in these areas.

August

Best Days Overall: 9, 10, 18, 26, 27
Most Stressful Days Overall: 4, 5, 11, 12, 24, 25, 31
Best Days for Love: 2, 3, 4, 5, 9, 10, 11, 12, 18, 19, 20, 21, 28, 29, 30, 31
Best Days for Money: 1, 2, 3, 6, 7, 11, 12, 16, 20, 21, 24, 25, 31
Best Days for Career: 1, 2, 11, 12, 20, 21, 29, 30

Retrograde activity increases this month – it's at its maximum for the year. From the 13th to the 25th half of the planets are travelling backwards, and 40 per cent of them are in retrograde motion both before and after this period. This affects the world and world events, but your career and finances don't seem affected. Prosperity is still happening. You're still in a yearly financial peak until the 22nd.

Last month the planetary power began to shift from the upper to the lower half of your chart. This month, as Venus crosses from the top to the bottom, the shift is even stronger. Now it is time to reduce your emphasis on career and focus more on the home, family and emotional wellness. The planetary shift symbolizes a psychological shift in you. Career opportunities are still happening (your career planet Mars is part of a Grand Trine in Fire), but you can be more choosy about them. You can opt for the ones that are emotionally more comfortable.

We have two eclipses this month. The first, the Lunar Eclipse of the 7th, is the stronger one – but you've gone through much stronger eclipses in recent years. You'll get through it just fine. This eclipse occurs in your 8th house of regeneration and affects the finances of the spouse, partner or current love interest. He or she is forced to make important financial changes. Their whole financial strategy will need to be changed. Every Lunar Eclipse has an impact on your image and personality, and this one is no different. Once again, the cosmos gives you the opportunity to redefine yourself. Your opinion of yourself hasn't been realistic and needs upgrading. It's always best if you do this redefining for yourself – if you don't, others will do it and it won't be so pleasant. Generally this redefinition brings wardrobe and image changes over the next six months. Often the hairstyle and overall presentation change.

This eclipse can bring encounters with death. Perhaps you have dreams about it or thoughts about it. Perhaps you read of some grisly death or watch a movie that triggers this. Sometimes one experiences 'close calls' – brushes with the dark angel. The cosmos intends you to get more serious about life.

The Solar Eclipse of the 21st brings financial changes to you. The earlier eclipse affected the beloved; this one affects you. Your financial thinking and strategy need changing. Since this eclipse occurs right on the cusp of your 3rd house, cars and communication equipment will get tested. There can be dramas in the lives of siblings and sibling figures. Students below college level are forced to make important educational changes.

September

Best Days Overall: 5, 6, 14, 15, 23, 24
Most Stressful Days Overall: 1, 7, 8, 20, 21, 28, 29
Best Days for Love: 1, 7, 8, 16, 17, 26, 27, 28, 29
Best Days for Money: 1, 3, 4, 10, 12, 13, 16, 17, 19, 20, 21, 30
Best Days for Career: 7, 8, 9, 10, 18, 19, 28, 29

Career is more or less in abeyance now. The bottom half of your chart is very dominant and the planetary power is moving away from the 10th house of career and towards the 4th house of home and family, and this is what you're doing. On the 22nd, the Sun will enter the 4th house, and other short-term planets will follow next month.

This is the time to build up the forces for your next career push, which will happen towards the end of the year. This is the time to prepare the ground for it. Now you can best serve your family by being there for them – by being available emotionally and in other ways. Your emotional wellness – feeling right – is more important than outer success. Cancerians have prodigious memories. They can tell you what they wore on their first date and every detail about it. But now – especially after the 22nd – it becomes even stronger. What seems like nostalgia to the human mind is really nature's therapeutic system. It brings up old memories in order to reprocess them. Generally, old traumas (and even happy events) get reinterpreted in the light of present consciousness. Something that seemed tragic when it happened, now brings only a smile. Healing happens.

Finance is still important this month, but the emphasis is winding down. The month begins with three planets in the money house – which shows a lot of focus – but by the 20th the money house will be empty. Short-term financial goals have been more or less achieved and you have no need to pay too much attention here now.

Your financial planet will be in your 3rd house until the 22nd. Thus, as we mentioned last month, good sales, marketing, PR and advertising are important in whatever you're doing. It is also a good period for trading – buying and selling. For investors, telecommunications, transportation and the health field look like promising areas. On the 22nd, the Sun moves on into your 4th house. This indicates spending on the home and family and earning money from home. It favours residential real estate, restaurants, the food business, hotels and industries that cater to the home. It shows good family support too. Family, and family connections especially, are very important (more so than usual) in the financial life.

Health is good this month – until the 22nd. After that date, make sure to get enough rest. In general you'll feel better and look better when the Moon waxes – from the 1st to the 6th and from the 20th onwards. Thus, though you should rest more after the 22nd, things won't be that bad. You look especially good – and have great confidence – on the 13th as the Moon is at her perigee. Rest and relax more on the 27th as the Moon is at her apogee, her most distant point from Earth.

October

Best Days Overall: 3, 4, 11, 12, 20, 21, 30, 31
Most Stressful Days Overall: 5, 6, 18, 19, 25, 26
Best Days for Love: 5, 6, 7, 8, 13, 14, 17, 18, 23, 24, 25, 26, 27, 28
Best Days for Money: 1, 9, 10, 11, 13, 14, 19, 20, 30
Best Days for Career: 5, 6, 7, 8, 15, 16, 27

Health and energy might be more stressful now but many nice things are happening still. Your 4th house of home and family is even stronger than last month, with 60 per cent of the planets either there or moving through there. This is definitely the major focus this month. Your family is your mission and career right now. Indeed, on the 22nd Mars, your career planet, moves into your 4th house. This additionally indicates working on your career from home, and working on the career by the methods of night – dreaming, visualizing what you want, and creating the internal infrastructure for outer career progress later on.

Everything centres round the home and family this month. If the domestic and emotional life are good, everything else – health, finance, career – will fall into place.

Health will improve somewhat later in the month – after the 23rd – but still needs watching. Review our discussion of health in the yearly report. The important thing, as always, is not to allow yourself to get over-tired. Listen to the body. If it is tired, just rest, take a nap or a break.

On the 11th your health planet Jupiter changes signs. He moves from Libra into Scorpio. This creates different health needs and different approaches. Detox regimes become more important. You could have a tendency towards surgery – or it could be recommended to you. The colon, bladder and sexual organs become important in health. Sexual moderation is important.

Mars, your career planet, has his solstice from the 23rd to the 30th. This reinforces what we mentioned above. A career pause is happening and then a change of direction. Don't be alarmed by this. It is a pause that refreshes.

You have a very nice payday on the 26th or 27th as your financial planet travels with Jupiter. A happy job opportunity can also come. When the Sun moves into Scorpio on the 23rd it will be good to use spare cash to pay off debts. Borrowing will be easier too – if you need it. There is luck in speculations after the 23rd, but this should only be done under the guidance of intuition and not blindly. Children and children figures are supportive financially. You're probably spending more on them too.

Sales and marketing people have good fortune on the 18th and 19th. The dream life is more active (and revelatory) on those days as well.

November

Best Days Overall: 7, 8, 16, 17, 26, 27
Most Stressful Days Overall: 1, 2, 14, 15, 21, 22, 29, 30
Best Days for Love: 2, 6, 7, 10, 16, 17, 20, 21, 22, 26, 27, 30
Best Days for Money: 7, 8, 9, 10, 16, 17, 18, 26, 27, 28, 29
Best Days for Career: 1, 2, 5, 6, 14, 15, 24, 25, 29, 30

Health and energy are much improved this month. There are still some planets in stressful alignment, but much fewer than last month. It is a fun kind of month; with some creativity you can even make your mundane tasks fun. The focus is still on the family (a fun activity for the Cancerian) but more on children. Your career planet is still in your 4th house all month – a clear message that your family and emotional and domestic wellness are the real career at the moment. As we mentioned last month, if these are right, the career will also be right.

You tend to look and feel better when the Moon, the ruler of your Horoscope, is waxing – from the 1st to the 4th and from the 18th onwards. The Full Moon and New Moon days (the 4th and the 18th) are especially good. The 5th and 6th are also good as the Moon is at perigee.

Jupiter will make beautiful aspects to Neptune towards the end of the month. This would indicate work-related travel. The Sun will Trine Neptune from the 2nd to the 4th, showing business-related travel (money is involved here). It is also a good financial period. The intuition is sharp.

These aspects are also good for college students and indicate success in their studies or with administrators. If you are involved in legal issues these too will go well in the month ahead.

The Sun, your financial planet, will be in Scorpio, your 5th house until the 22nd. Thus many of the financial trends that we discussed last month are still in effect. Money is earned in happy ways. You enjoy the act of money making. You are more speculative and lady luck seems with you. You spend more on fun kinds of activities. You spend on the children (or children figures in your life) but can earn from them as well. For investors, bonds and the bond market are interesting – also industries that cater to youth.

On the 22nd the Sun enters expansive Sagittarius. This is another good financial aspect. Again you are more speculative. You can be an impulse spender and investor – perhaps too quick in your decision making. For investors this aspect favours book publishing, the travel business and for-profit colleges. The health industry is also interesting. You are lucky, but basically you earn through your work. Your hard work creates the good luck.

Important career changes are happening this month, but perhaps behind the scenes. Parents and parent figures should take it easier from the 16th to the 20th and on the 30th.

December

Best Days Overall: 5, 6, 14, 15, 24, 25
Most Stressful Days Overall: 11, 12, 18, 19, 20, 26, 27
Best Days for Love: 7, 8, 16, 17, 18, 19, 20, 28
Best Days for Money: 5, 6, 7, 8, 14, 15, 16, 17, 24, 25
Best Days for Career: 3, 14, 24, 26, 27

Saturn's move into Capricorn on the 21st is going to make health an important priority for the next two years. Health is reasonably good until the 21st. Mars leaves his stressful aspect with you on the 9th and begins to make harmonious aspects to you. The short-term planets are leaving you alone until the 21st. But this is just a lull. From the 21st onwards husband your energy better. Schedule in more massages. Spend more time at a health spa, if possible. Enhance the health in the ways mentioned in the yearly report. The 19th seems a delicate health day, so try to rest more if possible.

The planetary power is now in the Western, social sector of your chart, and by the 21st it will be at its maximum Western position. Indeed, from the 12th to the 25th 90 per cent of the planets are in the Western sector. So perhaps it is good that energy is not up to its usual standard. It means you're forced to rely more on others and their good graces. It forces you to cultivate your social skills. You can't do everything by yourself right now – you need others. Let go of personal effort and self-will. Put others ahead of yourself. Allow good to happen rather than try to 'make' it happen.

If there are conditions and circumstances that irk you, make note of them. This is not a time to make changes – that will come in March and April next year – but at least you will know what needs to be changed.

Love is the main headline this month. Your 7th house of love becomes powerful from the 21st onwards and you enter a yearly love and social peak. You're spending more on the social life, but will be earning from here as well. Partnerships or joint venture opportunities will come. Finances will be easier in partnership than by going solo.

Saturn's move into your 7th house (and he will be there for the next two years) shows an attraction for older, more settled, more serious kinds of people. It indicates someone older coming into your love life. It shows a need to go slow in love and not to rush into anything. You will start to become more selective about who you date and the parties you attend. You're beginning to take a long-term perspective on love. Short-term relationships are becoming less interesting.

Your career planet Mars moves into your 5th house on the 9th. This shows that the children and children figures in your life are the career. But it also shows a need to enjoy your career path – to have fun with it. These opportunities will come.

Leo

♌

THE LION

Birthdays from
21st July to
21st August

Personality Profile

LEO AT A GLANCE

Element – Fire

Ruling Planet – Sun
    Career Planet – Venus
    Love Planet – Uranus
    Money Planet – Mercury
    Planet of Health and Work – Saturn
    Planet of Home and Family Life – Pluto

Colours – gold, orange, red

Colours that promote love, romance and social harmony – black, indigo, ultramarine blue

Colours that promote earning power – yellow, yellow-orange

Gems – amber, chrysolite, yellow diamond

Metal – gold

Scents – bergamot, frankincense, musk, neroli

Quality – fixed (= stability)

Quality most needed for balance – humility

Strongest virtues – leadership ability, self-esteem and confidence, generosity, creativity, love of joy

Deepest needs – fun, elation, the need to shine

Characteristics to avoid – arrogance, vanity, bossiness

Signs of greatest overall compatibility – Aries, Sagittarius

Signs of greatest overall incompatibility – Taurus, Scorpio, Aquarius

Sign most helpful to career – Taurus

Sign most helpful for emotional support – Scorpio

Sign most helpful financially – Virgo

Sign best for marriage and/or partnerships – Aquarius

Sign most helpful for creative projects – Sagittarius

Best Sign to have fun with – Sagittarius

Signs most helpful in spiritual matters – Aries, Cancer

Best day of the week – Sunday

Understanding a Leo

When you think of Leo, think of royalty – then you'll get the idea of what the Leo character is all about and why Leos are the way they are. It is true that, for various reasons, some Leo-born do not always express this quality – but even if not they should like to do so.

A monarch rules not by example (as does Aries) nor by consensus (as do Capricorn and Aquarius) but by personal will. Will is law. Personal taste becomes the style that is imitated by all subjects. A monarch is somehow larger than life. This is how a Leo desires to be.

When you dispute the personal will of a Leo it is serious business. He or she takes it as a personal affront, an insult. Leos will let you know that their will carries authority and that to disobey is demeaning and disrespectful.

A Leo is king (or queen) of his or her personal domain. Subordinates, friends and family are the loyal and trusted subjects. Leos rule with benevolent grace and in the best interests of others. They have a powerful presence; indeed, they are powerful people. They seem to attract attention in any social gathering. They stand out because they are stars in their domain. Leos feel that, like the Sun, they are made to shine and rule. Leos feel that they were born to special privilege and royal prerogatives – and most of them attain this status, at least to some degree.

The Sun is the ruler of this sign, and when you think of sunshine it is very difficult to feel unhealthy or depressed. Somehow the light of the Sun is the very antithesis of illness and apathy. Leos love life. They also love to have fun; they love drama, music, the theatre and amusements of all sorts. These are the things that give joy to life. If – even in their best interests – you try to deprive Leos of their pleasures, good food, drink and entertainment, you run the serious risk of depriving them of the will to live. To them life without joy is no life at all.

Leos epitomize humanity's will to power. But power in and of itself – regardless of what some people say – is neither good nor evil. Only when power is abused does it become evil. Without power even good things cannot come to pass. Leos realize this and are uniquely qualified to wield power. Of all the signs, they do it most naturally. Capricorn, the other power sign of the zodiac, is a better manager and administrator than Leo – much better. But Leo outshines Capricorn in personal grace and presence. Leo loves power, whereas Capricorn assumes power out of a sense of duty.

Finance

Leos are great leaders but not necessarily good managers. They are better at handling the overall picture than the nitty-gritty details of business. If they have good managers working for them they can become exceptional executives. They have vision and a lot of creativity.

Leos love wealth for the pleasures it can bring. They love an opulent lifestyle, pomp and glamour. Even when they are not wealthy they live as if they are. This is why many fall into debt, from which it is sometimes difficult to emerge.

Leos, like Pisceans, are generous to a fault. Very often they want to acquire wealth solely so that they can help others economically. Wealth to Leo buys services and managerial ability. It creates jobs for others and improves the general well-being of those around them. Therefore – to a Leo – wealth is good. Wealth is to be enjoyed to the fullest. Money is not to be left to gather dust in a mouldy bank vault but to be enjoyed, spread around, used. So Leos can be quite reckless in their spending.

With the sign of Virgo on Leo's 2nd money house cusp, Leo needs to develop some of Virgo's traits of analysis, discrimination and purity when it comes to money matters. They must learn to be more careful with the details of finance (or to hire people to do this for them). They have to be more cost-conscious in their spending habits. Generally, they need to manage their money better. Leos tend to chafe under financial constraints, yet these constraints can help Leos to reach their highest financial potential.

Leos like it when their friends and family know that they can depend on them for financial support. They do not mind – and even enjoy – lending money, but they are careful that they are not taken advantage of. From their 'regal throne' Leos like to bestow gifts upon their family and friends and then enjoy the good feelings these gifts bring to everybody. Leos love financial speculations and – when the celestial influences are right – are often lucky.

Career and Public Image

Leos like to be perceived as wealthy, for in today's world wealth often equals power. When they attain wealth they love having a large house with lots of land and animals.

At their jobs Leos excel in positions of authority and power. They are good at making decisions – on a grand level – but they prefer to leave the details to others. Leos are well respected by their colleagues and subordinates, mainly because they have a knack for understanding and relating to those around them. Leos usually strive for the top positions even if they have to start at the bottom and work hard to get there. As might be expected of such a charismatic sign, Leos are always trying to improve their work situation. They do so in order to have a better chance of advancing to the top.

On the other hand, Leos do not like to be bossed around or told what to do. Perhaps this is why they aspire so for the top – where they can be the decision-makers and need not take orders from others.

Leos never doubt their success and focus all their attention and efforts on achieving it. Another great Leo characteristic is that – just like good monarchs – they do not attempt to abuse the power or success they achieve. If they do so this is not wilful or intentional. Usually they like to share their wealth and try to make everyone around them join in their success.

Leos are – and like to be perceived as – hard-working, well-established individuals. It is definitely true that they are capable of hard work and often manage great things. But do not forget that, deep down inside, Leos really are fun-lovers.

Love and Relationships

Generally, Leos are not the marrying kind. To them relationships are good while they are pleasurable. When the relationship ceases to be pleasurable a true Leo will want out. They always want to have the freedom to leave. That is why Leos excel at love affairs rather than commitment. Once married, however, Leo is faithful – even if some Leos have a tendency to marry more than once in their lifetime. If you are in love with a Leo, just show him or her a good time – travel, go to casinos and clubs, the theatre and discos. Wine and dine your Leo love – it is expensive but worth it and you will have fun.

Leos generally have an active love life and are demonstrative in their affections. They love to be with other optimistic and fun-loving types like themselves, but wind up settling with someone more serious, intellectual and unconventional. The partner of a Leo tends to be more political and socially conscious than he or she is, and more libertarian. When you marry a Leo, mastering the freedom-loving tendencies of your partner will definitely become a life-long challenge – and be careful that Leo does not master you.

Aquarius sits on Leo's 7th house of love cusp. Thus if Leos want to realize their highest love and social potential they need to develop a more egalitarian, Aquarian perspective on others. This is not easy for Leo, for 'the king' finds his equals only among other 'kings'. But perhaps this is the solution to Leo's social challenge – to be 'a king among kings'. It is all right to be regal, but recognize the nobility in others.

Home and Domestic Life

Although Leos are great entertainers and love having people over, sometimes this is all show. Only very few close friends will get to see the real side of a Leo's day-to-day life. To a Leo the home is a place of comfort, recreation and transformation; a secret, private retreat – a castle. Leos like to spend money, show off a bit, entertain and have fun. They enjoy the latest furnishings, clothes and gadgets – all things fit for kings.

Leos are fiercely loyal to their family and, of course, expect the same from them. They love their children almost to a fault; they have to be careful not to spoil them too much. They also must try to avoid attempting to make individual family members over in their own image. Leos should keep in mind that others also have the need to be their own people. That is why Leos have to be extra careful about being over-bossy or over-domineering in the home.

Horoscope for 2017

Major Trends

You are coming off a few years of banner earnings. Jupiter is now in your 3rd house until October 10 and its time to enjoy the fruits of prosperity – the freedom to study, learn and pursue intellectual interests. The freedom for mental development. As long as we are tied up in the money game these pursuits are difficult. There's generally no time for them. Now you have it.

This is a very wonderful position for students below college level. The mind is sharp and clear and they succeed in their studies. Learning is a pleasurable thing these days. Teachers, writers, journalists and marketing people are also having a good year.

On October 11 Jupiter will move into your 4th house of home and family – basically a happy transit. It can bring moves, renovations and expensive items for the home. Leos of childbearing age become more fertile and a pregnancy wouldn't be a surprise. More on this later.

Saturn has been in your 5th house for the past two years and will be there for almost the whole year ahead. You are one of the great fun lovers in the zodiac, but over the past two years you've been toning it down. You've become more choosy – more selective – in the fun activities you pursue. This has been basically a good thing. Have no fear, you haven't lost the joy of life. Saturn will leave your 5th house at the end of the year, and next year the festivities begin anew.

Pluto has been in your 6th house of health for many, many years and will be there for many more. This gives a tendency towards surgery. But it also shows that detox regimes are beneficial. These should be explored more. More details below.

Neptune has been in your 8th house of regeneration since 2012. This shows a need to spiritualize – to elevate – the sexual drive. It has to be raised from animal lust into an act of worship.

Uranus, your love planet, has been in your 9th house since 2011. So many of the love trends we've written about in previous years are still in effect. Love is found in foreign lands and perhaps with foreigners. More on this later.

Your areas of greatest interest and focus this year are communication and intellectual interests (until October 10); home and family (from October 11 onwards); children, fun and creativity (until December 21); health and work; sex, personal transformation and reinvention and occult studies; religion, philosophy, higher education and foreign travel.

Your paths of greatest fulfilment this year are finance (until April 29); the body and image (from April 29 onwards); communication and intellectual interests (until October 10); home and family (from October 11 onwards).

Health

(Please note that this is an astrological perspective on health and not a medical one. In days of yore there was no difference, both of these perspectives were identical. But now there could be quite a difference. For a medical perspective, please consult your doctor or health practitioner.)

Health looks good this year. All the long-term planets are either making harmonious aspects to you or leaving you alone. On October 11 Jupiter will start to make a stressful aspect, but this is negligible – not enough to cause problems. With good planetary support pre-existing conditions should be much improved.

Your 6th house of health is very strong this year (and will get even stronger by the end of the year). Health is important and you're paying attention here. In fact, perhaps you're paying too much attention here, more than is needed. There's no need to panic over every little discomfort – which is the tendency with a strong 6th house. Many of these things are caused by the daily and monthly shifts of the planets. When they pass the discomfort passes.

Good though your health is, you can make it even better. Give more attention to the following areas – the vulnerable areas of your chart (the reflex points are shown overleaf).

- The heart. This is always important for a Leo. Most spiritual healers affirm that worry and anxiety (lack of faith) is the root cause of heart problems. So avoid this. Relax into life and develop more faith. Relaxation exercises are very helpful too.

- The spine, knees, teeth, bones, skin and overall skeletal alignment. These are also always important for Leo. Saturn, the ruler of these areas, is your health planet. So, regular back and knee massage should be a part of your normal health regime. Regular visits to a chiropractor or osteopath would be good. The vertebrae and skeletal bones need to be in right alignment. Therapies such as Rolfing, Feldenkrais and Alexander Technique are good (Alexander Technique is particularly good to prevent problems occurring). People often inadvertently throw the spine or skeleton out because of poor habits. The body needs to be retrained into a correct posture. Regular dental check-ups are important, and you should support the knees when exercising.
- The liver and thighs. Liver action seems sluggish of late and a herbal liver cleanse might be a good idea if you feel under the weather. Regular thigh massage will not only strengthen the thighs and liver, but the lower back as well. When Saturn moves into Capricorn at the end of the year, these areas will become less vulnerable.

Important foot reflexology points for the year ahead

Try to massage all of the foot on a regular basis – the top of the foot as well as the bottom – but pay extra attention to the points highlighted on the chart. When you massage, be aware of 'sore spots' as these need special attention. It's also a good idea to massage the ankles and below them.

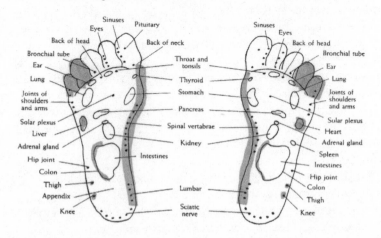

- The colon, bladder and sexual organs. These have been important areas since 2008 when Pluto entered your 6th house of health, and will remain so for many years to come. Many natural doctors claim that all disease begins in the colon, so keeping it clean is important. Herbal cleanses or herbal colonics would therefore be a good idea. Safe sex and sexual moderation is also important. Listen to your body. It will tell you when enough is enough.

Pluto in your house of health also gives other messages. It tends towards surgery, as we have mentioned. But it also shows that you respond well to detox regimes. Good health is not so much about adding new things to the body but about getting rid of things that don't belong there.

Since Pluto rules your 4th house of home and family, the Horoscope is saying that good emotional health is very important. There is a need for family harmony. Discord here (and there has been much in recent years) is a likely root cause of problems. Moods and feelings should be kept positive and constructive.

Home and Family

The home and family situation has been unstable for some years now. There have been major repairs in the home, sudden expenses and family shakeups. In many cases the family has broken up. In some cases there have been deaths in the family; in others, near-death experiences of family members. The worst of the instability is over with now – 2010 to 2014 were the most challenging years. If you got through that period, you will get through the year ahead.

Things start looking up after October 11 as Jupiter moves into your 4th house. A parent or parent figure (who has been severely stressed in recent years) starts to prosper. There is good family support. There will be many opportunities to create harmony in the family – to create reconciliation. There is an era of 'good feeling'.

You are generally not a depressive type of person. Your nature tends to be 'up' and optimistic. In recent years, though, it has been more difficult to be this way. Now, however, it does start to get easier. This will have a positive impact on your personal health as we have mentioned.

Jupiter moving into your 4th house indicates an expansion of the family circle. Generally this happens through birth or marriage. (Leos of childbearing age become more fertile this period – and even more fertile after December 21.) You have good emotional support from children or children figures in your life. And, you will meet people who become 'like family' to you – who give the unconditional emotional support that one should get from family.

Jupiter is the ruler of your 5th house of fun, joy and creativity. Thus you're having more fun at home and with family members. Family life in general becomes more joyful.

Your home is probably already like a playground – filled with games and entertainment devices. This is a Leo thing. But this year you add more to the mix. Perhaps you're updating the DVDs and players, or upgrading the home theatre system, or buying new games and toys (for children and adults).

For many years now (since 2008) you've been working to make the home healthier. You've been installing health gadgets in the home and exercise equipment or other medical paraphernalia. In some cases this was because someone in the family was ill; in other cases, it came from a desire to get fitter. This trend continues in the year ahead.

Jupiter in the 4th house often indicates a move, as we have mentioned – a happy move. In many cases it shows the purchase of an additional home or the renovation and enlarging of the present one. For those of you who actually move or get another home I can see it in a resort area, or perhaps near a place with ample recreation.

If you're planning to do construction work or major renovations, December 9 onwards is a good time for this. If you're planning to beautify the home in a cosmetic kind of way, November 7 to December 1 would be a good period.

Finance and Career

As we mentioned above, you're winding down from two years of excellent earnings. Most of your short-term financial goals have been achieved. This year, finance is not such a big issue. Your money house is empty (except for fast-moving, short-term planets) this year. The empty money house shows you're more or less content with the status quo. You don't have any major urge to make changes. You sort of take prosperity for granted. This is a good sign.

The Moon's North Node (an abstract point) is in the money house until April 29. This shows a sense of fulfilment about finances. It also tends towards 'excess'. Perhaps your problem is too much money (a nice problem to have)! The current spouse, partner or love interest could be having the opposite problem. His or her money house contains the Moon's South Node – this gives a feeling of 'deficiency'. Thus even if he or she is prospering, there is still this feeling of 'not enough'.

Jupiter spends most of the year in your 3rd house of communication and intellectual interests. This will expand your mind and knowledge base. From a financial perspective it shows 'wealth ideas' – intellectual wealth. Intellectual property you own increases in value. It shows earnings from trading activities – buying and selling. Many of you will be getting a new car and communication equipment – and good ones.

On October 11 Jupiter will enter your 4th house. This brings good financial support from the family, as we mentioned above. It shows the prosperity and generosity of a parent or parent figure, and it often shows a new and larger home and the fortunate sale or purchase of a home. This aspect favours earnings from residential real estate, restaurants and the food business. Psychological therapists should have a good year.

There are many short-term financial trends that can't be discussed here. We will cover them in the monthly reports. Mercury, your financial planet, is a fast-moving planet – only the Moon moves faster than him. He will move through your entire chart in the course of a year. Thus money and financial opportunity can come to you in a variety of ways and through a variety of people and places. It all depends where Mercury is at any given time and the kinds of aspects he receives. When it comes to finance, you're very flexible and changeable. You like to have a lot of irons in the fire.

Mercury in general favours trading (which is good this year) and the use of intellectual property. He will move backwards four times this year – usually he only does this three times. So, more than usual study and homework is necessary this year. (This was true last year too.)

Mercury will be retrograde from January 1 to January 8; April 9 to May 3; August 11 to September 5; and from December 3 to December 23. These are times to avoid major purchases or investments. Instead, use these times to review your finances to see where improvements can be made. These are times for getting mentally clear about your finances. Once this happens, decisions and plans will be good.

This year career is not a major issue. Your 10th house of career is basically empty, with only short-term planets moving through there. So, this is not an especially strong career year. Home and family (especially after October 11) are much more important. Enjoy the lull, Leo. In the next two years Uranus will move into your career house and will stay there for several years: then the career will be *very* busy and full of change and excitement.

Your career planet, Venus, like your financial planet, is very fast moving, and will move through your whole chart in any given year. So there are many short-term career trends that are best discussed in the monthly reports.

Love and Social Life

As in the area of finance you're coming off two strong romantic and social years. Many of you married or entered into romantic relationships and you seem satisfied with the status quo. You have no need to give this too much attention. A good signal. However, if love problems arise, lack of attention could be the root cause: you will have to start paying more attention.

Love is more or less stable this year. Singles will tend to stay single. Those who are married will tend to stay married.

A Lunar Eclipse on August 7 occurs in your 7th house of love. This will test existing relationships. Dirty laundry – suppressed grievances – is exposed so that it can be corrected. If there are flaws in your relationship, this is when you find out about them. Good relationships survive eclipses and get even better, but flawed ones can dissolve.

An eclipse in the 7th house need not bring 'bad' things. It shows a change in the marital status. Often singles will decide to marry on this kind of eclipse – the decision can be made this year, although the actual wedding could happen later on.

Your love planet, Uranus, has been in your 9th house of religion and philosophy for many years now, since 2011. So many of the love trends that we've written about in past years are still in effect. Love opportunities happen in foreign countries and sometimes with foreigners. The more exotic they are the better you like them. Love opportunities also happen at your place of worship or at college or university. Singles are advised to attend religious or educational functions. Fellow worshipers are likely to make introductions.

This is the kind of transit where one falls in love with the minister, priest, rabbi or imam – or with the professor. There is an attraction to mentor-type people. Learning is part of the romantic allure these days. Love is not just about love, but about education too.

The Love Planet in the 9th house also indicates how to help a troubled relationship. Going off on a foreign trip together – to some exotic, faraway place – would be beneficial. Worshiping together as a couple would be good, as would taking courses together as a couple.

Your love planet in hot fiery Aries exacerbates a natal tendency. You're a love-at-first-sight kind of person by nature, but these days even more so than usual. The tendency is to jump into serious things much too quickly. The problem with the love planet in Aries is that while the initial passion is overwhelming, it is difficult to maintain it over time. It tends to peter out.

Uranus is getting ready to move out of Aries next year. He will flirt, with the sign of Taurus in 2018, slipping in and out, before moving into Taurus for the long haul in 2019. This will bring important changes to the love attitudes and needs. The good news is that love will become more stable and enduring – at least you will be looking for that. You won't jump into things so fast. Singles will meet powerful people of high status.

Self-Improvement

Neptune, your planet of sex and personal transformation, has been in your 8th house of regeneration since 2012. He will be there for many more years. The transit of a long-term planet should not be considered an 'event' but more like a 'process' – a long-term process. So, as we have mentioned earlier, the sex life, the sexual urges and expression are getting refined, spiritualized and elevated. This is the cosmic agenda here. The process has begun but is far from finished. The sexual act is to be elevated from carnal desire into an act of worship. It will be elevated in its energy vibration (which is really the only safe sex there is). Many of you will wonder how this is done, but if you study Kundalini or Tantra yoga, hermetic science or Kabbala, you will learn how. There is a scientific process to it.

If you feel jaded with 'same old, same old', try spiritualizing the sexual act. You will be amazed. Pleasure is not only felt in the usual physical areas, but in the different chakras or energy centres in the different parts of the body. This kind of sex doesn't deplete, but actually leaves you more energized than before.

Elevating the sexual act is not only good for your spiritual life, but will improve the overall health as well. The sexual organs have been more vulnerable for some years.

Jupiter, as we have seen, will be in your 3rd house until October 11. The mind is sharp and clear. Learning is fast and easy. It is great to read those books you've always wanted to read, to take those courses you've always wanted to take, attend those seminars and workshops that interested you. Now is the time to do this. Learning is fun, and according to Aristotle one of the great pleasures of life. This is a year where you learn this. In a year or so, the career is going to be very active and you might not have the time for this. So take advantage of the cosmic gift.

Month-by-month Forecasts

January

Best Days Overall: 5, 6, 13, 14, 22, 23, 24
Most Stressful Days Overall: 1, 7, 8, 20, 21, 27, 28
Best Days for Love: 1, 2, 5, 6, 12, 13, 14, 20, 21, 23, 24, 27, 28, 31
Best Days for Money: 1, 6, 10, 15, 16, 18, 19, 25, 26, 28, 29
Best Days for Career: 2, 7, 8, 12, 20, 21, 31

To say that you begin your year with the Western, social sector of your chart dominant would be an understatement. From the 20th onwards, 90 per cent of the planets are in the social West. Your 7th house of love and social relationships will become powerful from the 19th onwards, while your 1st house of the self is empty (only the Moon will move through there on the 13th and 14th). This gives a very clear message. The cosmic energy supports others and so should you.

You are called to 'unselfishness' these days. Don't misunderstand this: concern with self – legitimate self-interest – is not a vice. It's just that you're not in that kind of cycle right now. Personal power and independence will increase in a few months' time, but the Eastern sector of self will never be as dominant this year as the Western sector. So, you're on a vacation from yourself. You're developing and honing your social skills. Personal ability and initiative don't count for much right now – it's your ability to get on with others, your like-ability, that will bring your good to you. The good news is that you're naturally inclined to this now and it's not a big struggle.

On the 19th the Sun, the ruler of your Horoscope, enters your 7th house – the house of social activities and love. In your case it makes for enhanced personal popularity. You're naturally looking out for others – and especially the spouse, partner or current love interest. His or her interest comes before your own – as it should be right now. It seems sacrificial, but it actually brings much good.

Love is a bit stressful until the 19th but afterwards becomes happy. Conflicts with the beloved – disagreements – are resolved and you're both in harmony. For singles, the online world seems a venue for romantic meetings after the 19th.

Finances are complicated as the year begins. Mercury, your financial planet, is retrograde so avoid important purchases or investments until after the 8th, when he starts to move forward again. You're always a speculator, but refrain from this between the 5th and the 8th. On the 13th Mercury moves into Capricorn, and financial judgement becomes more sound and stable. Financial decisions should be better. Money comes the old-fashioned way, through work and productive service. Mercury in Capricorn is a good period to set up long-term savings and investment plans. Think of wealth as a long-term process rather than trying to make a one-off 'killing' as the saying goes.

Your money house is empty this month (only the Moon moves through there on the 15th and 16th). You might not be paying enough attention to finance. On the other hand, this often shows contentment with the status quo.

Health is excellent all month. After the 19th the health and energy are a bit weaker (and so is self-confidence), but this is nothing serious. Only one planet, the Sun, is in a stressful aspect.

February

Best Days Overall: 1, 2, 9, 10, 19, 20, 28
Most Stressful Days Overall: 3, 4, 16, 17, 18, 24, 25
Best Days for Love: 1, 2, 9, 10, 19, 20, 24, 25, 28
Best Days for Money: 3, 4, 5, 6, 12, 13, 14, 15, 24, 25, 26
Best Days for Career: 3, 4, 9, 10, 19, 20, 28

We have two eclipses this month and both affect you strongly. Take it nice and easy a few days before and after each event.

The Lunar Eclipse of the 11th (in America it happens on the 10th) occurs in your own sign. Those of you born from August 9–13 will feel it most strongly, but all of you will be affected. It brings a redefinition of yourself – of your self-concept (how you think of yourself), your identity, your image and the look you present to the world. (These issues will come to the fore during the next eclipse too.) So it is time to define yourself for yourself. If you don't, others will do it for you and that won't be pleasant. If you haven't been careful in dietary matters a physical detox could happen. This is not sickness, but the symptoms are often the same. The body throws off effete material. It is a cleansing of the body. This eclipse will bring shakeups in a charity or spiritual organization you're involved in. There are dramas in the lives of gurus and guru-type figures. Often a person makes dramatic changes to their spiritual practice and teachings. Generally this is a 'spiritual course correction' – basically a healthy thing.

The Solar Eclipse of the 26th basically mirrors the Lunar Eclipse. Anything not completed by the Lunar Eclipse gets shaken up again. Events will happen that will force you to change your self-concept and image. Because this eclipse impacts on Neptune, the spiritual life is also affected. But this eclipse brings up more than the previous eclipse; it happens in your 8th house of regeneration and impacts (pretty directly) on the ruler of that house. So there can be encounters with death. The overwhelming majority are not going to physically die, but you will be dealing with death issues. Perhaps someone close to you dies. Perhaps you have a personal 'close call'. Perhaps you read of some grisly deaths in the papers and your mind starts thinking about it. Often there are dreams of death. The cosmos is sending a message to you to get more serious about life and your life purpose – the purpose you were born to fulfil. Also, in many cases, it will help you to understand death better and to lose any fear of it.

The spouse, partner or current love interest is forced to make dramatic financial changes by this eclipse. Often they change invest-ments, strategies and plans. The financial thinking has not been real-istic and the eclipse brings it to the surface.

Health is still good this month, though you should take it easier around the eclipse periods.

March

Best Days Overall: 1, 9, 10, 18, 19, 28
Most Stressful Days Overall: 2, 3, 16, 17, 23, 24, 30
Best Days for Love: 1, 9, 10, 18, 19, 20, 23, 24, 27, 28
Best Days for Money: 5, 6, 7, 8, 11, 12, 13, 14, 18, 19, 23, 24, 28, 29
Best Days for Career: 1, 2, 3, 9, 18, 27, 30

Last month, on the 7th, the planetary power shifted to the upper half of your chart – the half that represents the outer world and outer goals. So your outer life, your ambitions in the world are paramount now. You can safely downplay home and family issues and focus on the career. There are two ways we can serve our families. One way is by being there emotionally, attending school plays, soccer games, etc. The other way is by succeeding in the world and being the good provider. It is difficult to do both at the same time. That new deal or promotion might buy that coveted piece of equipment or pay for a good school. At this stage of the cosmic cycle, it is better to succeed in your career and pass on the soccer game.

Career is important but delicate now. There is much uncertainty, much lack of direction. Venus, your career planet, starts to move backwards on the 4th and will be retrograde until April 15. Mars in your 10th house of career from the 10th onwards suggests a need for more aggressive action. (You might have to travel this month.) Do what needs to be done, but spend time getting all the facts and doing your homework. The career situation is not as you think it is. There are twists and turns happening.

Finance doesn't seem a big issue this month. The money house is empty (only the Moon moves through there on the 11th and 12th). As we have mentioned before, this often shows contentment with the status quo. But sometimes it indicates complacency. And, if financial problems arise, it's because you haven't been paying enough attention here.

Until the 13th Mercury, your financial planet, is in Pisces, your 8th house. Thus it is a good time to pay down debt, and also to borrow or refinance debt. You seem very involved in the finances of the spouse, partner or current love. It is a good time to cut financial waste – a good detox of the financial life will do wonders. Get rid of excessive possessions – things that you don't need or use. Sell them or give them to charity.

On the 13th Mercury enters Aries, your 9th house. Earnings will increase and most likely come quickly. Your wealth goals are high and this tends to success. The financial planet in Aries tends towards risk taking and speculation. You are like that anyway – and now even more so. If you follow intuition (and not just blind greed) these risks will pay off.

The love life also seems happy from the 20th onwards. You and the beloved are on the same page – you are basically in harmony. Foreign venues (and this can mean online and not necessarily in a physical foreign country) are good for romance. Romance will get even better next month.

Health is super – especially after the 20th.

April

Best Days Overall: 5, 6, 14, 15, 16, 24, 25
Most Stressful Days Overall: 12, 13, 19, 20, 21, 26, 27
Best Days for Love: 4, 5, 6, 12, 13, 15, 16, 19, 20, 21, 23, 24, 25
Best Days for Money: 1, 7, 8, 10, 11, 18, 19, 20, 21, 24, 25, 28, 29
Best Days for Career: 4, 12, 13, 23, 26, 27

Continue to strive for clarity in your career. By the 15th, when Venus starts to move forward again, this should have been achieved; and when the Sun crosses your Mid-heaven on the 19th you'll be ready to act in a powerful way. You look very successful this month – especially after the 19th. You're on top of the world, in charge – right where you belong.

There is a lot of business-related travel this month. Your willingness to travel is important for your success. There is also much dealing with foreigners and foreign countries.

Mercury's move into your 10th career house on the 1st indicates pay rises (official or unofficial), and the financial favour of bosses and authority figures in your life. Your professional excellence brings happy financial opportunity to you. The only problem now is that Mercury goes retrograde on the 9th. This can create delays and glitches in the finances. The financial judgement might not be realistic (perhaps it's too pessimistic). As always when your financial planet is retrograde, avoid making major purchases or investments during this period. When the financial planet is retrograde, don't make matters worse by carelessness. Save every receipt. Make sure cheques are dated and addressed properly. There will be delays, but you don't need to contribute to them. On the 20th Mercury will move back into Aries. Resist the temptation to speculate or run after a quick buck.

Until the 19th you have the energy of ten people. Most likely you are hyperactive, flitting from one activity to the next without a break. You achieve much. However, after the 19th slow down a bit. Health is good – only two planets (both short-term ones) are in stressful alignment. On the 21st Mars moves into Gemini and into harmonious alignment.

But still, this is not your strongest health month. You're still going to be active, but schedule in more rest periods.

Love is very good this month. On the 13th and 14th (and some of you might feel this even before) the Sun and Uranus, your love planet, travel together. This shows an important romantic meeting for singles. It can happen online, at your place of worship or school. For those who are married or otherwise attached it shows a happy social invitation or a new friendship. Love is 'electric' this month. You and those you attract are 'love at first sight' people. Love moves quickly. You go for what you want – there's no shyness or game playing.

May

Best Days Overall: 2, 3, 12, 13, 21, 22, 29, 30
Most Stressful Days Overall: 9, 10, 17, 18, 23, 24
Best Days for Love: 2, 3, 12, 13, 17, 18, 21, 22, 30
Best Days for Money: 2, 3, 4, 5, 7, 8, 13, 16, 17, 18, 23, 24, 25, 26
Best Days for Career: 2, 3, 12, 13, 21, 22, 23, 24

In March and April the pace of life was fast – just as you like it. This month things are slowing down a bit. There is more retrograde activity for one thing. But mainly the Fire element is less intense than in the past two months. Enjoy the slow down. Most likely you've been over-active. It's refreshing to take a break.

Health is still good, but will get even better after the 20th. If you feel under the weather enhance the health in the ways mentioned in the yearly report.

Finances will be good this month – especially after the 3rd as Mercury starts moving forward. Speculations should be more favourable after this date. Your financial decision making is still very quick (perhaps rash) until the 16th, but with Mercury moving forward this should also be better.

Career is going great guns now. Your career planet Venus is moving forward and you're still in a yearly career peak. Much success is happening (and quickly too). Mercury's move back into your 10th house on the 16th brings pay rises (if they haven't already happened) and the financial favour of the authority figures in your life. If you have financial issues with the government, this is a good time to resolve them; you should get best case scenarios from the 16th onwards.

Mercury travels with Uranus for a relatively long time (Mercury is moving slowly this month) – from the 1st to the 11th. This shows important financial changes. Money can come to you unexpectedly. Your social contacts – and especially the current love interest – are supportive financially. Online activities bring profits. But sudden, unexpected expenses can also come and this can necessitate change. The Sun will Trine Pluto, your family planet, on the 9th and 10th. This indicates harmony with the family. On the 31st Mercury will Trine Pluto, showing good financial support from the family (and vice versa).

Mars makes beautiful aspects with Jupiter from the 10th to the 14th. This shows foreign travel (or the opportunity for foreign travel). It also shows good fortune for college students and those seeking places in college. Children and children figures prosper and there is luck in speculations.

The dream life should be hyperactive (and revelatory) on the 25th. Pay attention.

June

Best Days Overall: 8, 9, 18, 19, 26, 27
Most Stressful Days Overall: 5, 6, 7, 13, 14, 20, 21
Best Days for Love: 9, 10, 11, 13, 14, 19, 20, 21, 27, 28, 29
Best Days for Money: 1, 2, 3, 4, 13, 14, 22, 23, 24, 28, 29, 30
Best Days for Career: 10, 11, 20, 21, 28, 29

Last month, on the 6th, the planetary power began to shift to the Eastern half of your chart. This shift becomes even stronger on the 6th of this month as Venus crosses from the West to the East. You are entering a period of independence and personal power (very important to a Leo). Yes, it's nice to have friends and a happy social life, but these bring ties and obligations. Personal power is limited. It's more difficult to do the things that you really want to do. But this is changing now. The planetary power is moving towards you rather than away from you. It supports you. Your personal happiness – your self-interest – is important. Now is the time to follow it. Take responsibility for your own happiness and make the changes that need to be made. Let the world conform to you rather than the other way around.

Career is still important this month, but it is winding down. By the 6th only one planet, Venus, will be in your 10th house, indicating the importance of social connections in the career. Siblings and sibling figures seem successful this month and supportive. Your communication skills also seem important.

Finances are still not a big deal. The money house is still empty (only the Moon moves through there on the 1st, 2nd, 28th and 29th). The Moon is spending more time in the money house than usual, which tends to show good financial intuition (especially on those days). Mercury moves quickly this month. This shows confidence – someone who covers much financial ground quickly. The only issue is lack of attention here.

Mercury is strong in his own sign of Gemini from the 6th to the 21st. Your gift of the gab is your fortune. This aspect favours buying, selling and trading. Sales and marketing people should have a good month. On the 21st Mercury move into Cancer, your 12th house. This shows (as we have seen in other ways) a very solid financial intuition. Financial guidance will come in dreams or through psychics, astrologers, spiritual channels or ministers/guru types. Family support and family connections also seem important then.

The pace of life is more leisurely this month, and health is excellent.

Love doesn't seem a big issue at this time. Friendships and group activities seem more important now (and happy).

July

Best Days Overall: 5, 6, 15, 16, 23, 24
Most Stressful Days Overall: 3, 4, 10, 11, 17, 18, 30, 31
Best Days for Love: 6, 10, 11, 16, 19, 20, 24, 28, 29
Best Days for Money: 1, 4, 10, 11, 16, 19, 20, 25, 26, 28, 29
Best Days for Career: 10, 17, 18, 19, 20, 28, 29

The month ahead is happy and prosperous – one of the best in your year, Leo. Enjoy.

There are so many nice things happening we don't know where to begin. First off, during this month and the next you are in a period of maximum independence and personal power. You can shape and mould your life to your specifications. You can (and should) have things your way. Your happiness is up to you. If you haven't yet made the changes that you want to make, now (and August) is the time to make them.

Astrology confirms the spiritual teachings. Things – good or bad – have to happen internally before they can happen outwardly. These internal things are happening until the 22nd – with your spiritual 12th house very powerful. After the 22nd, the internal expansion will manifest outwardly. Spend the early part of the month on your spiritual practice, the results will be seen later on.

On the 6th Mercury crosses your Ascendant and enters your 1st house. This shows that money (and opportunity) pursues you. You can't avoid it. Financial windfalls happen. Friends bring financial opportunity. Online activities prosper. You spend on yourself. You dress more prosperously and look the part. This draws other financial opportunities to you.

Love is a bit challenging early in the month, but as the Sun enters your own sign on the 22nd there is great improvement. You look great for a start – Leo always has star quality, but in this period more so than usual. Mars will be in your sign from the 20th onwards too, and this just adds to your charisma. You are strong and energetic – with great magnetism. The opposite sex takes notice. With these kinds of aspects the actual shape of your physical body is not really the issue. It is the energy you exude that creates the charm. People are ultimately more attracted by a healthy energy field than by purely physical things.

Mars' move into your sign shows foreign travel and involvement with foreigners. Perhaps a foreign friend or associate is coming to stay with you. It is a wonderful aspect for college-level students. Schools are seeking you rather than vice versa.

Health and energy are super. There's nothing that you can't achieve this month.

August

Best Days Overall: 1, 2, 3, 11, 12, 20, 21, 29, 30
Most Stressful Days Overall: 6, 7, 8, 13, 14, 26, 27
Best Days for Love: 2, 3, 6, 7, 8, 9, 10, 11, 12, 18, 19, 20, 28, 29, 30
Best Days for Money: 4, 5, 6, 7, 13, 14, 16, 22, 23, 24, 25, 31
Best Days for Career: 9, 10, 13, 14, 18, 19, 28, 29

Two eclipses impact on you this month, but you have all the energy and help you need to deal with them. Even though your health is excellent, however, it won't hurt to reduce your busy schedule over the eclipse periods.

The Lunar Eclipse of the 7th occurs in your 7th house of love and tests the current relationship. Generally this testing arises as old baggage – long-repressed grievances (real or imagined) – come to the surface to be dealt with. Sometimes the relationship gets tested because of life-changing dramas in the life of the beloved. Either way, a good relationship will withstand the stresses and get better. It is the flawed ones that are vulnerable. Sometimes singles will decide to change their marital status under this kind of eclipse. They want to take their relationship on to the next stage.

Every Lunar Eclipse will activate the dream life – and generally not in a good way. Don't pay too much attention to this. The eclipse is stirring up the astral world and this gets reflected in your dream life. Every Lunar Eclipse produces spiritual changes – dramatic ones. Course corrections are needed in the spiritual life, a change of teachings and practice perhaps. There are shakeups and disruptions in spiritual or charitable organizations and guru figures in your life, and in your place of worship. Mars is affected strongly by this eclipse. Avoid foreign travel during this period. College or graduate-level students tend to make important changes to their educational plans. Legal issues can take a dramatic turn – one way or another.

The Solar Eclipse of the 21st affects you more intensely. It not only impacts on the ruler of your Horoscope, the Sun, but also occurs in your 1st house (close to the cusp of the 2nd). So once again, as in February, you're forced by events to redefine yourself. Once again you will be changing your image, look and presentation to the world. You will think differently of yourself and thus will want others to think differently of you as well. This will go on for another six months – it is a process rather than a one-off event.

As in February, detoxes of the body can happen – especially if you haven't been careful in dietary matters. The body throws off effete material. Since this eclipse is so close to the cusp of the money house, important financial changes are happening. However, as your financial planet is retrograde at this point, consider these changes carefully. It might be better to plan them now and put them into action next month, when Mercury moves forward again (on September 5). You are entering (on the 22nd) a yearly financial peak. Thus the changes are likely to be good – helpful.

Love is stormy early in the month (because of the eclipse) but gets better later. There is good harmony with the beloved, and the Solar Eclipse can also bring a happy romantic meeting. But your love planet, Uranus, is retrograde (from the 3rd onwards), so go slow in love. There's no need to rush into anything.

September

Best Days Overall: 7, 8, 16, 17, 25, 26
Most Stressful Days Overall: 3, 4, 10, 23, 24, 30
Best Days for Love: 3, 4, 7, 8, 16, 17, 27, 28, 30
Best Days for Money: 3, 4, 8, 9, 12, 13, 18, 19, 20, 21, 28, 29, 30
Best Days for Career: 7, 8, 10, 16, 17, 28

Last month on the 26th (as Venus crossed your Ascendant) the planetary power shifted from the top half of your chart to the bottom. This represents a psychological shift in you. Career is less of an issue now. Perhaps you have attained your short-term goals now – Venus in your sign shows that you look and feel successful – and others see you this way. It is time to regroup. Time to gather your forces for the next career push, which will happen next year. Now it's time to get the home and family life in order and to work on your emotional wellness. A harmonious domestic and emotional life is the foundation upon which the career rests. So you want this in order.

We have a lot of retrograde activity this month – although not as much as last month; 40 per cent of the planets are retrograde until the 5th (and 30 per cent after that). So, it won't hurt to take a career break now.

You're still in the midst of a yearly financial peak. Half the planets are either in the money house or passing through there this month – a lot of power. (The money house is not only strong quantitatively but qualitatively as well – the planets that are in there are very important ones.) Your financial planet moves forward on the 5th and enters the money house on the 10th. So earnings are strong. The financial judgement is also much better after the 10th than before. Up until the 10th you can be too impulsive, both in spending and investing. After that date, this is toned down.

Elders and authority figures in your life have been on your side since August 26, and this is the situation until the 20th of this month. After the 20th you have their financial favour. Mars (in your chart he is very beneficent – not the case for some other signs) moves into your money house on the 5th and stays there for the rest of the month. This shows financial expansion. It also brings business-related travel and good fortune with foreign companies or foreign investments.

The job situation looks hectic. You're working harder than usual. Be patient. The stresses will pass next month.

Health is excellent all month. If you feel under the weather, enhance the health in the ways mentioned in the yearly report.

October

Best Days Overall: 5, 6, 13, 14, 22, 23, 24
Most Stressful Days Overall: 1, 7, 8, 20, 21, 27, 28, 29
Best Days for Love: 6, 7, 8, 14, 17, 18, 23, 24, 27, 28
Best Days for Money: 1, 9, 10, 11, 15, 16, 20, 30, 31
Best Days for Career: 7, 8, 17, 18, 27, 28

Don't panic over the lull in your career. Your career planet (Venus) has her solstice from the 16th to the 19th (and most likely you will feel it even before then). The bottom half of your chart is still ultra-powerful and your 4th house of home and family becomes powerful from the

11th onwards. The lull is good. A change of direction is happening. Keep the focus on the home and your emotional wellness. This is a good time (especially from the 23rd onwards) to work on your career in 'interior' ways rather than overtly. Visualize where you want to be and what you want to achieve. Get into the mood and feeling of success. Then let go. These practices will lead to overt (and powerful) actions later on down the road.

Jupiter makes a major move (it only happens once a year) from Libra into Scorpio – from your 3rd house to your 4th. This is a major head-line for the month. The normal domestic life becomes more enjoyable. There is happiness from the family and good family support too. The family circle increases and widens. There are more children or children figures in your life. A parent or parent figure starts to prosper. The family as a whole seems more prosperous. There will be good fortune in the purchase or sale of a home.

Love is problematic this month. You and the beloved seem far apart. This can be physically, in terms of space, or psychologically (which is more likely). Two people can be in the same room physically but be universes apart psychologically and emotionally. It will take a lot more work than usual to bridge the differences. This is however a short-term trend, and love should improve after the 23rd. Your love planet, Uranus, is still retrograde – and this is not helping matters.

Finances are winding down. The month begins with two planets in the money house – Mars and Venus. By the end of the month, the money house will be empty. Earnings are still strong, but the interest and focus is waning. Most likely your short-term goals have been achieved and you don't feel pressure to focus overly much here. Mars in the money house expands earnings and indicates earnings from foreign companies or countries. It shows business-related travel, and that you are spending more on education and travel. Venus in the money house (until the 14th) indicates that you have the financial favour of elders, bosses, parents or parent figures. Your financial planet, Mercury, travels with Jupiter on the 18th and 19th. This shows a nice payday. There is luck in speculations too. The Sun travels with Jupiter on the 26th and 27th – another nice payday. This is also lucky for speculations.

November

Best Days Overall: 1, 2, 9, 10, 19, 20, 29, 30
Most Stressful Days Overall: 3, 4, 16, 17, 24, 25
Best Days for Love: 2, 6, 7, 10, 16, 17, 20, 24, 25, 26, 27, 30
Best Days for Money: 7, 8, 9, 12, 13, 16, 17, 19, 20, 26, 27, 29, 30
Best Days for Career: 3, 4, 6, 7, 16, 17, 26, 27

The 4th house of home and family is where the action is this month. Even your career planet, Venus, moves in there on the 7th. The home and family is the career. This is your mission, your priority for the month ahead. If your home base is in order, if there is emotional wellness, the outward career will take care of itself.

When the 4th house is strong people tend to have a passion for the past. There is a great need to come to terms with it. We don't really understand our present until we understand the events that led up to it. The past gives context for the present and the future. So, when these aspects are in effect there is a great interest in history, in family genealogy, in psychology. Nature, of course, is behind all this. This is a therapeutic exercise. Often we meet up or get calls from childhood friends. We connect via social media sometimes and rehash old times. We have dreams of old experiences – often the unpleasant ones. Looking at these things from your present state of maturity and understanding resolves many past issues and traumas. Yes, it is good to live in the now, as the gurus say. But in the now we can explore the past.

The 5th house of fun and creativity comes after the 4th house. The philosophy of astrology implies that we have to come to terms with the past, with our origins, first – then we can have fun and indulge in the pleasures of life. Your 5th house experience (which begins on the 22nd) will be affected by how well you do the work of the 4th house.

Health is still good overall, but rest and relax more until the 22nd. This is not your best health period (compared with other months). If you feel under the weather, enhance your health in the ways mentioned in the yearly report.

Though career is not a focus this month, there is a nice opportunity coming on the 12th and 13th. Career opportunities come for children and children figures too. The parents or parent figures in your life seem close. If they are single there is a strong romantic opportunity.

Your financial planet spends most of the month 'out of bounds' – from the 11th onwards. Thus your search for earnings and profits takes you outside your normal circles. You go into unknown areas – and this seems necessary. On the 6th, Mercury enters your 5th house and brings luck in speculations. Earnings increase. Money is earned in happy ways. You have a 'happy go lucky' attitude to money. It comes easily and you spend easily.

December

Best Days Overall: 7, 8, 16, 17, 26, 27
Most Stressful Days Overall: 1, 2, 14, 15, 21, 22, 28, 29
Best Days for Love: 7, 8, 16, 17, 18, 21, 22, 27, 28
Best Days for Money: 5, 6, 7, 8, 9, 10, 14, 15, 16, 17, 24, 25, 26, 27
Best Days for Career: 1, 2, 7, 8, 16, 17, 28, 29

Leo is the great fun lover of the zodiac. I would wager that if surveys were taken on any given night – in the nightclubs, theatres or casinos – one would find a disproportionate percentage of Leos there (or people strong in the sign). For the past two years you've been toning it down. But now, on the 21st, Saturn leaves your 5th house and moves into the 6th house (where he belongs). The inhibitions are gone now, Leo. You can let loose.

Last month on the 23rd you entered a yearly personal pleasure peak, and this continues until the 21st. (Next year's personal pleasure peaks will be a lot stronger, but you're in a yearly phase now.) This is the time to enjoy life and to do things that make you happy. Leos are creative people in general, and now even more so. Let it show.

Your love planet Uranus is still retrograde all month, so there is no need for major decision making but the love life *is* much better. There is more harmony with the beloved. Also, your more relaxed attitude is appealing.

Your financial planet spends the month in your 5th house, which is basically a happy and prosperous position. However, Mercury is retrograde from the 3rd to the 23rd. Try to tone down the speculations in this period. If you can't help yourself, wager with half of what you would normally do. Earnings will still happen during Mercury's retrograde but with delays and complications. This retrograde happens in the height of the holiday shopping season which complicates things. If possible, do your major shopping before the 3rd. If this is not possible, give more thought to your purchases. Set a realistic budget and make sure the stores have good returns policies.

This is a party-oriented month in general – but more so for you. By the 21st, you're more or less partied out and are ready for work.

Health is much improved over last month. Saturn's move into his own sign and house on the 21st shows a more serious attitude to health and work. You're ready to set up long-term health and fitness regimes – disciplined ones.

Children and children figures in your life have financial challenges for the next two years, but the month ahead is prosperous – especially after the 21st.

Virgo

♍

THE VIRGIN

Birthdays from
22nd August to
22nd September

Personality Profile

VIRGO AT A GLANCE

Element – Earth

Ruling Planet – Mercury
  Career Planet – Mercury
  Love Planet – Neptune
  Money Planet – Venus
  Planet of Home and Family Life – Jupiter
  Planet of Health and Work – Uranus
  Planet of Pleasure – Saturn
  Planet of Sexuality – Mars

Colours – earth tones, ochre, orange, yellow

Colour that promotes love, romance and social harmony – aqua blue

Colour that promotes earning power – jade green

Gems – agate, hyacinth

Metal – quicksilver

Scents – lavender, lilac, lily of the valley, storax

Quality – mutable (= flexibility)

Quality most needed for balance – a broader perspective

Strongest virtues – mental agility, analytical skills, ability to pay attention to detail, healing powers

Deepest needs – to be useful and productive

Characteristic to avoid – destructive criticism

Signs of greatest overall compatibility – Taurus, Capricorn

Signs of greatest overall incompatibility – Gemini, Sagittarius, Pisces

Sign most helpful to career – Gemini

Sign most helpful for emotional support – Sagittarius

Sign most helpful financially – Libra

Sign best for marriage and/or partnerships – Pisces

Sign most helpful for creative projects – Capricorn

Best Sign to have fun with – Capricorn

Signs most helpful in spiritual matters – Taurus, Leo

Best day of the week – Wednesday

Understanding a Virgo

The virgin is a particularly fitting symbol for those born under the sign of Virgo. If you meditate on the image of the virgin you will get a good understanding of the essence of the Virgo type. The virgin is, of course, a symbol of purity and innocence – not naïve, but pure. A virginal object has not been touched. A virgin field is land that is true to itself, the way it has always been. The same is true of virgin forest: it is pristine, unaltered.

Apply the idea of purity to the thought processes, emotional life, physical body and activities and projects of the everyday world, and you can see how Virgos approach life. Virgos desire the pure expression of the ideal in their mind, body and affairs. If they find impurities they will attempt to clear them away.

Impurities are the beginning of disorder, unhappiness and uneasiness. The job of the Virgo is to eject all impurities and keep only that which the body and mind can use and assimilate.

The secrets of good health are here revealed: 90 per cent of the art of staying well is maintaining a pure mind, a pure body and pure emotions. When you introduce more impurities than your mind and body can deal with, you will have what is known as 'disease'. It is no wonder that Virgos make great doctors, nurses, healers and dieticians. They have an innate understanding of good health and they realize that good health is more than just physical. In all aspects of life, if you want a project to be successful it must be kept as pure as possible. It must be protected against the adverse elements that will try to undermine it. This is the secret behind Virgo's awesome technical proficiency.

One could talk about Virgo's analytical powers – which are formidable. One could talk about their perfectionism and their almost superhuman attention to detail. But this would be to miss the point. All of these virtues are manifestations of a Virgo's desire for purity and perfection – a world without Virgos would have ruined itself long ago.

A vice is nothing more than a virtue turned inside out, misapplied or used in the wrong context. Virgos' apparent vices come from their inherent virtue. Their analytical powers, which should be used for healing, helping or perfecting a project in the world, sometimes get misapplied and turned against people. Their critical faculties, which should be used constructively to perfect a strategy or proposal, can sometimes be used destructively to harm or wound. Their urge to perfection can turn into worry and lack of confidence; their natural humility can become self-denial and self-abasement. When Virgos turn negative they are apt to turn their devastating criticism on themselves, sowing the seeds of self-destruction.

Finance

Virgos have all the attitudes that create wealth. They are hard-working, industrious, efficient, organized, thrifty, productive and eager to serve. A developed Virgo is every employer's dream. But until Virgos master some of the social graces of Libra they will not even come close to fulfilling their financial potential. Purity and perfectionism, if not handled correctly or gracefully, can be very trying to others. Friction in human relationships can be devastating not only to your pet projects but – indirectly – to your wallet as well.

Virgos are quite interested in their financial security. Being hard-working, they know the true value of money. They do not like to take risks with their money, preferring to save for their retirement or for a rainy day. Virgos usually make prudent, calculated investments that involve a minimum of risk. These investments and savings usually work out well, helping Virgos to achieve the financial security they seek. The rich or even not-so-rich Virgo also likes to help his or her friends in need.

Career and Public Image

Virgos reach their full potential when they can communicate their knowledge in such a way that others can understand it. In order to get their ideas across better, Virgos need to develop greater verbal skills and fewer judgemental ways of expressing themselves. Virgos look up to teachers and communicators; they like their bosses to be good communicators. Virgos will probably not respect a superior who is not their intellectual equal – no matter how much money or power that superior has. Virgos themselves like to be perceived by others as being educated and intellectual.

The natural humility of Virgos often inhibits them from fulfilling their great ambitions, from acquiring name and fame. Virgos should indulge in a little more self-promotion if they are going to reach their career goals. They need to push themselves with the same ardour that they would use to foster others.

At work Virgos like to stay active. They are willing to learn any type of job as long as it serves their ultimate goal of financial security. Virgos may change occupations several times during their professional lives, until they find the one they really enjoy. Virgos work well with other people, are not afraid to work hard and always fulfil their responsibilities.

Love and Relationships

If you are an analyst or a critic you must, out of necessity, narrow your scope. You have to focus on a part and not the whole; this can create a temporary narrow-mindedness. Virgos do not like this kind of person. They like their partners to be broad-minded, with depth and vision. Virgos seek to get this broad-minded quality from their partners, since they sometimes lack it themselves.

Virgos are perfectionists in love just as they are in other areas of life. They need partners who are tolerant, open-minded and easy-going. If you are in love with a Virgo do not waste time on impractical romantic gestures. Do practical and useful things for him or her – this is what will be appreciated and what will be done for you.

Virgos express their love through pragmatic and useful gestures, so do not be put off because your Virgo partner does not say 'I love you' day-in and day-out. Virgos are not that type. If they love you, they will demonstrate it in practical ways. They will always be there for you; they will show an interest in your health and finances; they will fix your sink or repair your video recorder. Virgos deem these actions to be superior to sending flowers, chocolates or Valentine cards.

In love affairs Virgos are not particularly passionate or spontaneous. If you are in love with a Virgo, do not take this personally. It does not mean that you are not alluring enough or that your Virgo partner does not love or like you. It is just the way Virgos are. What they lack in passion they make up for in dedication and loyalty.

Home and Domestic Life

It goes without saying that the home of a Virgo will be spotless, sanitized and orderly. Everything will be in its proper place – and don't you dare move anything about! For Virgos to find domestic bliss they need to ease up a bit in the home, to allow their partner and children more freedom and to be more generous and open-minded. Family members are not to be analysed under a microscope, they are individuals with their own virtues to express.

With these small difficulties resolved, Virgos like to stay in and entertain at home. They make good hosts and they like to keep their friends and families happy and entertained at family and social gatherings. Virgos love children, but they are strict with them – at times – since they want to make sure their children are brought up with the correct sense of family and values.

Horoscope for 2017

Major Trends

Last year was a year of prosperity and this year even more so. Jupiter is in your money house until October 10. More on this later.

Saturn has been in your 4th house of home and family for the past two years, and is there for almost the whole year ahead. Family life has been challenging. The emotional life is being reordered. Be careful not to repress feelings. Manage them, but don't repress them. More details on this later.

Pluto has been in your 5th house of fun and creativity since 2008 – a lot of years. He will be there for many more years to come too. Your creative life is getting a good detox – and the end result, still in the future, will be good. There have been life-and-death dramas with children and children figures in your life too. Childbirth probably happened via Caesarean section or there were other surgical procedures. (In some cases there were tendencies to abortion.)

Neptune has been in your 7th house of love since 2012 and will remain there for many more years. The love and social life – perhaps the existing marriage or relationship – is getting more refined and spiritual. This is a long-term process. You're attracting more spiritual friends these days. More on this below.

Uranus has been in your 8th house of regeneration since 2011 and he will still be there in the year ahead. This indicates much sexual experimentation. As long as it isn't destructive it's a good thing. This is how we learn what works for us.

Your main areas of interest this year are finance (until October 11); communication and intellectual interests (from October 11 onwards); home and family (until December 21); children, fun and creativity; love and romance; sex, personal transformation and reinvention, and occult studies.

Your paths of greatest fulfilment this year are the body and image (until April 29); finance (until October 10); communication and intellectual interests (from October 11 onwards); and spirituality (from April 29 onwards).

Health

(Please note that this is an astrological perspective on health and not a medical one. In days of yore there was no difference, both of these perspectives were identical. But now there could be quite a difference. For a medical perspective, please consult your doctor or health practitioner.)

Health will improve greatly by the end of the year as Saturn moves away from his stressful aspect with you. In the meantime health needs more attention. Two long-term planets – Saturn and Neptune – are in stressful alignment with you. By themselves they're not enough to cause serious problems, but when short-term planets join them in stressful aspect – this is when you really need to take precautions. These periods will be from February 18 to March 20, May 21 to June 20 and November 22 to December 21.

The good news is that you're a Virgo and you will always pay attention to your health – even though your 6th house is empty this year.

With two long-term planets in stressful alignment, your overall energy is not what you're used to. Thus, things you always did and felt fine doing might be harder to do now – or even cause injury. A friend of mine always climbed ladders to prune his trees. But when he tried it under a Saturn transit, he fell. His energy was not up to its usual standard.

So the most important thing is to maintain high energy levels. A strong aura (your spiritual immune system) will repel any disease. But let it weaken and a person becomes more vulnerable.

There are many things that can be done to enhance the health and prevent (or soften) problems. Give more attention to the following areas – the vulnerable areas this year (reflex points are shown in the chart below).

- The heart. This only became important in the past two years. Avoid worry and anxiety. Learn to relax into life. Relaxation exercises will be helpful.
- The small intestine. This is always an important area for you. Avoid foods (such as those containing gluten) that stress the small intestine.

Important foot reflexology points for the year ahead

Try to massage all of the foot on a regular basis – the top of the foot as well as the bottom – but pay extra attention to the points highlighted on the chart. When you massage, be aware of 'sore spots' as these need special attention. It's also a very good idea to massage the ankles and below them.

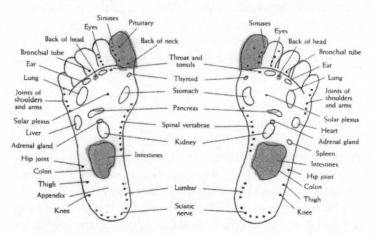

- The ankles and calves. These are always important for you and should be regularly massaged – this should be incorporated into your health regime. There are exercises that strengthen the calf muscles which are good to do. Give the ankles more support when exercising.
- The head, face and scalp. These have been important since 2011. Regular scalp and face massage will not only strengthen the area but the entire body as well. It's as if you give the entire body a workout when you massage these areas. There are reflexes there to the entire body.
- The adrenals. These too have only become important since 2011. The important thing here is to avoid anger and fear, the two emotions that stress them out.
- The musculature. Again, this has only been important since 2011. You don't need to become Arnold Schwarzenegger, but the muscles should be kept in tone. A weak muscle can knock the spine or skeleton out of alignment and cause many other problems. Vigorous exercise – according to your age and stage in life – is good.

Your health planet Uranus in your 8th house shows that safe sex is important this year. Since you're very experimental here, a word to the wise is sufficient. This aspect also shows tendencies towards surgery. But keep in mind, detox (which is good for you) will often do the same thing, although it usually takes longer.

If you take these precautions you should sail through the year disease free.

Home and Family

Saturn has been in your 4th house for the past two years. This is a difficult transit, and he will remain here for almost all of the year ahead. So home and family is a major focus.

Things are not easy at home. You've been taking on all kinds of extra responsibilities and burdens, and there is no way to get out of them. Space in the home seems cramped. Yet, a move doesn't seem practical just yet. You have to make do with what you have. A little bit of creativity – reordering things, using the space you have more efficiently – is the answer this year.

A parent or parent figure seems very stressed out. Stern and serious. Most likely he or she is over-demanding and over-controlling. His or her usual warmth is not there. This is hard on the family and is not helping this person's love and social life.

The home, which is a place for relaxation and nurturing, is being run like a business. It is cold and clinical. People are going through the motions but the warmth is not there.

Happily, by now, you're learning to handle this – after all, you've had two years of it. A human being can adjust to almost anything. Cheer up though, by the end of the year these trials will be over with. Saturn will leave the 4th house and enter your 5th house on December 21.

There is some good news here too. A parent or parent figure, while stern and business-like, seems to be prospering and is financially supportive. He or she has been receiving financial windfalls and having happy financial opportunities.

Saturn, as ruler of your 5th house of fun, indicates that you're trying to alleviate some of the gloom by installing sports, games and entertainment equipment in the home. You're working to make it more of a 'fun' place. This is a help.

You're spending on the home and family this year – more than usual – but you can also earn from here. Family connections seem important financially.

Renovations don't seem likely this year, but if you're redecorating or otherwise beautifying the home (and this is very likely), November 22 to the end of the year seems a good time.

Parents or parent figures are having a stable family year. Moves are not likely. Siblings and sibling figures are having a very spiritual kind of year and start to prosper after October 21. If they are of childbearing age they are more fertile then too. Their home life has been unstable for many years and there have probably been multiple moves. This trend continues in the year ahead. Children too have been moving around a lot lately.

Finance and Career

Finance, as we mentioned, is a major (and happy) focus this year. Jupiter in your money house is expanding your net worth. Assets that you own will increase in value. Happy financial opportunities will come to you and you'll have good financial ideas. You will end the year richer than when you began it.

Jupiter is your family planet. His position here in the money house gives many messages. It shows good family support, as we have already said. A parent or parent figure is very active (and in a positive way) in your financial life. It shows good fortune in residential real estate, the food business, restaurants and industries that cater to the home. It also shows, as we have mentioned, spending and investing in the home and family. Most likely you will be earning money from home – perhaps by working from home, perhaps by entertaining at home or having business functions in the home.

Jupiter in the money house brings good luck in finance. There is a feeling of optimism and faith here. You catch the lucky financial breaks and there is luck in speculations.

By October 11, as Jupiter moves out of your money house and into your 3rd house of communication, most of your short-term financial goals will have been achieved. And even though long-term goals might not have been realized, you will have made progress towards them. (We seldom achieve long-term goals in one year – progress is success.) So the attention will shift to communication and intellectual interests – to the life of the mind. This is as it should be.

There are many short-term trends in finance. Venus, your financial planet, moves quickly. In a given year she will move through your whole horoscope. These short-term trends depend on where Venus is and the aspects she receives at any given time, and are best covered in the monthly reports.

Venus will make one of her rare (once every two years) retrogrades this year – from March 4 to April 15. This is a period to avoid major financial decisions, purchases or investments. Sure, shop for necessities, but the big things need research and homework first. This will be a time for financial review, for seeing where improvements can be made, for gaining mental clarity on your financial affairs. Once this happens, decision making will be much easier.

There is a Lunar Eclipse in your 6th house of health and work on August 7. This often indicates job changes, which can happen either within your present company or with another one. The conditions of the workplace change dramatically.

Your 10th house of career is basically empty; only short-term planets will move through there this year. Moreover, the bottom half of your chart is stronger than the top half – on a long-term basis. (Of course, during the year short-term planets will energize your upper sector for a time, making you more ambitious, but the bottom half is stronger overall.) So there is more focus on the home and family – on your emotional wellness – than on the career. Career will tend to the status quo.

You're generally an ambitious person, but this year less so than usual. However, there will be many short-term career trends that are best covered in the monthly reports.

Love and Social Life

Neptune, the most spiritual of all the planets, has been in your 7th house for some years now and he will be there for many more years to come. Neptune is not only in your 7th house but he is also the ruler of that house – your love planet.

You are always idealistic about love, but these days a thousand times more so. Only the highest, most sublime love will satisfy you. Anything less (no matter how desirable from a worldly perspective) leaves you with vague feelings of dissatisfaction. To quote the well-known song: 'Is that all there is?'

In the worldly reading of things, Neptune is said to be the planet of scandals. This is good shorthand but not completely true. Neptune never sets out to create scandals. He is the planet of revelation. He shines light in the dark areas and so everything gets revealed – both the good and the bad. When this happens in the imperfect world we live in, scandals happen inevitably. Unpleasant revelations that people would rather keep secret. So a lot of revelation (and perhaps scandal) happens in your social and love life. This is basically good

- it is better to deal with reality than illusion - but it's not always very pleasant.

Love has been stressful these past two years. Not all of it is your fault. Saturn has been in adverse aspect with Neptune for two years so there have been obstructions here. Marriage wasn't likely (nor desirable). Perhaps there was excess fear in love - excess caution. Perhaps the current love was going through his or her own personal dramas and this complicated things. Infidelity could also have been a problem.

A Solar Eclipse on February 26 will further test love. It is a direct hit on your love planet and also occurs in your 7th house. So a lot of dirty laundry comes up for cleansing during that period. Long-repressed grievances now have to be dealt with. A good relationship will survive, but the faulty ones can end.

There is another issue we see in love. Many of you feel a conflict between serious, committed love and the fun-and-games variety. A part of you wants commitment; part just wants a love affair. This issue will resolve itself by the end of the year as Saturn moves away from his stressful aspect to Neptune.

The South Node of the Moon (not a planet but an abstract point) is in your 7th house until April 29. It spends a good deal of time near your love planet. This gives a feeling of deficiency - lack. So there could be feelings of 'lack of love' or 'lack of romance' even in the midst of a relationship. This is further testing love.

There is good news though. By the end of the year the love life should improve. Saturn will move away from his stressful alignment to Neptune and start to make harmonious aspects. The current love interest should be feeling better and this will improve things. You will be more able to express feelings of love.

In the course of a year Neptune will receive various kinds of aspects from the short-term planets. This will produce short-term trends in love which are best covered in the monthly reports.

Self-Improvement

The Moon's North Node (again, an abstract point) will spend most of the year – from April 29 onwards – in your spiritual 12th house. This shows good fortune and success in your spiritual life. You will see good results from your practice.

Spiritual growth and understanding is not just important for its own sake (which it is) but is very important in your love life. Your intuition is being trained in relationships and love this year. A good connection with the Divine Intelligence will do much to improve the love life.

There will be love challenges this year. You will often feel overwhelmed by them as in truth there is no concrete solution. The only solutions are spiritual – and this is the agenda. You have the kind of chart – and we have written of this in previous years – where one needs to 'cast the burdens of love' on the Divine and let go. There needs to be a complete surrender to the Divine. If this is done sincerely (with the heart and not just the lips) a tremendous peace will enfold you. Give the Divine complete charge of things. Get yourself out of the way. Little by little things will start to straighten out. Either the current relationship will straighten out or you'll meet someone new and better. Love is too complicated these days to handle on your own.

Your desire for ideal love is right and proper. You deserve it. Only one needs to know where to look. If you're looking outside yourself, you're on the wrong track. All these trials are leading you to Ideal Love – the pure Divine Love – sometimes referred to as *agape*. This is unconditional love. A love that encompasses every aspect of life – not just the romantic life. This *agape*, if allowed to develop, will often mend and heal (just by itself) a current love relationship. But even if the relationship goes, you will still have love. In a relationship or out of one will be the same to you. Every need in love (and every means every) will be taken care of.

Month-by-month Forecasts

January

Best Days Overall: 7, 8, 15, 16, 25, 26
Most Stressful Days Overall: 2, 3, 9, 10, 22, 23, 24, 30, 31
Best Days for Love: 2, 3, 11, 12, 20, 21, 30, 31
Best Days for Money: 1, 2, 10, 12, 17, 18, 19, 20, 21, 28, 29, 31
Best Days for Career: 6, 9, 10, 15, 25, 26

You begin your year with 80 per cent (and at times this rises to 90 per cent) of the planets in the Western, social sector of the chart – a huge percentage. Your 7th house of love and social activities is very strong, while your 1st house of self is empty (only the Moon moves through there on the 15th and 16th). So you are in a strong social period. You are on vacation from yourself temporarily. The needs of others come first. This is not necessarily saintly, just the cycle you're in right now. Things get done by consensus and through your social grace, not by your personal initiative or abilities. It is good every now and then to forget about self. Many psychological pathologies have their origin in too much self-centredness. When the West is strong in a chart there is less self-confidence and self-esteem (and here this is especially so until the 8th – Mercury, the ruler of your chart, is retrograde). Your way is probably not the best way these days. Let others have their way, so long as it isn't destructive.

The holidays are over, but you are still in party mode until the 19th. You're in one of your yearly personal pleasure peaks. To a Virgo even work is fun; you know how to enjoy your work – this month more so than usual. But many fun opportunities will come to you as the month progresses.

Health is good this month, but still needs some attention. Four planets (two of them long-term ones) are making stressful aspects to you. The good news is that being a Virgo you're always paying attention to this area – and especially so after the 19th. If you feel under the weather, enhance the health in the ways mentioned in the yearly report.

With Jupiter in your money house (right up to October 10) you're in a prosperous year. Your financial planet, Venus, has her solstice from the 29th to the 31st. This shows a pause in the financial life and then a change of direction. Interestingly we see the same phenomena in the finances of the spouse, partner or current love. Mars, the ruler of their finances, will have his solstice from the 27th to the 31st. So both you and the beloved are pausing and changing direction at the same (more or less) time. Your financial planet spends most of the month in your 7th house – from the 3rd onwards. This indicates opportunities for partnerships or joint ventures. The financial intuition will be very prominent from the 3rd onwards.

Love is challenging from the 5th to the 13th but will improve dramatically after that.

February

Best Days Overall: 3, 4, 12, 13, 21, 22
Most Stressful Days Overall: 5, 6, 19, 20, 26, 27
Best Days for Love: 7, 8, 9, 10, 16, 17, 19, 20, 26, 27, 28
Best Days for Money: 5, 6, 9, 10, 14, 15, 19, 20, 24, 25, 28
Best Days for Career: 3, 4, 5, 6, 14, 15, 25, 26

Two eclipses this month are shaking up your spiritual life. Both will make the dream life hyperactive and perhaps alarming. But don't pay too much attention to them. The dreams are just showing the disturbances in the astral plane. A course correction is needed in your spiritual life and the eclipses will force the issue.

The Lunar Eclipse of the 11th (in America it is on the 10th) occurs in your spiritual 12th house, and changes in your spiritual practice and attitudes – and perhaps changes in teachers or teachings. Spiritual and charitable organizations you're involved with are highly unstable right now. There are shakeups going on. Likewise there are dramas in the lives of gurus or guru figures in your life. You seem relatively unaffected on a personal level, but it won't hurt to take a more relaxed schedule over this period. Every Lunar Eclipse brings crisis with friends. Friendships get tested. Sometimes they break up. Often this happens because of life-changing events in their lives. (They can marry or move away, etc.) Sometimes the flaws in the relationship itself are revealed. Your high-tech equipment is more vulnerable in this period.

Make sure important files are backed up and that your anti-hacking software is up to date. Technology is a wonderful thing when it works, but when it doesn't it's a nightmare.

The Solar Eclipse of the 26th has a stronger effect on you personally. You need to reduce your schedule from the 18th onwards anyway – but especially for a few days before and after the eclipse. Those born early in the sign of Virgo – August 23 to September 3 – will feel this most strongly, but all of you will be affected. The eclipse occurs in your 7th house and impacts on the ruler of your 7th house – Neptune – so the love life, the current relationship, is affected here. The spouse, partner or current love can be having some health scare or job change. Old repressed grievances can come up that need to be dealt with. Flawed relationships are in danger; good ones will survive. Singles might decide to take the relationship a step further. Every Solar Eclipse affects your spiritual life, so there is also a replay of the effects of the Lunar Eclipse of the 11th.

The Solar Eclipse notwithstanding, the month ahead – from the 18th onwards – is a yearly love and social peak for you. You seem very devoted and engaged with others – as you should. Your relationship might be troubled, but you are socially popular.

March

Best Days Overall: 2, 3, 11, 12, 21, 22, 30
Most Stressful Days Overall: 4, 5, 18, 19, 25, 26
Best Days for Love: 1, 6, 7, 9, 15, 16, 18, 25, 26, 27
Best Days for Money: 1, 5, 6, 9, 13, 14, 18, 23, 24, 27
Best Days for Career: 4, 5, 7, 8, 18, 19, 28, 29

Your financial planet, Venus, has been in your 8th house of regeneration since February 3. She will be there all of this month too. This shows a need to prosper others. It shows much involvement in the finances of the spouse, partner or current love. It is an excellent time for estate planning (if you are of appropriate age), tax and insurance planning. The only issue now is Venus's rare retrograde, which begins on the 4th. This is not going to stop earnings, but it will introduce delays and complications.

This is a long retrograde – Venus won't go forward again until April 15. There is not much we can do about it – it is something cosmic beyond our control – but with some foresight we can mitigate some of the negative effects. First, we don't need to make matters more complicated by being careless. Sign and date all cheques properly. Save important receipts. Make sure your accounting is correct and up to date. When making a payment make sure you've addressed the envelope correctly. Little things like this can save much stress and heartache later. In America, this retrograde happens in the middle of the tax season. Take your time and make sure everything is perfect. Little mistakes can cause long delays. Avoid making major purchases or investments, if possible. Wait until after April 15 to do these things. Spend the retrograde period reviewing your financial situation and seeing where improvements can be made. It is a period for gaining mental clarity about your finances.

Now that the eclipses of last month are over, the love life seems quieter. On the 1st and 2nd the Sun travels with your love planet Neptune. The beloved is in a better frame of mind. There are romantic opportunities in the workplace. On the 4th and 5th Mercury travels with your love planet. This brings happy love and social experiences. You and the beloved are close, on the same page. For singles this augers an important romantic meeting.

Health still needs watching until the 20th. You will see great improvement in health and energy afterwards – quite naturally. The short-term planets leave their stressful aspect to you and your energy just rebounds.

There is some disturbance at the workplace on the 1st – keep the temper in check. A happy job opportunity will come on the 26th or 27th.

April

Best Days Overall: 7, 8, 17, 18, 26, 27
Most Stressful Days Overall: 1, 14, 15, 16, 22, 23, 28, 29
Best Days for Love: 3, 4, 12, 13, 22, 23, 30
Best Days for Money: 1, 4, 10, 11, 12, 13, 19, 20, 21, 23, 28, 29
Best Days for Career: 1, 7, 8, 18, 24, 25, 28, 29

The two planets involved in your finances – Jupiter, the occupant of your money house and Venus, your actual financial planet – are both retrograde this month (as was the case last month as well). Prosperity is happening, Virgo, but in convoluted and complicated ways. Financial deals seem to go backwards instead of forwards. Minds change and then change again. People sign contracts and then cancel them. Payments come later than expected. Communication with the money people in your life could be a lot better. Patience is called for now. Individual deals can fall through, but your overall prosperity is not in doubt. Other opportunities will come to replace them.

Venus moves backwards into your 7th house on the 2nd and spends most of the month there, until the 28th. This enhances your financial intuition (Venus will be in spiritual Pisces), but because she is retrograde intuitions should be confirmed before acting upon them – perhaps by consulting a spiritual channel or psychic. Get a few different opinions. This aspect shows a tendency to partnerships and joint ventures – but a lot more homework has to be done. The good news is that financial clarity starts to happen on the 15th.

Your 8th house of regeneration was powerful last month, from the 20th onwards, and is still powerful in the month ahead – until the 19th. The spouse, partner or current love is prospering and will be there to pick up the financial slack. You seem very involved – personally – in his or her earnings.

Health is good this month and gets even better after the 19th. There are some long-term planets (and Mars too) stressing you out, but you have help. Vitality seems good. Spiritual healing seems very effective on the 13th and 14th. Enhance the health in the ways mentioned in the yearly report.

In February the planetary power began to shift from the bottom to the top half of your Horoscope. The shift is even stronger now as Mars moves into your career house on the 21st. So, in general, you're more 'outer oriented'. The two planets involved with the home and family are retrograde this month – so family issues need time to resolve. Focus more on the career.

Mars in your 10th house shows much activity and aggressiveness in the career. You're fighting 'career wars' – not with guns and bullets, but perhaps in 'political' ways with competitors or at the office. This can bring 'near death' kinds of experiences in your company or industry, or with bosses or parent figures.

May

Best Days Overall: 4, 5, 14, 15, 23, 24
Most Stressful Days Overall: 12, 13, 19, 20, 25, 26
Best Days for Love: 1, 2, 3, 9, 10, 12, 13, 19, 20, 21, 22, 27, 28
Best Days for Money: 2, 3, 7, 8, 12, 13, 17, 18, 21, 22, 25, 26
Best Days for Career: 2, 3, 13, 16, 23, 24, 25, 26

Your 9th house – a very important and under-rated house – became strong on April 19 and is strong until the 20th. This is a happy time. Health is good – especially until the 20th. There will be happy travel opportunities – and you should take them (this could have already happened). Happy educational opportunities also come. When the 9th house is strong there is more interest in a juicy theological or philosophical discussion than in a night out on the town. There is a desire for understanding the 'meaning of life' and the spiritual laws. Often religious and philosophical kinds of breakthroughs happen.

This is a very good period for students at college level. There is more focus on their studies and this tends to success. Since Pluto is also receiving happy aspects, students below college level should also do well.

Mars has been in your 10th house since April 21. This month, on the 21st, the Sun will join him and you enter a yearly career peak. Psychologically you are in the 'noon' time of your year. Your ability to handle 'outer affairs' and ambitions is strongest. Now you handle them by the methods of day – by overt, physical ways. It is good now to detox the career, to get rid of attitudes and habits that are not helpful. The career is also furthered by charitable and altruistic activities. These are good in their own right, but this month will actually help the career – help your public status.

Health needs more attention after the 20th, when at least four (and on occasion five) planets will be in stressful alignment with you. As always rest and relax more. The career is demanding and you can't slack off there now. But you can work more intelligently – alternate activities – and schedule in more rest periods. Enhance the health in the ways mentioned in the yearly report. Low energy is the primal disease.

Your financial planet Venus, now moving forward, spends the month in your 8th house. This is a good aspect for paying down debt and for eliminating financial waste. With the financial planet in the 8th house one prospers by cutting back. You shouldn't cut the things that you really need – only the wasteful things. This is also a good aspect for estate, tax and insurance planning. Debt refinancing is easier with this position (this is another popular way to reduce debt). If you have good business ideas there are outside investors waiting for your call.

Love is happy this month. If there are problems in your relationship it doesn't seem your fault. The beloved has some stressful aspects. He or she is not him/her self.

June

Best Days Overall: 1, 2, 10, 11, 12, 20, 21, 28, 29
Most Stressful Days Overall: 8, 9, 15, 16, 22, 23
Best Days for Love: 5, 6, 10, 11, 15, 16, 20, 21, 24, 25, 28, 29
Best Days for Money: 3, 4, 10, 11, 13, 14, 20, 21, 22, 23, 28, 29, 30
Best Days for Career: 1, 2, 13, 14, 22, 23, 24

Your intense career activity seems to be working. You look very successful this month – especially from the 6th onwards. Mercury, the ruler of your Horoscope, is at the top of your chart. You seem above everyone in your world. You're in authority, calling the shots.

Health still needs keeping an eye on until the 21st. Keep in mind our discussion of this last month. Health and vitality will improve dramatically after the 21st, but in the meantime make sure you get enough rest.

Love still seems stressful for most of this month. You and the beloved are not in agreement. It doesn't mean a break-up necessarily, only that more work is needed to keep harmony between you. Perhaps your career focus is stressing the relationship. Sometimes this causes resentment in the beloved – he or she could feel that the career is more important to you than him or her. Perhaps you are unconsciously 'lording' it over the beloved. Some people have problems with this. Adding to the mix is Neptune's retrograde on the 16th. The beloved seems confused and lacking in direction. This is not a time to make important love decisions one way or the other. Your disagreements will, however, resolve after the 21st.

Finances are good this month. On the 6th Venus moves into Taurus in harmonious relationship with you. You are in harmony with the money people in your life. They seem favourably disposed to you. Venus is dignified in Taurus – she operates more powerfully – and this should reflect in your earnings. The financial planet's position in your 9th house – the luckiest of houses according to the Hindu astrologers – is another positive financial indicator. It shows financial expansion and good fortune. Your wealth goals are ambitious. You want more than just 'survival'. You're interested in really big wealth these days. This too tends to prosperity. The financial judgement is sound. You're more conservative in money matters (this has not been so in the past few months). Financial decisions should be good. Mercury makes beautiful aspects with Jupiter on the 13th and 14th. This looks like a nice payday.

Mercury, the ruler of your Horoscope, spends a good part of the month 'out of bounds'. Thus you're moving outside your normal sphere. You're going into unknown and strange places. You seem more adventurous.

Mars too spends almost all month 'out of bounds'. This would tend to show that the spouse, partner or current love is going outside the normal sphere in their financial dealings. Perhaps setting up accounts or companies 'offshore'. Perhaps exploring financial opportunities outside the normal sphere and with different sorts of people. This seems to work out for him or her – especially from the 25th to the 27th.

July

Best Days Overall: 8, 9, 17, 18, 23, 24
Most Stressful Days Overall: 5, 6, 13, 14, 19, 20
Best Days for Love: 3, 4, 10, 13, 14, 19, 20, 21, 22, 28, 29, 30, 31
Best Days for Money: 1, 10, 11, 19, 20, 28, 29
Best Days for Career: 4, 16, 19, 20, 25, 26

Overall health and energy are much improved over last month. You still have two long-term planets in stressful alignment with you, but almost all of the short-term planets are either in harmonious aspect or are leaving you alone. Health will be good this month. The 19th and 20th seem a little stressful (a short-term issue), so try to rest and relax more those days.

Love is bittersweet this month. On the one hand, the love planet receives very nice aspects until the 20th. This brings love and social opportunity. On the other hand, Mercury, the ruler of your Horoscope, moves in opposition to Neptune, the love planet, from the 6th onwards. The opposition aspect indicates 'maximum distance'. You and the beloved are very far apart – physically or psychologically. You have opposite perspectives on things and you can't seem to agree on anything. It will take much work to bridge your differences, but if you do, love will be better than ever. In astrology, the opposite is the natural love partner.

There is another issue in love too. You and the beloved are both more self-willed these days. Each wants their own way. Each feels he or she is right. The right way is somewhere in the middle. Even better, one time you lean in his or her direction, another time he or she leans in yours.

Speaking of self-will. The planetary power began to shift last month from the social West to the independent East. (This is also complicating love.) You're in a period of increased personal power and independence, which is growing stronger day by day. Now it is time for you and your interests to come first. This is not selfishness. As your interests are handled, you are more in a position to help others. This is the time (and over the next few months) to make the changes that need to be made in your circumstances. You have the energy and wherewithal to do it. You don't need to consult anyone. Take responsibility for your own happiness. Let the world conform to you.

Finances should be good this month. Your financial planet, Venus, moves into your 10th career house on the 5th, indicating a strong focus on finance. It is high on your priorities. Often this shows pay rises (official or unofficial) at work. Guard your professional reputation (always a good idea anyway) as this month it leads to financial opportunity. The authority figures in your life are supportive of your financial goals. Venus's Trine to Jupiter on the 18th and 19th brings financial increase and good fortune. A nice payday.

August

Best Days Overall: 4, 5, 13, 14, 22, 23, 31
Most Stressful Days Overall: 1, 2, 3, 9, 10, 16, 29, 30
Best Days for Love: 9, 10, 18, 19, 26, 27, 28, 29
Best Days for Money: 6, 7, 9, 10, 16, 18, 19, 24, 25, 28, 29
Best Days for Career: 4, 5, 13, 14, 16, 22, 23, 31

Your 12th house became powerful on July 20 as Mars entered this house. On July 22nd the Sun moved in as well. This is the situation until the 22nd of this month. (There will even be an eclipse in this house on the 21st.) This is a period for making spiritual kinds of breakthroughs. It is good for the study of sacred literature, for meditation and contemplation and other types of spiritual practice. There is an inner idealist in every person – this is the time to set it free.

We have a Lunar Eclipse on the 7th that seems to affect you strongly. It impacts on Mars, your planet of death and transformation. This generally doesn't show literal, physical death (you have to look at a lot more things to see that). But it generally indicates 'close encounters' with death – close calls. The dark angel comes calling and sends you a love message: 'Be about the business that you were born to do, life here on Earth is short – it can end at any time.' But this is only one of the meanings. This eclipse brings financial dramas to the beloved. Important changes will have to be made. If you are of an appropriate age you're making changes to your will and insurance policies. Since this eclipse occurs in your 6th house there can be turmoil at the job or in the workplace. Job changes are likely. Often there are health scares and a need to change the health regime. Take a nice easy schedule over this period – there's no need to tempt the dark angel more than is necessary.

The Solar Eclipse of the 21st occurs in your 12th house, but very close to the cusp of your 1st house and it affects both houses. If you were born early in the sign of Virgo – August 22–24 – you will feel it very strongly. Those born later in the sign won't feel it that much. Once again (as in February) important changes happen in your spiritual life. I feel this is because of interior revelation that happens (you're making spiritual breakthroughs this month). It would only be natural to change your practice and perhaps teachings as a result. Again, as in February, there are shakeups and upheavals in spiritual or charitable organizations that you're involved with, and dramas in the lives of gurus or guru figures.

On the 22nd, the Sun moves into your own sign and you enter into one of your yearly personal pleasure periods. This is a time for enjoying the pleasures of the body, for getting it into right shape. It's also a good time to get the image in right shape – the way you want it.

The issues in love that we discussed last month are even stronger this month. In love it's all about learning to bridge differences – agreeing to disagree but with love and respect.

September

Best Days Overall: 1, 10, 18, 19, 28, 29
Most Stressful Days Overall: 5, 6, 12, 13, 25, 26
Best Days for Love: 5, 6, 7, 8, 14, 15, 16, 17, 23, 24, 28
Best Days for Money: 3, 4, 7, 8, 12, 13, 16, 17, 20, 21, 28, 30
Best Days for Career: 8, 9, 12, 13, 18, 19, 28, 29

The planetary power is now in its maximum Eastern position. You have maximum personal power and independence. The planets are for you rather than others. Your personal goals – your personal happiness – receive strong cosmic support. You're supposed to have things your way these days. If others don't go along (most will) you can go it alone. You're not in need of social support systems. So take the bull by the horns. Create the conditions for your own happiness. Now is the time. If you wait too long it will become much harder.

Health and energy are super this month – perhaps the best they've been all year. Half the planets are either in your own sign or moving through there, and each is depositing a special gift and a special energy. The Sun in your 1st house until the 22nd bestows star quality and supernatural (unworldly) glamour to the image. Psychic and ESP abilities are greatly enhanced. Mars in your sign, from the 5th onwards, bestows sex appeal, physical strength and courage. (Be careful not to overdo a good thing.) Venus in your sign from the 20th onwards bestows beauty, grace and charm, and an excellent sense of style. (She also brings financial windfalls and opportunities.) Mercury brings self-confidence and self-esteem – and happy career opportunities. Life is good these days.

In spite of your wonderful personal appearance, your personal magnetism and charm – love still seems problematic. Yes, you're attracting the opposite sex but the problem seems to be in serious relationships. You are strong and want your way, and so do the people you meet. The issues we've written about in previous months are even more in effect now. The issue is learning to disagree respectfully – and especially to respect the other's position. (This can be difficult.) The tendency now (and for the past few months) would be to break up. But this need not happen. It will take more work though to keep things together. The 23rd to the 26th brings a love crisis – perhaps finance triggers it – but there's more to it than that. Ride it through – it is temporary.

Love could be better, but there are other kinds of happiness that happen for you. You're still in a yearly personal pleasure peak until the 22nd. And after the 22nd you enter a yearly earnings peak as the Sun moves into your money house. The month ahead is prosperous.

October

Best Days Overall: 7, 8, 15, 16, 25, 26
Most Stressful Days Overall: 3, 4, 9, 10, 22, 23, 24, 30, 31
Best Days for Love: 3, 4, 7, 8, 11, 12, 17, 18, 20, 21, 27, 28, 30, 31
Best Days for Money: 1, 7, 8, 10, 11, 15, 16, 20, 21, 25, 26, 30
Best Days for Career: 1, 9, 10, 20, 30, 31

Finance is the main headline this month. The money house is easily the most dominant house (and dominant interest), with 60 per cent of the planets either there or moving through there. This is a lot of financial power. Earnings increase dramatically. You're in a yearly period of peak earnings. The Sun in the money house until the 23rd makes you a 'financial star' – you shine in this world. Also it shows great financial intuition – great instincts. Mercury in the money house until the 17th shows earnings flowing from good communication – buying, selling, sales, marketing, advertising and PR. It also shows the financial favour of the elders and authority figures in your life. Sometimes this indicates money that comes from the government. Venus in this house, from the 14th onwards, also means increased earnings. She is now in her own sign and house, and she is naturally strong in this position.

The financial life will be good all month, but the interest wanes a bit as the month progresses. On the 11th Jupiter, which has been here since last year, will move into your 3rd house. Mercury will leave the money house on the 17th and the Sun on the 23rd. But by then, your main financial goals (the short-term ones at least) will have been attained and you won't need as much focus here.

Venus's solstice from the 16th to the 19th also indicates a pause in the financial affairs and then a change of direction. Moreover, Mars also has his solstice this month – from the 23rd to the 30th. This shows a pause in the financial affairs of the spouse, partner or current love too. These pauses are good.

Jupiter's move into your 3rd house shows earnings from sales, marketing, advertising, PR, blogging and writing. Trading is fortunate under this aspect too. A new car and communication equipment will likely come in the coming months (and perhaps next year too).

Intellectual interests will start becoming interesting to Virgos of all ages. It is especially good for students below college level. It shows success in their studies. Virgo is an intellectual sign and now you have the interest (and wherewithal) to indulge the intellect.

Health is still excellent. You can enhance it further in the ways mentioned in the yearly report.

November

Best Days Overall: 3, 4, 12, 13, 21, 22
Most Stressful Days Overall: 5, 6, 19, 20, 26, 27
Best Days for Love: 6, 7, 8, 16, 17, 26, 27
Best Days for Money: 3, 4, 7, 8, 12, 13, 14, 15, 16, 17, 21, 22, 26, 27
Best Days for Career: 5, 6, 9, 19, 20, 29, 30

The love life improved last month. It was not perfect, to be sure, but it was better than in previous months. This month love improves even further. You and the beloved are moving closer to each other. The distance between you is lessening day by day. There are still some disagreements after the 6th but these too will be temporary. If your relationship survived August and September it will survive the month ahead too. Jupiter's move into Scorpio last month was especially good for love. Singles are meeting serious love interests these days. The other good news is that the love planet, Neptune, is finally moving forward after many months of retrograde motion. This happens on the 22nd. The rest of this year and next year should bring happiness in love.

Health and energy are still good – especially until the 22nd. After that be sure to get enough rest. Enhance the health in the ways mentioned in the yearly report. Your health planet has been in retrograde motion since August, so avoid making drastic changes to the health regime. Changes need much homework.

The 3rd house is the main headline this month, with up to half the planets in there or moving through. So this is a month where students excel. They enjoy their studies. They don't need to be coaxed to learn – they want to study and read. There is success here.

You have an interest in all kinds of different books and periodicals these days – love stories, poetry, inspiration, erotica, financial and spiritual literature. Each has something to contribute to your store of knowledge.

The planetary power has been in the bottom half of your chart since September. Thus your focus has also shifted. Home, family and your emotional wellness are more important than the career now. You are always ambitious – you haven't lost it – but it's a time to 'regroup', to gather the forces you will need for your next career push, next year. A successful career rests on a solid psychological and domestic foundation. Working on this foundation will help the career later on.

Your 4th house of home and family becomes powerful from the 22nd onwards, while your 10th house of career is basically empty this month (only the Moon moves through there on the 5th and 6th). Another message from the cosmos. Let go of the career and focus on things at home. You're more involved with siblings, sibling figures and neighbours these days (and they seem to be prospering).

December

Best Days Overall: 1, 2, 9, 10, 18, 19, 20
Most Stressful Days Overall: 3, 4, 16, 17, 24, 25, 30, 31
Best Days for Love: 5, 6, 7, 8, 14, 15, 16, 17, 24, 25, 28
Best Days for Money: 5, 6, 7, 8, 11, 12, 14, 15, 16, 17, 24, 25, 28
Best Days for Career: 3, 4, 7, 8, 16, 17, 26, 27, 30, 31

Again, like last month, we find the 4th house of home and family ultra-powerful while the 10th house of career is empty (and again, only the Moon moves through there, on the 3rd, 4th, 30th and 31st). So continue to focus on the home and family situation. Continue to focus on attaining the 'right psychological state'. This is night time (symbolically speaking) of your year – the midnight hour. The outer world ceases to exist for us in the midnight hour. We are asleep to it. But inside, many things are happening that will set the stage for the next day – the next career push. Feeling right is more important than doing right these days. Being there for the family – in a physical and emotional way – is more important than making the right deal or getting that promotion. (Those things will happen in due course, but now be there for the family.)

Family issues are improving this month. Saturn is finally leaving the 4th house on the 21st. Family life (and perhaps a parent figure) has been a burden. This is over with now. Many of you have felt emotionally blocked for the past few years. You didn't feel safe in expressing your true feelings. Now this becomes much easier.

Saturn's move into your 5th house brings a focus on children and children figures. There is a need to discipline them correctly, which is an art. One neither overdoes it nor underdoes it. This is something you will learn over the next two years or so.

Health and energy still need watching until the 21st, but you will see a huge improvement afterwards. Saturn, who has been stressing you out for more than two years, starts to make harmonious aspects to you. After the 21st, there will be only one long-term planet – Neptune – in stressful alignment. You will feel this in your body.

Mercury is retrograde from the 3rd to the 23rd. Since Mercury is also your career planet, we have another indication to let go of the career and focus on the home. This is a time to review your personal and career goals and see where improvements can be made. You can put these improvements into action after the 23rd.

Mars makes dynamic aspects with Uranus from the 1st to the 3rd. Drive more carefully and avoid stressful activities.

Mars is in your money house until the 9th. It is a good time to use extra cash to pay down debt. This is also a good aspect for estate, tax and insurance planning (if you're of the appropriate age). The spouse, partner or current love seems supportive financially. Venus, your financial planet, spends most of the month in your 4th house, indicating that you're spending on the family and probably earning from them as well. There is good family support. There could be a tendency to overspend.

Libra

THE SCALES

Birthdays from
23rd September to
22nd October

Personality Profile

LIBRA AT A GLANCE

Element – Air

Ruling Planet – Venus
   Career Planet – Moon
   Love Planet – Mars
   Money Planet – Pluto
   Planet of Communications – Jupiter
   Planet of Health and Work – Neptune
   Planet of Home and Family Life – Saturn
   Planet of Spirituality and Good Fortune – Mercury

Colours – blue, jade green

Colours that promote love, romance and social harmony – carmine, red, scarlet

Colours that promote earning power – burgundy, red-violet, violet

Gems – carnelian, chrysolite, coral, emerald, jade, opal, quartz, white marble

Metal – copper

Scents – almond, rose, vanilla, violet

Quality – cardinal (= activity)

Qualities most needed for balance – a sense of self, self-reliance, independence

Strongest virtues – social grace, charm, tact, diplomacy

Deepest needs – love, romance, social harmony

Characteristic to avoid – violating what is right in order to be socially accepted

Signs of greatest overall compatibility – Gemini, Aquarius

Signs of greatest overall incompatibility – Aries, Cancer, Capricorn

Sign most helpful to career – Cancer

Sign most helpful for emotional support – Capricorn

Sign most helpful financially – Scorpio

Sign best for marriage and/or partnerships – Aries

Sign most helpful for creative projects – Aquarius

Best Sign to have fun with – Aquarius

Signs most helpful in spiritual matters – Gemini, Virgo

Best day of the week – Friday

Understanding a Libra

In the sign of Libra the universal mind – the soul – expresses its genius for relationships, that is, its power to harmonize diverse elements in a unified, organic way. Libra is the soul's power to express beauty in all of its forms. And where is beauty if not within relationships? Beauty does not exist in isolation. Beauty arises out of comparison – out of the just relationship between different parts. Without a fair and harmonious relationship there is no beauty, whether it in art, manners, ideas or the social or political forum.

There are two faculties humans have that exalt them above the animal kingdom: their rational faculty (expressed in the signs of Gemini and Aquarius) and their aesthetic faculty, exemplified by Libra. Without an aesthetic sense we would be little more than intelligent barbarians. Libra is the civilizing instinct or urge of the soul.

Beauty is the essence of what Librans are all about. They are here to beautify the world. One could discuss Librans' social grace, their sense of balance and fair play, their ability to see and love another person's point of view – but this would be to miss their central asset: their desire for beauty.

No one – no matter how alone he or she seems to be – exists in isolation. The universe is one vast collaboration of beings. Librans, more than most, understand this and understand the spiritual laws that make relationships bearable and enjoyable.

A Libra is always the unconscious (and in some cases conscious) civilizer, harmonizer and artist. This is a Libra's deepest urge and greatest genius. Librans love instinctively to bring people together, and they are uniquely qualified to do so. They have a knack for seeing what unites people – the things that attract and bind rather than separate individuals.

Finance

In financial matters Librans can seem frivolous and illogical to others. This is because Librans appear to be more concerned with earning money for others than for themselves. But there is a logic to this financial attitude. Librans know that everything and everyone is connected and that it is impossible to help another to prosper without also prospering yourself. Since enhancing their partner's income and position tends to strengthen their relationship, Librans choose to do so. What could be more fun than building a relationship? You will rarely find a Libra enriching him- or herself at someone else's expense.

Scorpio is the ruler of Libra's solar 2nd house of money, giving Libra unusual insight into financial matters – and the power to focus on these matters in a way that disguises a seeming indifference. In fact, many other signs come to Librans for financial advice and guidance.

Given their social grace, Librans often spend great sums of money on entertaining and organizing social events. They also like to help others when they are in need. Librans would go out of their way to help a friend in dire straits, even if they have to borrow from others to do so. However, Librans are also very careful to pay back any debts they owe, and like to make sure they never have to be reminded to do so.

Career and Public Image

Publicly, Librans like to appear as nurturers. Their friends and acquaintances are their family and they wield political power in parental ways. They also like bosses who are paternal or maternal.

The sign of Cancer is on Libra's 10th career house cusp; the Moon is Libra's career planet. The Moon is by far the speediest, most changeable planet in the horoscope. It alone among all the planets travels through the entire zodiac – all twelve signs and houses – every month. This is an important key to the way in which Librans approach their careers, and also to what they need to do to maximize their career potential. The Moon is the planet of moods and feelings – Librans need a career in which their emotions can have free expression. This is why so many Librans are involved in the creative arts. Libra's ambitions wax and wane with the Moon. They tend to wield power according to their mood.

The Moon 'rules' the masses – and that is why Libra's highest goal is to achieve a mass kind of acclaim and popularity. Librans who achieve fame cultivate the public as other people cultivate a lover or friend. Librans can be very flexible – and often fickle – in their career and ambitions. On the other hand, they can achieve their ends in a great variety of ways. They are not stuck in one attitude or with one way of doing things.

Love and Relationships

Librans express their true genius in love. In love you could not find a partner more romantic, more seductive or more fair. If there is one thing that is sure to destroy a relationship – sure to block your love from flowing – it is injustice or imbalance between lover and beloved. If one party is giving too much or taking too much, resentment is sure to surface at some time or other. Librans are careful about this. If anything, Librans might err on the side of giving more, but never giving less.

If you are in love with a Libra, make sure you keep the aura of romance alive. Do all the little things – candle-lit dinners, travel to exotic locales, flowers and small gifts. Give things that are beautiful, not necessarily expensive. Send cards. Ring regularly even if you have nothing in particular to say. The niceties are very important to a Libra. Your relationship is a work of art: make it beautiful and your Libran lover will appreciate it. If you are creative about it, he or she will appreciate it even more; for this is how your Libra will behave towards you.

Librans like their partners to be aggressive and even a bit self-willed. They know that these are qualities they sometimes lack and so they like their partners to have them. In relationships, however, Librans can be very aggressive – but always in a subtle and charming way! Librans are determined in their efforts to charm the object of their desire – and this determination can be very pleasant if you are on the receiving end.

Home and Domestic Life

Since Librans are such social creatures, they do not particularly like mundane domestic duties. They like a well-organized home – clean and neat with everything needful present – but housework is a chore and a burden, one of the unpleasant tasks in life that must be done, the quicker the better. If a Libra has enough money – and sometimes even if not – he or she will prefer to pay someone else to take care of the daily household chores. However, Librans like gardening; they love to have flowers and plants in the home.

A Libra's home is modern, and furnished in excellent taste. You will find many paintings and sculptures there. Since Librans like to be with friends and family, they enjoy entertaining at home and they make great hosts.

Capricorn is on the cusp of Libra's 4th solar house of home and family. Saturn, the planet of law, order, limits and discipline, rules Libra's domestic affairs. If Librans want their home life to be supportive and happy they need to develop some of the virtues of Saturn – order, organization and discipline. Librans, being so creative and so intensely in need of harmony, can tend to be too lax in the home and too permissive with their children. Too much of this is not always good; children need freedom but they also need limits.

Horoscope for 2017

Major Trends

This is your year, Libra – enjoy! Jupiter has been in your sign since September of last year and will be there until October 10. This brings optimism, good fortune (what the world calls good luck) and an abundance of sensual delights. No matter how much money you have (it's really not an issue) you will live on a higher standard – as if you were rich. The wherewithal for this will come naturally. On October 11 Jupiter will move into your money house, bringing financial expansion – real money. More on this later.

Saturn has been in your 3rd house for the past two years and is there almost to the year's end. For students, below college level, there is a need to work harder in school. Learning needs more discipline. If you apply self-discipline you will see success (Jupiter is helping you here). Even non students are going to become deeper, more serious thinkers this year. There will be more organization in the thought process. It might take you longer to learn but what you learn will be learned well.

Pluto in your 4th house (and he's been there for many years now) shows more spending on the home and family and perhaps renovations going on in the home. More details later.

Neptune has been in your 6th house of health and work since 2012 and will be there for many more years. This indicates someone who is going deeper (and getting good results) into spiritual healing. More on this later.

Uranus has been in your 7th house of love for many years (since 2011) and is there for the year ahead. This has tested many marriages and love relationships. Divorces (or near divorces) have been happening. The whole social life is highly unstable. By now you have learned to handle this, but it's been a challenge. Next year Uranus will start to move out of your 7th house and by 2019 he will be completely out of there. The love life is starting to become more stable. More on this later.

Your most important areas of interest this year are the body and image (until October 10); finance (from October 11 onwards); communication and intellectual interests (until December 21); home and family; health and work; love and romance.

Your paths of greatest fulfilment this year are the body and image (until October 10); finance (from October 11 onwards); spirituality (until April 29); friends, groups, group activities and online activities (from April 29 onwards).

Health

(Please note that this is an astrological perspective on health and not a medical one. In days of yore there was no difference, both of these perspectives were identical. Now there could be quite a difference. For a medical perspective, please consult your doctor or health practitioner.)

While health is much improved over the 2011 to 2014 period, it still needs watching. Two long-term planets – Uranus and Pluto – are in stressful alignment with you. At the end of the year – on December 21 – Saturn will also move into stressful alignment. This doesn't necessarily mean sickness, only that you have to pay more attention here. Your normal energy levels are not up to the usual standards. Thus, you can become more vulnerable to things. The good news here is that your house of health is prominent and you are paying attention.

There is much you can do to enhance the health and prevent problems from developing. The first and most important thing is to maintain high energy levels. Don't allow yourself to get over-tired. Don't waste energy on trivial, non-essential things. Keep your mind on the real priorities in your life and let lesser things go. This sounds easy but it's difficult in practice; often tough choices have to be made.

The second thing is to give more attention to the following areas – the vulnerable areas of your chart. These are where problems (if they happened) would most likely begin. Keeping them healthy and fit is sound preventive medicine. (The reflex points are shown in the chart below.)

- The heart. This is not normally a vulnerable area for you, but in recent years – since 2011 – it has become so. Avoid worry and anxiety. Cultivate a relaxed approach to life. One can be more effective without being tense. Develop more faith.
- The kidneys and hips. These are always important for you. Regular hip massage (and the buttocks too) should be incorporated into your health regime. Herbal kidney cleanses are good too.

Important foot reflexology points for the year ahead

Try to massage all of the foot on a regular basis – the top of the foot as well as the bottom – but pay extra attention to the points highlighted on the chart. When you massage, be aware of 'sore spots' as these need special attention. It's also a good idea to massage the ankles and below them.

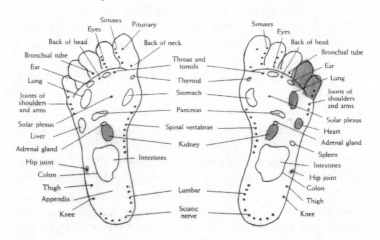

- The feet. These too are always important for you. Neptune, your health planet, rules the feet. But ever since 2012 when Neptune moved into Pisces, they have become even more important. Regular foot massage – see our chart above – should be part of your health regime. There are gadgets on the market that massage the feet and some even give foot whirlpool treatments. These would be great (over time they pay for themselves). Wear shoes that fit right and that you can balance well in. It's better to sacrifice fashion for comfort – although this is a difficult thing for Libra to do. If you can have both – fashion and comfort – all the better.

Neptune, the most spiritual of all the planets, as the health planet shows that you respond well to spiritual therapies, as we have mentioned. This was always the case for you but more so since 2012. If you feel under the weather, see a spiritual healer.

Your health planet rules from a Water sign. Thus you have a special connection to the healing powers of the Water element. Water is weak in the horoscope this year (until October 11), so make sure you're drinking enough water. Dehydration could be an issue for you. Water aerobics and water sports are healthy kinds of exercises. It will be good to spend more time on the water – especially if you feel under the weather. Get on a boat or go to the beach, river or lake. Hang out near water. Soaking in a natural spring, lake, river or ocean will be healing. At a pinch, soaking in the tub will also be beneficial.

If you pay attention and take these precautions you should sail through the year with few problems.

Home and Family

Home and family has been an important focus in your life for many years now – since 2008. It been tumultuous to say the least. There have been death and near-death experiences in the family circle. There have been major repairs and renovations in the home. Perhaps even break-ups in the family unit. None of this should be considered punishment. A cosmic detox is happening in the family (and in your emotional life). The cosmic construction crews are hard at work creating the dream home and the ideal family relationship. A Pluto transit is not an 'event' but a long-term process; a series of events that go on and on until the job is done. This is what is happening now. The job is far from finished. Pluto will be in your 4th house for many more years.

Anyone who has ever had major renovations done knows the chaos of the experience. Furniture is all over the place. You can't walk in certain areas. It's noisy and often smelly. Sometimes you have to leave the house and sleep elsewhere. You're forced out of your comfort zone for a while. But the end result! Ah! That's when you see that it was worth it. Pluto is a master craftsman. He knows exactly what he's doing. It will all work out well in the end.

There's another upside to all of this. Family support seems good. You're spending on the home but can earn from it as well. Family connections are important financially.

Pluto, your financial planet, in your 4th house shows good fortune with mortgages and lines of credit based on your home equity. Money can come from insurance claims related to the home. It's wise to have a good homeowner's insurance policy these days. Repairs can be needed at any time.

This transit also shows someone who earns money from home. Many of you are setting up home offices or home-based businesses. The home is as much an office as a home. All these things seem worthwhile this year.

Repairs and renovations can happen at any time, as we mentioned. But if you have some free will in the matter, January 28 to March 20 and July 20 to September 5 are good times for this. The work will go better and quicker. If you're planning to redecorate or otherwise beautify the home (a never-ending process for Libra), November 22 to the end of the year is good.

With Jupiter in your own sign, Libras of childbearing age are much more fertile than usual.

A parent or parent figure seem stressed out but financially supportive. He or she is also involved in endless renovations – and perhaps even moves. The home base seems very unstable. He or she seems emotionally temperamental too, and subject to swift changes of mood. Therapy would be helpful here. Siblings and sibling figures will feel better by the end of the year. A move is likely from October 21 onwards. Children or children figures are having a stable family year.

Finance and Career

This is a prosperous year. Since September 2016 you have been in a multi-year cycle of prosperity. Sure there will be work involved. Sure there will be some challenges. But the end result will be increased earnings.

Jupiter, as we have said, spends most of the year in your 1st house. So, you're dressing more expensively. You're taking on the 'image' of wealth. Others see you as wealthy, and this brings financial opportunity to you. You spend on yourself too.

We mentioned earlier that Jupiter in your 1st house shows the 'good life' - the high life. You spend more on - or have access to - personal indulgences. The year ahead is about personal pleasure, personal pampering, fine clothes, good food, good wine and personal luxuries. (The weight will need watching this year - this is the price of excessive good living.)

There is a temptation to overspend on these things so be careful about this. However, you will have the wherewithal to enjoy these good things. If you keep things within budget, there will be less financial stress. If you overspend, you will be able to cover it, but with more stress.

You're spending more on the home and family this year, as we have mentioned. You might be overspending in this area too. (Jupiter's influence tends to excess.) But these kinds of investments are basically good - and in your Horoscope.

These aspects favour earnings from residential real estate, restaurants, the food business, the lodging industry and industries that cater to the home. Being a Libra, interior designers, furniture makers and makers of luxury items for the home are also good investments.

Your financial planet Pluto has been in the sign of Capricorn since 2008. This is a good financial position. It show sound financial judgement - a conservative, long-term approach to wealth. Wealth is built up in a methodical, step-by-step fashion over time. This aspect is excellent for budgeting and financial planning. Libras are not known for their financial skills - their strengths are elsewhere - but since 2008 your financial management skills are much improved. When the money starts to roll in after October 11, you'll know what to do with it.

Jupiter in the sign of Scorpio after October 11 shows that those of an appropriate age are doing estate planning. Tax issues and estates are determining the financial decision making.

The year ahead – but especially after October 11 – is good for paying down debt. But much depends on your personal needs. You will find it easier to borrow money too. Your line of credit will increase. You have good access to outside capital. Learning to manage debt properly is one of the important lessons in this life. If you use it properly it can make you rich. If misused, it becomes (as the financial savants say) a weapon of mass destruction.

Career doesn't seem a big issue this year. Some years are like that. The focus is more on finance and the home. Nevertheless there will be many short-term trends in the career which are best dealt with in the monthly reports.

Love and Social Life

Love is always important to Libra – the reason for their existence (as many will say if you talk to them). But since 2011 when Uranus entered your 7th house, it has become more important and more challenging (not to mention more fun and exciting).

Uranus is the planet of freedom and sudden change – lightning-like change. This makes the love life very exciting. Lightning can strike at any moment, in any place. Love can happen at any time. There is always this feeling of anticipation – today it can happen. But this also creates instability. Lightning generally doesn't last very long. The feelings of love that were so intense last week are over this week. But no matter, something new can happen today.

Uranus in the 7th house is not good for committed relationships. Marriages have been in serious trouble for some years now. Many a divorce has happened. And though divorce doesn't have to happen, keeping an existing relationship together will take a *lot* of work and effort. If the work is put in – and the relationship is basically sound – I've seen marriages survive this kind of aspect. (Not many though.)

Singles are not advised to marry this year. Enjoy the love life for what it is. There's no need to project anything onto it. The instability in love is in effect all year, but next year it will start to fade. By 2019 some normality enters the love life. You, and the people you attract, will be more settled. The rebellion will be out of the system.

There are many short-term trends in love. Your love planet, Mars, is relatively fast moving. He won't move through every area of your chart, but through many of them in a given year. Thus the love life will be affected by where Mars is at any given time and the kinds of aspects he receives. These are best covered in the monthly reports.

Those working on your second marriage are having a stable year: if you are already married, you'll likely stay married; if single, you'll likely stay single. The same is true for those working on or in the third marriage. Those working on the fourth marriage have wonderful romantic aspects, but marriage is better delayed for a later time.

Children and children figures are having a good social year. If anything they can be socializing to excess (especially from April 29 onwards). Grandchildren of the appropriate age (if you have them) are struggling socially.

Love might be unstable, but friendships seem happy this year – especially after April 29 as the North Node of the Moon enters your 11th house. The problem could be too many, rather than too few friends.

Self-Improvement

Both 2015 and 2016 were strong spiritual years. Much growth happened. There were many spiritual breakthroughs. Your ESP abilities were enhanced and you had many supernatural experiences. The spiritual life is still happy this year but less active. The Moon's North Node will be in your 12th house until April 29.

Uranus in your 7th house of love has been difficult to deal with, but this aspect has brought some important personal growth. You've been learning to deal with love and social insecurity – to be comfortable about it and to be at ease with the sudden changes that happen. After six years of this you've lost much of your anxiety.

Spiritual healing, as we've mentioned, is a big issue these days and you're going deeper into it. This is a long-term trend and we've written about it in previous years. Spiritual healing is a huge, huge subject. This is not something you learn in a year or two or three. It takes many years and this is the message of your chart. Neptune is going to be in your health house for many more years.

As you go deeper into spiritual healing, you will see, for yourself, that the current scientific understanding of the body is not adequate. It is true up to a point. The body does have a mechanical and a chemical aspect to it. But above these purely physical levels – the levels that can be measured by instruments – are many other finer levels. There is an energy body (sometimes called the etheric body). There is a feeling body and above that a mental body and upper mental body. Above these are other spiritual bodies, which are given different labels by different systems. In astrology we understand that each of the planets has its own body in each person. The higher bodies are 'causitive' relative to the lower ones. A change in a higher body (higher in energy vibration) will produce a change in the body beneath it, which will create a change in the body beneath that, and so forth until the chemical-physical level gets affected.

Mind-body medicine is more or less mainstream these days. But there are limits to it. Problems in the mind, where the seeds of pathology lie, can't be dealt with by the human mind. (The human mind is in itself the problem.) What is needed is the intervention of a power which is above the human mind to clear these issues. And here we have the spiritual approach to healing. It is about the invocation of a power that is above the mind, to come in and do its perfect work.

As the power descends, it will heal the mind – the problems there that were causing the physical condition. Then, by a beautiful natural process, the feelings will get healed, and then, the physical body. Sometimes the effect is speeded up and we don't notice the stages. But generally healing happens by a gradual kind of process.

The important thing is to be persistent in your practice and allow for the gradual dissipation of the health problem. It is seldom instantaneous.

Month-by-month Forecasts

January

> Best Days Overall: 1, 9, 10, 17, 18, 19, 27, 28
> Most Stressful Days Overall: 5, 6, 11, 12, 25, 26
> Best Days For Love: 2, 3, 4, 5, 6, 11, 12, 20, 21, 31
> Best Days For Money: 1, 7, 8, 10, 15, 16, 18, 19, 20, 21, 25, 26, 28, 29
> Best Days For Career: 7, 8, 11, 12, 16, 27, 28

You begin your year with the Western, social sector of your chart over-whelmingly dominant. All this month between 70 and 80 per cent of the planets are in the social West. You are other-oriented by your nature and now even more so. This situation is comfortable for you – much more so than for other signs such as Aries or Leo. You enjoy being dependent. You enjoy exercising your social gifts. You know how to manoeuvre here. You are already adept at getting cooperation from others, so the month ahead should be happy and successful.

Health needs some attention – especially until the 19th – but it won't hurt to rest and relax more afterwards too. The good news is that Venus moves into your 6th house of health on the 3rd and spends the rest of the month here. You're on the case in health matters. You're focused here. Health is enhanced in the ways mentioned in the yearly report. Spiritual-healing techniques are especially powerful from the 3rd onwards – and particularly on the 11th and 12th. If you feel under the weather, see a spiritual healer, or apply the techniques on your own.

Your focus on health has other side benefits too. Your love planet, Mars, spends most of the month – until the 28th – in your 6th house. Thus your focus on health can also lead to romance and social oppor-tunity. You could be attracted to health professionals or people involved in your health. Love could be more idealistic during this period and spiritual compatibility would be important. Health problems could have love issues as their root causes. If this happens restore harmony as quickly as possible. A visit to a health professional or a health semi-nar could lead to social and romantic opportunities.

Pluto, your financial planet, is receiving positive aspects this month until the 19th. So prosperity is happening. Friends and family seem especially supportive. High tech and online activities also bring profits. The 7th seems an especially good financial day.

Your 4th house of home and family is powerful until the 19th. The planetary power is mostly below the horizon of your chart, signalling that career is not a big issue this month. Focus on the home, family and your emotional wellness. This will set the stage for this year's career push, which will begin in March and April. This is the time to build the psychological infrastructure for future career success.

February

Best Days Overall: 5, 6, 14, 15, 24, 25
Most Stressful Days Overall: 1, 2, 7, 8, 21, 22, 28
Best Days for Love: 1, 2, 9, 10, 19, 20, 28
Best Days for Money: 3, 4, 5, 6, 12, 13, 14, 15, 16, 17, 18, 21, 22, 24, 25
Best Days for Career: 5, 6, 7, 8, 14, 15, 26, 27

Towards the end of last month both Venus and Mars had their solstices. In the case of Venus it happened from January 29–31. In the case of Mars it happened from the 27th to the 31st. This brought a temporary pause in your love life and personal affairs. And now you're going in a different direction. Taking a new tack.

We have two eclipses this month. These always bring change and disturbance. In your case, these will be mild. You don't seem too personally affected. It won't hurt though to take it a little easier over the eclipse periods.

The Lunar Eclipse of the 11th (in America it's on the 10th) occurs in your 11th house. Not only that, but it impacts on the ruler of your 11th house – the Sun* – as well. The eclipse brings dramas in the lives of friends. Friendships get tested and friends can be more temperamental this period, so be patient. Computers, mobile devices and other high-

---

* Every Lunar Eclipse impacts on the Sun even though it is the Moon that is getting eclipsed.

tech gadgetry could malfunction – they tend to be sensitive to cosmic energy. In many cases the malfunction will clear up after the eclipse passes, but sometimes equipment or software needs replacement. It would be a good idea to have your important files backed up. Hacking and viruses could be a problem too. Every Lunar Eclipse affects the career and this one is no different. Often it indicates dramatic changes in your company or industry. The rules of the game change. Often it shows life-changing events in the lives of bosses, parents or parent figures.

The Solar Eclipse of the 26th occurs in your 6th house of health and work, and it also impacts on Neptune, the ruler of this house. So there can be health scares or job changes. There are disruptions in the work-place. If you hire others there is employee turnover and unrest. There are dramatic changes in your health regime over the next six months. The health regime needs a change of course now and the eclipse will force the issue. Since the eclipsed planet, the Sun, is the ruler of your 11th house there is more testing of your high-tech equipment and gadgetry happening. There are more dramas in the lives of friends.

March

Best Days Overall: 4, 5, 13, 14, 23, 24
Most Stressful Days Overall: 1, 6, 7, 21, 22, 28
Best Days for Love: 1, 9, 10, 18, 20, 21, 27, 28, 30
Best Days for Money: 2, 3, 5, 6, 11, 12, 13, 14, 16, 17, 21, 22, 23, 24, 31
Best Days for Career: 6, 7, 16, 27, 28

The planetary power starts to shift after the 20th. The upper half of the Horoscope begins to become stronger. It is time to focus on your career and outer goals. Now, because of the way the long-term planets are aligned, the bottom half of your chart is still pretty strong, with four long-term planets there. So home, family and emotional wellness continue to be important – you can't ignore these things – but you can start giving more focus to your outer life and ambitions. You're basically balancing a successful career with a happy and harmonious family life. You're juggling the two.

Your good career days are shown above. In general you have more enthusiasm and drive from the 1st to the 12th and from the 28th onwards, as the Moon (your career planet) waxes. There is more success during those periods. The 3rd and 30th are also very good – though the aspects are a bit lacklustre. This is when the Moon is at her perigee, her closest point to Earth.

The focus is on health and work until the 20th. Your 6th house is very strong. This is a good thing. You need to build up strength for when the health becomes more problematic. Make sure to get enough rest from the 20th onwards.

Power in the 6th house is excellent for job seekers. The 1st and the 2nd seem exceptionally good days. Children and children figures in your life are prospering during this period. There is romance in store for them later in the month too.

On the 20th you enter one of your yearly love and social peaks. Your 7th house of love is chock-full of planets – 60 per cent of the planets are either there or moving through there this month. It is a socially active month and there are many romantic opportunities for singles. The problem is that with Venus retrograde from the 4th onwards, you're not sure of what you want. Personal confidence is not what it should be. (The Western sector is very powerful and the ruler of your Horoscope, Venus, is far, far from home. In the sign of Aries she is much weaker than usual.) In a way this is good. You're not about to be overly assertive with others. You'll tend to go with the flow. You'll be more popular than usual. There is a love relationship here but you seem to be backing away from it.

Finances are good until the 20th but get more stressful afterwards. This does not affect your overall prosperity – which is excellent this year – but there are more challenges to deal with. More work than usual is needed to attain your goals.

April

Best Days Overall: 1, 10, 11, 19, 20, 21, 28, 29
Most Stressful Days Overall: 3, 4, 17, 18, 24, 25, 30
Best Days for Love: 4, 7, 8, 12, 13, 18, 23, 24, 25, 28
Best Days for Money: 1, 7, 8, 10, 11, 12, 13, 17, 18, 19, 20, 21,
    26, 27, 28, 29
Best Days for Career: 3, 4, 5, 6, 15, 16, 26, 27, 30

In March you seemed very impulsive in love – more than usual. Most likely you paid the price for it. This month you seem more cautious. Venus, the ruler of your Horoscope, will spend most of the month in Pisces. (Last month she was in impulsive Aries.) The love life is still very active and you're still in a yearly love and social peak. But this seems more about friendship and group activities than romance. Venus is still retrograde until the 15th, so use the time to get clear about your personal goals. It seems you need to decide what kind of 'look' you want to project – how you want others to see you.

On the 28th Venus moves back into Aries and into your 7th house – this time in a healthier kind of way. She is moving forwards instead of backwards. You still need to be careful about jumping into relationships too quickly, but the judgement is better now. Personal popularity is much stronger than usual and you have no problem putting other people first. You seem proactive in love – more so than usual.

If you talk to a Libra – or someone with many planets there – they will tell you that 'life is all about relationship. Relationship is everything. You only learn about yourself through relationships.' Not everyone thinks this way. But you do – and these days more than usual.

Your love planet, Mars, spends most of the month in your 8th house of regeneration. This shows the importance of sexual magnetism in love. If you're not feeling this way, you're attracting people who do. While this magnetism is important, it won't hold a relationship together for the long haul. On the 21st, Mars moves into intellectual Gemini and into your 9th house. This introduces more depth to the romantic life. Sex is still important, but now you also want good communication and philosophical compatibility. The person with the gift of the gab (and who has something to say) is the one that attracts you. The college or educational function is the venue for love. As is your place of worship.

Health still needs watching until the 19th, but improves greatly afterwards. As always, make sure to get enough rest until the 19th. High energy is better than hosts of pills and potions.

You're still in a prosperity period overall, but until the 19th you have to work harder for earnings. Finances improve after the date – although be aware that on the 20th your financial planet, Pluto, starts to go backwards (this will go on for many months). Earnings will happen, but perhaps a bit slower than usual.

May

Best Days Overall: 7, 8, 17, 18, 25, 26
Most Stressful Days Overall: 1, 14, 15, 21, 22, 27, 28
Best Days for Love: 2, 3, 7, 8, 12, 13, 17, 18, 21, 22, 25, 26
Best Days for Money: 4, 5, 7, 8, 9, 10, 14, 15, 17, 18, 23, 24, 25, 26
Best Days for Career: 1, 4, 5, 14, 15, 25, 26, 27, 28

Health and energy are getting better and better day by day. If you feel under the weather, you can enhance things in the ways discussed in the yearly report.

Your 8th house became powerful on April 19 and is still strong until the 20th. The spouse, partner or current love is prospering; he or she is in a period of peak earnings. Your finances are also good until the 20th. But Pluto, your financial planet is still retrograde. There will be delays, glitches and perhaps misunderstandings. Try not to make matters worse through financial carelessness. Study the fine print of all guarantees or extended warranties. Make sure you're not slipshod in writing or addressing cheques. Make sure account numbers are correct. Little mistakes can cause big problems later on.

Power in the 8th house tends towards more sexual activity and a stronger libido. But it also indicates more than that. It shows an interest in death and life after death. It shows an interest in occult studies. Many of you are involved in projects of self-transformation and this is a good month for these things. In-depth psychology and the exploration of past incarnations are also more interesting.

The 8th house is related to death. But in astrology death has many more meanings than just the death of the physical body. Death involves dying to the old and useless in our lives – to old patterns, habits and conditions. On a deeper level, the 8th house is about 'renewal' or, to use the old-fashioned term, 'resurrection'. Renewal and resurrection always follows death. If you observe life, you will see this for yourself. Something old dies – perhaps a relationship, a business venture, a beloved pet, or some object. Very soon after, something new is born to take its place. This is the nature of life and this is the message of the Horoscope. There is no death without resurrection. So this is a month to resurrect things in your life that need it. But first you must die to the old.

It is wonderful for weight loss regimes (if you need them) and for detox regimes. In the 8th house we get rid of whatever is no longer useful or needed. (The things might not necessarily be evil, they might be harmless in fact, but if something is just taking up space, get rid of it.)

Your love planet will be in your 9th house all month. Thus there are love opportunities in foreign countries or with foreigners. Foreign travel is very much in the chart after the 20th and singles might want to take the opportunity. Students will have love opportunities at school or school functions. If a current relationship is stressed a foreign trip together could bring healing.

June

Best Days Overall: 3, 4, 13, 14, 22, 23, 30
Most Stressful Days Overall: 10, 11, 12, 18, 19, 24, 25
Best Days for Love: 4, 5, 10, 11, 15, 16, 18, 19, 20, 21, 24, 25, 28, 29
Best Days for Money: 1, 2, 3, 4, 5, 6, 7, 10, 11, 13, 14, 20, 21, 22, 23, 28, 29, 30
Best Days for Career: 3, 4, 13, 14, 24, 25

Career is the main headline of the month. Mars, the love planet, enters the 10th house on the 4th. The Sun and Mercury will enter on the 21st. The New Moon of the 24th will also occur in your 10th house. So this is a powerful career period coming up. Much progress will be made here.

Mars in the career house gives many meanings. The spouse, partner or current love is successful and active in your career – perhaps opening doors for you. Social contacts in general are helpful. The right social events are helpful career-wise – attending or hosting the right kind of parties or gatherings. Mars in your 10th house also shows that you are active and aggressive in the career. Bold actions are necessary now.

This New Moon of the 24th will be an exceptionally powerful career day and will bring much success. (Every New and Full Moon boosts the career, but this one is a 'super New Moon' – it occurs near the Moon's perigee or closest point to Earth.)

The Sun's entry into the 10th house also shows the importance of your social connections in your career. But in addition it highlights that your high-tech prowess and skills play important roles too. (Online social networking, especially, helps the career.) Mercury's entry into the 10th house shows that being involved in charities or altruistic activities helps the career. You have a good intuition when it comes to career matters.

Those of you who are job seekers have excellent opportunities all month, but especially after the 21st.

Finance becomes more stressful after the 21st. You just have to work harder than usual. Things happen for you but not smoothly.

Your love planet spends most of the month 'out of bounds'. This shows that in your love and social life you're outside your normal sphere. Your normal circle doesn't have what you want, so you go outside it into unknown territory.

In love, your attitudes change after the 4th. You're attracted to the 'power people' – the high and mighty. Social and professional status are romantic turn-ons. Often this shows romantic opportunities with bosses or superiors – clandestine kinds of things. Sometime it merely indicates dating high-powered people – people above you in status.

Health needs more attention after the 21st. As always make sure to get enough rest.

July

Best Days Overall: 1, 10, 11, 19, 20, 28, 29
Most Stressful Days Overall: 8, 9, 15, 16, 21, 22
Best Days for Love: 3, 4, 10, 13, 14, 15, 16, 19, 20, 23, 28, 29, 30, 31
Best Days for Money: 1, 3, 4, 8, 9, 10, 11, 17, 18, 19, 20, 25, 26, 28, 29, 30, 31
Best Days for Career: 3, 4, 13, 14, 21, 22, 23, 24

Career is still the main headline this month. Your yearly career peak continues until the 22nd. Much progress and much success is happening. Your good career days are shown above, but keep in mind that your career energy will tend to be strongest from the 1st to the 9th and from the 23rd onwards, as the Moon, your career planet, waxes. The 21st will also be successful as the Moon will be at her perigee.

The career trends that we wrote of last month are still in effect now. Review our discussion of this.

Health still needs watching until the 22nd. So it is still important to get enough rest. Continue to enhance the health in the ways mentioned in the yearly report. Health and energy will get much better after that date as the short-term planets move away from their stressful aspect to you.

Love is always important to a Libra, but especially now. Your love planet, Mars, occupies your 10th house. Thus he is more prominent than usual. In many cases this would show that your love life – your social life – *is* the career, your spiritual mission this month. You need to be there for the spouse, partner or current love – for friends too. In many cases people are following a worldly career but the social life is the real calling – the highest priority. This tends to success.

Many of the love trends that we wrote about last month are still in effect now (until the 20th). You are attracted to people of power and prestige. The love life is not just romantic, but it aids the career. You are attracted to people who can help you career-wise. Power is the most alluring thing right now.

On the 20th, Mars enters Leo, your 11th house. This too gives many messages. Love opportunities happen online or as you get involved with groups, group activities and professional organizations. Power and status are no longer so alluring; you want to have fun with the beloved. Now you gravitate to those you can have fun with, to people who are enjoying their lives. Mere ambition is less attractive. You like a more egalitarian relationship.

Finances are still a bit stressful until the 22nd, but they will improve afterwards. The 18th and 19th bring an especially nice cosmic payday. But Pluto is still retrograde this month, so be cautious contemplating large purchases or investments.

August

Best Days Overall: 6, 7, 8, 16, 24, 25
Most Stressful Days Overall: 4, 5, 11, 12, 18, 31
Best Days for Love: 1, 2, 9, 10, 11, 12, 18, 19, 20, 21, 28, 29, 30
Best Days for Money: 4, 5, 6, 7, 13, 14, 16, 22, 23, 24, 25, 26, 27, 31
Best Days for Career: 1, 2, 3, 11, 12, 18, 20, 21, 31

Your 11th house of friends and group activities became very powerful on July 22, and is even stronger this month. So the month ahead is very social - a happy month. This house is more about platonic kinds of relationships rather than romantic ones, yet because your love planet Mars will be here all month, romance is likely to happen from these kinds of activities. Something nice happens romantically on the 1st.

Health is good this month. Not perfect, but good. With more energy available to you, pre-existing conditions either fade away or lessen considerably.

Though your yearly career peak is over, we still see you successful this month. Venus crosses the Mid-heaven on the 1st and enters your career house. Venus, the ruler of your Horoscope, is the most elevated planet in your chart this month. (The Moon will briefly be more elevated on the 17th and 18th - but this is a short-term condition.) This shows that you are above everyone in your world. You are elevated. People look up to you and aspire to be like you. It shows authority and power. Honours and recognition are likely this month. In general you'll have more enthusiasm and zest for the career from the 1st to the 7th and from the 21st onwards – as the Moon waxes. A Lunar Eclipse on the 7th impacts on the career and brings dramatic changes – I feel they will be good ones. Doors open for you (shakeups in your company or industry – and perhaps with bosses – achieve this). There can be dramas in the lives of parents and parent figures too.

This Lunar Eclipse impacts on your love planet, Mars. So a current relationship will get some testing. Sometimes this kind of eclipse signals a change of the marital status. (Singles often marry or get engaged under this kind of eclipse.)

There is also a Solar Eclipse on the 21st. This occurs in your 11th house and impacts on the ruler of that house, the Sun. You have been through this in February (twice). Once again friendships get tested. Your high-tech equipment and gadgetry get tested. Some will need replacement. Computers and online activity can be erratic this period. Make sure important files are backed up and do your best to protect yourself against hackers and viruses. Children and children figures in your life have social dramas. If they are of an appropriate age, marriages get tested. Younger ones have friendships tested.

September

Best Days Overall: 3, 4, 12, 13, 20, 21, 30
Most Stressful Days Overall: 1, 7, 8, 14, 15, 28, 29
Best Days for Love: 7, 8, 9, 10, 16, 17, 18, 19, 28, 29
Best Days for Money: 1, 3, 4, 10, 12, 13, 18, 19, 20, 21, 23, 24, 28, 29, 30
Best Days for Career: 1, 10, 14, 15, 19, 30

The planetary power is now mostly in the East – not your favourite sector. This has been the case since July, but now the power is getting stronger. You are entering a period of maximum personal power and independence. One of the problems with too much 'other conscious-ness' is that one can lose one's centre – one's own sense of self. One can be too vulnerable to peer pressure – to people pleasing – and of the wrong kind. Now is the time to assert yourself more. To get in touch with what you like and what you feel. To get in touch with yourself and follow your personal path of happiness. Fear not, you will not lose friends. Most likely they will support this. The fact is one cannot be a real friend or lover if one is not oneself. So if there are changes to be made in your conditions or circumstances, now is the time to make them. (Next month is also good for this.) If you wait too long, changes can still be made, but with much more difficulty.

Career is winding down this month. There is a rhythm to life – a rhythm to things. You've had much success these past few months and the career urges are less imposing now. You can devote yourself to other things – and especially to your spiritual life. Your 12th house of spirituality is easily the most dominant house this month – half the planets (and important ones too) are either there or moving through there. This is a month for spiritual – interior – progress. For getting in touch with the Divinity within. For spiritual studies such as meditation, the study of sacred literature and for 'good works'. One need not be involved in an official charity to practise charity. Every day brings opportunity.

Mars, your love planet, moves into your 12th house on the 5th and stays there the rest of the month. This gives many messages. You feel closest to the Divine when you are in love. It favours the Shakti path – love, love, love and everything will be all right. Venus moves into your spiritual house on the 20th and just reinforces this message. The presence of Mercury and the Sun in the 12th house shows that the path of knowledge and rationality is also important, however. You benefit from the combination of love and reason.

Mars in this house indicates that the spiritual connection and compatibility is important in love these days. You and the beloved need to share the same spiritual ideals and support each other's growth. It shows that love and romantic opportunities happen as you follow your spiritual path and with people involved in this. This is not a month to look for love in bars and clubs. Attend a spiritual workshop or a prayer meeting. Attend a charity event. Here is where you will find it.

On the 22nd the Sun enters your own sign and you begin another one of your personal pleasure periods. A happy time. Health is good and it shows in your physical appearance.

October

Best Days Overall: 1, 9, 10, 18, 19, 27, 28, 29
Most Stressful Days Overall: 5, 6, 11, 12, 25, 26
Best Days for Love: 5, 6, 7, 8, 15, 16, 17, 18, 27, 28
Best Days for Money: 1, 7, 8, 10, 11, 15, 16, 20, 21, 25, 26, 30
Best Days for Career: 1, 9, 10, 11, 12, 19, 30

This month the congregation of planets in your own sign is the main headline – 60 per cent of them are either in your sign or moving through there this month. (No other sign or house comes even close to this.) Each brings its gifts and abilities. This month your personal independence and power is even stronger than last month. It is time to be yourself. It is wonderful to be you – unapologetically. Review our discussion of this from last month.

Health is super this month. If anything, it might be too good. You have so much energy and drive that unless it is directed properly, it can be misused and lead to problems. Use it well; don't abuse it.

Everything you could want or need is coming to you – yearning for you, searching ardently for you. Love and friendship seek you. Mars moves into your sign on the 22nd. There is nothing special you need to do to find love – just show up. Just go about your daily business. If you are in a relationship, this aspect shows that the beloved is totally devoted to you. He or she puts you first – ahead of him or herself. You're being pampered this month. The Sun, the planet of friends, has been in your 1st house since September 22. And the same is true with your friends.

You've been living the 'high life' all year, and this month perhaps even more so. This is not only good for indulging in the sensual pleasures, but also for getting the body and image in right shape – the way that you want it to be.

Jupiter makes a major move this month, from your 1st house to your 2nd money house. Thus there is prosperity happening well into next year. The Sun moves into the money house a bit later on – on the 23rd – and you enter a yearly financial peak. The 26th and 27th seem especially good financial days. Friends are prospering and providing financial opportunity. Children or children figures in your life have romantic opportunities those days.

You have love, money, health and good looks these days. Is there anything more that you need?

November

Best Days Overall: 5, 6, 14, 15, 24, 25
Most Stressful Days Overall: 1, 2, 7, 8, 21, 22, 29, 30
Best Days for Love: 1, 2, 5, 6, 7, 14, 15, 16, 17, 24, 25, 26, 27, 29, 30
Best Days for Money: 3, 4, 7, 8, 12, 13, 16, 17, 21, 22, 26, 27
Best Days for Career: 7, 8, 17, 18, 28, 29

Another happy and *very* prosperous month ahead, Libra. Enjoy!

Love and money are the main headlines this month. Your money house is even stronger than it was last month (and that's saying something). It is not only chock-full of planets, but chock-full of the most important ones (especially on the 16th and 17th). Not only that, but Pluto, your financial planet, is moving forward again (indeed, he has been since late September). All the financial systems are go. Everything you touch turns to gold. Venus moves into your money house on the 7th and spends the rest of the month there. On the 12th and 13th she travels with Jupiter bringing a very nice financial bonanza. But the whole month is filled with financial bonanzas!

Venus's move into the money house shows personal involvement with finance. You're not delegating things to others. You're taking personal charge. It shows someone who spends on him or herself. You look rich. You're a money person to those around you – people tend to see you that way. Since Venus also rules your 8th house of regeneration, this is a great period to use spare cash to pay off debt. You have a real opportunity to get out of debt right now and you should take it.

Last month the planetary power began to shift from the upper to the lower half of your chart. Now, from the 15th to the 27th, 90 per cent of the planets are in the lower half of the chart. (Before and after that it is 80 per cent.) This is huge dominance. It is time now to de-emphasize the career and focus on the home, family and your emotional well-being. It is time to gather the forces for the next career push that will happen next year.

This is a month where you value hard cash over prestige and status. A career opportunity that gives prestige but little cash is not likely to interest you. Nor will a career opportunity that disturbs your emotional equilibrium. In spite of its lack of importance, you won't be able to ignore the career altogether. Your best career days are shown above. In general you will have more enthusiasm (and power) for your career from the 1st to the 4th and from the 18th onwards – as the Moon waxes. The Full Moon of the 4th is a particularly strong career day as the Moon is near perigee – her closest distance to Earth. But, as we mentioned above, the thrust now is towards home and family.

Health is still good this month. Mars in your sign all month shows drive and energy. You're physically dynamic now. You excel in sports and exercise regimes. You have good muscle tone and self-confidence. Also, you have love – and devoted love to boot. The beloved doesn't have wandering eyes these days. He or she is completely devoted and on your side.

December

Best Days Overall: 3, 4, 11, 12, 21, 22, 30, 31
Most Stressful Days Overall: 5, 6, 18, 19, 20, 26, 27
Best Days for Love: 3, 7, 8, 14, 16, 17, 24, 26, 27, 28
Best Days for Money: 1, 2, 5, 6, 9, 10, 14, 15, 19, 20, 24, 25, 28, 29
Best Days for Career: 5, 6, 7, 8, 16, 17

Home and family issues are even more important this month than last. Your 4th house becomes ultra-powerful from the 21st onwards. Your 10th house by contrast is basically empty – only the Moon will move through there on the 5th and 6th.

For many people, the holiday season is a party period. You will have some of this – the ruler of your 5th house of fun receives nice aspects until the 21st. But for you celebrating with the family seems the ticket. I wouldn't be surprised if you spend New Year's Eve at home in a quiet kind of way – with the family. It's not that you can't go out; you just seem to want to be there.

Saturn's move into the 4th house (where he will be for the next two years) shows a sense of duty – a sense of family responsibility. You show your love through taking on more responsibility. Family life can be a burden these days, but you can't avoid it. Pick up the burden and handle it. This will bring much personal growth and unexpected help.

Saturn in the 4th house initiates a period where you need to manage the emotional life. There is a tendency to repress emotions under this aspect. But this never works – not for long anyway. Managing the feelings is not repression. One takes charge of them and directs them in the proper way – in constructive kinds of ways. Meditation is a big help here.

Finances are still excellent. Jupiter has been in the money house since October 11, and on the 9th Mars moves in and spends the rest of the month there too. This tends to show the active financial support of the spouse, partner or current love. It brings partnership and joint venture opportunities. Your friends are prospering and providing financial opportunity.

Mars in the money house indicates a change in your love preferences. Now material wealth is a romantic turn-on. Singles gravitate to the 'good providers'. Love is shown in material ways – financially or through material gifts. This is how you feel loved, this is how you show it. For the past couple of months, with Mars in your own sign, love was romantic. The romantic niceties were important. But now (after the 9th) with Mars in Scorpio, it is the sexual magnetism that attracts.

Health is good until the 21st, but after that date you need to pay it a lot more attention. It's not just the short-term planets (the Sun and Venus) that stress you out. Now Saturn will be making stressful aspects to you too, and this is a long-term trend. Tough choices have to be made in the coming years. You can't do everything and please everyone. You will have to focus on what's really important.

Scorpio

♏

THE SCORPION

Birthdays from
23rd October to
22nd November

Personality Profile

SCORPIO AT A GLANCE

Element – Water

Ruling Planet – Pluto
  Co-ruling Planet – Mars
  Career Planet – Sun
  Love Planet – Venus
  Money Planet – Jupiter
  Planet of Health and Work – Mars
  Planet of Home and Family Life – Uranus

Colour – red-violet

Colour that promotes love, romance and social harmony – green

Colour that promotes earning power – blue

Gems – bloodstone, malachite, topaz

Metals – iron, radium, steel

Scents – cherry blossom, coconut, sandalwood, watermelon

Quality – fixed (= stability)

Quality most needed for balance – a wider view of things

Strongest virtues – loyalty, concentration, determination, courage, depth

Deepest needs – to penetrate and transform

Characteristics to avoid – jealousy, vindictiveness, fanaticism

Signs of greatest overall compatibility – Cancer, Pisces

Signs of greatest overall incompatibility – Taurus, Leo, Aquarius

Sign most helpful to career – Leo

Sign most helpful for emotional support – Aquarius

Sign most helpful financially – Sagittarius

Sign best for marriage and/or partnerships – Taurus

Sign most helpful for creative projects – Pisces

Best Sign to have fun with – Pisces

Signs most helpful in spiritual matters – Cancer, Libra

Best day of the week – Tuesday

Understanding a Scorpio

One symbol of the sign of Scorpio is the phoenix. If you meditate upon the legend of the phoenix you will begin to understand the Scorpio character – his or her powers and abilities, interests and deepest urges.

The phoenix of mythology was a bird that could recreate and reproduce itself. It did so in a most intriguing way: it would seek a fire – usually in a religious temple – fly into it, consume itself in the flames and then emerge a new bird. If this is not the ultimate, most profound transformation, then what is?

Transformation is what Scorpios are all about – in their minds, bodies, affairs and relationships (Scorpios are also society's transformers). To change something in a natural, not an artificial way, involves a transformation from within. This type of change is radical change as opposed to a mere cosmetic make-over. Some people think that change means altering just their appearance, but this is not the kind of thing that interests a Scorpio. Scorpios seek deep, fundamental change. Since real change always proceeds from within, a Scorpio is very interested in – and usually accustomed to – the inner, intimate and philosophical side of life.

Scorpios are people of depth and intellect. If you want to interest them you must present them with more than just a superficial image. You and your interests, projects or business deals must have real substance to them in order to stimulate a Scorpio. If they haven't, he or she will find you out – and that will be the end of the story.

If we observe life – the processes of growth and decay – we see the transformational powers of Scorpio at work all the time. The caterpillar changes itself into a butterfly; the infant grows into a child and then an adult. To Scorpios this definite and perpetual transformation is not something to be feared. They see it as a normal part of life. This acceptance of transformation gives Scorpios the key to understanding the true meaning of life.

Scorpios' understanding of life (including life's weaknesses) makes them powerful warriors – in all senses of the word. Add to this their depth, patience and endurance and you have a powerful personality. Scorpios have good, long memories and can at times be quite vindictive

- they can wait years to get their revenge. As a friend, though, there is no one more loyal and true than a Scorpio. Few are willing to make the sacrifices that a Scorpio will make for a true friend.

The results of a transformation are quite obvious, although the process of transformation is invisible and secret. This is why Scorpios are considered secretive in nature. A seed will not grow properly if you keep digging it up and exposing it to the light of day. It must stay buried - invisible - until it starts to grow. In the same manner, Scorpios fear revealing too much about themselves or their hopes to other people. However, they will be more than happy to let you see the finished product - but only when it is completely unwrapped. On the other hand, Scorpios like knowing everyone else's secrets as much as they dislike anyone knowing theirs.

Finance

Love, birth, life as well as death are Nature's most potent transformations; Scorpios are interested in all of these. In our society, money is a transforming power, too, and a Scorpio is interested in money for that reason. To a Scorpio money is power, money causes change, money controls. It is the power of money that fascinates them. But Scorpios can be too materialistic if they are not careful. They can be overly awed by the power of money, to a point where they think that money rules the world.

Even the term 'plutocrat' comes from Pluto, the ruler of the sign of Scorpio. Scorpios will - in one way or another - achieve the financial status they strive for. When they do so they are careful in the way they handle their wealth. Part of this financial carefulness is really a kind of honesty, for Scorpios are usually involved with other people's money - as accountants, lawyers, stockbrokers or corporate managers - and when you handle other people's money you have to be more cautious than when you handle your own.

In order to fulfil their financial goals, Scorpios have important lessons to learn. They need to develop qualities that do not come naturally to them, such as breadth of vision, optimism, faith, trust and, above all, generosity. They need to see the wealth in Nature and in life, as well as in its more obvious forms of money and power. When they develop generosity their financial potential reaches great heights, for Jupiter, the Lord of Opulence and Good Fortune, is Scorpio's money planet.

Career and Public Image

Scorpio's greatest aspiration in life is to be considered by society as a source of light and life. They want to be leaders, to be stars. But they follow a very different road than do Leos, the other stars of the zodiac. A Scorpio arrives at the goal secretly, without ostentation; a Leo pursues it openly. Scorpios seek the glamour and fun of the rich and famous in a restrained, discreet way.

Scorpios are by nature introverted and tend to avoid the limelight. But if they want to attain their highest career goals they need to open up a bit and to express themselves more. They need to stop hiding their light under a bushel and let it shine. Above all, they need to let go of any vindictiveness and small-mindedness. All their gifts and insights were given to them for one important reason – to serve life and to increase the joy of living for others.

Love and Relationships

Scorpio is another zodiac sign that likes committed clearly defined, structured relationships. They are cautious about marriage, but when they do commit to a relationship they tend to be faithful – and heaven help the mate caught or even suspected of infidelity! The jealousy of the Scorpio is legendary. They can be so intense in their jealousy that even the thought or intention of infidelity will be detected and is likely to cause as much of a storm as if the deed had actually been done.

Scorpios tend to settle down with those who are wealthier than they are. They usually have enough intensity for two, so in their partners they seek someone pleasant, hard-working, amiable, stable and easy-going. They want someone they can lean on, someone loyal behind them as they fight the battles of life. To a Scorpio a partner, be it a lover or a friend, is a real partner – not an adversary. Most of all a Scorpio is looking for an ally, not a competitor.

If you are in love with a Scorpio you will need a lot of patience. It takes a long time to get to know Scorpios, because they do not reveal themselves readily. But if you persist and your motives are honourable, you will gradually be allowed into a Scorpio's inner chambers of the mind and heart.

Home and Domestic Life

Uranus is ruler of Scorpio's 4th solar house of home and family. Uranus is the planet of science, technology, changes and democracy. This tells us a lot about a Scorpio's conduct in the home and what he or she needs in order to have a happy, harmonious home life.

Scorpios can sometimes bring their passion, intensity and wilfulness into the home and family, which is not always the place for these qualities. These traits are good for the warrior and the transformer, but not so good for the nurturer and family member. Because of this (and also because of their need for change and transformation) the Scorpio may be prone to sudden changes of residence. If not carefully constrained, the sometimes inflexible Scorpio can produce turmoil and sudden upheavals within the family.

Scorpios need to develop some of the virtues of Aquarius in order to cope better with domestic matters. There is a need to build a team spirit at home, to treat family activities as truly group activities - family members should all have a say in what does and does not get done. For at times a Scorpio can be most dictatorial. When a Scorpio gets dictatorial it is much worse than if a Leo or Capricorn (the two other power signs in the zodiac) does. For the dictatorship of a Scorpio is applied with more zeal, passion, intensity and concentration than is true of either a Leo or Capricorn. Obviously this can be unbearable to family members - especially if they are sensitive types.

In order for a Scorpio to get the full benefit of the emotional support that a family can give, he or she needs to let go of conservatism and be a bit more experimental, to explore new techniques in childrearing, be more democratic with family members and to try to manage things by consensus rather than by autocratic edict.

Horoscope for 2017

Major Trends

Saturn in your money house these past two years has placed additional financial burdens and responsibilities on you. There's been no way you could avoid them, so there has been a feeling of financial 'tightness'. This is not what it seems. The cosmos has been calling you to reorganize this area. Make it healthier. Manage your money and resources better. This trend continues in the year ahead.

In spite of this feeling of tightness, you will end the year richer than when you began. Your financial planet, Jupiter, will move into your sign on October 11. This begins a multi-year cycle of prosperity. More on this later.

Pluto, the ruler of your Horoscope, has been in your 3rd house of communication since 2008. You have been more conservative and traditional of late (and perhaps took a lot of flak over this – it probably didn't make you popular). You have been focused on intellectual activities – writing, blogging, teaching, sales and marketing. Many of you have been taking courses in subjects that interest you. You've been exploring the intellectual world – the life of the mind. Whatever the level of your previous education, you're becoming more intellectual than usual. This trend will continue for many more years.

Neptune has been in your 5th house since 2012. Your view of fun is becoming more refined and spiritualized. Spiritual forms of entertainment have become more interesting. Spiritual and inspirational films and plays are attracting you now. Children and children figures in your life are more spiritual, but in some cases this can show more involvement with drugs and alcohol.

Uranus has been in your 6th house of health since 2011. He will be there for the rest of the year ahead, but is getting ready to leave in the next two years. This aspect indicates much experimentalism in health matters. You have been making many dramatic changes to the health regime and this is an ongoing process. More on this later.

Jupiter spends most of the year in your spiritual 12th house, making it a very spiritual year. You'll discover that spiritual understanding is not just something abstract or nebulous. It has very practical – and bottom line – consequences. More on details later.

Your most important interests in the year ahead are the body and image (from October 11 onwards); finance; communication and intellectual interests; children, fun and creativity; health and work; and spirituality (until October 11).

Your paths of greatest fulfilment this year are spirituality (until October 11); the body and image (from October 11 onwards); friends, groups, group and online activities (until April 29); and career (from April 29 onwards).

Health

(Please note that this is an astrological perspective on health and not a medical one. In days of yore there was no difference, both of these perspectives were identical. Now there could be quite a difference. For a medical perspective, please consult your doctor or health practitioner.)

Health looks good this year Scorpio. There are no long-term planets in stressful alignment with you, and by the end of the year four long-term planets will be in harmonious aspect with you – a very good health signal. You have lots of energy. Of course, there will be periods in the year where health and energy are less easy than usual. However, these are temporary things caused by short-term transits. They're not trends for the year ahead. When the difficult transits pass your normal health and energy return.

This is good news for those of you with pre-existing conditions. They should ease up this year and not be so troublesome. In many cases there will be actual healing. Perhaps some health professional, or therapy, or medication, or supplement will get the credit, but the truth is that the cosmic energy was supporting you.

Good though your health is, power in your 6th house indicates that there is great focus here. Perhaps you are overly focused – more than you need to be. You could be so focused that every little twinge or ache gets magnified beyond proportion. Most likely there is nothing to these things. (The Moon could be in the wrong place at the time; when she moves away, the ache disappears.)

Your health is good, although you can make it even better. Give more attention to the following – the vulnerable areas in your chart (the reflex points are shown below):

- The colon, bladder and sexual organs. These are always important for a Scorpio. It is important to keep the colon clean. Herbal colonics are generally good for you. Safe sex and sexual moderation are also important. (Scorpio tends to overdo this area.)
- The head, face and scalp. These are also always important for you. These areas should be regularly massaged. This will not only strengthen these areas but the whole body too. There are reflexes in these areas that help the whole body. Craniosacral therapy is a generally good therapy for Scorpio.
- The musculature. Muscles need to be kept in tone. A weak muscle can knock the spine and skeleton out of alignment and this will cause hosts of other problems. Vigorous physical exercise (according to your age and stage in life) is important.

Important foot reflexology points for the year ahead

Try to massage all of the foot on a regular basis – the top of the foot as well as the bottom – but pay extra attention to the points highlighted on the chart. When you massage, be aware of 'sore spots' as these need special attention. It's also a good idea to massage the ankles and below them.

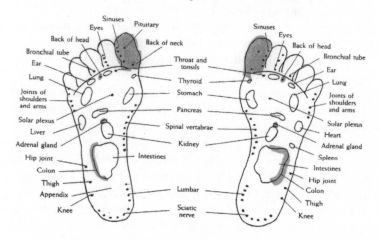

- The adrenals. Again, very important for you, Scorpio. Avoid anger and fear – the two emotions that stress the adrenal glands.
- The ankles and calves. These have only become important since 2011. Both areas should be regularly massaged as part of your normal health regime. Give the ankles more support when exercising.

Uranus in your 6th house shows an affinity for alternative rather than orthodox medicine. But the new cutting-edge technologies in orthodox medicine could be alluring. You love what is new and trendy.

There are many short-term trends in health. Mars, your health planet, moves fairly quickly. He changes signs and houses approximately every 45 days. These trends are best covered in the monthly reports.

Home and Family

The home and family arena has been turbulent for many years now. You don't seem in harmony with them – and especially with one of the parents or parent figures in your life. The good news is that things are easier than the period of 2011 to 2014. But it's still not the way it should be.

The important thing with a long-term struggle is to not make things worse than they need to be. Do your best to keep negativity to the minimum. There will be negativity – there are personal and financial disagreements these days – the issue is, how you handle it. There are no rules about this, only the principle of minimum negativity. Each will apply it in their own way.

The financial disagreements should resolve themselves after October 11. But the personal issues still remain. It will take much effort to maintain some semblance of harmony here.

Your health is good this year as we mentioned. But family or emotional discord could affect it adversely. So maintaining as much harmony as possible is actually a health issue. (If health problems arise (God forbid), restore harmony as quickly as possible.)

Your family planet Uranus has been in your 6th house of health since 2011, and many of the trends we've written about in previous years are still very much in effect. You're installing health equipment – health gadgets – in the home. You're getting rid of any kind of toxic materials in the home (and probably spending on this). The health of your family is a major priority. The home is becoming a health spa as much as a home.

Your family planet in the 6th house also indicates someone who works from home. So home offices and perhaps home-based businesses are being set up or being expanded. Family members could also be your employees (which is another complication in your relationship).

With Uranus as your family planet you're someone who likes to upgrade the home continually. You like the modern, high-tech look. Your home is probably filled with gadgets – and when new products come on the market you're one of the first to get them. You tend to move a lot. This year though, a move doesn't seem likely; 2018 is a more likely year for this.

Siblings and sibling figures are also experiencing family instability. A move though is not likely this year. (There's nothing against it however.) A parent or parent figure can move from October 11 onwards – there is good fortune in the purchase or sale of a home. Children and children figures in your life are having stable family years. Grandchildren (if you have them) are likely to move after October 11.

If you're planning to redecorate or to buy decorative objects for the home, January 29 to February 18 is a good time. If you're planning construction work or major repairs in the home, January 28 to March 10 is a good time for this.

Finance and Career

The year ahead, as we mentioned, will be prosperous. But until October 11, you're in a preparation period. Ninety per cent of life is preparation. The actual happenings – the results – are only a small fraction of it. Jupiter, your financial planet, spends most of the year in your spiritual 12th house. This means that spiritual – interior – revelation is happening in your financial life and attitudes. Revelation is a great thing, but while it's happening it is not so pleasant. Light shining in a dark room reveals jewels and hidden treasures, but also many unpleasant things. There can be scandals involving the money people in your life. Secret machinations in your financial life or investments are going on and you'll probably find out about them. But along with this – if you're open to guidance – will be revelation on how to deal with these things.

Jupiter in the 12th house shows that you are developing financial intuition this year. Intuition is always the short-cut to wealth. Generally work is involved, but intuition guides you to the fastest way.

You seem more philanthropic in the year ahead. More generous. You're giving to charities and to altruistic causes. When you hear a tale of woe or sob story, the wallet opens.

Jupiter in Libra shows a good affinity for the beauty industry this year – for art, fashion, cosmetics, jewellery and antiques. These are interesting investments – either in a physical way or through buying shares in companies involved in these things. You're probably spending more on these things. This aspect of Jupiter also shows an affinity for oil, natural gas, shipping, shipbuilders, the fishing industry and industries involved with water.

The most important development with Jupiter in the 12th house is learning about (and in many cases going deeper into) the spiritual dimensions of wealth. This is a year where you learn to 'tap into' the resources of the universe, rather than just working with your own resources. More on this later.

There is a danger of overspending on the home and family. This can be a stress.

Saturn, as we have mentioned, is in your money house. He's been there for the past two years (since Christmas 2014). This is also part of the preparation that you're going through. If you're to attain the financial goals you aspire to – and they seem high – you need preparation. The intuition is getting trained (with Jupiter in your 12th house) and the financial life in general needs to be reorganized – restructured. This restructuring is almost over, but you've got a year to go. You've got to use the resources you have more effectively. In many cases assets and investments – or spending – need to be shifted around. Waste is being eliminated. A solid foundation is being built. Long-term financial plans – investment and savings plans – are being created. And, if you stick to them, wealth will be assured over the long haul.

Jupiter will move into your own sign on October 11. This is when the money starts rolling in. Financial windfalls will happen. The money people in your life will cater to you and offer you opportunities. There will be luck in speculations. Children and children figures will be financially supportive. You will dress more expensively. People will see you as someone who is prospering. You will be the 'money person' to many others in your life. Most importantly, you will feel wealthy. Finally, when Saturn leaves your money house at the end of the year (on December 21) the prosperity increases even further. It was all worth the wait.

There are a lot of career changes happening this year. There are two Solar Eclipses and these always affect your career, company and industry. There is also a third eclipse – a Lunar Eclipse on February 11 – that impacts on the career as it occurs in your career house. So there is a lot of drama here. I feel the changes will be good ones and the dramas will work in your favour. The Moon's North Node enters your 10th career house on April 29.

Love and Social Life

Your 7th house of love and social activities is not strong this year. It is not prominent. Only short-term (fast-moving) planets will move through there in the year ahead. This tends to the status quo. Those who are married will most likely stay married and singles will stay single. You seem more or less at ease with things as they are and have no need to make major changes, or to focus here unduly.

This situation – this lull – is only temporary. Enjoy the quiet. Next year Uranus will start his move into your 7th house and by 2019 will be established there for the long haul. This is when the excitement begins. There will not be a dull moment in love for seven more years. The whole social life will undergo dramatic change. We will cover this more fully next year.

Venus, your love planet, is a fast-moving planet. In a given year she will move through every sector of your chart. Only the Moon and Mercury move faster than her. So, love, romantic and social opportunities can happen in many ways and through many people – depending on where Venus is at a given time and the aspects she receives. Also, it shows that you're a person whose needs in love change quickly. Those involved romantically with a Scorpio need to understand this. They are not being 'fickle'. They are just responding to Venus's different moves. These short-term trends are best dealt with in the monthly reports.

Your love planet will make one of her rare retrogrades this year. She does this once every two years (all the other planets that retrograde, with the exception of Mars, regularly retrograde every year – and Mercury goes backwards four times this year). So a Venus retrograde is a headline. She will be retrograde from March 4 to April 15. This is a time for a romantic review. The romantic life will tend to slow down; relationships can seem to go backwards. None of this should be taken too seriously. It is a pause – a regrouping – a space where clarity can be attained. Don't make important love decisions during that period.

Venus will spend a lot of time in Aries this year – over three months, triple her usual time in a sign. Thus there are love opportunities at the workplace, with co-workers or with people involved in your health.

Your 11th house of friendships seems happy. The Moon's North Node will be in this house until April 29. This indicates excess. Perhaps your problem is too many friends. But this is a good problem to have.

Self-Improvement

Your 12th house of spirituality is strong this year, as we mentioned above. This is a year for much internal growth. Great things are happening to you internally, but it's not yet visible to the world. These changes will start to be visible after October 11 and well into next year. Those of you already on a spiritual path will make great progress this year. There will be many spiritual breakthroughs – and these are most joyous when they happen. Your spiritual abilities – ESP abilities – are greatly enhanced. The dream life becomes very active and often prophetic. Your dreams should be written down and studied; they are significant.

Those of you not yet on a spiritual path, or who are just dabbling (a normal stage on the road) will perhaps embark on such a path this year. You will probably experience many strange coincidences – the spirit's way to call you closer.

This year spiritual practice is not a 'discipline' where one 'sets the jaw like flint'. It is fun and enjoyable (and profitable too). It is something you will look forward to.

Scorpio is a warrior soul. The world is a dangerous place and only the strong and the smart survive. But in spiritual matters, this tendency must be laid aside. With Venus as your spiritual planet, love is the way. There is a need to develop the love nature. So, mantra chanting, singing, drumming and dancing are valid spiritual paths for you. Any practice that strengthens your love and devotion is good.

Jupiter is your financial planet. His presence in your 12th house shows you're developing your financial intuition this year. You're making it a tool in your financial arsenal. But there's more to it than that. This is a year where you go deeper into the spiritual dimensions of wealth. There is Wall Street's perspective and there is the Divine perspective and they are radically different. Everyone yearns for financial freedom and independence. But in truth these things are impossible without a spiritual understanding of supply. Even the richest of worldly people are dependent on many things – the market, the economy, government decisions, etc., etc. But a person who understands the spiritual dimension is free of all of this. He or she relies only on the Divine Supply – nothing else matters.

No matter what is going on at the job or in the worldly economy, the Divine Supply will happen – the need of the hour will always be met. Others might have larger portfolios than you, but how much you own is never the issue. The issue is only 'how much the Divine has' – and he has it all.

The laws of spiritual supply are not complex to understand, but they are usually difficult to put into practice. Some people manage it more easily than others. There is much 'human learning' – many subconscious fears and beliefs – that must be overcome. And this is what takes time. Many of you already understand much about this. This is a year to go deeper into it. Read as much as you can on the subject – there is much literature out there if you look. Practise what you learn. The practice will bring results.

Financial guidance will come to you in dreams and through astrologers, psychics, tarot readers, spiritual channels, gurus or guru-type figures this year. If you feel confused, see one of these people.

Month-by-month Forecasts

January

Best Days Overall: 2, 3, 11, 12, 20, 21, 30, 31
Most Stressful Days Overall: 1, 7, 8, 13, 14, 27, 28
Best Days for Love: 2, 7, 8, 12, 20, 21, 31
Best Days for Money: 1, 10, 18, 19, 22, 23, 24, 28, 29
Best Days for Career: 7, 8, 13, 14, 16, 27, 28

You're in a very good period for starting new projects and ventures this month. Both your personal Solar cycle and the Universal one are waxing (growing). Best of all, the planetary momentum is strongly forward this month. After the 7th *all* the planets are moving forward. The 1st to the 12th and the 28th to the 31st are especially good, as the Moon is also waxing. Spring is generally a good time to start new things, but retrograde activity will be stronger then. Now seems better in your case.

You begin your year with the bottom half of your chart dominant. From the 1st to the 6th and from the 21st onwards 90 per cent of the planets are below the horizon. So, career is not much of an issue for you right now. This is a time for inner wellness, for getting the home base in right order. You're building up the forces for the next career push later in the year. Nature is never go-go-go. She has a rhythm. It is good to work with this rhythm.

Your overall health is excellent this year and this month. But after the 19th it is a little less so. This is nothing serious; the Sun moves into stressful alignment and will pass by next month. If you feel under the weather, foot massage is powerful until the 28th, and head and scalp massage will be powerful after then.

Your mission this month (your spiritual career) is to gain knowledge and information, until the 19th. For some of you it might mean teaching what you know to others. It is important for you to be there for siblings and sibling figures in your life. After the 19th your mission is the home, family and your emotional wellness. Without this there will be no lasting outer career success.

Gaining and disseminating knowledge is not only interesting in its own right but it also helps the bottom line. Spending on books or periodicals seems a good investment. Your financial intuition is important and this will improve after the 19th. The gut feelings are more reliable too. Prosperity is better after the 19th than before (although it's OK earlier in the month).

Your love planet Venus enters Pisces on the 3rd and spends the rest of the month there. This makes love idealistic and tender. The spouse, partner or current love seems unusually sensitive, so tread lightly and watch your voice tone and body language.

Venus has her solstice from the 29th to the 31st. This indicates a pause in your social life and then a change of direction. Mars's solstice from the 27th to the 31st shows a pause in the workplace. These pauses are good – like holidays. You come back refreshed.

February

Best Days Overall: 7, 8, 16, 17, 18, 26, 27
Most Stressful Days Overall: 3, 4, 9, 10, 24, 25
Best Days for Love: 3, 4, 9, 10, 19, 20, 28
Best Days for Money: 5, 6, 14, 15, 19, 20, 24, 25
Best Days for Career: 5, 6, 9, 10, 14, 15, 26, 27

This is still a great period to start new projects, launch new ventures or products now. Up to February 6 is the optimal time: the Moon will be waxing and all the planets are moving forward. On the 6th, your financial planet, Jupiter, starts to go into retrograde motion, so you want to start before that.

Though we have two eclipses this month, you're basically in a happy period. On the 18th you enter one of your yearly personal pleasure peaks. So although there is much change and upheaval going on, you're managing to enjoy yourself.

The Lunar Eclipse of the 11th (in America this happens on the 10th) has a strong effect on you, so take it easy that period. You don't need to be involved in daredevil stunts or break any athletic records. This eclipse occurs in your 10th house of career and signals career changes. These changes can take many forms. There can be shakeups in your company or industry. There can be changes in the top management of your company or changes in company policy. Often government changes regulations in your industry. Sometimes people actually change their career path. There are dramas in the lives of bosses, elders, parents or parent figures – life-changing events. Since the Moon, the eclipsed planet, rules your 9th house, foreign travel is best avoided this period. (If you have to, you have to – but unnecessary travel should be avoided.) There are shakeups in your place of worship. Students at college level make important changes to their educational plans. Often they change institutions or courses.

The Solar Eclipse of the 26th does not affect you as strongly – actually, it makes harmonious aspects to you. It won't hurt, however, to reduce your schedule anyway. It might not be so kind to the people around you. This eclipse occurs in your 5th house and impacts on children or children figures in your life. They experience some dramatic change. Often this is quite normal; it can show puberty, sexual awakening, graduation – important, life-changing events. But children should be kept out of harm's way over that period. Speculations are best avoided.

The dream life will probably be hyperactive this period – and not in a good way. The Solar Eclipse occurs in Pisces and very near to Neptune. Don't pay too much attention to your dreams or be overly disturbed. The astral plane (the dream dimension) is stirred up and that is all that you're seeing. Every Solar Eclipse affects the career, the industry and your company. Also bosses, parents and parent figures. It is, in this regard, more or less a repeat of the Lunar Eclipse of the 11th. Because Neptune is involved in this eclipse there can be scandals or unpleasant revelations in your company or industry.

Finances are good this month – especially until the 18th. But try to wrap up important purchases or investments before the 6th and Jupiter's retrograde. Your financial planet will be retrograde for a few months now. This will slow things down, but it won't stop earnings.

March

Best Days Overall: 6, 7, 16, 17, 25, 26
Most Stressful Days Overall: 2, 3, 9, 10, 23, 24, 30
Best Days for Love: 1, 2, 3, 9, 18, 27, 30
Best Days for Money: 5, 6, 13, 14, 18, 19, 23, 24
Best Days for Career: 7, 9, 10, 16, 27, 28

The Western, social sector of your chart has been dominant since last month (from February 7), and this sector will be strong for many more months. The planetary power is moving away from you and towards others. This means that you should start focusing more on others rather than your own self-interest. You're cultivating your social skills now. You have many skills and gifts but these things are not the issue, now. How well you get on with others is what is important in this period. Hopefully you are in happy conditions and circumstances. If there are problems here, make note, and wait until the planets shift back to the East (in about five months' time) to make changes. Things get done by consensus now and not by direct action.

You're still in a yearly personal pleasure peak until the 20th. It is important for you to have some fun and to enjoy your life. Doing things you love fosters emotional wellness, which is important now. Your outer career is not that important now. Your children and children figures in your life are more important.

Your 6th house of health and work is very strong this month. It's not wise to overly focus on your health. Your health is good. There's no need to magnify every little ache or pain into something serious. Better to focus on your work. It is a very good time to do those boring, detailed tasks, now such as filing, bookkeeping, tax returns, etc. You have the energy and the mood for this. Job seekers have good fortune this month – especially from the 20th onwards. Likewise those who hire others.

Your health planet, Mars, moves into your 7th house on the 10th and spends the rest of the month there. Thus, love becomes an issue in health. If there are problems in love, the physical health can be affected. Should this happen (God forbid), restore harmony as quickly as possible. Neck and throat massage will enhance the health (as well as the ways mentioned in the yearly report).

Love is complicated this month. Your love planet, Venus, goes retrograde on the 4th (until April 15). Thus a current relationship can be stalled or feel like it's going backwards. You and the beloved are not in agreement. Perhaps you're in conflict. But don't make any important decisions one way or another, not yet. By April 15 things will be clearer. Mars in your 7th house is not the best aspect for love either. It can bring power struggles in love – and that's guaranteed to kill any kind of romantic feeling. Also it can bring too much perfectionism into the relationship, too much criticism. Be careful of this.

April

Best Days Overall: 3, 4, 12, 13, 22, 23, 30
Most Stressful Days Overall: 5, 6, 19, 20, 21, 26, 27
Best Days for Love: 4, 12, 13, 23, 26, 27
Best Days for Money: 1, 10, 11, 14, 15, 16, 19, 20, 21, 28, 29
Best Days for Career: 5, 6, 15, 16, 26, 27

The love life is improving this month. Venus retrogrades back into Pisces on the 2nd and spends most of the month there, and so there is more harmony with the beloved. But Mars is still in your 7th house until the 21st. You still have to be careful of power struggles and too much criticism. Perfection is good, but go about it in a gradual and loving way. The good news is that the Sun moves into your 7th house of love on the 19th. This initiates a yearly love and social peak. It shows that you're focused on your relationship. It's important, and you're trying very hard. This will tend to save a relationship. Venus's forward motion on the 15th will also help matters.

The Sun's move into your 7th house indicates career-related social events. You should attend these as much as possible. It shows that you are mixing with power people in your world. Your social grace will help the career (as well as many other areas of your life).

For singles love opportunities happen in the usual places this month – at parties, gatherings, nightclubs, resorts and places of entertainment. Have fun with the beloved. Do fun kinds of things. This will do much to ease any tension between you.

Your health is still very good. Even after the 19th, as the Sun moves into stressful alignment with you, health will still be good. The Sun will be the only planet in stressful alignment after the 21st, when Mars moves away from his stressful aspect. So although this is not your optimal health period in the year, it's nothing to be concerned about. Enhance the health in the ways mentioned in the yearly report. Until the 21st add neck and throat massage; after that date add arm and shoulder massage instead.

Finances have been challenging since March 20. Your financial planet is not only retrograde, but he's receiving stressful aspects. Important deals hit snags and miss deadlines. Clients can change their minds (perhaps a few times). Earnings will come but they'll need more work. Be patient now.

The New Moon of the 26th is a 'Super New Moon'. It occurs very near the Moon's perigee (her closest distance to Earth). Thus it has more impact than the average New Moon. This will be a good career day for you. (Career is starting to become more important.) It is also an excellent day for college or postgraduate-level students. There is success at school. If you're involved in legal issues, this is a good day for those things too.

May

Best Days Overall: 1, 9, 10, 19, 20, 27, 28
Most Stressful Days Overall: 2, 3, 17, 18, 23, 24, 29, 30
Best Days for Love: 2, 3, 12, 13, 21, 22, 23, 24
Best Days for Money: 7, 8, 12, 13, 17, 18, 25, 26
Best Days for Career: 2, 3, 4, 5, 14, 15, 25, 26, 29, 30

The upper half of your chart – the sector of the outer life – will never be really dominant this year (and this has been the case for many years now). This is because the long-term planets (with the exception of Jupiter) are all in the bottom half of your chart. So, in general your life has been about emotional wellness and functioning from your emotional comfort zone for quite a while. But now, as the short-term planets begin to shift to the upper half of your chart, you can start paying more attention to the career. This shift begins to happen on the

6th – next month it will be stronger. The trick now is to pursue your career from a place of emotional harmony. Try not to violate that.

You're still in a yearly love and social peak until the 20th. And, like last month, there is a lot of career-related social activity. Elders, bosses, parents and parent figures seem very interested in your love life and want to foster it along. (Perhaps they're playing Cupid – making introductions, setting up blind dates, etc.) Venus in your 6th house all month (and now moving forwards) shows an attraction to health professionals or people involved in your health. Venus in Aries makes you more of a love-at-first-sight kind of person these days. Perhaps too impulsive in love. The workplace also seems a venue for romance.

Health is much improved after the 20th. There's nothing seriously wrong before the 20th, but overall energy is slightly less than usual. Enhance your health in the ways mentioned in the yearly report. Add some arm and shoulder massage too. Plain old fresh air is wonderful if you feel under the weather. Get out in the fresh air and just breathe deeply. The health planet Mars in the 8th house of regeneration all month shows that detox regimes are beneficial.

Though your financial planet is still retrograde this month, finances are much improved. Earnings come more easily than last month. Earning power is stronger. Finances will improve further after the 20th. You have excellent financial intuition this year – Jupiter is in your spiritual 12th house – but his retrograde suggests you need to verify such intuition.

We have another 'Super New Moon' this month on the 25th. (It occurs with the Moon very near her perigee.) So this will be a good career day and an excellent day for college or postgraduate students.

June

Best Days Overall: 5, 6, 7, 15, 16, 24, 25
Most Stressful Days Overall: 13, 14, 20, 21, 26, 27
Best Days for Love: 10, 11, 20, 21, 28, 29
Best Days for Money: 3, 4, 8, 9, 13, 14, 22, 23, 30
Best Days for Career: 3, 4, 13, 14, 24, 26, 27

Your 8th house of regeneration (your favourite house) became power-ful on May 20 and is still powerful until the 21st. So this is a month of high libido. With your health planet still here until the 4th there is no need to overdo things. Listen to your body; it will tell you when enough is enough.

The 8th house deals with all of your important interests – sex, personal transformation, personal reinvention, death and resurrection. This is a great month to pursue these interests and you will see much progress here. When this house is strong it is a good time to get rid of the effete and useless material in our lives. This can be possessions, excess weight, toxins or effete material in the body – outmoded thought and emotional patterns. In the 8th house we renew ourselves by 'elimination'. We grow by pruning and cutting. (The 9th house of expansion comes after the 8th house of elimination.)

This is a great month for tax and estate planning (if you are of the appropriate age). It is good for negotiating credit or refinancing debt. The spouse, partner or current love is prospering now – in a yearly financial peak. It is good (and you do this naturally anyway) to make other people rich – to put their financial interests ahead of your own. This concern will bring your own prosperity to you naturally.

Health is good all month and gets even better after the 21st. There is only one planet in stressful alignment with you at any one time – Mercury until the 6th, and Venus after the 6th. Swimming, water aerobics and water sports are healthy kinds of exer-cises from the 4th onwards. Diet becomes more of an issue after the 4th too. If you feel under the weather, the chances are you're not eating right.

The beloved should stay out of harm's way from the 2nd to the 4th. On the 6th Venus moved into your 7th house and starts to make very nice aspects to the ruler of your Horoscope, Pluto. Love is happy this month. There is harmony with the beloved. Singles will have romantic opportunity (the 23rd to the 25th looks especially good). You're in the mood for love.

Mars, your health and work planet, spends most of the month 'out of bounds'. Thus your work takes you outside your normal sphere. For job seekers, there is a need to go outside your usual boundaries for work opportunities. You seem this way in health matters too – though there's nothing wrong. Perhaps you're just exploring exotic kinds of therapies, health regimes or workouts.

July

Best Days Overall: 3, 4, 13, 14, 21, 22, 30, 31
Most Stressful Days Overall: 10, 11, 17, 18, 23, 24
Best Days for Love: 10, 17, 18, 19, 20, 28, 29
Best Days for Money: 1, 5, 6, 10, 11, 19, 20, 28, 29
Best Days for Career: 3, 4, 13, 14, 23, 24

Health is excellent until the 20th, but afterwards you need to rest and relax more. Fatigue seems the main problem – overwork. The career is very successful from the 22nd onwards, but you're earning every bit of it. If you feel under the weather, heat-oriented therapies are good from the 20th onwards. The steam room, sauna or hot bath – things that heat up the body and relax the muscles – are beneficial. Also pay more attention to the heart. Don't become so busy that there's no time to get out in the Sun. These health issues are short-lived and will pass next month.

The career is the main headline this month. This is the focus and rightly so. Home and family are always important these days, but you serve your family (and increase your emotional well-being) by succeeding in your outer life.

Mars, your health and work planet, crosses the Mid-heaven and enters your 10th house on the 20th. This shows that your good work ethic brings success. Superiors make note of this. It indicates much activity and aggressiveness in the career. Competitive battles are being fought. Good leadership is as important as your professional skills. (This aspect also shows that health is a priority and that you're paying attention here.)

On the 22nd the Sun moves into your 10th house and you enter a yearly career peak. The Sun, your career planet, is very powerful in his own sign and house, and this foretells success. Your career abilities are enhanced.

Venus, your love planet, moves into Gemini, your 8th house, on the 5th. Good sex covers many sins in a relationship. The sexual chemistry is the main attraction, but it's not everything. Good communication seems important too. Good communication these days is a form of sexual foreplay. Sexual magnetism is important but so is the gift of the gab. There is a happy romantic opportunity for singles on the 18th and 19th. For those of you who are attached it shows a happy social experience. Your erotic zones (aside from the normal ones) are the chest until the 16th and the abdomen afterwards. Arms and shoulders always tend to be erotic zones for you.

A parent or parent figure has a strong social month from the 20th onwards. If he or she is single there is romantic opportunity.

August

Best Days Overall: 9, 10, 18, 26, 27
Most Stressful Days Overall: 6, 7, 8, 13, 14, 20, 21
Best Days for Love: 9, 10, 13, 14, 18, 19, 28, 29
Best Days for Money: 1, 2, 3, 6, 7, 16, 24, 25, 29, 30
Best Days for Career: 1, 2, 3, 11, 12, 20, 21, 31

Career is still the main headline this month. Not only is your 10th house powerful, but there is a Solar Eclipse in this house on the 21st. So, there is a lot of activity and change happening in the career. Continue to watch the health this month – especially around the eclipse period. Those of you born late in the sign of Scorpio (November 19 to 22) are most affected – but all of you will feel it.

Health and energy should improve dramatically from the 23rd onwards (and most of you will feel better from the 22nd). In the meantime try to schedule more rest periods – though you still seem extremely busy. Enhance the health in the ways mentioned in the yearly report and continue to give special attention to the heart. Heat-oriented therapies – discussed last month – are still very effective.

There is a Lunar Eclipse on the 7th that affects you strongly. Reduce your schedule over that period and spend more quiet time at home. This eclipse occurs in your 4th house and affects the home and family. If there are hidden problems in the home, this is when you find out about them and can make the corrections. Family members (and especially a parent or parent figure) are more temperamental now and need more patience. Often this shows that they are experiencing life-changing kinds of events. Every Lunar Eclipse affects college-level students. They make changes in their educational plans. Foreign travel is best avoided during this period. If you must travel, try to schedule your trip round the eclipse – try not to be on the road or in the air at that time.

There are shakeups in your place of worship. Your religious and philosophical beliefs get tested. (This is a good thing, by the way – sometimes they need revision or discarding.) Since this eclipse impacts on Mars, job changes or changes in the conditions of work are afoot. Sometimes there are health scares too.

The Solar Eclipse of the 21st is technically in your 10th house, but it occurs very close to the cusp (the border) of the 11th house so it affects both houses. There are career changes – changes in your corporate hierarchy, corporate policy or your industry. There are personal dramas in the lives of bosses, parents or parent figures. Friends have life-changing dramas too. Your high-tech equipment gets tested.

September

Best Days Overall: 5, 6, 14, 15, 23, 24
Most Stressful Days Overall: 3, 4, 10, 16, 17, 30
Best Days for Love: 7, 8, 10, 16, 17, 28
Best Days for Money: 3, 4, 12, 13, 20, 21, 25, 26, 30
Best Days for Career: 1, 10, 16, 17, 19, 30

Last month on the 26th the planetary power made a major shift from the social West to the independent East. The planetary power now moves away from others and towards you. Personal independence and personal power is increasing day by day. You have the power to create your own happiness now. You need to start thinking about 'Number One' – yourself. The cycle of people pleasing is mostly over with. Now you have to please yourself. The cosmos is supporting you. This is not selfish as most people think. If you are happy, the world as a whole becomes a happier place. If every person takes responsibility for their own happiness, the overall happiness in the world will increase.

The career focus tapers off this month. Mars moves out of your 10th house on the 5th. Things are quieter. Less hectic. Mercury leaves on the 10th and Venus leaves on the 20th. Along with these moves come big improvements in health and overall energy. Probably the mood will improve as well. Health is enhanced through paying more attention to the small intestine. Abdominal massage would be good too.

Your 11th house of friends became powerful on August 22 and is even more powerful in the month ahead. Thus the social life is prominent now. The social life of the 11th house is different from the social life of the 7th house – it is more about friendships and platonic relationships than relationships of the heart. But Venus's move into your 11th house (on the 20th) shows that romance can happen in this venue too. You can be involved in a group activity or organizational function and meet someone special. Sometimes friends like to play Cupid. And, sometimes someone whom you thought of as a friend becomes more than that. The online world is socially good this month – especially the social networks.

Venus in Virgo (from the 20th onwards) is not your best position for love. Venus is not comfortable in the sign of Virgo. She cannot function in her full strength. So your social magnetism is not up to its usual standards.

There is a very happy career opportunity between the 8th and 10th. You seem successful during that period.

Finances are good this month too. On the 22nd, as the Sun starts to travel with Jupiter, there will be financial expansion. Next month will be even better.

October

Best Days Overall: 3, 4, 11, 12, 20, 21, 30, 31
Most Stressful Days Overall: 1, 7, 8, 13, 14, 27, 28, 29
Best Days for Love: 7, 8, 17, 18, 27, 28
Best Days for Money: 1, 10, 11, 20, 22, 23, 24, 30
Best Days for Career: 1, 9, 10, 13, 14, 19, 30

A happy, healthy and prosperous month ahead Scorpio. Enjoy!

Jupiter, your financial planet, makes a major (once in a year) move this month, from Libra into your own sign. This initiates a multi-year cycle of prosperity, bringing financial windfalls and happy opportunities. You have the image – the appearance – of wealth. You are the 'money person' to the people around you. This image of wealth brings all kinds of opportunities to you by the law of attraction – like attracts like. You spend on yourself and live a 'higher' kind of lifestyle. You can afford to. Financial opportunities seek you out. You just go about your daily business and they find you. The money people in your life are devoted to you.

The Sun, your career planet, will cross your Ascendant and enter your 1st house on the 23rd. This brings happy career opportunities to you. There's no rush to accept anything, but the offers are there and you can be choosy. You not only look rich, but you look successful too. People see you this way. You are one of the 'high and mighty' these days.

The planetary power is now at its maximum Eastern position (and will remain there through next month as well). If you haven't yet made the changes that make you happy, now is the time. You have the power and the money to create your own happiness. If you wait too long, the changes can still be made but with more difficulty.

The spiritual life is the other important headline this month: 60 per cent of the planets are either in your 12th house or moving through there this month. This is a lot of power. So, this is a month for spiritual breakthroughs, for direct and personal spiritual experiences. It is one thing to read something in a book or hear something in a workshop, but quite another to have the direct experience of a thing. This is what is happening for you this month. Get the spiritual life right – stay in harmony and attuned with the Divine within – and everything else will fall into place.

Health is excellent this month. You have the energy of ten people. There are no long-term planets stressing you out – in fact only the Moon will do so occasionally, but these stresses are mild and short term. Mars's move into your 12th house on the 22nd shows that you benefit from spiritual-healing techniques. In the unlikely event that you feel under the weather, see a spiritual healer.

November

Best Days Overall: 7, 8, 16, 17, 26, 27
Most Stressful Days Overall: 3, 4, 9, 10, 24, 25
Best Days for Love: 3, 4, 6, 7, 16, 17, 26, 27
Best Days for Money: 7, 8, 16, 17, 19, 20, 26, 27
Best Days for Career: 7, 8, 9, 10, 17, 18, 28, 29

You have love, money, health and independence this month. There's not much more one can ask from life. You're very much your own person, having things your way. So long as these gifts are not abused, things are wonderful. Abuses can lead to problems later on down the road.

Health is fabulous this month. Imagine, there are no planets in stressful aspect with you. Only the Moon – and only occasionally – will make stressful aspects. And these pass very quickly. If there have been any pre-existing conditions, these seem in abeyance or much reduced. You'll need to watch your weight these days though – the good life can make you pile on the pounds. Scorpios of childbearing age are much more fertile than usual now.

The physical appearance shines now. There is more than usual appeal to the opposite sex. Physical beauty is as much a function of energy as it is of form. Energy might even be more important than form. You look like someone who is 'on top of the world'. You look and dress for success, and expensively. Scorpios are not usually flamboyant people, but these days you like to flaunt your wealth.

Venus moves into your sign on the 7th. For women this increases the physical beauty and grace. There is a natural sense of style. For a man it tends to bring younger women into the personal sphere. Venus's move into your sign brings love that pursues you – whether you are male or female. It's as if you can't escape romance. If you are already in a relationship the beloved is very devoted to you – at your beck and call.

The 12th and 13th is an especially good love and financial period.

Jupiter in your sign is bringing money and financial opportunity, as we have mentioned. On the 22nd, as the Sun enters your money house, wealth increases even further. You enter a yearly financial peak. You have the financial favour of bosses, elders, parents or parent figures. They all seem financially supportive and provide financial opportunity.

Jupiter in your sign shows a good eye for companies involved with water – water utilities, water bottlers or purifiers, ships and shipping. Some of you might be buying your own boat these days. This position is also good for companies that make surgical supplies or that supply intelligence agencies.

Your health planet Mars spends the month in the 12th house. Your health is good, but this is a good month to explore spiritual healing – the role that spirit plays on the physical body.

December

Best Days Overall: 5, 6, 14, 15, 24, 25
Most Stressful Days Overall: 1, 2, 7, 8, 21, 22, 28, 29
Best Days for Love: 1, 2, 7, 8, 16, 17, 28, 29
Best Days for Money: 5, 6, 14, 15, 16, 17, 24, 25
Best Days for Career: 7, 8, 16, 17

The rich get richer. Finances are even better this month than last (and that's saying something). On the 21st, Saturn moves out of your money house, where he's been for over two years. He has been a drag on the financial life. He slowed things down. He brought extra financial burdens that you couldn't escape. He forced a reshuffling and reorganization of your finances. Worst of all, he brought a sense of financial pessimism. After the 21st, this is all over. Financial confidence is restored. Financial burdens seem removed (and if not removed, they are now so easily handled as to not feel like burdens). Saturn has done his job and now moves into your 3rd house to reorganize your intellectual life. Scorpios are deep thinkers by nature. But Saturn will take you even deeper. Your speech, thinking and writing will be more organized. You will be forced to do more homework before you talk – to know what you're talking about. Frivolous speech will be a big no-no for the next two or so years.

Saturn's move into your 3rd house impacts on your siblings or the sibling figures in your life. They are forced to take on more responsibility, to be more serious about life. Saturn knows how to do this.

You are still in the midst of a yearly financial peak until the 21st. So earnings are still very strong. Venus, the love planet, will move into the money house on the 1st and spend almost all month here. This shows the financial support of the spouse, partner or current love. It shows opportunities for financial partnerships or joint ventures. For singles it shows an allurement to wealth. Wealth is as much a turn-on as sexual magnetism (perhaps even more so). You like the good provider. Material gifts and financial support turn you on. Love opportunities come as you pursue your financial goals and with people involved in your finances.

Mars moves into your sign on the 9th, bringing energy and dynamism to your image. In a woman's chart it brings younger men into the picture. In a man's chart it increases physical energy and 'macho' flair. The testosterone levels soar.

Mars is your health and work planet. Thus job opportunities come to you. If you hire others, good employees find you. There's nothing much you need to do – it happens naturally. Just go about your daily business.

Health is still very good. Mars in your sign shows that you look healthy too. (One can be healthy, but not necessarily appear that way.) You look physically fit. Good exercises now are swimming, water sports and water aerobics.

Sagittarius

THE ARCHER

Birthdays from
23rd November to
20th December

Personality Profile

SAGITTARIUS AT A GLANCE

Element – Fire

Ruling Planet – Jupiter
  Career Planet – Mercury
  Love Planet – Mercury
  Money Planet – Saturn
  Planet of Health and Work – Venus
  Planet of Home and Family Life – Neptune
  Planet of Spirituality – Pluto

Colours – blue, dark blue

Colours that promote love, romance and social harmony – yellow,
  yellow-orange

Colours that promote earning power – black, indigo

Gems – carbuncle, turquoise

Metal – tin

Scents – carnation, jasmine, myrrh

Quality - mutable (= flexibility)

Qualities most needed for balance - attention to detail, administrative and organizational skills

Strongest virtues - generosity, honesty, broad-mindedness, tremendous vision

Deepest need - to expand mentally

Characteristics to avoid - over-optimism, exaggeration, being too generous with other people's money

Signs of greatest overall compatibility - Aries, Leo

Signs of greatest overall incompatibility - Gemini, Virgo, Pisces

Sign most helpful to career - Virgo

Sign most helpful for emotional support - Pisces

Sign most helpful financially - Capricorn

Sign best for marriage and/or partnerships - Gemini

Sign most helpful for creative projects - Aries

Best Sign to have fun with - Aries

Signs most helpful in spiritual matters - Leo, Scorpio

Best day of the week - Thursday

Understanding a Sagittarius

If you look at the symbol of the archer you will gain a good, intuitive understanding of a person born under this astrological sign. The development of archery was humanity's first refinement of the power to hunt and wage war. The ability to shoot an arrow far beyond the ordinary range of a spear extended humanity's horizons, wealth, personal will and power.

Today, instead of using bows and arrows we project our power with fuels and mighty engines, but the essential reason for using these new powers remains the same. These powers represent our ability to extend our personal sphere of influence – and this is what Sagittarius is all about. Sagittarians are always seeking to expand their horizons, to cover more territory and increase their range and scope. This applies to all aspects of their lives: economic, social and intellectual.

Sagittarians are noted for the development of the mind – the higher intellect – which understands philosophical and spiritual concepts. This mind represents the higher part of the psychic nature and is motivated not by self-centred considerations but by the light and grace of a Higher Power. Thus, Sagittarians love higher education of all kinds. They might be bored with formal schooling but they love to study on their own and in their own way. A love of foreign travel and interest in places far away from home are also noteworthy characteristics of the Sagittarian type.

If you give some thought to all these Sagittarian attributes you will see that they spring from the inner Sagittarian desire to develop. To travel more is to know more, to know more is to be more, to cultivate the higher mind is to grow and to reach more. All these traits tend to broaden the intellectual – and indirectly, the economic and material – horizons of the Sagittarian.

The generosity of the Sagittarian is legendary. There are many reasons for this. One is that Sagittarians seem to have an inborn consciousness of wealth. They feel that they are rich, that they are lucky, that they can attain any financial goal – and so they feel that they can afford to be generous. Sagittarians do not carry the burdens of want and limitation which stop most other people from giving generously. Another reason for their generosity is their religious and philosophical idealism, derived from the higher mind. This higher mind is by nature generous because it is unaffected by material circumstances. Still another reason is that the act of giving tends to enhance their emotional nature. Every act of giving seems to be enriching, and this is reward enough for the Sagittarian.

Finance

Sagittarians generally entice wealth. They either attract it or create it. They have the ideas, energy and talent to make their vision of paradise on Earth a reality. However, mere wealth is not enough. Sagittarians want luxury – earning a comfortable living seems small and insignificant to them.

In order for Sagittarians to attain their true earning potential they must develop better managerial and organizational skills. They must learn to set limits, to arrive at their goals through a series of attainable sub-goals or objectives. It is very rare that a person goes from rags to riches overnight. But a long, drawn-out process is difficult for Sagittarians. Like Leos, they want to achieve wealth and success quickly and impressively. They must be aware, however, that this over-optimism can lead to unrealistic financial ventures and disappointing losses. Of course, no zodiac sign can bounce back as quickly as Sagittarius, but only needless heartache will be caused by this attitude. Sagittarians need to maintain their vision – never letting it go – but they must also work towards it in practical and efficient ways.

Career and Public Image

Sagittarians are big thinkers. They want it all: money, fame, glamour, prestige, public acclaim and a place in history. They often go after all these goals. Some attain them, some do not – much depends on each individual's personal horoscope. But if Sagittarians want to attain public and professional status they must understand that these things are not conferred to enhance one's ego but as rewards for the amount of service that one does for the whole of humanity. If and when they figure out ways to serve more, Sagittarians can rise to the top.

The ego of the Sagittarian is gigantic – and perhaps rightly so. They have much to be proud of. If they want public acclaim, however, they will have to learn to tone down the ego a bit, to become more humble and self-effacing, without falling into the trap of self-denial and self-abasement. They must also learn to master the details of life, which can sometimes elude them.

At their jobs Sagittarians are hard workers who like to please their bosses and co-workers. They are dependable, trustworthy and enjoy a challenge. Sagittarians are friendly to work with and helpful to their colleagues. They usually contribute intelligent ideas or new methods that improve the work environment for everyone. Sagittarians always look for challenging positions and careers that develop their intellect, even if they have to work very hard in order to succeed. They also work well under the supervision of others, although by nature they would rather be the supervisors and increase their sphere of influence. Sagittarians excel at professions that allow them to be in contact with many different people and to travel to new and exciting locations.

Love and Relationships

Sagittarians love freedom for themselves and will readily grant it to their partners. They like their relationships to be fluid and ever-changing. Sagittarians tend to be fickle in love and to change their minds about their partners quite frequently.

Sagittarians feel threatened by a clearly defined, well-structured relationship, as they feel this limits their freedom. The Sagittarian tends to marry more than once in life.

Sagittarians in love are passionate, generous, open, benevolent and very active. They demonstrate their affections very openly. However, just like an Aries they tend to be egocentric in the way they relate to their partners. Sagittarians should develop the ability to see others' points of view, not just their own. They need to develop some objectivity and cool intellectual clarity in their relationships so that they can develop better two-way communication with their partners. Sagittarians tend to be overly idealistic about their partners and about love in general. A cool and rational attitude will help them to perceive reality more clearly and enable them to avoid disappointment.

Home and Domestic Life

Sagittarians tend to grant a lot of freedom to their family. They like big homes and many children and are one of the most fertile signs of the zodiac. However, when it comes to their children Sagittarians generally err on the side of allowing them too much freedom. Sometimes their children get the idea that there are no limits. However, allowing freedom in the home is basically a positive thing – so long as some measure of balance is maintained – for it enables all family members to develop as they should.

Horoscope for 2017

Major Trends

Saturn, your financial planet, has been in your sign for the past two years and will be there almost till the end of the year ahead. While this is bringing prosperity and financial opportunity, it has made you a bit cold, business-like and standoffish to others. The social life has been affected by this. More on this later.

The year ahead looks prosperous, with Saturn remaining in your sign almost all year. On December 21, he moves into your money house – a strong position. He is powerful on your behalf. More on this later.

Jupiter, the ruler of your Horoscope, spends most of the year in your 11th house. This is a year for friendships and group activities. A year for manifesting 'fondest hopes and wishes'. New and important friends are coming into the picture. On October 11, Jupiter will move into your spiritual 12th house, and spirituality will start to become important. This will be the case well into next year. You enter a period of spiritual growth.

Spirituality is important in other ways too. Pluto, your spiritual planet, has been in your money house since 2008. Your spiritual understanding and insight is having concrete bottom-line results and this is a long-term trend. Pluto will be here for many more years.

Neptune has been in your 4th house since 2012 and will be there for many more years. The family relationship is becoming elevated and spiritualized – a long-term process.

Uranus has been in your 5th house since 2011. Children and children figures in your life have been more rebellious and difficult to handle. Give them as much freedom as possible, so long as it isn't destructive. They should be taught safe ways to test the limits of their bodies.

Your areas of greatest interest this year are the body and image; finance; home and family; children, fun and creativity; friends, groups, group and online activities (until October 11); and spirituality (from October 11 onwards).

Your paths of greatest fulfilment this year are career (until April 29); religion, philosophy, higher education and foreign travel (from April 29 onwards); friends, groups, group and online activities (until October 11); and spirituality (from October 11 onwards).

Health

(Please note that this is an astrological perspective on health and not a medical one. In days of yore there was no difference, both of these perspec-tives were identical. But now there could be quite a difference. For a medi-cal perspective, please consult your doctor or health practitioner.)

Health is much improved over last year and will improve even further towards the end of the year. In the meantime there are two long-term planets stressing you out. Of itself this is not enough to cause disease, but still overall energy is not what it should be. The periods to watch this year are when the short-term planets put addi-tional stress on you. This is when you become more vulnerable to problems. These periods are from February 19 to March 20; April 20 to June 21; and August 22 to September 22. Be sure to rest and relax more over these times and do your best to maintain high energy levels.

I would rate your health as OK. Not spectacular but adequate. Your empty 6th house (only short-term planets move through there) is a good sign. You don't have a need to overly focus here.

There is much you can do to improve your health and energy and prevent problems from developing. Give more attention to the following – the vulnerable areas of your chart (the points are shown opposite):

• The liver and thighs. These are always important for Sagittarius. Regular thigh massage should be a part of your normal health regime. Regular herbal liver cleansings too. (Liver action has been sluggish in recent years and needs more energy.)

- The neck and throat. These too are always important for Sagittarius. Regular neck massage will release tension and strengthen the whole area. Craniosacral therapy is also good here.
- The kidneys and hips. These are also another important area. Hips (and buttocks) should be regularly massaged. A herbal kidney cleanse every now and then would also be good – especially if you feel under the weather.
- The heart. This has only become important in recent years (since Christmas 2014). You're very much involved in worldly affairs these days – especially business. Avoid worry and anxiety, the two emotions that stress the heart. Develop more faith.

Venus as your health planet indicates the importance of social harmony in health. For you, good health means a healthy love and social life. Even if you have no physical symptoms, if the love life isn't right, you

Important foot reflexology points for the year ahead

Try to massage all of the foot on a regular basis – the top of the foot as well as the bottom – but pay extra attention to the points highlighted on the chart. When you massage, be aware of 'sore spots' as these need special attention. It's also a good idea to massage the ankles and below them.

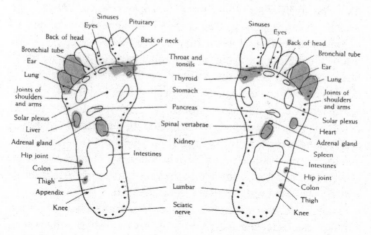

probably won't feel well. If the discord is prolonged, it can produce pathologies in the body. So, if health problems arise (God forbid), restore harmony in the social life as quickly as you can.

Venus is a fast-moving planet. She will move through all the signs and houses of your horoscope in any given year. Thus there are many short-term trends in health – different needs and different effective therapies – depending on where she is and the aspects she receives. These are best covered in the monthly reports.

Venus will make one of her rare (once every two years) retrogrades this year – from March 4 to April 15. Avoid making dramatic dietary or health regime changes during that period. Do more research. Your thinking on these matters is not realistic then.

Home and Family

This has been a troubling area these past few years and has required much of your attention and focus. This trend continues in the year ahead, but is less severe than in the past two years. By the end of the year, things at home get much happier.

A parent or parent figure in your life seems very stressed out. You and this person are having financial disagreements. Family obligations seem to stress you financially.

Family members are much more sensitive than usual and are easily hurt. You are by nature an 'up front' kind of person. You say what you want to say forthrightly. You tend to be bluntly honest. But this doesn't sit well with family members. They can see this as 'cruelty' or gross insensitivity. From your point of view you don't see it this way. You're just being forthright. But they would see it this way. So, make more of an effort to be more diplomatic in your speech and opinions.

The family's sensitivities go deeper than just speech. They tend to react to voice tone and body language too. If, for example, you were annoyed by something that happened at work, and you came home and had a conversation, your tone of irritation would impact on them. (They could feel it was directed at them.) A little more care in these matters will save much heartache down the road.

Finance, as we mentioned, is an important area this year. Family could feel that you care more about your business affairs than you do for them. From their perspective you're putting business first.

There is a Solar Eclipse on February 26 that not only occurs in your 4th house but also impacts on Neptune, the ruler of that house. Family and family relationships seem very stressed by this. There could be personal, life-changing dramas in their lives. Passions run high. Sometimes repairs are needed in the home. Be more patient with the family at this time.

On October 11, as Jupiter moves into Scorpio, moves could happen. You will start to get on better with the family and especially with a parent or parent figure. But the financial disagreements are not fully resolved until the end of the year.

When Jupiter moves into Scorpio the family circle will expand – usually through birth or marriage. Sometimes the circle expands through meeting people who 'play the role' of family in your life.

Children and children figures in your life have been difficult to handle for many years now. They don't respond well to the 'authoritarian' approach. They are more rebellious than usual. However, if they are made to understand the 'why' of your requests, things should go much better. Many children these days are addicted to the internet and high-tech gadgetry, but yours more so than others.

You always like large, spacious homes Sagittarius, but these days (especially since 2012) waterfront homes are most attractive. If you're planning major repairs or renovations, January 1–28, June 4 to July 20, and December 9–31 are good times. If you're redecorating or otherwise beautifying the home, January 3 to February 3 and February 18 to March 20 seem good for this.

Finance and Career

Prosperity has been happening since Christmas 2014 as your financial planet, Saturn, moved into your sign, and he remains here for almost all of the year ahead. The prosperity continues. Money is on your mind. You're focused here.

You have naturally good intuition for the travel business, airlines, foreign investments and for-profit colleges, but now it is even better than normal. Invest in the things that you love – that interest you.

Of course, the best investment is in yourself. You're spending on yourself these days. You're dressing expensively and creating an image of wealth. Others are seeing you this way. The money people in your life are devoted to you, on your side and helping out. And you seem like a 'money person' in your own right – especially with others.

Personal appearance and overall presentation are very important financially and this could be reason for the spending. It's more like a 'business investment' than vanity.

The good thing about your financial planet's position in your own sign is that there's nothing special you need to do to attract earnings or financial opportunities. These are seeking you out. You just go about your daily affairs and money will find you.

There is a down side to this, however. There could be a tendency to define yourself in terms of money. The financial statement is me. If I make more, then I am more. If I make less, then I'm somehow diminished. This can distort the financial judgement and lead to losses. You need to keep the ego out of the way in your financial decision making.

Generally you're a risk taker in finance, but less so these past few years. This is a good thing. The financial judgement is sound and conservative (and will become more so after December 21). You have a good long-range perspective on wealth – a good sense of what an investment will be worth many years down the road.

These past few years (and this continues in the year ahead) has been a great time to set up savings and investment plans, budgets and the like. There's something comforting about a good plan. Once it's set up, you don't need to think too much about it. Just follow it and wealth will happen more or less on schedule.

Pluto, as we have mentioned, has been in your money house for many years and will be there for many more to come. A Pluto transit is a long-term process. So, this shows that you're forging your financial intuition. This is, and will become ever more so, an important tool in your financial arsenal – perhaps the most important one. But this transit also shows other things. Those of you of appropriate age are doing estate planning now. Younger Sagittarians have inherited substantial sums and now need to invest the windfalls properly. Taxes and estate issues are governing much of your financial decision making.

The North Node of the Moon will be in your 10th house until April 29. So the career should be going well – a source of fulfilment. This would also show strong and perhaps excessive ambition – which tends to success. Perhaps you're more ambitious than you need to be.

After April 29 ambitions taper off and career is not such a big factor for you. Wealth is more important than status or prestige.

Love and Social Life

Your 7th house hasn't been strong for some years now. Romance doesn't seem a big issue this year. Some years are like that. Generally this shows a stable year tending towards the status quo. Those who are married will tend to stay married and singles will tend to stay single. You have a lot of social freedom this year. There's nothing against marriage or a serious relationship, just lack of interest. The cosmos in not impelling you one way or the other.

The overall social life is another story. This is active and happy. But this social life is more about friendship – platonic kinds of relationships – not romance. You seem very focused here and proactive. You're cultivating friendships and group activities. New and happy friendships are happening.

Your love planet, Mercury is, second to the Moon, the fastest moving of all the planets. He is also one of the most erratic. Sometimes he moves ultra-fast, sometimes slow, sometimes (four times this year) he moves backwards, sometimes he is motionless. This can make you seem fickle and difficult to please – difficult to figure out in love. Yes, at different times your needs and desires in love change. Sometimes one thing pleases you, sometimes another. Sometimes you show love one way, sometimes another. This is just your nature. You follow Mercury's movements. This being the case, there are many short-term trends in love that depend on where Mercury is and the aspects he receives. These short-term trends are best covered in the monthly reports.

Anyone in love with a Sagittarius will have to learn many roles. He or she will need great flexibility.

Saturn, as we have mentioned, has been in your sign for some time now. While this has many good points, which we have mentioned, it is not the greatest aspect for love. We have written of this in previous years and the tendency is still in effect. You seem too serious, too business-like, too cool, too aloof and distant. Now, you're not really like this. There is no warmer, more ebullient person on the planet than Sagittarius. Yet, these days, people can see you this way if you're not careful. The Saturn influence is like a drug (a serious drug). You can be emanating this vibration or feeling without intending to. The solution, as we have said in previous years, is to make a project of sending love and warmth to others. Normally you wouldn't have to do this, it would come out naturally. But now you must do it consciously. This will help the love life a lot.

Saturn will move out of your sign on December 21. The love life should improve after that.

What we've said applies to all of you but especially those of you in or working on the first, second or fourth marriage. Those working on the third marriage have excellent aspects this year. Serious romance is very likely.

Children and children figures in your life have beautiful romantic aspects this year. If they are of appropriate age, marriage could happen. Whatever their age they are making new and happy friendships. Siblings and sibling figures have a stable romantic year. Those who are married will tend to stay married, and singles will tend to stay single.

Self-Improvement

Your spiritual planet, Pluto, has been in your money house for many years, as we have mentioned. For you, spirituality – your spiritual understanding of how things work – is far from 'pie in the sky' abstraction. It has strong financial consequences. You're always intuitive in finances, but now even more so. Yes, you put on an exterior of logic and finance-speak for the world, but in truth your intuition is the deciding factor.

We have written of this in previous years, but the trend (and process) is still in effect. You're going deeper into the spiritual (not so much the worldly) laws of wealth. This is a huge subject. We don't learn it in a few years. It's not like getting a business degree. There are many personal experiments that need to be made. There is much delving into the subconscious blockages and human learning that has to be unpicked. We cannot access the spiritual supply with only intellectual knowledge. One must practise. One must contact the 'spirit of afflu-ence' itself, allow it to come in and teach us how to be affluent. Affluence knows how. There is a need to set aside all 'human wisdom' on the subject and allow the pure spirit to teach us directly.

If you do this, and many of you are, you will see that the economic laws taught in school are not the way they are being taught. There is a 'spiritual economics' which supersedes all of that. You're getting initi-ated into this 'spiritual economics' these days.

Spiritual economics is not concerned with any material condition. A person attuned to the Spiritual Affluence could be on a desert island and he or she would still be supplied with everything needed in that environ-ment. Spiritual Affluence is never about how much we have, but about how much we can receive. In many cases (this is not true for you, but for many others) the wealth concepts – the mental containers – are not big enough to hold the spiritual supply. If one goes to the ocean with only a cup, one will only take away a cupful – though there are huge amounts of water to be had. If one comes with a barrel, one will take away a barrel – but that is not all there is to be had. The ocean doesn't care how much you take. The thing is one must know that there IS an ocean there.

Your spiritual lessons will intensify after October 11 as Jupiter enters your 12th house. This will not only assist in finances, but in your personal growth and in your ability to handle the family.

Month-by-month Forecasts

January

Best Days Overall: 5, 6, 13, 14, 22, 23, 24
Most Stressful Days Overall: 2, 3, 9, 10, 15, 16, 30, 31
Best Days for Love: 2, 6, 9, 10, 12, 15, 20, 21, 25, 26, 31
Best Days for Money: 1, 5, 6, 10, 13, 14, 18, 19, 23, 24, 25, 26, 28, 29
Best Days for Career: 6, 15, 16, 25, 26

You begin your year with most of the planets in the independent East of your chart. This will soon change. If there are important changes to be made in your personal life – in conditions and circumstance – now is the time to make them. It will be more difficult to make them later on. Success comes through personal initiative now.

The bottom half of your Horoscope is hugely dominant as the year begins – 80 per cent of the planets are energizing the lower half. From the 1st to the 6th and from the 22nd onwards, 90 per cent of the planets will be there. So ambition is not very strong this period. Career is not a big issue. Your 10th house is basically empty (only the Moon moves through there on the 15th and 16th) while your 4th house of home and family is ultra-powerful. The Horoscope gives a clear message. Focus on getting the home base in order. Focus on your emotional wellness. Now is the time to build up the forces for your next career push later on in the year. You are in the night time of your year. Night is for rest and recuperation. It is said that in winter nature dreams and in the spring she manifests her dreams outwardly. So it is with you. Now you dream of where you want your career to go, in your spring – the daytime of your year – you will act out your dreams.

The month ahead is prosperous. You entered a yearly financial peak last month on the 21st and this continues until the 19th. Your financial planet is still in your 1st house, prospering you, and he receives mostly good aspects.

This month is an excellent time for starting new projects or ventures. Perhaps even better than the Spring. Your personal solar cycle is waxing and so is the universal solar cycle. Most importantly the planetary momentum is overwhelmingly forward (which you won't have in the spring). There is never less than 90 per cent of the planets in forward motion this month, and after the 7th *all* the planets will be forward. The 7th to the 12th and the 28th to the 31st would be the best times of the month to launch your new venture. (The Moon will be waxing and all the planets are moving forward.)

Health is good this month, but not perfect. There are a few planets stressing you out. You can enhance the health through foot massage and spiritual techniques from the 2nd onwards. You will respond very well to a spiritual healer if you feel under the weather.

February

Best Days Overall: 1, 2, 9, 10, 19, 20, 28
Most Stressful Days Overall: 5, 6, 12, 13, 26, 27
Best Days for Love: 3, 4, 5, 6, 9, 10, 14, 15, 19, 20, 25, 26, 28
Best Days for Money: 1, 2, 5, 6, 9, 10, 14, 15, 19, 20, 21, 22, 24, 25, 28
Best Days for Career: 3, 4, 12, 13, 14, 15, 25, 26

Love has improved over last month. Your love planet Mercury was retrograde last month (until January 8) and now he is moving forward – and very quickly. Perhaps the problem now is your changeability (fickleness?) in your love needs. On the other hand, love opportunities happen in different places and different ways this month. Until the 7th love opportunities happen as you handle your financial goals – and perhaps with people involved in your finances. Material wealth is the romantic turn-on. (This was the case all last month too.) From the 7th to the 25th you gravitate to those who have the gift of the gab. Good communication is a romantic turn-on. Intellectual intimacy is as important as the physical side. Your love planet in Aquarius shows that you gravitate to very brilliant kinds of people – scientists, astronomers, astrologers, inventors and innovators. Romantic meetings can happen online. After the 25th you crave emotional intimacy (though you still like the intellectual side). You also gravitate to spiritual kinds of people.

Mercury's fast motion shows good social confidence. Probably you're dating more. You seem to cover a lot of territory.

We have two eclipses this period. This is guaranteed to shake things up. The Lunar Eclipse of the 11th (in the Americas it's on the 10th) occurs in your 9th house and impacts mostly on students at college level. There are dramatic changes to their educational plans. It is not advisable to be on the road or in the air over that period. It will bring shakeups in your place of worship and a testing of your religious and philosophical beliefs. They get 'reality therapy'. Some will have to be revised, some discarded altogether. The eclipsed planet, the Moon, is the ruler of your 8th house and this gives many messages. The spouse, partner or current love is forced to make important course corrections in their financial life. Most likely the thinking and strategy is unrealistic.

The eclipse can bring encounters with death – close calls, near-death kinds of experiences, dreams of death, etc. The cosmos sends a gentle reminder to get more serious about life – it can end at any time. Avoid dangerous kinds of activities this period.

The Solar Eclipse of the 26th affects you more strongly. Reduce your schedule. (You should reduce your schedule from the 18th onwards anyway, but especially during this eclipse period.) This eclipse also impacts on college students, on your place of worship and on your religious and philosophical beliefs. The Sun is the ruler of your 9th house and these areas of life are getting shaken up by the two eclipses. But this one also impacts on the home and family, and especially one of the parents or parent figures in your life.

March

Best Days Overall: 1, 9, 10, 18, 19, 28
Most Stressful Days Overall: 4, 5, 11, 12, 25, 26
Best Days for Love: 1, 4, 5, 7, 8, 9, 18, 19, 27, 28, 29
Best Days for Money: 1, 5, 6, 10, 13, 14, 19, 20, 21, 22, 23, 24, 28
Best Days for Career: 7, 8, 11, 12, 18, 19, 28, 29

Your 4th house became powerful on February 18 and is still powerful until the 20th of this month. Most of the planets are still in the bottom half of your chart. Your 10th house of career is still empty (only the Moon moves through there on the 11th and 12th), so the focus remains on home and family. This is the magical, mystical midnight hour of your year. This is when miracles happen – but internally. They are unseen. This is when the patterns are set for the day ahead. So respect the midnight hour. With a good night's sleep we have a good chance of a successful day. Without it, the day most likely won't be successful.

Health needs watching until the 20th. The most important thing is to get enough rest. You can further enhance the health through head, face and scalp massage. Craniosacral therapy is also good. Mars, the ruler of these areas, moves into your 6th house of health on the 10th and spends the rest of the month there. Exercise is also good – as vigorous as you can handle. It's very important to keep good muscle tone. Health will improve dramatically after the 20th.

Your health planet goes retrograde on the 4th, so avoid making major changes to the diet or health regime after that date. If changes have to be made, do a lot more research and study. You will think differently about these things next month.

Finances have been more stressful since February 18. This is the case until the 20th. Of course earnings will happen, but they come with much more work and effort. Things are more complicated than usual. But after the 20th it is all systems go. The financial planet, Saturn, starts to receive wonderful aspects.

When the Sun enters Aries on the 20th you enter one of your yearly personal pleasure peaks. A holiday period. A time for enjoying your life and doing the things that you most love to do. As you do the things you love, love and romance will find you. Your love planet Mercury enters the 5th house on the 13th.

You are a love-at-first-sight kind of person by nature, and especially so after the 13th. You could be too impulsive in relationships. You leap before you look. The good thing about this is that relationships can start and develop very quickly.

April

Best Days Overall: 5, 6, 14, 15, 16, 24, 25
Most Stressful Days Overall: 1, 7, 8, 22, 23, 28, 29
Best Days for Love: 1, 4, 7, 8, 12, 13, 18, 23, 24, 25, 28, 29
Best Days for Money: 1, 5, 6, 10, 11, 15, 16, 17, 18, 19, 20, 21, 24, 25, 28, 29
Best Days for Career: 7, 8, 18, 24, 25

You're still very much in a yearly personal pleasure peak until the 19th. It is time for R&R. Time to let go of your cares and worries and do the things that you love to do. Miraculously you will find that the things you worried about are resolved naturally. Often after a period of fun, we see solutions to problems that we didn't see before. Too much focus on the problem was blocking the solution.

With the Sun in your 5th house this is a month for pleasure-oriented travel. Students are enjoying their studies and tend to be successful. Children and children figures in your life are more fertile this period (if they are of appropriate age). They are also prospering – especially from the 19th onwards. However, with their financial planet retrograde until the 15th they need more caution in finances.

Your personal finances are excellent until the 19th. They are good afterwards too, but much better before the 19th. Saturn, your financial planet starts to travel backwards on the 6th and this will continue for several months. You shouldn't shut down all financial activity – you can't – but you should avoid, where possible, making major purchases or investments. Put them on the back-burner and study them further. It is guaranteed that you will have a different attitude to them a few months from now. These things are not as urgent as you might think. In the meantime you buy your necessities, of course – the groceries, clothing, etc. The important thing now is to gain clarity on your financial life and dealings. When this happens you will be in a good position to implement big plans when Saturn starts to move forward again in August.

Health is good this month. It is especially good until the 19th, but it is reasonable afterwards too. You respond very well to spiritual-healing techniques from the 2nd to the 28th – most of the month. Foot massage is also a great 'pick me up'.

Love is complicated this month. For one thing, your love planet Mercury goes retrograde on the 9th and this tends to weaken the social confidence and judgement. Mars will enter the 7th house on the 21st and spend the rest of the month there. This is not especially good for love as it tends to conflict and power struggles. Since Mars rules your 5th house of fun, it shows a lack of seriousness about love. This aspect favours a love affair rather than a real romance.

Avoid speculations after the 21st.

May

Best Days Overall: 2, 3, 12, 13, 21, 22, 29, 30
Most Stressful Days Overall: 4, 5, 19, 20, 25, 26
Best Days for Love: 2, 3, 12, 13, 21, 22, 23, 24, 25, 26
Best Days for Money: 3, 7, 8, 13, 14, 15, 17, 18, 22, 25, 26, 30
Best Days for Career: 2, 3, 4, 5, 13, 16, 23, 24

The planetary power has been in the Western, social sector of your chart since February and now the planets are at their maximum Western position. These days life is about others and not so much about your self-interest. If conditions or circumstance disturb you, make note of them. The time for making changes will come in a few months. Your good happens through others now. Let others have their way so long as it isn't destructive. On the 20th the Sun enters your 7th house of love and you begin a yearly love and social peak. Love should be much improved this month as Mercury, your love planet, starts moving forward again on the 3rd. The mind is clear about love. There is more social confidence.

Mercury spends most of the month, from the 6th onwards, in your 6th house of health and work. Thus there is an attraction to health professionals and people at the workplace. There is more socializing with people at work. This also shows that for you - these days - good health also means good social health. If there are problems in love, the physical health can be affected. So, if problems arise restore harmony with the beloved as quickly as possible. In general you're attracted to foreigners, and this month especially so - from the 20th onwards. You're also attracted to the clergy and mentor types. Love can happen through introductions made by people in your place of worship or at university functions. Your professors are alluring romantically. Mars is still in your house of love, so be careful of power struggles. Avoid them as much as possible.

Health needs more attention this month - especially from the 20th onwards. You respond beautifully to head and face massage this month. Physical exercise is also good. Keep the muscles well-toned.

The love planet in the sign of Taurus slows you down a bit in love - a good thing. You're less likely to leap into something prematurely. Also it gives more stability.

Finances become more rocky after the 20th. Saturn, your financial planet, is still retrograde and he receives challenging aspects. So, you just have to work harder for earnings than usual.

The spouse, partner or current love has better earning power from the 1st to the 10th and from the 25th onwards - as the Moon waxes. (These are periods of increased libido as well.) The New Moon of the 25th seems an especially good financial day for him or her as it is a

'Super New Moon' – the Moon is very near her perigee (her closest point to Earth).

June

   Best Days Overall: 8, 9, 18, 19, 26, 27
   Most Stressful Days Overall: 1, 2, 15, 16, 22, 23, 28, 29
   Best Days for Love: 1, 2, 10, 11, 13, 14, 20, 21, 22, 23, 24, 28, 29
   Best Days for Money: 3, 4, 9, 10, 11, 12, 13, 14, 19, 22, 23, 27,
      30
   Best Days for Career: 1, 2, 13, 14, 24, 28, 29

Love is still the main headline this month. You're still in the midst of a yearly love and social peak until the 21st. Love is very interesting as you seem to go outside your normal sphere in search of it. Perhaps you're meeting an 'outsider' and having a relationship. Mercury is 'out of bounds' from the 18th onwards. The love life seems happy.

There is foreign travel and increased earnings from the 2nd to the 5th. Singles have a strong romantic opportunity on the 13th and 14th. Those who are married or in relationships have happy social invitations that period. Their relationship becomes more romantic.

The planetary power begins to shift this month from the lower half to the upper half of your chart – for the first time this year. Day is dawning in your year and it's time to be up and about and focused on your outer life. Time to take objective, physical actions to further your career. A good work ethic is important until the 6th. Afterwards your social connections play a big role, and a lot of your socializing is career-related. It will be beneficial to attend or host the right parties or gatherings. You're meeting people socially who can help your career.

Mercury's 'out of bounds' from the 18th onwards affects the career. You're thinking outside the box, going into unknown territory, in your career path. You're a bit unconventional now.

Health still needs some attention until the 21st. Make sure to get enough rest – this is always the most important thing. Enhance the health with head, face and scalp massage and regular exercise until the 6th. After the 6th follow our discussion of this in the yearly report. You have good recuperative powers after that date: Venus, your health planet, will be in her own sign and house and thus she is strong on your behalf.

The spouse, partner or current love is having a good financial month. On the 21st he or she enters a yearly financial peak. The New Moon of the 24th is an especially powerful financial day for him or her. Not only is it a 'Super New Moon' but it also occurs in his or her money house.

July

Best Days Overall: 5, 6, 15, 16, 23, 24
Most Stressful Days Overall: 13, 14, 19, 20, 25, 26
Best Days for Love: 4, 10, 16, 19, 20, 25, 26, 28, 29
Best Days for Money: 1, 5, 6, 8, 9, 10, 11, 15, 16, 19, 20, 23, 24, 28, 29
Best Days for Career: 4, 16, 25, 26

Health and energy are very good now and should improve even further from the 20th onwards. Your health planet moves into your 7th house on the 5th. In the unlikely event that you feel under the weather, arm and shoulder massage will boost your energy. You have a good connection with the healing powers of the Air element from the 5th onwards. Getting out in the fresh air and just breathing deeply will be a nice tonic. If you do develop a health problem, check your love life and restore harmony there as quickly as you can.

Sagittarians are expansive kinds of people. They want to expand, expand, expand. Grow, grow, grow. But since June 21 your 8th house has become very strong, and now it's all about cutting back – removing waste, removing the things that block expansion. It's a time to 'de-clutter' the life. Expansion will happen later on – after the 22nd – but until then prepare the ground. Go through your possessions and take stock. Are you holding on to things that you don't use or need? Get rid of them. Do you have too many old bank accounts? Old savings accounts? Too many credit cards? Close down the obsolete and excess. There is a time to breathe out and a time to breathe in. Until the 22nd, you're in an 'out breath' period. Empty the lungs (figuratively speaking) so that the next in-breath will be full and strong.

The 8th house is about dying and being reborn. This need not be taken too literally. In order to give birth to the person we want to be, we must die to the old one (or allow that old person to die). Birth and death are two sides of the same coin. Nothing is born without some kind of death. This is a month where you go deeper into these issues.

On the 22nd (and probably you will feel the effects a bit earlier) the Sun enters your 9th house – Sagittarius's natural territory. You become a 'super Sagittarius' that period. All your natural inclinations are reinforced. There is foreign travel, higher education and religious and philosophical breakthroughs. Much is written of Sagittarius's love for travel – their love for the 'jet set' life. Not so much is written of their love for theology and philosophy. If one did a random survey of the ranks of the clergy, I would wager there would be a disproportionate percentage of Sagittarians there (or people strong in the sign). Underneath every 'jet setter' is a budding priest or minister.

Finances are OK as the month begins – nothing special one way or another – but they get really good from the 22nd onwards. Until the 22nd use spare cash to pay off any debts.

August

Best Days Overall: 1, 2, 3, 11, 12, 20, 21, 29, 30
Most Stressful Days Overall: 9, 10, 16, 22, 23
Best Days for Love: 4, 5, 9, 10, 13, 14, 16, 18, 19, 22, 23, 28, 29, 31
Best Days for Money: 2, 3, 6, 7, 8, 11, 12, 16, 20, 21, 24, 25, 29, 30
Best Days for Career: 4, 5, 13, 14, 22, 23, 31

Another healthy and happy month. You're doing the things that you love to do and that you are good at. You're travelling (or making travel plans), learning and having religious and philosophical insights. Though your financial planet Saturn is still retrograde (he begins moving forward on the 25th) finances are good – though there can be some delays involved.

Health is excellent as we have mentioned. But after the 22nd, you will need to rest and relax more. Diet seems important in health until the 26th. Detox regimes are beneficial too. This is a very good month for losing weight (if you need to).

We have two eclipses this month shaking things up in the world and in your environment, but you seem fairly unaffected. The Solar Eclipse of the 21st affects you more strongly than the Lunar Eclipse of the 7th.

The Lunar Eclipse of the 7th occurs in your 3rd house of communication. This will test cars and communication equipment. Some of it will need repair or replacement. Sibling and sibling figures in your life are experiencing life-changing dramas – perhaps near-death experiences. You could be experiencing encounters with the dark angel too (he is really an angel of light, but we visualize him as dark because we fear him). If you're having dreams of death – which often happens – understand them for what they are: love messages from above urging you to get on with your true purpose in life. The spouse, partner or current love is forced to make major financial changes by this eclipse. Sometimes there are dramas with insurance companies or to do with taxes. Children and children figures should stay out of harm's way this period. Speculations are not advisable either.

The Solar Eclipse of the 21st is stronger on you (but mostly for those of you born early in the sign – from November 21 to November 23). This eclipse occurs right on the cusp or border of your 9th and 10th houses and impacts on both of them. So foreign travel should be avoided – try not to be on the road or in the air during the eclipse period. Schedule travel plans around it. College-level students can change institutions or courses, their educational plans have to be changed. There are shakeups in your place of worship, and in your company and industry.

This eclipse seems to open career doors for many of you. Sometimes the cosmos uses dramatic means to manifest its plans. On the 22nd you enter a yearly career peak and much progress will be made.

September

Best Days Overall: 7, 8, 16, 17, 25, 26
Most Stressful Days Overall: 5, 6, 12, 13, 18, 19
Best Days for Love: 7, 8, 9, 12, 13, 16, 17, 18, 19, 28, 29
Best Days for Money: 1, 3, 4, 7, 8, 12, 13, 16, 17, 20, 21, 26, 27, 28, 29, 30
Best Days for Career: 8, 9, 18, 19, 28, 29

You're still in the midst of your yearly career peak and push. Home and family issues will just have to wait right now as you give your attention to the outer life. Your 10th house of career is well-stocked with planets. You have a lot of career support and you need to take advantage of the opportunities happening.

Mars enters the 10th house on the 5th and spends the rest of the month there. This shows a lot of frenetic career activity. There is aggressiveness and conflict. You're fending off competitors. Good leadership skills are as important as your professional abilities. Venus enters your 10th house on the 20th and this indicates a need for a good work ethic.

Health needs more attention than last month as there are a lot of planets in stressful aspect with you. No doubt but the demands of the career are contributing to the problem. Succeed, by all means, but schedule regular rest breaks. Delegate tasks wherever possible. Enhance the health with chest massage, and generally pay more attention to the heart until the 20th. After the 20th abdominal massage will be powerful.

The love life seems improved over last month. Your love planet (and also your career planet) Mercury moves forward on the 5th. On the 10th he enters your 10th house – his own sign and house. Mercury is thus more powerful on your behalf and this is good for the career and for love. Until the 10th love and social opportunities happen at your place of worship, school or on one of your foreign trips. After the 10th you find love as you pursue your career goals. Strategic skills and courage are important in the career, but so is your social grace. You need both. Sometimes you wield the sword and sometimes you offer the rose. In love, from the 10th onwards, you look to those who can help you career-wise. You're attracted by power and position. There are romantic opportunities with bosses and with those above you in status. The danger here is getting involved in a relationship of convenience rather than true love.

The Sun leaves your 10th house on the 22nd although the career remains very powerful. The Sun in the 11th house promotes the social life, but not the romantic kind. It's more about friends and group activities. This has been an important interest all year and after the 22nd even more so. New friends are coming into the picture.

October

Best Days Overall: 5, 6, 13, 14, 22, 23, 24
Most Stressful Days Overall: 3, 4, 9, 10, 15, 16, 30, 31
Best Days for Love: 1, 7, 8, 9, 10, 17, 18, 20, 27, 28, 30, 31
Best Days for Money: 1, 5, 6, 10, 11, 13, 14, 20, 23, 24, 25, 26, 30
Best Days for Career: 3, 4, 11, 12, 20, 21, 30, 31

An eventful and happy month ahead. Health is improving day by day. By the 22nd, as Mars leaves his stressful aspect with you, the short-term planets will either be in harmony with you or leaving you alone. Your health planet is still in Virgo, your 10th house, until the 14th. Abdominal massage will remain powerful (there are reflexes there to the intestines – a more vulnerable area during this period). On the 14th Venus will move into Libra, your 11th house. Health is now enhanced through paying more attention to the kidneys and hips. Hip and buttock massage will be a good tonic this period. Your health planet in the 11th house makes you more experimental in health matters – more open to new and untried therapies.

Your 11th house of friends has been powerful all year, and it is the major headline of the month ahead. It is a social house but not gener-ally romantic. It deals with Platonic friendships – friendships of the mind, friendships of people with similar interests. Yet, because your love planet is here until the 17th, these shared interests can lead to romance as well. Singles should get more involved in groups and group activities. Friends can make romantic introductions. Someone you considered merely a friend can become more than that.

This power in the 11th house will bring you more scientific and astrological knowledge. I've seen many cases where people who had never been interested in astrology had their charts done when their 11th house became strong. It is a great period also for honing and expanding your knowledge of technology. It is good for buying high-tech equipment (your judgement will be good) and for online activities.

The other major headline – and it is important too – is Jupiter's move from the 11th house to the spiritual 12th house, which takes place on the 11th. The ruler of your Horoscope – Jupiter – has equal importance to the Sun and the Moon. He is one of the most important planets in your chart. This transit indicates a major shift for you personally. You enter a very spiritual period in your life which will go on well into next year. If you are not yet on some kind of spiritual path, you will enter one in the year ahead. If you are on a path you will see a lot of progress – a lot of growth and development.

On the 17th your love planet moves into your 12th house, and on the 23rd the Sun joins him. The month ahead is a spiritual kind of month, good for the study of sacred literature, spiritual practice, meditation and charitable activities. Get the spiritual life right and love, career and personal issues will fall into place.

November

Best Days Overall: 1, 2, 9, 10, 19, 20, 29, 30
Most Stressful Days Overall: 5, 6, 12, 13, 26, 27
Best Days for Love: 5, 6, 7, 9, 16, 17, 19, 20, 26, 27, 29, 30
Best Days for Money: 2, 7, 8, 10, 16, 17, 20, 21, 22, 26, 27, 30
Best Days for Career: 9, 12, 13, 19, 20, 29, 30

In September the planetary power shifted from the social West to the independent East. Day by day, personal power and independence is growing. This month (and next) the planetary power is moving in its maximum Eastern position with at least 70 per cent (and often 80 per cent) of the planets in the East. The planetary power moves towards you – it supports you and your personal goals. You have the power to create the conditions of your happiness. To have life your way and on your terms. Your love planet Mercury is also in the East (on the 6th it moves into your sign), thus others will support your actions. The cosmos wants you to be happy. Take the steps that are needed to achieve this.

Health and energy are good this month. If you would like to enhance the health further pay more attention to the kidneys and hips (until the 7th) and to the colon, bladder and sexual organs afterwards. Abdominal massage will also help the colon. Spiritual healing becomes a strong interest this month (from the 7th onwards). You respond well to it. In the unlikely event that you feel under the weather, see a spiritual healer.

Job seekers have a beautiful opportunity on the 12th and 13th. Likewise those who hire others.

Like last month, love can be found in spiritual settings, until the 6th. You will find it at the meditation seminar, the charity event or the prayer meeting – as you pursue your spiritual interests and perhaps with people involved in your spiritual life. Your career also benefits from your spiritual interests and practice.

On the 6th your love planet crosses your Ascendant and enters your 1st house. Love pursues you. You won't escape it. If you are in a relationship already, the beloved is doting on you – he or she is very devoted. You're having your way in love. You do seem to be meeting people who are outside your normal circle. Mercury is 'out of bounds' from the 11th onwards. Your career will also pull you outside your normal sphere.

Mercury's move into your sign brings happy career opportunities. It brings the favour of bosses, elders and authority figures in your life. They are devoted to you.

The Sun's move into your sign on the 22nd brings happy travel and educational opportunities, and you'll probably take them. Any excuse to travel – even the flimsiest – is enough to start you packing.

Children and children figures are having an active social life these days. They seem very popular.

December

Best Days Overall: 7, 8, 16, 17, 26, 27
Most Stressful Days Overall: 3, 4, 9, 10, 24, 25, 30, 31
Best Days for Love: 3, 4, 7, 8, 16, 17, 26, 27, 28, 30, 31
Best Days for Money: 5, 6, 8, 14, 15, 17, 18, 19, 20, 24, 25, 28
Best Days for Career: 7, 8, 9, 10, 16, 17, 26, 27

A happy and prosperous month ahead, Sagittarius. Enjoy!

When the Sun entered your 1st house last month (on the 22nd) you began one of your yearly personal pleasure periods. And, this continues until the 21st. You're living the good life now – travelling, enjoying sensual pleasures, eating good foods and drinking good wines. Health is good too and it shows in your personal appearance. Energy is more important in personal appearance than physical form. It is definitely more important than hosts of lotions and potions. A homely person looks beautiful if the cosmic energy is flowing properly. One forgets about the form and sees only the radiance. So, you're more magnetic and attractive this period. Yet, in spite of this, love is more complicated. The beloved is devoted to you to be sure, and singles are attracting happy romantic opportunities. It is Mercury's retrograde motion that is the issue. Your love planet moves backwards from the 3rd to the 23rd. Love seems to go backwards instead of forwards. There are delays and glitches in the love life. This passes by the 23rd; love will be much happier after that.

There is another factor that helps the personal appearance and the overall demeanour. Saturn is moving out of your sign on the 21st. He has been there for more than two years. While many of you lost weight and got your body in shape, it gave you a cold (and often forbidding) demeanour. Now you can be your natural sunny Sagittarius self, bubbly and full of fun. Saturn's move out of your sign will do much for the love life too. You should see big improvements (you'll see it more next year).

The month ahead will be prosperous too. Saturn's move into the money house (this coincides with the Sun's move there) will bring a more stable and conservative financial judgement. You're be less speculative and more rational about finances. You will take a long-term perspective on wealth. Also, the ego will be less involved and this will improve your judgement. From the 21st onwards you will be in a yearly financial peak.

The planetary power is now below the horizon of your chart. You have achieved your short-term career goals (and people see you as successful now) and it's time to focus more on the home, family and your emotional well-being. It's time now to build up the forces for your next career push in the coming year.

Capricorn

♑

THE GOAT

Birthdays from
21st December to
19th January

Personality Profile

CAPRICORN AT A GLANCE

Element – Earth

Ruling Planet – Saturn
  Career Planet – Venus
  Love Planet – Moon
  Money Planet – Uranus
  Planet of Communications – Neptune
  Planet of Health and Work – Mercury
  Planet of Home and Family Life – Mars
  Planet of Spirituality – Jupiter

Colours – black, indigo

Colours that promote love, romance and social harmony – puce, silver

Colour that promotes earning power – ultramarine blue

Gem – black onyx

Metal – lead

Scents – magnolia, pine, sweet pea, wintergreen

Quality – cardinal (= activity)

Qualities most needed for balance – warmth, spontaneity, a sense of fun

Strongest virtues – sense of duty, organization, perseverance, patience, ability to take the long-term view

Deepest needs – to manage, take charge and administrate

Characteristics to avoid – pessimism, depression, undue materialism and undue conservatism

Signs of greatest overall compatibility – Taurus, Virgo

Signs of greatest overall incompatibility – Aries, Cancer, Libra

Sign most helpful to career – Libra

Sign most helpful for emotional support – Aries

Sign most helpful financially – Aquarius

Sign best for marriage and/or partnerships – Cancer

Sign most helpful for creative projects – Taurus

Best Sign to have fun with – Taurus

Signs most helpful in spiritual matters – Virgo, Sagittarius

Best day of the week – Saturday

Understanding a Capricorn

The virtues of Capricorns are such that there will always be people for and against them. Many admire them, many dislike them. Why? It seems to be because of Capricorn's power urges. A well-developed Capricorn has his or her eyes set on the heights of power, prestige and authority. In the sign of Capricorn, ambition is not a fatal flaw, but rather the highest virtue.

Capricorns are not frightened by the resentment their authority may sometimes breed. In Capricorn's cool, calculated, organized mind all the dangers are already factored into the equation – the unpopularity, the animosity, the misunderstandings, even the outright slander – and a plan is always in place for dealing with these things in the most efficient way. To the Capricorn, situations that would terrify an ordinary mind are merely problems to be managed, bumps on the road to ever-growing power, effectiveness and prestige.

Some people attribute pessimism to the Capricorn sign, but this is a bit deceptive. It is true that Capricorns like to take into account the negative side of things. It is also true that they love to imagine the worst possible scenario in every undertaking. Other people might find such analyses depressing, but Capricorns only do these things so that they can formulate a way out – an escape route.

Capricorns will argue with success. They will show you that you are not doing as well as you think you are. Capricorns do this to themselves as well as to others. They do not mean to discourage you but rather to root out any impediments to your greater success. A Capricorn boss or supervisor feels that no matter how good the performance there is always room for improvement. This explains why Capricorn supervisors are difficult to handle and even infuriating at times. Their actions are, however, quite often effective – they can get their subordinates to improve and become better at their jobs.

Capricorn is a born manager and administrator. Leo is better at being king or queen, but Capricorn is better at being prime minister – the person actually wielding power.

Capricorn is interested in the virtues that last, in the things that will stand the test of time and trials of circumstance. Temporary fads and fashions mean little to a Capricorn – except as things to be used for profit or power. Capricorns apply this attitude to business, love, to their thinking and even to their philosophy and religion.

Finance

Capricorns generally attain wealth and they usually earn it. They are willing to work long and hard for what they want. They are quite amenable to foregoing a short-term gain in favour of long-term benefits. Financially, they come into their own later in life.

However, if Capricorns are to attain their financial goals they must shed some of their strong conservatism. Perhaps this is the least desirable trait of the Capricorn. They can resist anything new merely because it is new and untried. They are afraid of experimentation. Capricorns need to be willing to take a few risks. They should be more eager to market new products or explore different managerial techniques. Otherwise, progress will leave them behind. If necessary, Capricorns must be ready to change with the times, to discard old methods that no longer work.

Very often this experimentation will mean that Capricorns have to break with existing authority. They might even consider changing their present position or starting their own ventures. If so, they should be willing to accept all the risks and just get on with it. Only then will a Capricorn be on the road to highest financial gains.

Career and Public Image

A Capricorn's ambition and quest for power are evident. It is perhaps the most ambitious sign of the zodiac – and usually the most successful in a worldly sense. However, there are lessons Capricorns need to learn in order to fulfil their highest aspirations.

Intelligence, hard work, cool efficiency and organization will take them a certain distance, but will not carry them to the very top. Capricorns need to cultivate their social graces, to develop a social style, along with charm and an ability to get along with people. They need to bring beauty into their lives and to cultivate the right social contacts. They must learn to wield power gracefully, so that people love them for it – a very delicate art. They also need to learn how to bring people together in order to fulfil certain objectives. In short, Capricorns require some of the gifts – the social graces – of Libra to get to the top.

Once they have learned this, Capricorns will be successful in their careers. They are ambitious hard workers who are not afraid of putting in the required time and effort. Capricorns take their time in getting the job done – in order to do it well – and they like moving up the corporate ladder slowly but surely. Being so driven by success, Capricorns are generally liked by their bosses, who respect and trust them.

Love and Relationships

Like Scorpio and Pisces, Capricorn is a difficult sign to get to know. They are deep, introverted and like to keep their own counsel. Capricorns do not like to reveal their innermost thoughts. If you are in love with a Capricorn, be patient and take your time. Little by little you will get to understand him or her.

Capricorns have a deep romantic nature, but they do not show it straightaway. They are cool, matter of fact and not especially emotional. They will often show their love in practical ways.

It takes time for a Capricorn – male or female – to fall in love. They are not the love-at-first-sight kind. If a Capricorn is involved with a Leo or Aries, these Fire types will be totally mystified – to them the Capricorn will seem cold, unfeeling, unaffectionate and not very spontaneous. Of course none of this is true; it is just that Capricorn likes to take things slowly. They like to be sure of their ground before making any demonstrations of love or commitment.

Even in love affairs Capricorns are deliberate. They need more time to make decisions than is true of the other signs of the zodiac, but given this time they become just as passionate. Capricorns like a relationship to be structured, committed, well regulated, well defined, predictable and even routine. They prefer partners who are nurturers, and they in turn like to nurture their partners. This is their basic psychology. Whether such a relationship is good for them is another issue altogether. Capricorns have enough routine in their lives as it is. They might be better off in relationships that are a bit more stimulating, changeable and fluctuating.

Home and Domestic Life

The home of a Capricorn – as with a Virgo – is going to be tidy and well organized. Capricorns tend to manage their families in the same way they manage their businesses. Capricorns are often so career-driven that they find little time for the home and family. They should try to get more actively involved in their family and domestic life. Capricorns do, however, take their children very seriously and are very proud parents – particularly should their children grow up to become respected members of society.

Horoscope for 2017

Major Trends

Saturn's position in your spiritual 12th house for the past two years shows that you're bringing your natural organizational and management skills to the realm of spirituality. You will go far. On December 21 Saturn crosses your Ascendant and enters your 1st house – your own sign. He will be there through 2018 and 2019. The spiritual insights you've garnered will now be applied in physical and material ways.

Capricorn is always ambitious and career driven, and this year especially so. Jupiter entered your 10th career house in September 2016 and will be there for most of the year ahead (until October 10). This is a banner career year. You're ultra-successful. This is the main headline of the year ahead. More on this later.

On October 11 Jupiter will enter your 11th house of friends. New and significant friendships are being made. You're very involved with groups and professional organizations; it seems as if they are spiritual or charitable ones.

Pluto has been in your sign since 2008 and will be there for many more years. This shows the reinvention of your image and personality – a focus on personal transformation. You're giving birth to the person you want to be, your ideal self. This never happens overnight, but is a long-term process that will continue for many more years.

Neptune has been in your 3rd house of communication since 2012, raising and refining your intellectual processes – your taste in reading as well. You are able to communicate in a refined and elegant way. This too is a long-term process that will go on for many more years.

Uranus has been in your 4th house of home and family since 2011. This has created great turmoil in the family and most likely brought multiple moves or renovations. The whole family circle has been unstable. Happily this is almost over with. Next year Uranus will flirt with your 5th house, and in 2019 will enter there for the long haul. More on this later.

Your areas of greatest focus this year are the body and image (and this will become even stronger after December 21); communication and intellectual interests; home and family; career (until October 10); friends, groups, group and online activities (from October 11 onwards); and spirituality (until December 21).

Your paths of greatest fulfilment this year are religion, philosophy, higher education and foreign travel (until April 29); sex, personal transformation and reinvention (from April 29 onwards); career (until October 10); friends, groups, group activities and technology (from October 11 onwards).

Health

(Please note that this is an astrological perspective on health and not a medical one. In days of yore there was no difference, both of these perspectives were identical. But now there could be quite a difference. For a medical perspective, please consult your doctor or health practitioner.)

I would rate your health as 'adequate' this year. Not spectacular but not disastrous either. So-so. However, it is a vast improvement over the years 2011 to 2014. Then it was actually dangerous. If you got through that period with wellness, you'll get through the year ahead.

You have three long-term planets in stressful alignment with you. One of them (Jupiter) moves away on October 11 and the other will move away in the next few years. So a gradual improvement is happening.

Your empty 6th house is seen as a positive for health. You don't feel a need to overly focus here. Generally this is because nothing is wrong. As our regular readers know, there is much you can do to improve your health and prevent problems from developing. Give special attention to the following – the vulnerable areas of your chart (the reflex points are shown below):

- The heart. This has only become important in recent years. Capricorns tend to worry a lot. They like to look at worst-case scenarios. Avoid this as much as possible. This is said to be the root cause of heart problems. Relaxation exercises will be helpful.
- The spine, knees, teeth, bones, skin and overall skeletal alignment. These are always important for Capricorn. Regular back and knee massage should be part of your normal health regime. Regular visits to a chiropractor or osteopath are also beneficial. You want to make sure that the vertebrae and skeleton are in right alignment. Regular dental check-ups are important. Give the knees more support when exercising. There are massage chairs out on the market that give great back massages – this might be a good investment for you; over time it will pay for itself.

Important foot reflexology points for the year ahead

Try to massage all of the foot on a regular basis – the top of the foot as well as the bottom – but pay extra attention to the points highlighted on the chart. When you massage, be aware of 'sore spots' as these need special attention. It's also a good idea to massage the ankles and below them.

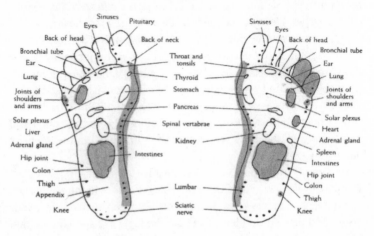

- The lungs, arms, shoulders and respiratory system. Again, these are always important for Capricorn. Mercury, the ruler of these areas, is your health planet. Arms and shoulders should be regularly massaged.

Mercury, your health planet, is a fast-moving planet. Only the Moon moves faster than him. Not only is he fast moving, but he's also nimble and erratic. Sometimes he moves quickly, sometimes slowly; sometimes he stands still, sometimes he moves backwards (four times this year). This gives him his reputation for 'flexibility'. Flexibility is something for you to cultivate from a health perspective. The body of Capricorn can become too rigid and calcified. It must be made more flexible. But this also shows that you respond well to many kinds of therapies, depending on where Mercury is at any given time. Your health needs tend to be fluid. These short-term trends are best dealt with in the monthly reports.

Home and Family

As we mentioned this has been a volatile and challenging area since 2011. Behind all this volatility is a spiritual agenda. Family can be both a womb and a tomb. It is a survival mechanism to be sure, but if carried too far it can be a tomb, stifling a person's independence and creativity. So, if the family relationship has become too 'tomb-like' Uranus comes in and explodes things. He brings more freedom into the family relationship – often in dramatic kinds of ways. So, there have been family break-ups (or near break-ups). All kinds of stresses are put on the family so that more freedom is given. Family members are subject to wild and extreme mood swings. You never know where you stand with them from moment to moment. Things can change in a trice. (And most likely they accuse you of this too.) Relations with siblings and sibling figures have been particularly stressful. This should improve after December 21.

The home itself is just a work in progress. It is never finished. It is constantly being renovated or upgraded. One can hear the banging of hammers and screech of saws as we study this chart. Every time you think you have things right, a new idea comes, and a new upgrade happens. Most likely there have been multiple moves since 2011. And it could happen again this year – suddenly and unexpectedly.

Capricorns are traditional people. Though it is not politically correct to admit this, they believe, deep down, in a hierarchical order and that they are 'born' to be in charge. But this kind of thinking doesn't sit right with family members these days. There is a need to make the family function like a team – a team of equals.

Uranus is your financial planet. His position in your 4th house gives many messages. You're spending a lot on the home and family. You seem unusually financially supportive of them. Most likely you're working more from home – making money from home. The family seem to be financially supportive of you too – especially a parent or parent figures. Family contacts and connections are important in your financial life.

This would also indicate a home office or home-based business. You've been installing a lot of technological gadgetry in the home, and will probably install more this year.

Renovations can happen at any time. But if you have free will, between January 28 and March 10 is a good time. If you're redecorating (this too could happen at any time), February 3 to April 4 and April 19 to June 6 would be good.

The parents or parent figures in your life have had troubling marriages these past few years. A divorce wouldn't be a surprise, but this year there is good social opportunity if they are single. Moves are not likely this year. Siblings are having a stable family year. A move is not likely, though there's nothing against it. The spouse, partner or current love most likely wants to move. Children and children figures are also having a stable family year.

Finance and Career

The year ahead is much more of a career year than a financial one. Your money house is basically empty (only short-term planets will move through there this year), while your 10th house of career is prominent. There is much career success – elevation, promotion at the job or company, status and prestige. There is more recognition this year too

- not just for your professional achievements, but for your charitable and philanthropic work.

Career success seems to entail some short-term financial sacrifices. Sometimes this means choosing status over earnings. It seems you're willing to make these sacrifices and it seems wise. Career elevation generally leads to greater earnings down the road.

Financial problems – if they happen – are likely to be the result of taking your eye off the ball – of lack of attention. You have to force yourself to pay more attention here. Also you might be over-giving to charities, or spending too much time on charitable or idealistic projects (generally non-paying ones) so that you feel some financial stress.

A Lunar Eclipse on August 7 occurs in the money house. Events will happen that will force you to make some financial 'course corrections'.

Finances should improve after October 11, as Jupiter moves away from his stressful aspect to Uranus.

Many of the financial trends that we've written about in previous years are still very much in effect. This is because your financial planet, Uranus, is very slow moving. He has been in Aries since 2011. Thus you're much more of a risk-taker than usual. You favour start-ups and new enterprises rather than long-established investments. Conservative by nature, these days you're quick to make important financial decisions and purchases. When the transits are favourable these things work out and you cover a lot of financial territory quickly. But when they were unkind, you've been burned.

Finance and financial attitudes will soon change. Uranus is getting ready to move out of Aries. He will be there this year, but next year will start to flirt with Taurus. The financial judgement is going to become more conservative again. Generally, Capricorn abhors the 'quick buck'. But these days – since 2011 – you've fallen under this allure a few times.

Three eclipses impact on the earnings of the spouse, partner or current love (and business partners). This is highly unusual. There will be two Solar Eclipses that affect them and one Lunar Eclipse. These bring much turmoil and change to their earnings. They have to make very dramatic changes – to thinking, planning and strategy.

You've been in a very spiritual period for two years now. Your spiritual planet, Jupiter, is in your career house. This transit gives a very strong message – you further your career through charitable and altruistic activities. Many of you will take management positions in non-profit corporations or in charitable foundations. These things attract you. In some cases Capricorn, you will actually opt for a spiritual career – ministry as an example – or will make the spiritual practice the actual career.

Love and Social Life

This is not an especially strong romantic year. Your 7th house of love is empty (only short-term planets will move through there). Love is not a strong focus this year. Of course, singles will date and go out, and there will be parties and gatherings. But nothing special. A stable romantic year. Those who are married will stay married and singles will most likely remain single. The empty 7th house shows that you have much freedom in this area. There is nothing opposing romance, but nothing that supports it either. You seem content with things as they are.

Your love planet, the Moon, is the fastest moving of all the planets. Where even the other fast-moving planets (the Sun, Mercury or Venus) take a year to go through all the sectors of the chart, the Moon does this every month! So love and love opportunities change every few days for you. It all depends on where the Moon is and the aspects she receives. These short-term trends are best covered in the monthly reports.

In general, your social magnetism will be stronger when the Moon is waxing (getting larger) than when she is waning (getting smaller). These periods begin at the New Moon and culminate at the Full Moon.

The social status quo we've discussed applies to those in or working on the first, second or fourth marriages. Those working on the third marriage have excellent opportunities from October 11 onwards. These opportunities happen in spiritual-type settings – at the spiritual lecture, prayer meeting or meditation seminar – or at charitable events.

Romance is stable this year, but the social life overall will be good – especially after October 10. (We have already mentioned this.) This is where you make new friends, strengthen old ones and get more involved in group kinds of activities. Many prefer these kinds of relationships to the romantic kind. There is total freedom and no commitment.

A parent or parent figure is having a strong social year. Very active. Very happy. If he or she is single, marriage can happen. Meetings happen at their place of worship, in foreign lands or at educational-type functions. Siblings and sibling figures in your life are having an active social life too – perhaps over-active. They seem successful here. Children or children figures are having a very active social year from October 11 onwards. If they are of appropriate age a serious love relationship is likely – perhaps even marriage. But whatever their age, they are making new friends. Grandchildren of appropriate age (if you have them) are having their marriages tested this year. This has been going on for a few years now. A Solar Eclipse on February 26 will further test the marriage.

Self-Improvement

Pluto, the planet of transformation has been in your own sign since 2008. The 1st house relates to the body and image. Saturn, the ruler of your Horoscope, has been in your 12th house of spirituality for two years now, and as the ruler of your Horoscope rules your body and image. So we have a very strong message here. There is spiritual transformation happening in your body. Many of you are involved in these kinds of projects – transforming and reinventing the body. Some of you have tried cosmetic surgery to effect this. (And many of you are still thinking about it.) Some of you have used diet as a means to do this. Some are using technology. All with so-so success.

The important thing to understand is that, spiritually speaking, it is within your power and ability to utterly and totally transform your body. Many of you know this and have received teaching on this. The skinny weakling can become a muscleman. The obese can become slim and trim. The old can regain youthfulness. You have the power to shape your body exactly as you see fit. The body doesn't have a will of its own. It has appetites, habits and momentums, to be sure – but no independent will. Sooner or later it *must* take on the image that you create. It has no choice in the matter.

Your job is to hold the appropriate image – your personal image of perfection. Also it is good to make positive affirmations – positive statements about the body – according to your desire. If you want, for example, a flat stomach, you would visualize it flat and you would make the appropriate affirmation – i.e. I have a flat stomach now. Repeat this daily and preferably a few times a day. When you start, there's no need to worry about how this will happen. This is not your business. It is the business of a Higher Intelligence which knows the body and its needs intimately. As you continue (and persistence is a very important element here), ways and means will come to you in interesting ways. Perhaps you will start exercising. Often the food cravings will change, normally and naturally. You won't feel that you're depriving yourself of anything. You will just crave different kinds of foods – foods more suitable to the image you want to manifest. If a certain therapy or supplement is needed, this too will come to you quite naturally.

Don't expect instant results overnight. This is a trap for many people. After a week or so, if nothing discernible happens, they give up and say 'it doesn't work'. The truth is, on a day-by-day basis, you won't notice much. But over time, the results will be dramatic indeed. It is much like watching a plant or tree grow. Day to day nothing seems to be happening. But many things are happening internally. Look at the plant in three weeks. Look at the tree in three months and you will see important change. Take your time. Let things happen gradually. Persist. Over time you will be amazed. After a year of persistent work, you won't even recognize the body.

A year is not a long time. If you consider that the present condition of the body took many, many years (and in some cases thousands of years) to be what it is. One year of spiritual work is nothing. It is actually miraculous.

Month-by-month Forecasts

January

Best Days Overall: 7, 8, 15, 16, 25, 26
Most Stressful Days Overall: 5, 6, 11, 12, 17, 18, 19
Best Days for Love: 2, 7, 8, 11, 12, 16, 20, 21, 27, 28, 31
Best Days for Money: 1, 5, 6, 10, 13, 14, 18, 19, 23, 24, 27, 28, 29
Best Days for Career: 2, 12, 17, 18, 19, 20, 21, 31

You're in an amazing career year in 2017, but right now, with most of the planets below the horizon, it is time to build up the forces for your next career push in the summer. This is a time for pursuing career objectives by the methods of night – by internal rather than external methods – through meditation, controlled day dreaming, and by putting yourself in the 'mood' of what you want to achieve. As you do this, you set the forces into motion that will make career success happen later on down the road.

Your career planet, Venus, has her solstice from the 29th to the 31st. This shows a pause in your career and then a change of direction. It is a pause that refreshes and is not anything to be alarmed about.

The month ahead is happy and prosperous. The planetary power is mostly in the independent East and is 'on your side' – supporting you and your goals. So, if there are changes to be made – changes that increase your personal happiness – now is the time to make them. You have the power, the will and the resources.

Health is good this month. You look healthy and feel healthy. Your good health does more for your looks than hosts of powders and cosmetics. You can enhance it further through back massage (until the 5th and after the 13th) and thigh massage (from the 5th to the 13th). The retrograde of your health planet Mercury until the 8th shows a need for caution in making drastic changes to the health regime.

Love is not a big issue this month. Your 7th house is empty (only the Moon moves through there on the 11th and 12th). In general you'll have more social magnetism (and more zest for social matters) from the 1st to the 12th and from the 28th onwards – as the Love Planet waxes. The Moon moving through your sign on the 25th and 26th will bring love and social opportunity to you. Though the love aspects on the 10th are lacklustre, it should be a good love day – the Moon will be at her perigee – her closest position to Earth.

February

Best Days Overall: 3, 4, 12, 13, 21, 22
Most Stressful Days Overall: 1, 2, 7, 8, 14, 15, 28
Best Days for Love: 5, 6, 7, 8, 9, 10, 14, 15, 19, 20, 26, 27, 28
Best Days for Money: 1, 2, 5, 6, 9, 10, 14, 15, 19, 20, 24, 25, 28
Best Days for Career: 9, 10, 14, 15, 19, 20, 28

The Sun moved into your money house on January 19 and is there until the 18th of the month ahead. You're in the midst of a yearly financial peak (one of them). This is a great month for attracting outside investors to your projects (if you have good ideas), for paying down debt, for tax and insurance planning. If you are of appropriate age it is good for estate planning too. The spouse, partner or current love seems financially supportive. Money can come from tax savings, refunds and insurance payments. Mercury will move into the money house on the 7th and stay there until the 25th. This shows you earning money from the health field (and spending on this too). Good sales and marketing are important in whatever you're doing.

We have two eclipses this month. These seem to affect the spouse, partner or current love more than you. But of course there will be some impact on you as well.

The Lunar Eclipse of the 11th occurs in your 8th house of regeneration. Thus the spouse, partner or current love will make important financial changes (and these will go on for the next six months). Financial course corrections are needed and the eclipse provides the impetus. Every Lunar Eclipse will test your love relationship and this one is no different. Old unresolved grievances can arise that need to be dealt with. Since there is a Lunar Eclipse twice a year (usually) you've dealt with this very often. Be more patient with the beloved. Allow the dirty laundry to be revealed and see what can be fixed. Good relationships survive these things. The 8th house connection can bring near-death experiences or encounters with death (rarely does it bring actual physical death, though sometimes it does). You're supposed to gain a deeper understanding of death and overcome your fears.

The Solar Eclipse of the 26th brings more of the same. The eclipsed planet, the Sun, rules your 8th house. So again the spouse, partner or current love has to make important financial changes. There can be more encounters with death. There can be upheavals with your insurance company and in tax issues. This eclipse occurs in your 3rd house of communication, and so cars and communications equipment will get tested – some of it will need repair or replacement. Siblings and sibling figures in your life have personal dramas. There are disruptions in your neighbourhood.

March

Best Days Overall: 2, 3, 11, 12, 21, 22, 30
Most Stressful Days Overall: 1, 6, 7, 13, 14, 28
Best Days for Love: 1, 6, 7, 9, 16, 18, 27, 28
Best Days for Money: 1, 5, 6, 10, 13, 14, 19, 20, 23, 24, 28
Best Days for Career: 1, 9, 13, 14, 18, 27

Your 3rd house became powerful on February 18 and remains strong until the 20th of this month. If you need a new car or updated communications equipment this is a good time to shop for these things. It is also a great month for learning and/or teaching others. Students below college level should do better in school. (The last eclipse, of February 26, brought changes in their educational plans.) It's a very good time to catch up on your reading and on those letters and emails that you need to write.

On the 20th the Sun enters your 4th house of home and family and you enter the midnight hour of your year. The focus should be on internal activities; on getting the home and family life in right order, on healing your past, your old traumas. Those of you involved in psychological therapy should make good progress now. On a deeper level, you're building the internal infrastructure – the psychological foundations – for future career success.

Health will need more attention from the 20th onwards. Many planets are in stressful alignment with you. The effect is often subtle. Things that you used to do with ease are suddenly more difficult. If you're used to doing ten push-ups, now you can only do five. Perhaps you climbed a flight of stairs with ease, now the same climb leaves you breathless and gasping. The usual energy is not there. The natural protection of a strong aura is weaker. So there is greater vulnerability to microbes and other opportunistic invaders. Health can be enhanced in the ways mentioned in the yearly reports. After the 20th pay more attention to the scalp, head and face. Scalp and face massage will be very beneficial for you (it not only strengthens the given area, but the entire body too). Physical exercise is also called for – gear it to your age and stage in life. Good muscle tone is important.

Though overall energy is not what it should be, the financial life sparkles after the 20th. We could call this another yearly financial peak. Your financial planet, Uranus, is receiving much positive stimulation and he is more powerful on your behalf.

Venus, your career planet, goes retrograde on the 4th. This is another reason why career should be de-emphasized now. During this retrograde (which lasts until April 15) don't make judgements about what's happening in the career. They will most likely be wrong. Things are not as they seem. Focus on the home, family and emotional wellness. Career issues will be clarified next month.

April

Best Days Overall: 7, 8, 17, 18, 26, 27
Most Stressful Days Overall: 3, 4, 10, 11, 24, 25, 30
Best Days for Love: 3, 4, 5, 6, 12, 13, 15, 16, 23, 26, 27, 30
Best Days for Money: 1, 5, 6, 10, 11, 15, 16, 19, 20, 21, 24, 25, 28, 29
Best Days for Career: 4, 10, 11, 12, 13, 23

A hectic, active month, with many changes going on. Perhaps you're too active. Health is still delicate, but improving after the 19th. In the meantime try to schedule in more rest periods. Your health planet Mercury is retrograde from the 9th onwards. Avoid making drastic changes to the health regime or diet until next month. If you must make changes (diet does seem an issue after the 20th) do your home-work. Enhance the health through neck and throat massage. Craniosacral therapy will also be good. After the 20th, as Mercury retrogrades back into Aries, give more attention to the head, face and scalp. Massage of these areas will be good. Physical exercise becomes important then too. Mars moves into your 6th house of health on the 21st and this reinforces the above.

Job seekers need to analyse offers more closely from the 9th onwards. Don't just accept an offer blindly. Resolve your doubts. Ask questions. There's no need to rush into anything, though you will be tempted to.

Yes, things are hectic, but you're prospering. Uranus, your financial planet, receives positive aspects this month. The 13th and 14th look like nice financial days – both for you, the spouse, partner or current love. There is good financial cooperation between you.

Your career planet, Venus, is still retrograde until the 15th. Jupiter, the occupant of your career house, is also retrograde at the moment, so career issues are more or less in a holding pattern now. Continue to give attention to the home, family and your physical and emotional well-being. Your career planet was in your 4th family house last month and she will be there for part of this month too – on the 1st and from the 28th onwards. Home and family is the real career. Being there for siblings and neighbours also seems important – especially from the 2nd to the 28th.

Love is not a major focus this month, which can be seen as a good thing. It shows satisfaction with the status quo. Your social magnetism will be strongest from the 1st to the 11th and from the 26th onwards. The New Moon of the 26th – a Super New Moon – seems an excellent love and social day. Libido seems very strong. A good financial day for the spouse, partner or current love.

May

Best Days Overall: 4, 5, 14, 15, 23, 24
Most Stressful Days Overall: 1, 7, 8, 21, 22, 27, 28
Best Days for Love: 1, 2, 3, 12, 13, 21, 22, 27, 28
Best Days for Money: 3, 7, 8, 13, 17, 18, 22, 25, 26, 30
Best Days for Career: 2, 3, 7, 8, 12, 13, 21, 22

The planetary power shifted on April 28 from the Eastern, independent sector to the Western, social sector. The planetary power moves away from you and towards others. The focus is now on others and their needs. Yield to others' will, especially if it is not destructive. Self-confidence and self-esteem are not at their best right now. And, your way might not be the best way. It is your ability to get on with others – to gain their cooperation and their grace – that brings success.

The planetary power is still mostly below the horizon – in the bottom half of your chart. Even your career planet will spend the entire month in your 4th house. The home and family is the career these days. This is your mission. Venus is now moving forward however, and career issues are becoming clearer. But you're still building the psychological foundations for your next career push – which will begin very soon.

Health is much improved this month. If there are any pre-existing conditions they seem in abeyance now. Mars in your 6th house shows the importance of physical exercise and scalp, face and head massage. This is important all month. After the 6th, neck and throat massage once again become powerful. A sense of joy will greatly enhance the health from the 6th onwards. If you feel under the weather, do fun kinds of things.

Mercury travels with Uranus, your financial planet, for an unusually long time – from the 1st to the 11th. This is a good financial period. It shows financial increase and good financial ideas. Perhaps you're spending more on health but you can earn from this as well. There is good communication with the money people in your life. Mars, your family planet, makes very nice aspects to Jupiter from the 10th to the 14th. This shows good family support, the prosperity of a parent or parent figure and luck in speculations (for this parent or parent figure).

On the 20th the Sun enters your 6th house of health and work, making it a house of power for the rest of the month. This is wonderful for job seekers. (Mercury, the work planet, moves forward on the 3rd, so there is more clarity here now as well.)

The overall social life becomes stronger from the 20th onwards. There is more involvement with groups and group activities. The spouse, partner or current love has good financial intuition. Financial guidance will come to him or her in dreams or through psychics, spiritual channels or spiritual types.

June

Best Days Overall: 1, 2, 10, 11, 12, 20, 21, 28, 29
Most Stressful Days Overall: 3, 4, 18, 19, 24, 25, 30
Best Days for Love: 3, 4, 10, 11, 13, 14, 20, 21, 24, 25, 28, 29
Best Days for Money: 3, 4, 9, 13, 14, 19, 22, 23, 27, 30
Best Days for Career: 3, 4, 10, 11, 20, 21, 28, 29, 30

Health is good until the 21st, but after that it becomes more delicate. It needs some watching. Your health planet will spend a good deal of the month 'out of bounds' – from the 18th onwards. This shows that you're going outside your normal sphere in the search for health and therapies. What's available doesn't suffice and you must look elsewhere. Mercury is also moving very quickly this month, so the health needs are changing rapidly. They are in a state of flux. Until the 6th enhance the health through neck and throat massage. From the 6th to the 21st, arm and shoulder massage is good. Fresh air will be beneficial this period. Get out in the fresh air and just breathe deeply. After the 21st, diet becomes an issue. It is important to maintain positive, constructive moods. Good family relations also seem important.

A parent or parent figure is also outside his or her usual boundaries this month. He or she is moving in 'unknown and unfamiliar territory'.

Love is the major headline in the month ahead. Up to now it hasn't been a major factor or focus, but this changes from the 4th onwards. On the 4th Mars moves into your 7th house. And on the 21st Mercury and the Sun enter. You are in a yearly love and social peak. If you are single you're meeting rich and successful kinds of people. They seem ambitious and worldly. If you're in a relationship, the spouse, partner or current love is prospering and receiving happy career opportunities. The New Moon of the 24th – another Super New Moon – presages a powerful love and social day (and a great financial day for the beloved). It will clarify love issues as the month progresses – until the next New Moon new month. Your social magnetism is especially strong from the 1st to the 9th and from the 24th onwards – as the love planet waxes.

The spouse, partner or current love is having a good financial month from the 21st onwards, as we have mentioned. But he or she also has a nice payday between the 2nd to the 5th. Venus travels with your financial planet from the 2nd to the 4th and brings financial increase and sudden career opportunity.

July

Best Days Overall: 8, 9, 17, 18, 23, 24
Most Stressful Days Overall: 1, 15, 16, 21, 22, 28, 29
Best Days for Love: 3, 4, 10, 13, 14, 19, 20, 21, 22, 23, 24, 28, 29
Best Days for Money: 1, 6, 10, 11, 16, 19, 20, 24, 28, 29
Best Days for Career: 1, 10, 19, 20, 28, 29

The planetary power is now in the upper half of your chart. Jupiter, in your 10th house started to move forward on June 9. It is time to make the career push. Time to take overt, physical actions to advance the career. The time for interior work is over. Dreams have to be implemented in physical ways. Next month, the career energy will be even stronger. Much success is happening.

Your career planet, Venus, will spend almost all month (from the 5th onwards) in your 6th house of health and work. You always have a good work ethic, but now even more so than usual. This good work ethic will advance the career. Good communication – good PR and advertising – will also advance the career. It goes without saying that without good health, there is no career. So this needs watching and you seem on the case. We could say that staying healthy is your real mission this month.

Love is the other major headline this month. You're still in the midst of a yearly love and social peak. Many of the love trends that we wrote of last month are still in effect. Family (and especially a parent or parent figure) seems very involved in your love life. (Sometimes they meddle too much, but they mean well.) The attraction is to money people and to the sexual magnetism.

The spouse, partner or current love is still having a great financial month – this gets even stronger after the 22nd, and he or she will be more generous with you.

In general your social magnetism is strongest from the 1st to the 9th and from the 23rd onwards – as the Moon, your love planet, waxes. The 21st seems especially good for love as the Moon is at perigee (her closest distance to Earth – she has more power that day). Full Moons are generally good for love but this Full Moon, which happens when the Moon is in apogee (furthest away from Earth) is not as strong as usual. These phenomena explain all the various nuances experienced in love.

Health, as we mentioned, needs watching, until the 22nd. The most important thing is to get enough rest. Enhance the health through eating right until the 6th. Detox regimes will be beneficial (and are probably what you need). From the 6th to the 16th give more attention to the heart (don't worry so much). After the 16th, abdominal massage will be good.

August

Best Days Overall: 4, 5, 13, 14, 22, 23, 31
Most Stressful Days Overall: 11, 12, 18, 24, 25
Best Days for Love: 1, 2, 3, 9, 10, 11, 12, 18, 19, 20, 21, 28, 29, 31
Best Days for Money: 2, 3, 6, 7, 8, 11, 12, 16, 20, 24, 25, 29, 30
Best Days for Career: 9, 10, 18, 19, 24, 25, 28, 29

Your 8th house of regeneration became powerful on July 22 and is even more powerful this month. A major focus. A Solar Eclipse on the 21st occurs in this house adding to its importance.

When the 8th house is strong we are concerned with death – not just physical death but the death of old conditions and circumstances. The cosmos urges us to get rid of the impediments to further progress and this takes many forms. Perhaps there is too much clutter in our life. The home is filled with things we don't need or use. This is so for the physical body and the emotional life too. There is a need to get rid of the substances or emotional patterns that are no longer necessary. Perhaps at one time they were needed – they are not necessarily bad – but now they are just 'clutter'.

We have two eclipses this month so it is a tumultuous kind of month. However, you don't seem overly affected, compared with other signs. Still it won't hurt to reduce your schedule over these periods.

The Lunar Eclipse of the 7th occurs in the money house. Thus you're forced to make important financial changes. (Finances are good this month, by the way, and most likely your strategy was too pessimistic.) Every Lunar Eclipse tests the love life and the current relationship – you went through this in February. Be more patient with the beloved and try not to make things worse than they need to be. The grievances and dramas that arise can be a stepping stone to an even better relationship. Business partnerships also get tested. Mars, your family planet is affected here. Thus there are shakeups at home; perhaps repairs are needed. A parent or parent figure has personal dramas. Emotions run high in the family.

The Solar Eclipse of the 21st occurs right on the cusp (border) of your 8th and 9th houses and impacts on both of them. Thus there are dramatic financial changes for the spouse, partner or current love – it's not just you. Business partnerships are also getting tested (financially). Because the 9th house is involved here, students at college level are making more changes to their educational plans – this also happened in February. There are more shakeups in your place of worship. Once again, as in February, there are encounters with death. This is not any sort of punishment (the planets never punish), only a kindly reminder to get on with the really important things of life – the reason you were born.

September

Best Days Overall: 1, 10, 18, 19, 28, 29
Most Stressful Days Overall: 7, 8, 14, 15, 20, 21
Best Days for Love: 1, 7, 8, 10, 14, 15, 16, 17, 19, 28, 30
Best Days for Money: 3, 4, 8, 12, 13, 17, 20, 21, 27, 30
Best Days for Career: 7, 8, 16, 17, 20, 21, 28

The planetary power is still mostly in the social West and Saturn, the ruler of your Horoscope, receives stressful aspects. Health is good, but self-esteem and self-confidence could be better. But no matter, self-confidence is not an important issue right now. It's the social graces that continue to be important. There is no need for undue self-asser-tion. Yield to the will of others so long as it isn't destructive. Your personal weakness allows for other strengths to come through.

Your 9th house became strong on August 22 and is even stronger in the month ahead. Thus it is a month for travel and for the expansion of your horizons. It is excellent for students as there is great focus on their studies – this tends to success. You've been in a spiritual period for two years now and this power in the 9th house emphasizes it. Your interest in the 'Higher Laws', in religion and philosophy, is much enhanced. Philosophy is more important than psychology. A person's philosophy will shape the psychology. This is a time to delve deeper into these things. Many of you will have religious or philosophical insights.

Health is good, as we mentioned – especially until the 22nd. Any doubts about it are resolved after the 5th as Mercury starts to move forward. (Travel is better after the 5th too.) Health can be improved even further through detox regimes, until the 10th. Good heart health is also important until the 10th. After the 10th, abdominal massage will be powerful. There are reflexes in the abdomen that help the small intestine, an area that needs work that period. After the 22nd, make sure to get enough rest, and eat foods that are easily digested.

Career is another major headline this month. Jupiter has been in your 10th house all year. The planetary power is in the upper half of your chart (moving towards the career and way from the home). On the 22nd the Sun enters your 10th house and you begin a yearly career peak. For many of you it will be a lifetime peak. (Much depends on your age.) The planets are supporting your outer ambitions. Have no fear – press forward and succeed.

Love is not a big issue this month. Your 7th house is basically empty – only the Moon moves through there on the 14th and 15th. Love goals basically have been achieved over the past few months and you have no need to focus greatly here. In general your social magnetism is stronger from the 1st to the 6th and from the 20th onwards – as the Moon waxes. Though the love aspects are lacklustre on the 13th it should be a good love day. The Moon is close to Earth, at her perigee.

October

Best Days Overall: 7, 8, 15, 16, 25, 26
Most Stressful Days Overall: 5, 6, 11, 12, 18, 19
Best Days for Love: 1, 7, 8, 9, 10, 11, 12, 17, 18, 19, 27, 28, 30
Best Days for Money: 1, 6, 10, 11, 14, 20, 23, 24, 27, 28, 29, 30
Best Days for Career: 7, 8, 17, 18, 19, 27, 28

Career is the main headline of the month. It is frenetic, active, competitive, but successful. Sixty per cent of the planets are either in your 10th house or moving through there this month. There is a cosmic conspiracy to make you successful – to elevate you. Nothing can stop it. Do the logical things that need to be done and allow the cosmic surge to carry you to your goals.

By the end of the month the career surge will start to abate. It will still be important, but not as much as in the early part of the month. This I read as the attainment of short-term goals and good progress towards your long-term goals.

Career is successful but you might not see the financial rewards right away. Give it time; it will happen (most likely next month). Uranus, your financial planet, is retrograde and receiving stressful aspects. Finances are more challenging than usual. Continue to focus on the career and the money will follow eventually.

Health is a bit stressed this month. You will see improvements after the 23rd, but it's stressful all month. Most likely you're overworking. Try to schedule some extra rest periods this month. Enhance the health by giving more attention to the hips and kidneys, until the 17th. Hip and buttock massage will be powerful. (This will not only strengthen the kidneys and hips but the lower back as well.) After the 17th detox regimes will be beneficial. A herbal colonic might be the ticket if you feel under the weather. Safe sex and sexual moderation are important.

Jupiter makes a major move out of your 10th house and into your 11th house on the 11th. He will be there well into next year – a long-term transit. This will activate your social life and bring new friends into the picture. You start to reap the rewards of success – entering a new social circle of friends. Children and children figures in your life will have an excellent social month and year ahead. If they are of appropriate age, marriage could happen.

The social life of the 11th house is different to the social life of the 7th house. The 7th house (which is basically empty this month) involves relationships of the heart – it is a more romantic kind of social life. The social life of the 11th house involves Platonic kinds of relationships – relationships of the mind and with people who share your interests. So friendships – non-committed kinds of relationships – are what's happening this month (and for the next year).

November

Best Days Overall: 3, 4, 12, 13, 21, 22
Most Stressful Days Overall: 1, 2, 7, 8, 14, 15, 29, 30
Best Days for Love: 6, 7, 8, 16, 17, 18, 26, 27, 28, 29
Best Days for Money: 2, 7, 8, 10, 16, 17, 20, 24, 25, 26, 27, 30
Best Days for Career: 6, 7, 14, 15, 16, 17, 26, 27

Your 11th house continues to be strong this month – until the 22nd. Aside from the new friends and social activities, it brings an enlargement of your understanding of technology, science, astrology and astronomy. Most likely you will be getting new high-tech equipment or gadgetry now. It is a good time to buy these things as your judgement will be good. Many people have their full Horoscopes done when the 11th house is powerful and many embark on a serious study of astrology.

Jupiter is your spiritual planet. His position in your 11th house shows that much of your spiritual studies are verified scientifically. Also it indicates a more scientific approach to your innate spirituality.

Finances are much improved this month. Uranus is still moving backwards, but the stressful aspects are mostly over with. Earnings might be slow or delayed, but they do happen.

Jupiter makes beautiful aspects with Neptune on the 29th and 30th – and you will probably feel the effects even earlier. This aspect can bring a new car or communication equipment to you. Also, it indicates earning from trading – buying or selling. Siblings and sibling figures have a good financial period and seem successful in their career.

Children and children figures of appropriate age seem involved in romance – and with someone rich, a money person. This person seems generous with them – especially on the 12th and 13th. The 12th and the 13th are excellent days for them to pay down debt.

Love is not a big issue this month. Your 7th house of love is basically empty – only the Moon moves through there on the 7th and 8th. In general your social magnetism is strongest from the 1st to the 4th and from the 18th onwards. The Full Moon of the 4th, a Super Full Moon, should be especially good socially and romantically. It occurs with the Moon close to perigee (her closest point to Earth).

Health is much improved this month, and will improve further next month too. You can enhance the health through paying more attention to the colon, bladder and sexual organs until the 6th and to the thighs and liver afterwards. Thigh massage will strengthen the liver (and also the lower back). Spiritual-healing techniques are powerful after the 6th and if you feel under the weather a spiritual-type healer might do the trick.

December

Best Days Overall: 1, 2, 9, 10, 18, 19, 20
Most Stressful Days Overall: 5, 6, 11, 12, 26, 27
Best Days for Love: 5, 6, 7, 8, 16, 17, 28
Best Days for Money: 5, 6, 8, 14, 15, 17, 18, 21, 22, 24, 25, 27
Best Days for Career: 7, 8, 11, 12, 16, 17, 28

The month ahead is very spiritual – a spiritual month in a two-year period that has been spiritual. This focus is soon to change. On the 21st Saturn, the ruler of your Horoscope (and a very important planet in your chart) moves out of your 12th house and into the 1st house – your own sign. The Sun will also cross your Ascendant and enter your 1st house on the 21st. So you've achieved your spiritual goals of the past two years. Whatever enlightenment was needed has happened. Now (from the 21st onwards) it's about putting it into practice – manifesting your understanding in the world and in your body.

Saturn's move into your sign is perhaps the major headline of the month. Saturn only changes signs every two to two and a half years. This move will strengthen you. You become more of a Capricorn than you already are. All your natural organizing and management skills get stronger than ever. The only pitfall now is that you might 'overdo' things – become too cold, too business-like, too aloof. This will put a damper on your love and social life for sure.

The month ahead is happy. The planetary power is now at its maximum Eastern position (and will be so during next month too). You're at the maximum of your personal power and independence. You can and should have your way in life. Your way is the best way. The planetary power supports you rather than others. So make the moves and changes needed to create your personal happiness.

Saturn in one's own sign is generally not a good health indicator, but for you it's OK. You're comfortable under Saturn's rays. Health will be good. You can enhance it further through more focus on the liver and thighs (like last month) and on spiritual-healing techniques.

Uranus, your financial planet, is still moving backwards, but receives beautiful aspects until the 21st. Prosperity is happening but perhaps more slowly and with more delays. This month is a shopping season and the retrograde of your financial planet could cause you to overspend. Study things more carefully.

Love is not a big issue this month. The Moon is the only planet that will move through your 7th house in December (on the 5th and 6th). This can be seen as a good thing – a contentment with the status quo. You have no need to overly focus here. In general your social magnetism will be strongest from the 1st to the 4th and from the 18th onwards. The Full Moon of the 4th – a Super Full Moon – should be an exceptionally strong love and social day – the Moon is at her perigee.

Aquarius

THE WATER-BEARER

Birthdays from
20th January to
18th February

Personality Profile

AQUARIUS AT A GLANCE

Element – Air

Ruling Planet – Uranus
  Career Planet – Pluto
  Love Planet – Sun
  Money Planet – Neptune
  Planet of Health and Work – Moon
  Planet of Home and Family Life – Venus
  Planet of Spirituality – Saturn

Colours – electric blue, grey, ultramarine blue

Colours that promote love, romance and social harmony – gold, orange

Colour that promotes earning power – aqua

Gems – black pearl, obsidian, opal, sapphire

Metal – lead

Scents – azalea, gardenia

Quality – fixed (= stability)

Qualities most needed for balance – warmth, feeling and emotion

Strongest virtues – great intellectual power, the ability to communicate and to form and understand abstract concepts, love for the new and avant-garde

Deepest needs – to know and to bring in the new

Characteristics to avoid – coldness, rebelliousness for its own sake, fixed ideas

Signs of greatest overall compatibility – Gemini, Libra

Signs of greatest overall incompatibility – Taurus, Leo, Scorpio

Sign most helpful to career – Scorpio

Sign most helpful for emotional support – Taurus

Sign most helpful financially – Pisces

Sign best for marriage and/or partnerships – Leo

Sign most helpful for creative projects – Gemini

Best Sign to have fun with – Gemini

Signs most helpful in spiritual matters – Libra, Capricorn

Best day of the week – Saturday

Understanding an Aquarius

In the Aquarius-born, intellectual faculties are perhaps the most highly developed of any sign in the zodiac. Aquarians are clear, scientific thinkers. They have the ability to think abstractly and to formulate laws, theories and clear concepts from masses of observed facts. Geminis might be very good at gathering information, but Aquarians take this a step further, excelling at interpreting the information gathered.

Practical people – men and women of the world – mistakenly consider abstract thinking as impractical. It is true that the realm of abstract thought takes us out of the physical world, but the discoveries made in this realm generally end up having tremendous practical consequences. All real scientific inventions and breakthroughs come from this abstract realm.

Aquarians, more so than most, are ideally suited to explore these abstract dimensions. Those who have explored these regions know that there is little feeling or emotion there. In fact, emotions are a hindrance to functioning in these dimensions; thus Aquarians seem – at times – cold and emotionless to others. It is not that Aquarians haven't got feelings and deep emotions, it is just that too much feeling clouds their ability to think and invent. The concept of 'too much feeling' cannot be tolerated or even understood by some of the other signs. Nevertheless, this Aquarian objectivity is ideal for science, communication and friendship.

Aquarians are very friendly people, but they do not make a big show about it. They do the right thing by their friends, even if sometimes they do it without passion or excitement.

Aquarians have a deep passion for clear thinking. Second in importance, but related, is their passion for breaking with the establishment and traditional authority. Aquarians delight in this, because for them rebellion is like a great game or challenge. Very often they will rebel strictly for the fun of rebelling, regardless of whether the authority they defy is right or wrong. Right or wrong has little to do with the rebellious actions of an Aquarian, because to a true Aquarian authority and power must be challenged as a matter of principle.

Where Capricorn or Taurus will err on the side of tradition and the status quo, an Aquarian will err on the side of the new. Without this virtue it is doubtful whether any progress would be made in the world. The conservative-minded would obstruct progress. Originality and invention imply an ability to break barriers; every new discovery represents the toppling of an impediment to thought. Aquarians are very interested in breaking barriers and making walls tumble – scientifically, socially and politically. Other zodiac signs, such as Capricorn, also have scientific talents. But Aquarians are particularly excellent in the social sciences and humanities.

Finance

In financial matters Aquarians tend to be idealistic and humanitarian – to the point of self-sacrifice. They are usually generous contributors to social and political causes. When they contribute it differs from when a Capricorn or Taurus contributes. A Capricorn or Taurus may expect some favour or return for a gift; an Aquarian contributes selflessly.

Aquarians tend to be as cool and rational about money as they are about most things in life. Money is something they need and they set about acquiring it scientifically. No need for fuss; they get on with it in the most rational and scientific ways available.

Money to the Aquarian is especially nice for what it can do, not for the status it may bring (as is the case for other signs). Aquarians are neither big spenders nor penny-pinchers and use their finances in practical ways, for example to facilitate progress for themselves, their families, or even for strangers.

However, if Aquarians want to reach their fullest financial potential they will have to explore their intuitive nature. If they follow only their financial theories – or what they believe to be theoretically correct – they may suffer some losses and disappointments. Instead, Aquarians should call on their intuition, which knows without thinking. For Aquarians, intuition is the short-cut to financial success.

Career and Public Image

Aquarians like to be perceived not only as the breakers of barriers but also as the transformers of society and the world. They long to be seen in this light and to play this role. They also look up to and respect other people in this position and even expect their superiors to act this way.

Aquarians prefer jobs that have a bit of idealism attached to them – careers with a philosophical basis. Aquarians need to be creative at work, to have access to new techniques and methods. They like to keep busy and enjoy getting down to business straightaway, without wasting any time. They are often the quickest workers and usually have suggestions for improvements that will benefit their employers. Aquarians are also very helpful with their co-workers and welcome responsibility, preferring this to having to take orders from others.

If Aquarians want to reach their highest career goals they have to develop more emotional sensitivity, depth of feeling and passion. They need to learn to narrow their focus on the essentials and concentrate more on the job in hand. Aquarians need 'a fire in the belly' – a consuming passion and desire – in order to rise to the very top. Once this passion exists they will succeed easily in whatever they attempt.

Love and Relationships

Aquarians are good at friendships, but a bit weak when it comes to love. Of course they fall in love, but their lovers always get the impression that they are more best friends than paramours.

Like Capricorns, they are cool customers. They are not prone to displays of passion or to outward demonstrations of their affections. In fact, they feel uncomfortable when their other half hugs and touches them too much. This does not mean that they do not love their partners. They do, only they show it in other ways. Curiously enough, in relationships they tend to attract the very things that they feel uncomfortable with. They seem to attract hot, passionate, romantic, demonstrative people. Perhaps they know instinctively that these people have qualities they lack and so seek them out. In any event, these relationships do seem to work, Aquarian coolness calming the more passionate partner while the fires of passion warm the cold-blooded Aquarius.

The qualities Aquarians need to develop in their love life are warmth, generosity, passion and fun. Aquarians love relationships of the mind. Here they excel. If the intellectual factor is missing in a relationship an Aquarian will soon become bored or feel unfulfilled.

Home and Domestic Life

In family and domestic matters Aquarians can have a tendency to be too non-conformist, changeable and unstable. They are as willing to break the barriers of family constraints as they are those of other areas of life.

Even so, Aquarians are very sociable people. They like to have a nice home where they can entertain family and friends. Their house is usually decorated in a modern style and full of state-of-the-art appliances and gadgets – an environment Aquarians find absolutely necessary.

If their home life is to be healthy and fulfilling Aquarians need to inject it with a quality of stability – yes, even some conservatism. They need at least one area of life to be enduring and steady; this area is usually their home and family life.

Venus, the generic planet of love, rules the Aquarian's 4th solar house of home and family, which means that when it comes to the family and child-rearing, theories, cool thinking and intellect are not always enough. Aquarians need to bring love into the equation in order to have a great domestic life.

Horoscope for 2017

Major Trends

Saturn has been in your 11th house for two years now (since Christmas 2014) and will be there in the year ahead. The social life is being reordered. You're becoming more selective about your friends and in your online activities. This is a good thing. Saturn is your spiritual planet, thus you're making spiritual-type friends and getting involved in spiritual groups and group activities.

Saturn will join Pluto in your 12th house of spirituality on December 21. This will make your 12th house the strongest, on a long-term basis, of any of the houses. Spirituality has been important for many years – Pluto has been in this house since 2008 – but come December 21 (and for the next two years) it becomes even more prominent. More on this later.

Pluto is your career planet. His position in your 12th house shows the need for an idealistic 'spiritually correct' career. Just being successful and making money is not enough for you. More details later.

Neptune has been in your money house since 2012. This is a good financial position. He is in his own sign and house and powerful on your behalf. You're going deeper into 'spiritual economics' these days. More on this later.

Jupiter moved into your 9th house in September 2016, and will be there until October 11. This is an excellent transit for college students; it show success in their studies. It is also wonderful for those applying to college. There will be good fortune – best-case scenarios. Non students will travel more in the year ahead.

On October 11, Jupiter will cross your Mid-heaven and enter your 10th house. This shows career success – elevation, promotion and perhaps honours and recognition. Most of the year ahead is simply preparation for this. More details later.

Your areas of greatest interest this year are finance; communication and intellectual interests; religion, philosophy, higher education and foreign travel (until October 10); career (from October 11 onwards); friends, groups, group and online activities; and spirituality.

Your paths of greatest fulfilment this year are sex, personal transformation and re-invention, and occult studies (until April 29); love, romance and social activities (from April 29 onwards); religion, philosophy, higher education and foreign travel (until October 10); and career (from October 11 onwards).

Health

(Please note that this is an astrological perspective on health and not a medical one. In days of yore there was no difference, both of these perspectives were identical. But now there could be quite a difference. For a medical perspective, please consult your doctor or health practitioner.)

Health looks good this year, Aquarius – enjoy! For most of the year there are no long-term planets in stressful aspect with you. On October 11, as Jupiter moves into Scorpio, he will be the only one long-term planet stressing you, and his stresses are mild.

Health is another form of wealth. With high energy there's almost nothing that can't be attained. All kinds of possibilities open up. Things that seem impossible when energy is low are eminently possible with high energy levels.

Your 6th house of health is basically empty this year. You're more or less taking good health for granted and not paying too much attention to it. Of course, there will be periods during the year when health and energy are less easy than usual. But these are temporary things caused by the transits of short-term planets. They are not trends for the year.

There's not much you need to do to enhance the health this year, but if you like you can give more attention to:

Important foot reflexology points for the year ahead

Try to massage all of the foot on a regular basis – the top of the foot as well as the bottom – but pay extra attention to the points highlighted on the chart. When you massage, be aware of 'sore spots' as these need special attention. It's also a good idea to massage the ankles and below them.

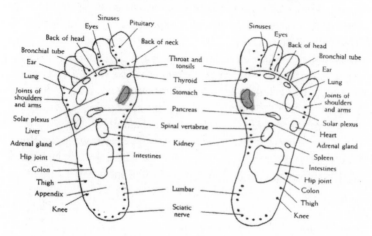

- The stomach. (For women, the breasts also need some more attention.) The stomach is always important for Aquarius. Your health planet, the Moon, rules the stomach. Eating right is always an important issue in health (not so for all people, but for you certainly). *What* you eat should be checked with a professional (although there is no consensus among them on diet). *How* you eat is perhaps just as important, however. Try to slow down when you eat. Chew the food well. Eat in a calm, relaxed state and enjoy what you're eating. Have nice soothing music – relaxing music – playing in the background. Give thanks for the meal. Say grace in your own words before and after eating. Bless the food (in your own words). These practices will elevate the energy vibrations of both the food and the body and digestive system. Food will be digested better and you will receive only the highest energies of the food.
- The ankles and calves. These are also always important for Aquarius. Ankle and calf massage should be part of your regular health regime. Give the ankles more support when exercising.

The most vulnerable health periods this year are from April 20 to May 20, July 23 to August 23 and October 23 to November 21. These won't bring anything serious, but it's be a good idea to rest and relax more.

Your health planet is the Moon. She is the fastest and most change-able of all the planets. Where the other fast-moving planets make a circuit of your chart in a year, the Moon will do so every month. Thus you benefit from a wide variety of therapies and have changing health needs – it all depends on where the Moon is at any given time. So a therapy that works well for two days, when the Moon is one sign, might not work that well when the Moon changes signs. This is why it is good to throw out all the rule books and see what works for you. Your intuition of the moment is very important for this reason. These short-term trends are best dealt with in the monthly reports.

Speaking generally, health and energy will be better when the Moon waxes (grows) than when she wanes (gets smaller). Detox regimes will work better when the Moon wanes than when she waxes.

Home and Family

Your 4th house of home and family hasn't been strong for some years now. And this is still the case for the year ahead. The cosmos grants great latitude in home and domestic issues – you can forge them as you desire. The only problem is lack of interest. This tends to the status quo.

You should enjoy this lull. Savour it. Boring is sometimes beautiful. Next year and in ensuing years there will be never-ending change and disruption in the family circle. Some of you – the more sensitive ones – are beginning to feel this already.

Venus is your family planet. She is, as our regular readers know, a fast-moving planet. During the course of a year she will move through all the signs and houses of your chart and will be subject to all kinds of aspects – some harmonious, some discordant. These short-term trends are best dealt with in the monthly reports.

Venus will make one of her rare (once in two years) retrogrades, from March 4 to April 15. This is not a time to make important home or family decisions or to buy expensive items for the home. (You might be tempted, but don't go with it.) This is a time for review. A time to see where improvements can be made. A time to gain clarity on the actual situation (which might not be as you think). When Venus moves forward you'll be in a position to forge ahead with confidence.

Both the parents, or parent figures in your life, are having spiritual kinds of years. Much internal growth is happening. One of them prospers from October 11 onwards. He or she might not move, but will be travelling more than usual. Another parent or parent figure will have an excellent social kind of year. If he or she is single, romance could happen. A move seems unlikely, though there are various kinds of family crises happening.

Siblings and sibling figures are restless and probably living in various places for extended periods, but a formal move is not likely.

Children and children figures are having a stable kind of family year. Grandchildren (if you have them) are likely to move after October 11. (Their personal rooms or living spaces can be expanded as well.)

If you're planning renovations or major repairs, March 10 to April 21 would be a good time. If you're redecorating and beautifying the home on a more cosmetic kind of level, April 19 to May 20 and June 6 to July 4 are good times.

Finance and Career

It's good that your money house is powerful these days. With Saturn stressing out your financial planet Neptune for the past two years, there's a need for a strong focus here. You can't just take earnings for granted. If you give the focus needed – and it seems that you will – the year ahead should be prosperous. Yes, you'll work harder to attain your goals, but they will happen.

There's a lot of good financial news this year. The year ahead should be more prosperous than last year. You will start to feel the 'shift' from April 29, as the Moon's South Node moves out of your money house. The South Node creates a feeling of 'deficiency' – lack. No matter how much one has, one still feels 'deficient'. The prosperity shift increases further from October 11 onwards, as Jupiter starts to make beautiful aspects to Neptune. Then, towards the end of the year, Saturn will move away from his stressful aspect. We get a sense of steady improvement as the year progresses. Prosperity happens well into 2018.

Saturn is your spiritual planet. Neptune is the generic spiritual planet. These two spiritual planets are in conflict with each other (this has been going on for two years now). Thus two spiritual attitudes – both good in themselves – are inhibiting earnings. One attitude is 'practical' – an idealistic kind of practical. One should be business-like in one's giving. One should be systematic about it. Orderly. The other is a more transcendental perspective, which counsels: 'never mind the rules of the earth, follow only the spirit. Sell all that you have and give it to the poor.' This kind of conflict often manifests through others. Two respected spiritual leaders in your life disagree about the role of money – and you're caught in the middle.

You've been charitable and philanthropic for some years now, and in the past few years even more so. Probably you're involved in 'sacrificial' giving and this seems to stress the finances. Giving should be 'proportional' to income.

Neptune as your financial planet shows an affinity for industries involving water – water utilities, water bottlers and purifying companies, the fishing industry, shipping and shipbuilders. It would also favour oil, natural gas, retirement homes, hospices and companies that make mood enhancers and anaesthetics. This has been the case for some years now and will be in effect for many more years. (Neptune is a very slow-moving planet – only Pluto is slower than him.)

A Solar Eclipse on February 26 occurs in your money house and will force dramatic changes. These will work out over the long haul, but can feel stressful while they're happening. (There's much insecurity about it.)

Career will also be super this year, as we mentioned. Jupiter crosses your Mid-heaven on October 11 and enters your 10th house. So, you are elevated in your profession or company. Pay rises and promotions are likely. Friends are also succeeding and they seem helpful – they open doors for you. Your technological expertise seems very important in the career.

Your career planet, Pluto, has been in your spiritual 12th house since 2008 – many years now. Thus whatever your outer career is, being involved in charitable activities will enhance the career. These things are good in their own right, but have practical consequences – you make important connections that you never would have made otherwise.

Love and Social Life

There's a lot of change and drama happening in love this year. The end result, though, should be happy.

The tumult is being caused by three eclipses, which affect the life and social life. That's a lot of eclipse energy! Every Solar Eclipse tests love, since the Sun, the eclipsed planet, is your love planet. But the Solar Eclipse of August 21 is unusually severe as it occurs in your 7th house of love. The other Solar Eclipse – on February 26 – will also test love, as well as finances. This year a Lunar Eclipse on February 11 also tests love. Generally such eclipses do not, but this one occurs in your 7th house.

If your current relationship is fundamentally sound, it should survive all this pounding. Repressed grievances will surface, and you and the beloved will make the necessary corrections. But if the relationship is lukewarm – so-so – it is in danger.

Eclipses in the 7th house are not always 'bad'. They show a change in the marital or relationship status. In some cases, the current relationship will improve – a change in status. In other cases singles decide to marry. The marriage might not happen right away, but the inner decision is made.

The North Node of the Moon will enter your 7th house of love on April 29. This is considered good. It shows fulfilment in love. Often it shows 'excess'. This can mean a hyperactive social life or, in the case of singles, 'excess' love opportunities. Excess can be problematic, but it's certainly better than deficiency.

Your love planet, the Sun, is a fast-moving planet. In any given year he will move through your entire Horoscope. Not only will he be in different sectors of your chart from month to month but he will make and receive all kinds of aspects in his travels. So, there are many short-term love trends, depending on where the Sun happens to be (and the kinds of aspects he receives). These are best discussed in the monthly reports.

Aquarians love friendships and group activities naturally. No one is better at this than you, Aquarius. This year, as we mentioned, you're being more selective about this. You tend to have many, many friends and acquaintances. Now (and this has been going on for some years) it's time to separate the wheat from the chaff – the true friends from the lukewarm ones. Better fewer friends, but good ones, than hosts of lukewarm ones. This is the feeling these days.

Saturn, your spiritual planet, is in your 11th house of friends. Thus you're making spiritual kinds of friends. You're more involved with spiritual and altruistic groups than secular ones. Spiritual compatibility is a big factor in friendship these days. You need friends who are supportive of your spiritual path and ideals.

Self-Improvement

Spirituality is all over the chart this year. No matter where we look, we see it. Your 12th house of spirituality is strong and will get even stronger by the end of the year. Jupiter, the generic planet of religion, spends most of the year in your 9th house – the house of religion. Neptune, the most spiritual of the planets, is in his own sign (enhancing his power and influence) and in your money house. Your spiritual planet, Saturn, spends almost all year in your house of friends. Spirituality dominates the career (Pluto, your career planet, is in your 12th house), finances (Neptune, the financial planet, in your money house) and a good part of your social life (Saturn in your 11th house of friends). All roads lead to Rome.

The basic message here is 'get the spiritual life in order and everything else will just fall into place'. Your spiritual understanding and inner guidance will lead you to success in all these outer areas.

The spiritual life and the spiritual guidance are going to be ultra-practical this year. It often seems like they are 'other worldly' and 'abstract' – but the consequences will be practical. You'll feel it in your career, finances and social life.

If you need financial or career guidance, psychics, tarot readers, astrologers, ministers and spiritual channels all have important knowledge to give you. And good ones should be consulted. Guidance will also come in dreams and flashes of intuition. You need to stay open to them.

Perhaps the most important revelation will be that the Divine cares about your worldly well-being – your finances, career and social life. Yes, even these seemingly trivial and unimportant things (from the grand perspective) are under its care. 'Not a leaf falls that your Heavenly Father doesn't know about it.'

Prayer will solve most problems. But meditation – prayer that is prolonged – will do even more for you. It will not only solve the problem but also clear the root issues that caused the problem in the first place. Regular daily meditation – perhaps half an hour to an hour a day – is a must. If you're having a crisis of some kind, you may need to increase your meditation periods.

With spirituality so prominent, this is a year for miracles and supernatural kinds of experiences. It's great fun.

Your spiritual planet spends most of the year in Sagittarius, the sign of religion. This would show an affinity for the mystical paths of your own native religion – whatever it is. Every religion has its mystical side.

There's no need to run off to foreign lands to gain spirituality. Go deeper into what you already have.

Month-by-month Forecasts

January

Best Days Overall: 1, 9, 10, 17, 18, 19, 27, 28
Most Stressful Days Overall: 7, 8, 13, 14, 20, 21
Best Days for Love: 2, 7, 8, 12, 13, 14, 16, 20, 21, 27, 28, 31
Best Days for Money: 1, 2, 3, 10, 11, 18, 19, 20, 28, 29, 30, 31
Best Days for Career: 7, 8, 15, 16, 20, 21, 25, 26

The Eastern, independent sector of your chart is overwhelmingly dominant as your year begins. From the 1st to the 6th and from the 21st onwards, 90 per cent of the planets are in the East, with 80 per cent in the East during the rest of the month. Not only that but you're in your period of maximum independence and personal power. Self-confidence and self-esteem is very strong right now. If you direct this properly almost anything is possible. For both this month and the next it's not about pleasing others (though we are always respectful of them). Others are pleasing you. You're learning now that the cosmos wants you to be happy and supports your legitimate self-interest. It is not selfish to pursue your own interest (so long as it's not destructive). You have the power and support to create your personal nirvana now – so you might as well.

Until the 19th you're in a spiritual period. Spiritual insights always precede personal ones. Things have to happen 'through you' before they can happen to you. The battles of life are won far from the actual battle field – they are won in the chambers of the heart and the closet of meditation. Everything else is pure side effect.

Until the 19th love happens in spiritual venues – at the yoga studio, at a spiritual lecture or seminar, at charity events and at prayer meetings. If you're looking elsewhere you're wasting your time. On the 19th, as the Sun, your love planet, crosses the Ascendant and enters your 1st house, love pursues you. There's no need to look for it or do anything special. You won't escape it. Those of you already in a relationship will find that the beloved dotes on you now. He or she puts your interest ahead of his or her own. Love is happy this month.

The year ahead is going to be a very strong career year. At the moment you're preparing for it. There is career success this month, but nothing compared to what will happen later on. You have the support of the spouse, partner or current love as well as friends. Charity events (of a social nature) will foster the career.

Finances are good too. Your money house is strong. There is good family support. Your communication skills are like money in the bank until the 28th. Continue to trust your financial intuition.

Health is good this month. There are no planets in stressful alignment with you. In general health and energy will be best when the Moon (your health planet) waxes – from the 1st to the 12th and the 28th onwards. The New and Full Moons are always high energy days for you. The 10th seems an especially high energy day as the Moon is at her closest to Earth, her perigee.

February

Best Days Overall: 5, 6, 14, 15, 24, 25
Most Stressful Days Overall: 3, 4, 9, 10, 16, 17, 18
Best Days for Love: 5, 6, 9, 10, 14, 15, 19, 20, 26, 27, 28
Best Days for Money: 5, 6, 7, 8, 14, 15, 16, 17, 24, 25, 26, 27
Best Days for Career: 3, 4, 12, 13, 16, 17, 18, 21, 22

When the Sun entered your sign on January 19 you began a yearly personal pleasure peak. Also a yearly love and social peak. (You will have others in the year ahead too.) So this is a period where you enjoy the sensual delights – good food and wine, good restaurants and nice clothing. It is also good for getting your body and image in right shape. The ruler of your 5th house of fun enters your 1st house on the 7th, which just reinforces the personal happiness. The physical appearance shines these days and the opposite sex takes notice.

We have two eclipses this month. The Lunar Eclipse of the 11th (in the Americas it's on the 10th) occurs in your 7th house of love. This eclipse affects you strongly, so take it easy over this period. It will test your current love relationship. It need not break it up, but it will put some stress on it. Dirty laundry surfaces for cleansing. If your relationship is a good one, these things can make it even better (let the dust settle first). Corrections can be made that will improve things. If the relationship is fundamentally flawed it can dissolve. Friendships of the heart also get tested – generally because of life-changing events that friends experience.

Every Lunar Eclipse causes shakeups at the job and the workplace. Generally job changes happen or there are changes in the conditions of work. There could be a health scare, but since your health is good, it won't be more than that. The spouse, partner or current love is going through some spiritual changes. He or she could change teachers or teachings.

The Solar Eclipse of the 26th brings more of the same. It tests the love life and the current relationship. Things you didn't resolve from the Lunar Eclipse get resolved now. (These effects often last for six months – until the next set of eclipses.) This eclipse occurs in your money house and forces course corrections in your finances. Your financial thinking and strategy wasn't right and the events of the eclipse will show you why. The changes you make (you're forced into it) will be good – and this is the purpose of the eclipse.

Health is still good. Self-esteem and confidence are still high. You can make the changes you need to make for your personal happiness. In general health and energy will be strongest from the 1st to the 11th and from the 26th onwards, as the Moon waxes.

March

Best Days Overall: 4, 5, 13, 14, 23, 24
Most Stressful Days Overall: 2, 3, 9, 10, 16, 17, 30
Best Days for Love: 1, 7, 9, 10, 16, 18, 27, 28
Best Days for Money: 5, 6, 7, 13, 14, 15, 16, 23, 24, 25, 26
Best Days for Career: 2, 3, 11, 12, 16, 17, 21, 22, 31

On February 18 you began a yearly financial peak, and this continues until the 20th. Earnings are strong. The spouse, partner or current love is financially supportive – very active in your finances. Partnerships and joint ventures are likely (especially on the 1st or 2nd). Investors will see increases in dividends or other investment income this month. Mercury in the money house until the 13th shows happy money, luck in speculations, and the financial favour of children or children figures. They seem helpful.

Love attitudes seem more 'materialistic' this month – especially until the 20th. Wealth is a turn-on. Singles gravitate to the good provider, the giver of material gifts. On the 20th, as your love planet moves into your 3rd house, you gravitate to the good communicators – the people with the gift of the gab. Good communication is a form of foreplay from the 13th onwards. Love seems happy this month. For singles love is in the neighbourhood, or perhaps with neighbours. There's no need to travel far and wide. Love is also in educational setting – at lectures, seminars or school.

Last month, on the 7th, the planetary power began to shift from top half of your Horoscope to the bottom. It is time to let go of career matters (although you won't ignore them altogether) and give more attention to the home and family. Finding and functioning from your emotional comfort zone is also very important. It's nice to be successful, but good emotional wellness will prepare the way and will set it on a good foundation.

You family planet, Venus, goes retrograde on the 4th. So family issues aren't what they seem. Take the time to gain clarity before acting. This would not be a good time to complete on a house purchase. There's no rush. Next month after the 15th will be much better.

Health is still good. There will be only one planet – Mars – in stressful alignment with you (from the 10th onwards); all the rest are either in harmony or leaving you alone. As always, health and energy will be strongest during the waxing Moon periods – from the 1st to the 12th and from the 28th onwards. The 3rd and 30th bring stressful aspects to you, but you have the energy to handle them – your health planet is very close to Earth.

Mars in your 4th house is wonderful for doing construction work or major house repairs. However with Venus going backwards, wait until next month to do this work. In the meantime you can get quotes and information.

April

Best Days Overall: 1, 10, 11, 19, 20, 21, 28, 29
Most Stressful Days Overall: 5, 6, 12, 13, 26, 27
Best Days for Love: 4, 5, 6, 12, 13, 15, 16, 23, 26, 27
Best Days for Money: 1, 3, 4, 10, 11, 12, 13, 19, 20, 21, 22, 23, 28, 29, 30
Best Days for Career: 7, 8, 12, 13, 17, 18, 26, 27

You're approaching the magical midnight hour of your year. By the 19th you will be in it. Career success is happening – almost as a side effect – but this isn't the main focus now. The focus is on the home, family and your emotional well-being. You need to feel right about things, to be in the right mood, to be in emotional harmony. Everything else will proceed from that. Serena Williams, the tennis champion, was interviewed after winning at Wimbledon. She said that the 'match is won or lost before one gets on the court – in the mind'. This is a deep spiritual truth. Attain your career goals in the mind and the feelings now, and the rest will happen naturally later. This is the psychological preparation month for future success.

Health needs more attention after the 19th. Nothing serious seems amiss – the long-term planets are either in harmony with you or leaving you alone. This is a short-term issue. Overall energy is not up to par. Make sure to get enough rest. Your most vulnerable period this month is from the 19th to the 26th. The Moon, your health planet, is waning and other short-term planets are in stressful alignment with you.

This is not a month – until the 15th anyway – for long-haul travel. The two planets that rule this in your chart – Venus (the actual ruler) and Jupiter (the generic ruler) are both retrograde. Travel will go better after the 15th than before that date.

This month you have a mini love and social peak. Your love planet, the Sun, travels with Uranus, the ruler of your Horoscope, until the 19th. For singles this brings romantic meetings. For those who are married or in a relationship there is more closeness – togetherness – with the beloved. Love is happy.

On the 19th the Sun moves into your 4th house and the love needs change once again. The gift of the gab is always important for an

Aquarian, but now you want more emotional intimacy. You gravitate to those with whom you feel emotionally comfortable, with whom you can share feelings – good or bad. Family values are important in a partner.

Sometimes with this position there is a tendency to recreate the past. One constantly compares the current relationship to previous ones. Thus you can lose the immediacy of the moment. Old love experiences from the past come up for resolution and healing. Often an old flame (or someone who reminds you of the old flame) will come into the picture. This may or may not lead to something, but the real reason is to heal the past.

May

Best Days Overall: 7, 8, 17, 18, 25, 26
Most Stressful Days Overall: 2, 3, 9, 10, 23, 24, 29, 30
Best Days for Love: 2, 3, 4, 5, 12, 13, 14, 15, 21, 22, 25, 26, 29, 30
Best Days for Money: 1, 7, 8, 9, 10, 17, 18, 19, 20, 25, 26, 27, 28
Best Days for Career: 4, 5, 9, 10, 14, 15, 23, 24

Love is still close to home this month. There is more socializing from home and with family members. Love opportunities can come through family members or family connections. This is a period (until the 20th) where a romantic evening at home is more enjoyable than a night out on the town. (This will change after the 20th.) From a therapeutic perspective, this is a good period to review your old love experiences and look at them from your present perspective. Much healing will happen and many psychological obstructions to love can be resolved.

On the 20th your love planet moves on into your 5th house of fun and creativity. The whole love attitude shifts. Now you want fun (you're entering a yearly personal pleasure peak anyway). The person who can show you a good time is the one you're attracted to. Love, you feel, should be fun. You're not interested in the responsibilities and burdens (perhaps abstractly, but not emotionally). Love becomes much happier and there is more harmony with the current love.

Mercury spends an unusually long time with Uranus this month, from the 1st to the 11th (he is beginning to move forward again and is travelling very slowly). This indicates a growing desire for more fun in your life (and this will flower after the 20th). It shows good fortune in your efforts of personal transformation. There is more sex appeal to the image. Sexual opportunities come and performance sizzles. Whatever your age or stage in life, libido will be stronger that period.

Mars makes beautiful aspects with Jupiter from the 10th to the 14th. This shows good fortune for students below college level. Writers sell their work. Sales and marketing people make fortunate sales.

Health improves greatly after the 20th. Positive feelings and sensations course through the body. You can enhance your health further in the ways mentioned in the yearly report. In general health and energy will be best from the 25th onwards. The New Moon of the 25th seems an especially good health day as it is very near the Moon's perigee – her closest point to Earth. This is a Super New Moon – a stronger than usual New Moon.

Though May is not a strong career month – home and family seem more important – career success is happening, but there are delays involved.

June

Best Days Overall: 3, 4, 13, 14, 22, 23, 30
Most Stressful Days Overall: 5, 6, 7, 20, 21, 26, 27
Best Days for Love: 3, 4, 10, 11, 13, 14, 20, 21, 24, 26, 27, 28, 29
Best Days for Money: 3, 4, 5, 6, 13, 14, 15, 16, 22, 23, 24, 25, 30
Best Days for Career: 1, 2, 5, 6, 7, 10, 11, 20, 21, 28, 29

You're still in the midst of one of your yearly personal pleasure peaks. A time to enjoy your life and especially your love relationships. This is a time to do fun things together. Since your love planet is in Gemini until the 21st, the gift of the gab is still part of the appeal. Love equals good communication and intellectual compatibility. Love opportunities happen at school functions, lectures or seminars – as well as at the usual places: clubs, resorts and places of entertainment.

On the 6th, as Venus moves into your 4th house, the planetary power shifts from the East to the West. This means that the planetary power is moving away from you and towards others. And, this is how you should be. It is time to let go of self and self-interest for a while (though there's nothing wrong with it) and focus on others. This is the cosmic energy right now. So, take a vacation from yourself for a while. Move with the universe. Cultivate the social graces. Yield to others' will so long as it isn't destructive. Your way is not the best way these days. For the next few months it will be more difficult to make changes in the conditions and circumstances of your life. Adapt to what is as best you can. The time will come, in four or five months when the planets shift again, when these changes will happen more easily.

Mercury spends a good part of the month 'out of bounds' – from the 18th onwards. This is how you are intellectually – taking in ideas outside the mainstream. Your love of fun also takes you outside your normal circles. Children and children figures go off exploring the wider world for a while.

We see this intellectual 'out-of-bounds' condition in another way too. Mars, your planet of communication and intellectual interests, spends almost all month 'out of bounds' – from the 1st to the 29th. The mind is not getting what it wants from the mainstream and needs to find it elsewhere.

Health is excellent this month. After the 6th only one planet is in stressful aspect with you – Venus – and she usually doesn't cause much trouble. On the 21st, your 6th house of health becomes prominent and there is great focus here. (Hopefully you won't focus too hard and create problems where there are none.) Mars in your 6th house suggests a need for more physical exercise.

Job seekers have a good month from the 21st onwards. There are many opportunities – many choices.

July

Best Days Overall: 1, 10, 11, 19, 20, 28, 29
Most Stressful Days Overall: 3, 4, 17, 18, 23, 24, 30, 31
Best Days for Love: 3, 4, 10, 13, 14, 19, 20, 23, 24, 28, 29
Best Days for Money: 1, 3, 4, 10, 11, 13, 14, 19, 20, 21, 22, 28, 29, 30, 31
Best Days for Career: 3, 4, 8, 9, 17, 18, 25, 26, 30, 31

The love attitudes and needs shifted again on June 21. Emotional intimacy is again important. You want someone you feel safe with to express your feelings. Love has to have some therapeutic value to it. You're attracted to health professionals and to people involved in your health. The person who can relieve your emotional stress or discomfort is the one that attracts you. Love is expressed through emotional support and through practical service to the beloved. This is how you show love; and this is how you feel loved.

On the 22nd there will be another shift in love as your love planet, the Sun, enters your 7th house of love. Love once again is about fun. The joy aspect is alluring. Love is also more romantic than usual. The romantic niceties seem important – the flowers, the walks on the beach, the whispering of sweet nothings in the ear.

You enter a yearly love and social peak on the 22nd. The social life is hyperactive. Four planets are in or moving through the 7th house this month. It is easily the strongest house and strongest interest. So, there are more parties and gatherings. More social invitations. More weddings to attend. Love seems very happy now. Singles have many romantic opportunities.

If you're in a relationship, the spouse, partner or current love is prospering this month. Next month will be even better.

Your personal finances are excellent until the 22nd. But your financial planet, Neptune, is retrograde at the moment and there can be delays involved here.

Health needs watching after the 20th. Drive more defensively during that period. There is nothing seriously wrong, but temporarily your overall energy is not up to scratch and this can create vulnerabilities.

So make sure to get more rest. Enhance the health in the ways mentioned in the yearly report.

This month and the next, the planetary energy is in its most Western position. It is far away from you. Self-esteem and self-confidence are not at their usual levels, but there is less need for self now. Self-assertion is not called for. Cultivate the social skills and put others first. Your own good will come to you through others.

August

Best Days Overall: 6, 7, 8, 16, 24, 25
Most Stressful Days Overall: 13, 14, 20, 21, 26, 27
Best Days for Love: 1, 2, 3, 9, 10, 11, 12, 18, 19, 20, 21, 28, 29, 31
Best Days for Money: 6, 7, 9, 10, 16, 18, 24, 25, 26, 27
Best Days for Career: 4, 5, 13, 14, 22, 23, 26, 27, 31

Retrograde activity is at its maximum for the year this month. From the 13th to the 25th half of the planets are moving backwards. Things are slowing down in the world and in your personal life. Uranus, the ruler of your Horoscope, is also retrograde – from the 3rd onwards. Things might be slow but not boring. Two eclipses this month, both of which affect you strongly, will liven things up. You need to take a more relaxed schedule anyway until the 22nd, but especially around the eclipse periods.

The Lunar Eclipse of the 7th occurs in your own sign. This impacts on your body and image. You're forced to re-evaluate yourself, to redefine yourself, to change how you think about yourself. This is always a good thing to do, but better when it is done voluntarily. Here you seem forced into it. Over the coming months you will present a new image, a new 'look' to the world. The wardrobe often changes, the hairstyle and colouring – things of this nature. Since the Moon is your health planet, there could be a health scare (it will probably be no more than that) and important changes to the health regime. If you haven't been careful in dietary matters, the eclipse can bring a detox of the body. Job changes can happen too. Since Mars is affected, students below college level make dramatic changes in their educational plans. Sometimes they change schools. There are dramas in the lives of siblings and sibling figures. Drive carefully this period.

The Solar Eclipse of the 21st is also strong in its effect on you – especially on those of you born between February 16 and February 18. It occurs on the cusp of your 7th and 8th houses and thus affects the affairs of both. So, the current relationship gets a testing. This looks like a serious testing. You go through these things twice every year, but this one is stronger than usual. Be patient with the beloved. He or she can be having personal dramas and this impacts on your relationship. This is, in many respects, a repeat of the February Solar Eclipse. The good news is that relationship issues will be clarified for the next 30 days – until the New Moon next month. The spouse, partner or current love is having financial dramas now and this could be part of the problem. Important changes have to be made. There can be encounters with death – close calls and exposures to it, either through events or dreams. This is supposed to help you come to terms with death and lose your fear of it.

Sensitive people often feel the onset of an eclipse weeks before they happen. All of you will get your 'personal announcement' of when you're in the eclipse period. Something strange will happen, or you'll hear of some strange kind of event. This is the cosmos telling you to start taking it easy.

September

Best Days Overall: 3, 4, 12, 13, 20, 21, 30
Most Stressful Days Overall: 10, 16, 17, 23, 24
Best Days for Love: 1, 7, 8, 10, 16, 17, 19, 28, 30
Best Days for Money: 3, 4, 5, 6, 12, 13, 14, 15, 20, 21, 23, 24, 30
Best Days for Career: 1, 10, 18, 19, 23, 24, 28, 29

Aside from the two strong eclipses last month, there was a planetary shift from the lower half to the upper half of the Horoscope. Venus crossed over on August 26 and the upper half of your chart is now dominant. The planetary power is moving away from the 'internal' side of your life to the external. Your outer affairs – your career – are becoming important. This is a time for taking overt, physical steps to further the career. Emotional well-being will come from achieving your outer goals.

Your 7th house of love is still strong this month, but its power is winding down. Short-term social goals have been achieved and you don't need to focus too much here. Venus in your 7th house is a classic romance indicator. It shows that the family is very involved in the social life and that there are more family gatherings to attend. Mars leaves the 7th house on the 5th, which is good. Mars often creates social strife and power struggles. The Sun, your love planet, is in your 8th house until the 22nd. This shows that sexual magnetism is the prime romantic attraction (this will change later in the month). It shows an allurement for money people (and the current love interest seems to prosper now). Your personal finances are stressful this month – especially until the 22nd. Neptune is still retrograde and is receiving stressful aspects. You and the partner don't seem in financial agreement. There are financial conflicts with siblings and sibling figures too. Earnings will happen but you'll have to work a lot harder for them.

On the 22nd your love planet moves into your 9th house and the sign of Libra. This shows an attraction for foreigners and highly educated or religious-type people. It is a more romantic kind of energy, not just sexual. The only problem is that you and the beloved are distant with each other. You're seeing things in opposite ways. Distance doesn't always mean physical distance, it often means 'psychological distance'. Your challenge now will be to bridge your differences. It's hard work but it can be done.

Health and energy are improving day by day. By the 20th there will be no planets in stressful aspect with you and you will feel revitalized.

The 8th house, which has been powerful since August 22, is all about 'removing things from your life' that don't belong there. It's not about adding things. That will happen later. It might be a good idea to read Marie Kondo's *The Life-Changing Magic of Tidying Up*. It's a very 8th-house kind of book. These projects go well now.

October

Best Days Overall: 1, 9, 10, 18, 19, 27, 28, 29
Most Stressful Days Overall: 1, 7, 8, 13, 14, 20, 21
Best Days for Love: 1, 7, 8, 9, 10, 13, 14, 17, 18, 19, 27, 28, 30
Best Days for Money: 1, 3, 4, 10, 11, 12, 20, 21, 30, 31
Best Days for Career: 7, 8, 15, 16, 20, 21, 25, 26

An eventful, but ultimately successful kind of month – very hectic, Aquarius. Early in the month there's a lot of upheaval and stress in the career. Perhaps there is a change of management at your company, or changes in the rules. A parent or parent figure seems stressed out. But all these seeming disturbances are preparing the way for your good. Don't judge things by what happens early in the month. Career is ultra-successful.

On the 11th Jupiter crosses the Mid-heaven and enters your 10th house of career – a classic signal of expansion and good fortune. On the 23rd the Sun will enter the 10th house and you begin a yearly career peak. For many (it depends on your age) this is a lifetime career peak. For older Aquarians, it will be one of your lifetime peaks. This will continue well into next year.

You have friends in high places opening doors for you. Your high-tech expertise (and Aquarius is naturally good at this) is an important factor. Your ability to network – your natural Aquarian gift – is another important factor. The spouse, partner or current love is also successful and supportive of your career goals. You're mingling with the high and mighty socially after the 23rd.

The other important headline this month is the power in your 9th house. This is easily the strongest house in the Horoscope this month and this is a happy and expansive kind of period. There is travel, optimism and the expansion of horizons. It is especially good for college or postgraduate students; they have success in their studies. Your understanding of religion, philosophy and metaphysics is greatly expanded. Even non-students will have happy educational opportunities.

When the 9th house is strong, it's the juicy theological or philosophical event or discussion that appeals – more so than a night out on the town. And whereas the 8th house is about 'getting rid' of things, the 9th house is about acquiring things. In this case, it indicates more friends, perhaps more furniture, and more high-tech equipment.

Love happens in religious or educational settings, at events in your place of worship or university. There are romantic opportunities in foreign lands and with foreigners too. The 26th and 27th seem especially good love days.

Health needs more attention after the 23rd. Career success has a price. You expend more energy on it.

November

Best Days Overall: 5, 6, 14, 15, 24, 25
Most Stressful Days Overall: 3, 4, 9, 10, 16, 17
Best Days for Love: 6, 7, 8, 9, 10, 16, 17, 18, 26, 27, 28, 29
Best Days for Money: 7, 8, 16, 17, 26, 27
Best Days for Career: 3, 4, 12, 13, 16, 17, 21, 22

Finance and career are the main headlines this month. Both areas are going well. You're still in the midst of a yearly career peak, until the 22nd. You have a lot of support here; in particular, there is much family support after the 7th. And the family as a whole seems more successful. Your career is almost like a 'family project'. The beloved, and social contacts in general, are supporting the career. You have friends in high places and this is a big help.

Jupiter's move into Scorpio last month presages a prosperous year ahead. Neptune, your financial planet, is receiving beautiful aspects (especially on the 29th and 30th). Best of all Neptune will start to move forward on the 22nd after many months of retrograde motion. Financial clarity is happening. The financial life will start moving forward again. Career success is producing financial success.

When the Sun moves into Sagittarius on the 22nd, there can be some financial stress, but this is a short-term problem. The overall prognosis is prosperity.

On the 7th the planetary power begins to shift to the independent East of your chart. The planets are now moving towards you – supporting you and energizing you. Other people are always important but you're not so dependent on them as you have been. Your personal initiative and skills matter now. Day by day personal power and independence grow stronger. This is a time to start making the changes in your life that need to be made. Take responsibility for your happiness.

Health still needs watching until the 22nd. As always, when planetary stress is high, make sure to get enough rest. Keep the energy levels high. Maintain a strong aura. Enhance the health in the ways mentioned in the yearly report.

Much of your socializing (until the 22nd) seems career-related, and this is good. Socializing helps the career. Like last month there is an attraction to power and authority. For singles this shows romantic opportunities with bosses or other authority figures. After the 22nd, love will be happier. It's more about friendship. Your lover is also your best friend. Romantic opportunities come as you get involved in groups and group activities. The online world and online activities can lead to romance. Friends can play Cupid.

December

    Best Days Overall: 3, 4, 11, 12, 21, 22, 30, 31
    Most Stressful Days Overall: 1, 2, 7, 8, 14, 15, 28, 29
    Best Days for Love: 7, 8, 16, 17, 28
    Best Days for Money: 5, 6, 14, 15, 24, 25
    Best Days for Career: 1, 2, 9, 10, 14, 15, 19, 20, 28, 29

Another eventful month. In October, Jupiter made a major move. This month, Saturn makes a major move that will have important consequences. He leaves your 11th house and enters your spiritual 12th house on the 21st. There he will stay for two to two and a half years. Thus for the next two and a half years or so, two long-term planets will be in your 12th house. This emphasizes the spiritual life and spiritual activities. These things are not seen by the public but are very real. It is a period of inner growth. You will need to balance your spiritual ideals and practice with a successful outer life – a successful career. This can be a challenge as the values of the world are very different from spiritual values. You will have to marry these two areas of life.

Every person finds their own solution to this. There are no hard and fast rules.

Saturn's move out of Sagittarius and into Capricorn will enhance the financial life. He has been making a stressful aspect with your financial planet Neptune for more than two years. Earnings are still challenging until the 21st, but there will be a big improvement afterwards. Overall, you're in a prosperity period. You're working a bit harder this month, but prosperity is happening.

The love life is happy this month. Your love planet is in the 11th house until the 21st. This, like last month, shows romantic opportunities as you involve yourself in groups and group activities. Power and status are less important now. Your lover has to be a friend - a peer - as well as a lover. You're always an experimental kind of person, and this month, even more so - especially when it comes to love. Experimental - outside the norm - relationships are appealing. You seem to be enjoying this as love seems happy this month. Someone you considered only a friend can become more than that.

On the 21st the Sun moves on into your spiritual 12th house and the love needs change once again. Spiritual compatibility - spiritual intimacy - becomes important. You have to be able to share your spiritual ideals and yearnings with the beloved, and vice versa. Love opportunities happen in spiritual settings - at a spiritual lecture, meditation seminar or at a charity event. Altruism is a romantic turn-on. The love planet will travel with Saturn from the 20th to the 23rd and this is likely to bring this kind of person into the picture.

Career is successful this month and seems very hectic. Mars will move into your 10th house on the 9th and will stay there for the rest of the month. You need to be aggressive and fearless in your career. You are fighting off competitors. Martial skills are as important as your professional skills.

Health is good.

Pisces

THE FISH

Birthdays from
19th February to
20th March

Personality Profile

PISCES AT A GLANCE

Element – Water

Ruling Planet – Neptune
  Career Planet – Jupiter
  Love Planet – Mercury
  Money Planet – Mars
  Planet of Health and Work – Sun
  Planet of Home and Family Life – Mercury
  Planet of Love Affairs, Creativity and Children – Moon

Colours – aqua, blue-green

Colours that promote love, romance and social harmony – earth tones,
  yellow, yellow-orange

Colours that promote earning power – red, scarlet

Gem – white diamond

Metal – tin

Scent – lotus

Quality – mutable (= flexibility)

Qualities most needed for balance – structure and the ability to handle form

Strongest virtues – psychic power, sensitivity, self-sacrifice, altruism

Deepest needs – spiritual illumination, liberation

Characteristics to avoid – escapism, keeping bad company, negative moods

Signs of greatest overall compatibility – Cancer, Scorpio

Signs of greatest overall incompatibility – Gemini, Virgo, Sagittarius

Sign most helpful to career – Sagittarius

Sign most helpful for emotional support – Gemini

Sign most helpful financially – Aries

Sign best for marriage and/or partnerships – Virgo

Sign most helpful for creative projects – Cancer

Best Sign to have fun with – Cancer

Signs most helpful in spiritual matters – Scorpio, Aquarius

Best day of the week – Thursday

Understanding a Pisces

If Pisces have one outstanding quality it is their belief in the invisible, spiritual and psychic side of things. This side of things is as real to them as the hard earth beneath their feet – so real, in fact, that they will often ignore the visible, tangible aspects of reality in order to focus on the invisible and so-called intangible ones.

Of all the signs of the zodiac, the intuitive and emotional faculties of the Pisces are the most highly developed. They are committed to living by their intuition and this can at times be infuriating to other people – especially those who are materially, scientifically or technically orientated. If you think that money, status and worldly success are the only goals in life, then you will never understand a Pisces.

Pisces have intellect, but to them intellect is only a means by which they can rationalize what they know intuitively. To an Aquarius or a Gemini the intellect is a tool with which to gain knowledge. To a well-developed Pisces it is a tool by which to express knowledge.

Pisces feel like fish in an infinite ocean of thought and feeling. This ocean has many depths, currents and undercurrents. They long for purer waters where the denizens are good, true and beautiful, but they are sometimes pulled to the lower, murkier depths. Pisces know that they do not generate thoughts but only tune in to thoughts that already exist; this is why they seek the purer waters. This ability to tune in to higher thoughts inspires them artistically and musically.

Since Pisces is so spiritually orientated – though many Pisces in the corporate world may hide this fact – we will deal with this aspect in greater detail, for otherwise it is difficult to understand the true Pisces personality.

There are four basic attitudes of the spirit. One is outright scepticism – the attitude of secular humanists. The second is an intellectual or emotional belief, where one worships a far-distant God-figure – the attitude of most modern church-going people. The third is not only belief but direct personal spiritual experience – this is the attitude of some 'born-again' religious people. The fourth is actual unity with the divinity, an intermingling with the spiritual world – this is the attitude of yoga. This fourth attitude is the deepest urge of a

Pisces, and a Pisces is uniquely qualified to pursue and perform this work.

Consciously or unconsciously, Pisces seek this union with the spiritual world. The belief in a greater reality makes Pisces very tolerant and understanding of others – perhaps even too tolerant. There are instances in their lives when they should say 'enough is enough' and be ready to defend their position and put up a fight. However, because of their qualities it takes a good deal to get them into that frame of mind.

Pisces basically want and aspire to be 'saints'. They do so in their own way and according to their own rules. Others should not try to impose their concept of saintliness on a Pisces, because he or she always tries to find it for him- or herself.

Finance

Money is generally not that important to Pisces. Of course they need it as much as anyone else, and many of them attain great wealth. But money is not generally a primary objective. Doing good, feeling good about oneself, peace of mind, the relief of pain and suffering – these are the things that matter most to a Pisces.

Pisces earn money intuitively and instinctively. They follow their hunches rather than their logic. They tend to be generous and perhaps overly charitable. Almost any kind of misfortune is enough to move a Pisces to give. Although this is one of their greatest virtues, Pisces should be more careful with their finances. They should try to be more choosy about the people to whom they lend money, so that they are not being taken advantage of. If they give money to charities they should follow it up to see that their contributions are put to good use. Even when Pisces are not rich, they still like to spend money on helping others. In this case they should really be careful, however: they must learn to say no sometimes and help themselves first.

Perhaps the biggest financial stumbling block for the Pisces is general passivity – a *laissez faire* attitude. In general Pisces like to go with the flow of events. When it comes to financial matters, especially, they need to be more aggressive. They need to make things happen, to create their own wealth. A passive attitude will only cause loss and missed opportunity. Worrying about financial security will not provide that security. Pisces need to go after what they want tenaciously.

Career and Public Image

Pisces like to be perceived by the public as people of spiritual or material wealth, of generosity and philanthropy. They look up to big-hearted, philanthropic types. They admire people engaged in large-scale undertakings and eventually would like to head up these big enterprises themselves. In short, they like to be connected with big organizations that are doing things in a big way.

If Pisces are to realize their full career and professional potential they need to travel more, educate themselves more and learn more about the actual world. In other words, they need some of the unflagging optimism of Sagittarius in order to reach the top.

Because of all their caring and generous characteristics, Pisces often choose professions through which they can help and touch the lives of other people. That is why many Pisces become doctors, nurses, social workers or teachers. Sometimes it takes a while before Pisces realize what they really want to do in their professional lives, but once they find a career that lets them manifest their interests and virtues they will excel at it.

Love and Relationships

It is not surprising that someone as 'otherworldly' as the Pisces would like a partner who is practical and down to earth. Pisces prefer a partner who is on top of all the details of life, because they dislike details. Pisces seek this quality in both their romantic and professional partners. More than anything else this gives Pisces a feeling of being grounded, of being in touch with reality.

As expected, these kinds of relationships – though necessary – are sure to have many ups and downs. Misunderstandings will take place because the two attitudes are poles apart. If you are in love with a Pisces you will experience these fluctuations and will need a lot of patience to see things stabilize. Pisces are moody, intuitive, affectionate and difficult to get to know. Only time and the right attitude will yield Pisces' deepest secrets. However, when in love with a Pisces you will find that riding the waves is worth it because they are good, sensitive people who need and like to give love and affection.

When in love, Pisces like to fantasize. For them fantasy is 90 per cent of the fun of a relationship. They tend to idealize their partner, which can be good and bad at the same time. It is bad in that it is difficult for anyone to live up to the high ideals their Pisces lover sets.

Home and Domestic Life

In their family and domestic life Pisces have to resist the tendency to relate only by feelings and moods. It is unrealistic to expect that your partner and other family members will be as intuitive as you are. There is a need for more verbal communication between a Pisces and his or her family. A cool, unemotional exchange of ideas and opinions will benefit everyone.

Some Pisces tend to like mobility and moving around. For them too much stability feels like a restriction on their freedom. They hate to be locked in one location for ever.

The sign of Gemini sits on the cusp of Pisces' 4th solar house of home and family. This shows that Pisces likes and needs a home environment that promotes intellectual and mental interests. They tend to treat their neighbours as family – or extended family. Some Pisceans can have a dual attitude towards the home and family – on the one hand they like the emotional support of the family, but on the other they dislike the obligations, restrictions and duties involved with it. For Pisces, finding a balance is the key to a happy family life.

Horoscope for 2017

Major Trends

Psychics and spiritual channels have been talking about a 'shift' – a spiritual influx – happening on the planet for some years now. Astrologically speaking this corresponded to Neptune's move into your own sign in 2012. Everyone is feeling this 'shift' but no one more than you, Pisces. Your body is becoming evermore refined. You see that it is not this 'solid' thing that you've always imagined, but extremely malleable to spiritual energy. It is good to have your head in the clouds these days, but keep both feet firmly on the ground. You are still living on Earth.

You're coming out of a very strong love and social period. Over the past two years many of you married or entered into serious love relationships. This year love is not a big issue.

Jupiter spends most of the year in your 8th house of regeneration, and there is success in projects involving personal transformation and re-invention. On October 11 Jupiter will move into Scorpio, your 9th house. This shows foreign travel happening this year – much of it career-related. Students at college level become more successful in their studies. Those applying to colleges should hear good news after this date.

Saturn has been in your 10th house of career for the past two years and will be there for almost all of the year ahead. Career has been demanding under this transit. You've had to discipline yourself here. Bosses could have been demanding and perhaps even unreasonable, and you've had to earn your success the hard way. Much of this testing is almost over with. By the end of the year, the career will be less demanding. There's more on this later.

Pluto has been in your 11th house for many years now, since 2008. A cosmic detox is going on – a long, long process – in your friendships. By the time Pluto is finished with you, you will be in a completely different social circle. More on this later.

Uranus has been in the money house since 2011, and will still be there in the year ahead. This has made the financial life exciting – filled with sudden and unexpected changes – but also highly unstable. You've been learning to deal with financial instability and change these past few years, and this continues. There's never a dull moment in the financial life these days. More details later.

Your areas of greatest focus and interest this year will be the body and image; finance; sex, personal transformation and reinvention, and occult studies (until October 10); religion, metaphysics, philosophy, higher education and foreign travel (from October 11 onwards); career (until December 21); and friends, groups, group and online activities.

Your paths of greatest fulfilment this year are health and work (from April 29 onwards); love and romance (until April 29); sex, personal transformation and reinvention, and occult studies (until October 10); and religion, philosophy, metaphysics, higher education and foreign travel (from October 11 onwards).

Health

(Please note that this is an astrological perspective on health and not a medical one. In days of yore there was no difference, both of these perspectives were identical. But now there could be quite a difference. For a medical perspective, please consult your doctor or health practitioner.)

Health looks good this year, and certainly much improved over last year. Only one long-term planet is in stressful alignment with you – Saturn. All the other long-term planets are either in harmony with you or leaving you alone. Good though health is, it will get even better after October 11, as Jupiter moves into harmonious aspect with you. And it gets better still after December 21 as Saturn leaves his stressful alignment.

Those of you with pre-existing conditions should hear good news. Either the condition resolves itself or it is in abeyance and not bothering you. Perhaps some new pill, supplement or therapy will get the credit, but the reality is that the planetary power has shifted in your favour.

Good though your health is, you can make it even better. Give more attention to the following – the vulnerable areas of your chart (the reflex points are shown overleaf):

- The heart. This is always important for Pisces as the Sun, the ruler of the heart, is your health planet. As our regular readers know, the important thing with the heart is to avoid worry and anxiety, the two emotions that stress the heart. In the grip of these emotions the heart rate shoots up, burning needed energy. Blood pressure increases. The whole circulatory system is under stress. Replace worry with faith. Practise the 'relaxation response' to problems. Relaxation exercises are good.
- The feet. These too are always important for Pisces. Regular foot massage (and foot reflexology) should be part of your regular health regime. When you do this, you not only strengthen the feet,

but the entire body as well (see our chart above). There are inexpensive gadgets out on the market that massage the feet automatically. Some will give foot whirlpool treatments too. These are good investments for you – it can get quite expensive to see a reflexologist regularly. Wear shoes that fit and that don't knock you off balance. Comfort and good fit is more important than fashion. Sometimes you can have both – this would be the best of both worlds.

Your health planet, the Sun, is a fast-moving planet. He will move through different houses of your chart every month. In the course of a year he will move through your entire chart. Thus there are many short-term health trends that depend on where the Sun is and the aspects he receives. These are best dealt with in the monthly reports.

Your health is good, yet we see many changes in your health regime and health attitudes this year. Three eclipses are having an impact here. Two Solar Eclipses (on February 26 and August 21) and one

Important foot reflexology points for the year ahead

Try to massage all of the foot on a regular basis – the top of the foot as well as the bottom – but pay extra attention to the points highlighted on the chart. When you massage, be aware of 'sore spots' as these need special attention. It's also a good idea to massage the ankles and below them.

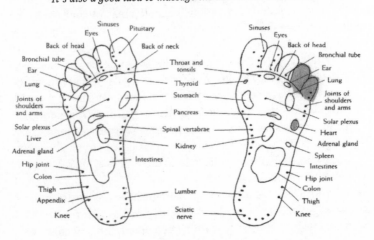

Lunar Eclipse on February 11 (which occurs in your 6th house). These could bring health 'scares' but they probably won't be more than that – health, as we mentioned above, is good. But the eclipses will produce needed changes.

Neptune has been in your own sign for some years now. The physical body is much more sensitive these days. Drugs and alcohol should be avoided as you can overreact to them. Not every pain or twinge you feel in the body denotes illness. In most cases it's not even you. Your sensitized body picks up energy vibrations from others and it feels like it's happening to you. Understanding this will save much heartache and aggravation.

Home and Family

Your 4th house of home and family hasn't been prominent for some years now. Thus it hasn't been a major focus in life. Generally this shows contentment with things as they are. The tendency is to the status quo. The empty 4th house this year (except for short-term planets that move through there) doesn't gainsay a move or home improvements, but neither does it support these things. You have more freedom in this area, but lack interest.

If family problems arise this year, they are probably due to this lack of interest.

Your family planet, Mercury, is a fast-moving planet. Only the Moon moves faster than him. Thus there are many short-term home and family trends that depend on where Mercury is and the aspects he receives. These are best covered in the monthly reports.

Mercury is both your family and love planet. He serves double duty in your chart. This tends to show someone who likes to entertain from home and who likes to socialize with family and family connections. You would see the purpose of marriage as about creating a family – not just something romantic.

A parent or parent figure (the father in a man's chart and the mother in a woman's) has been stressed for the past few years. He or she could have had surgery or near-death kinds of experiences. He or she is prospering this year (and for the past few years) but seems over-controlling – a bit tyrannical. You and this person are not in financial agreement.

(This will improve by the end of the year.) He or she could move after October 11. There are good opportunities for this.

The other parent or parent figure is having marital and social challenges. A divorce or separation could have happened in the past two years. A move was more likely in the past two years than now.

Siblings and sibling figures in your life have wonderful employment opportunities this year and are prospering. There is love in their lives after October 11 and possibly marriage. They are making important repairs in the home (probably a few times) but a move is not likely.

Children or children figures are likely to move this year and the move seems happy. If they are of appropriate age their marriages or current relationship is being tested. After December 21, the testing will be even more severe.

Grandchildren (if you have them) are prospering this year, but moves aren't likely.

If you're planning to do major repairs or renovations, April 21 to June 4 is a good time. If you're redecorating, repainting or otherwise beautifying the home, May 20 to June 21 and July 4–31 are good times.

Finance and Career

As we mentioned, your money house has been strong for many years now. And your 10th house of career has been strong for the past two years. So, this is a strong money and career year. It's true that you're having to work hard and earn your success, but it is happening.

Uranus in your money house shows, as we mentioned, much financial instability. Earnings can soar beyond your imagination, and then sink very low. The highs are unusually high and the lows unusually low – a rollercoaster ride. Your challenge these days, as has been the case for many years, is to smooth out your earnings. Set aside money from the good times to cover the low times.

With Mars as your financial planet you tend to be a risk-taker in finance. There's a reason for this. You came here to develop financial courage – fearlessness. Thus, even if the risks don't pan out (and often they don't), if you conquered your fears, you've won. But these days you seem much more of a risk-taker than normal. Perhaps you're too quick to jump into a purchase or investment. There is a need to slow down a bit, sleep on things, and calculate the ramifications of a purchase or investment. You seem to especially favour new, high-tech start-ups.

Technology in general attracts you. Even if you're not yet an investor, your high-tech expertise is important in whatever you're doing. You're spending on this too. (But do more research before you splash out.)

The finances are OK for most of the year. But when Jupiter moves into Scorpio on October 11 and starts to make nice aspects to you, there will be much improvement.

Mars is a relatively fast-moving planet. He will move to a different house of your Horoscope every 45 days or so, thus there are many short-term financial trends during the year that depend on where Mars is at any given time and the aspects he is receiving. These are best covered in the monthly reports.

Career, as we mentioned, has been difficult. Saturn in your 10th house shows much discipline and hard work involved. You certainly can't coast. You have to give your best every day – and probably a bit extra. If you take up the challenge, you will see much success happening, and your success will be more enduring. Saturn is the ruler of your 11th house of friends and technology. Thus technology is not only involved in finance but in the career as well. You have successful friends who are supportive of your career goals.

Your career planet Jupiter spends most of the year in Libra. This also shows a social dimension to the career. Social contacts and your personal 'likeability' are playing a huge role in the career. It's good to have the right social contacts, but with Saturn in your 10th house it won't be enough. You have to perform. Libra is your 8th house of regeneration. This indicates that a 'detox' happening in your career, in your attitudes, your approach and your plans. Impurities in these things have to be got rid of. There are probably all kinds of dramas – life and death issues – in your company, industry and profession. This could be happening with bosses and authority figures too.

Jupiter's move into Scorpio on October 11 is not just good for your finances. It will bring career elevation and happy opportunities to you, either within your present company or situation or with new ones. Your willingness to travel is an important factor.

The past few years (and most of the year ahead too) have been about 'paying your dues' for the success that you crave. When Saturn leaves your 10th house on December 21, the dues will have been paid. 2018 will be a very strong and successful career year – even more than this year.

Love and Social Life

As we mentioned earlier, you're coming to the end of two years of wonderful social and romantic aspects. Love is still happy, but doesn't seem like a major focus this year. This would indicate contentment with the status quo. There's no compelling need to make dramatic changes, one way or another (though you're free to do so). Singles will most likely remain single, and those who are married will most likely remain married.

The year ahead is sexually more active than usual. Regardless of your age or stage in life the libido is stronger than usual. Though sex and love are two different things, it does show that singles are dating more and married couples are having more sex.

We saw a lot of business- and career-related socializing last year, and we see it again in the year ahead. The ruler of your 11th house of friends is right on the Mid-heaven. Your career planet Jupiter is in social Libra for most of the year.

Your love planet Mercury is, as we have mentioned, a very fast-moving planet. In any given year he will move through all the sectors of your Horoscope; in a given month he might move through two (and sometimes three) houses. Thus, you're someone who is changeable in love. Your needs change constantly. You show love in different ways. Your partner or spouse could call you fickle, but you're just following Mercury. Mercury is not only fast-moving but can be erratic. Where most of the planets move steadily, with little variation, Mercury will sometimes move extremely fast, sometimes rather slowly, sometimes he stands still and sometimes moves backwards (four times this year). This is how you are in love. (And you tend to attract people who are like this.) Anyone romantically involved with a Pisces needs to understand this. These short-term trends are best covered in the monthly reports.

Mercury is both your love planet and your family planet. This shows that you gravitate to intellectual kinds of people. You're attracted by the mind and communication skills. You gravitate to people who are easy to talk to. But mind is only one part of the equation. You like emotional intimacy as much as intellectual intimacy (the 4th house rules the moods and emotions). You like sharing ideas, but you also like sharing feelings.

The North Node of the Moon (an abstract point, although Hindu astrologers consider it a planet) will be in your 7th house of love until April 29. This is another indicator of happiness in love. Since the North Node (Rahu, according to the Hindus) shows 'excess', your problem might be too much love – not a bad problem to have. Sometimes this 'excess' shows 'obsessive' love. Obsessive love relationships tend not to end too well, but enjoy it while it lasts.

Like last year, Mercury will retrograde four times this year (usually this happens only three times). During these periods love seems to go backwards. It is a time for both parties to take stock of things and see where improvements can be made. It's not a good idea to make important love decisions then – though you will be tempted. Things are not as they seem – neither as bad nor as good. Take the time to gain mental clarity. This year Mercury is retrograde from January 1-8, April 9 to May 3, August 11 to September 5 and December 3-23.

Self-Improvement

Neptune, the ruler of your Horoscope, has been in your own sign since 2012, as we have mentioned. Here, in his own sign and house, he is ultra-powerful. So you are under intense spiritual energies these days. Most importantly there is spiritual revelation about the body. The body is not some solid, intractable 'lump'. It is a dynamic thing, easily moulded and shaped, if we know the rules for it. You are in a cycle now – and this will continue for many more years – where you can (if you choose and do the necessary spiritual work) completely transform your body. You are discovering – or soon will – the spiritual laws behind it. The rest is just application.

Theoretically the body can be transformed regardless of a person's age or state of health. But, practically speaking, it might be harder for an older person or someone with a terminal condition to do it as there are stronger karmic momentums (habits, appetites, negative attitudes) to be overcome. But still great improvements can be made, if one takes a 'gradualist' kind of approach to it.

The spiritual power you invoke can't wait to come in and clean things up and restore order. But you must allow it to have its own way in your body. There will be a lot of 'unlearning' of human thought and opinion that will happen.

The body, you will discover, has no will of its own. It is totally, 100 per cent under the control of the mind. (I realize this is controversial, but this is the spiritual teaching.) The mind, the way it was designed, was supposed to be controlled by the Divine. If this were the case, sickness, age and imperfection would be impossible. Unfortunately, this is not the case. Humans have free will, and the abuse of this has created the seeds of pathology. New free will can, with time, upend the old free will, and the mind gradually comes into ever-greater alignment with Spirit. The physical body will just naturally reflect this. There will be intuitive guidance happening. Eat this. Don't eat that. You don't need that second helping of potatoes. Eat half the dessert. And much much more.

If exercise is needed (and often this is the case) you will be guided to the right ones. If certain therapies or therapists are needed they will come to you normally and naturally. This is not a 'rule book' approach to reshaping the body, but an intuitive one. One let's go of all human thinking and allows the 'spirit of health and beauty' to teach us – to have its way in the body.

Jupiter's presence in your 8th house of personal transformation for most of the year shows success in these endeavours – and happiness.

Month-by-month Forecasts

January

Best Days Overall: 2, 3, 11, 12, 20, 21, 30, 31
Most Stressful Days Overall: 9, 10, 15, 16, 22, 23, 24
Best Days for Love: 2, 6, 12, 15, 16, 20, 21, 25, 26, 31
Best Days for Money: 1, 3, 4, 5, 6, 10, 11, 12, 18, 19, 20, 21, 28, 29
Best Days for Career: 1, 10, 18, 19, 22, 23, 24, 28, 29

It's nice to have friends and happy social relationships, but this month, with so many planets in the Eastern half of your chart, it's more about you and your self-interest. You have much personal power and independence now (next month even more). You have the power and the wherewithal to make the changes necessary for your happiness. You don't have to consult anyone or get anyone's approval. You can act independently. So, if there are conditions that irk you, change them, make them more harmonious. The world will conform to you now, rather than vice versa.

Health is excellent this month. From the 13th onwards there is only one planet in stressful alignment with you (and this has been the case for the past two years). You can enhance your already good health through back and knee massage until the 19th and through calf and ankle massage afterwards. If you're into exercise, give more support to the knees until the 19th, and to the ankles afterwards.

The month ahead is very prosperous. Mars, your financial planet, is in your own sign until the 28th. This brings all kinds of happy financial opportunities to you – windfalls as well. It's as if money is pursuing you rather than vice versa. The money people in your life are firmly on your side and eager to help. You spend on yourself and dress expensively; there's a tendency to flaunt your prosperity and good fortune. The personal appearance seems an important factor in earning. The financial intuition – perhaps the most important thing in finance – is excellent this month.

While Mars in your sign brings prosperity and energy, there is a downside here too. It can make you impatient; there's a tendency to rush and to get things done in a hurry. Sometimes people speed on the road without realizing it. This hastiness can lead to accident or injury. So, as the ancients said, 'make haste slowly'. Mars in your sign can also make a person more combative than usual. Little slights that you would normally ignore in other circumstances can elicit an overreaction. Watch the temper.

Venus moves into your sign on the 3rd – a happy transit. It brings beauty to the image and a sense of style. You walk and move with more grace. In a woman's chart it enhances her personal beauty (and sex appeal). In a man's chart it brings younger women into the life.

Love is not such a big issue this month. Your 7th house is empty (only the Moon moves through there on the 15th and 16th). Mercury, your love planet, is retrograde until the 5th and moves slowly afterwards. You're attracting the opposite sex, but a relationship is another story.

February

Best Days Overall: 7, 8, 16, 17, 18, 26, 27
Most Stressful Days Overall: 5, 6, 12, 13, 19, 20
Best Days for Love: 3, 4, 9, 10, 12, 13, 14, 15, 19, 20, 25, 26, 28
Best Days for Money: 1, 2, 5, 6, 9, 10, 14, 15, 19, 20, 24, 25, 28
Best Days for Career: 5, 6, 14, 15, 19, 20, 24, 25

The planetary power enters its maximum Eastern position this month on the 18th. Review our discussion of this last month. It seems that you are making the changes that need to be made – a Solar Eclipse on the 26th occurs in your sign and very near the ruler of your Horoscope, Neptune. Health is excellent, but reduce your schedule that period.

We have two eclipses this month and so there will never be a dull moment. The eclipses bring about the changes needed to manifest a higher cosmic plan.

The Lunar Eclipse of the 11th occurs in your 6th house of health and work. Thus job changes – or changes in the conditions of work – are happening. The job changes can happen within your present company or with another one. There will be dramatic changes – important changes – in your health regime too. Sometimes this kind of eclipse brings a health scare, but your health is good Pisces, and it is not likely to be more than that.

If you employ others there can be employee turnover now. There are dramas in the lives of employees and those who are involved in your health. Every Lunar Eclipse impacts on children and children figures in your life. So they should stay out of harm's way for a few days before and after the eclipse. Children and children figures are redefining themselves now, changing how they think of themselves and how they want others to see them. This is a healthy thing and they get to do this twice a year.

The Solar Eclipse of the 26th also impacts on health and work – you get a double dose this month. The Sun, the eclipsed planet, is your health and work planet. So this eclipse basically repeats the phenomena of the Lunar Eclipse. Since it occurs in your own sign it shows that you too are redefining yourself – changing how you see yourself and how you want others to see you. As we mentioned, this is a healthy exercise, but it is best when done voluntarily. Here it seems forced.

The love life is much improved this month. Your love planet, Mercury, is moving forward and very quickly. Singles are dating more and covering a lot of territory. Mercury's speedy motion shows social confidence. But it also shows a kind of 'fickleness' in love. The love needs change very rapidly – a bewilderment to you and those you're involved with. On the 25th Mercury will enter your own sign and you begin a yearly love and social peak (you will have another one from August 23 to September 22). Love pursues you now and you won't escape it.

March

Best Days Overall: 6, 7, 16, 17, 25, 26
Most Stressful Days Overall: 4, 5, 11, 12, 18, 19
Best Days for Love: 1, 7, 8, 9, 11, 12, 18, 19, 27, 28, 29
Best Days for Money: 1, 5, 6, 10, 13, 14, 20, 21, 23, 24, 28, 30
Best Days for Career: 5, 6, 13, 14, 18, 19, 23, 24

When the Sun entered your sign on February 18 you began one of your yearly personal pleasure peaks. This continues until the 20th of this month and brings the physical pleasures to you – good food, good wine, nice clothing and accessories. The body is being pampered and it feels good. The personal appearance shines with the light of the Sun. You have star quality now. Regardless of your age or stage in life, the light of the Sun creates beauty and radiance (on an energetic level).

The Sun's entry into your sign last month also brought (and is still bringing) happy job opportunities for job seekers. The beauty of this is that there's nothing much you need to do. They seek you out. You can either accept or reject them, but the offers come.

The love planet, Mercury, is still in your sign until the 13th. Love is still very happy and there's not much you need to do to have it. It's just there. If you're in a relationship the beloved dotes on you and is very devoted. He or she puts your interest ahead of his or her own. Love is still very much on your terms. You don't need to 'people please', just to be yourself.

On the 20th the Sun enters the money house and you begin a yearly financial peak. The financial intuition is still very powerful (this has been the case for many years now). Money comes from your work – the normal way – and also through social contacts and family. A partnership or joint venture could offer itself this month.

In your chart Venus is the planet of communication. She rules your 3rd house. She makes one of her rare retrogrades on the 4th so be more careful in your communications. Make sure emails and letters are addressed properly. Make sure you say what you mean and that the other person understands what you mean. Also, don't be afraid to ask questions and resolve your doubts when speaking. This will save a lot of heartache down the road. This is not a time to buy a car or new communication equipment. Wait until April 15, when Venus starts to move forward again, before you do. In the meantime you can do your research.

Venus's retrograde seems to have financial implications too. Your financial planet, Mars, moves into your house of communication on the 10th. Deals or sales can be delayed or seem to go backwards. Give special care to financial communication. Handle all the details perfectly. Venus's retrograde won't stop your prosperity but it will slow things down a bit.

Health is good this month. You can enhance it further through foot massage (always important for you) until the 20th, and through head, face and scalp massage afterwards. Exercise is beneficial after the 20th too.

April

Best Days Overall: 3, 4, 12, 13, 22, 23, 30
Most Stressful Days Overall: 1, 7, 8, 14, 15, 16, 28, 29
Best Days for Love: 4, 7, 8, 12, 13, 18, 23, 24, 25
Best Days for Money: 1, 7, 8, 10, 11, 18, 19, 20, 21, 24, 25, 28, 29
Best Days for Career: 1, 10, 11, 14, 15, 16, 19, 20, 21, 28, 29

Venus retrogrades back into your own sign on the 2nd and spends most of the month – until the 28th – there. This is basically a happy transit. She enhances the physical appearance and gives grace and charm to your demeanour – the way you move and walk. This is another good period (especially from the 15th to the 28th) to buy clothing or personal accessories. Good to do things that enhance the image.

You're still in a yearly financial peak until the 19th. So prosperity is happening. All those obligations will be handled; although there could be delays (Venus is retrograde until the 15th) everything will be handled.

On the 19th the Sun enters your 3rd house of communication and intellectual interests. Venus, your communication planet, will also be moving forward now, so this is an excellent period for students below college level. They are focused on their studies and this should bring success. It will be a good period for writers, teachers, journalists, sales and marketing people – they are at the top of their game.

Your financial planet moves into your 4th house on the 21st. This indicates that you are spending more on the home and family (perhaps you're doing renovations or major repairs) but it also shows you're earning from this area. Family support should be good. Family connections become important financially.

Mars in your 4th house shows that it's a good time to review your financial past. Good to re-examine old financial traumas (they will probably arise anyway) and look at them from your present state. This will bring healing. Often financial problems stem from old childhood experiences. Good to clear and resolve these things now.

Love is not a big issue this month. Your 7th house is basically empty – only the Moon moves through there on the 7th and 8th. Your love planet Mercury goes retrograde on the 9th. So although singles will certainly date and meet people, it is not a great period for serious kinds of relationships.

The planetary power has been mostly in the bottom half of your chart since February 25, and very soon we will be approaching its maximum point. Career is still important, but home, family and the emotional well-being are more important right now. You're preparing the psychological ground for your next career push in a few months.

These preparation periods are just as important as the overt actions you will take. Health is still good.

May

> Best Days Overall: 1, 9, 10, 19, 20, 27, 28
> Most Stressful Days Overall: 4, 5, 12, 13, 25, 26
> Best Days for Love: 2, 3, 4, 5, 12, 13, 16, 21, 22, 23, 24
> Best Days for Money: 7, 8, 17, 18, 21, 22, 25, 26
> Best Days for Career: 7, 8, 12, 13, 17, 18, 25, 26

This month the planetary power will be at the lowest level of your chart. The planetary power is 'most distant' from the career (the 10th house). So, you should be focused on getting the home and domestic situation in order. Do your best to make it stable. This will enable future career success to happen.

Health needs more attention from the 20th onwards. Three (and on the 25th four) planets are in stressful alignment with you. This shouldn't cause any serious problem, but could make you vulnerable to things if you get over-tired. Until the 20th your health can be enhanced through neck and throat massage; after the 20th through arm and shoulder massage. Fresh air is a healing tonic after the 20th. Get out in the fresh air and just breathe deeply. Emotional wellness is extremely important after the 20th. It's not just a career issue but an actual health issue. Depression should be avoided like the plague. It is good to work from home if you can arrange this – some people find it less stressful than going to the office.

Your love planet, Mercury, starts moving forward on the 3rd. Until the 16th love opportunities happen as you pursue your normal financial goals. Wealth is a romantic turn-on. You show love through giving material gifts – in tangible ways – and this is how you feel loved. This attitude prevails after the 16th too, as Mercury moves into your 3rd house. Wealth and material gifts are still important but you also want good communication and a good exchange of ideas. Love is good communication. There are love opportunities at lectures, seminars or school functions. Love opportunities can be found in your neighbourhood, and most likely there will be more socializing with neighbours.

Though your financial peak is technically over with, this is still a strong financial month. Your money house is very strong. Mercury is there until the 16th and Venus and Uranus are there all month. Venus in the money house shows earnings from sales, marketing, PR and advertising. There is a need to use the media properly and to let people know about your product or service. Mars is still in your 4th house of home and family, which indicates (like last month) good family support. Mars will make beautiful aspects to Jupiter from the 10th to the 14th. This brings a nice payday. There is luck in speculations. There can be pay rises at work. A parent or parent figure is unusually generous. You have the financial favour of the authority figures in your life that period.

June

Best Days Overall: 5, 6, 7, 15, 16, 24, 25
Most Stressful Days Overall: 1, 2, 8, 9, 22, 23, 28, 29
Best Days for Love: 1, 2, 10, 11, 13, 14, 20, 21, 24, 28, 29
Best Days for Money: 3, 4, 5, 13, 14, 15, 16, 18, 19, 22, 23, 24, 25, 30
Best Days for Career: 3, 4, 8, 9, 13, 14, 22, 23, 30

Your 4th house of home and family is still very strong this month. So continue to focus on home life. With your health planet the Sun in your 4th house until the 21st, emotional wellness is a health issue. Good health these days *means* good emotional health. If there are health problems (and health is more delicate until the 21st) check your family relationships and restore harmony as quickly as possible.

A strong 4th house is excellent for those of you undergoing psychological therapy. There will be much progress and insights occurring this month. But even if you're not involved in a formal kind of therapy, psychological therapy will happen through nature. Old memories (love, family and financial ones) are going to arise spontaneously. Sometimes through dreams, sometimes when you're awake. Suddenly, for no apparent reason, an old event comes to mind – and often with the same emotions as when the event occurred. It is good to just look at these things impersonally. If you can't be impersonal

– if they overwhelm you – it might be good to discuss it with a friend or counsellor. In my book *Technique for Meditation* we give methods for dealing with these things. The important thing is to stay in the present as you observe and analyse. The emotion will soon dissipate and you'll feel free.

On the 21st the Sun enters your 5th house of fun and creativity and you begin another of your yearly personal pleasure peaks. All kinds of opportunities for 'fun' activities will come to you. You should take them. Very often the solution to a problem happens when we let go of it and do something enjoyable. When we come back, the solution presents itself.

Your financial planet in the 5th house from the 4th onwards shows that you will have the wherewithal to enjoy yourself. You spend on fun things. You enjoy the wealth that you have. You earn money or find financial opportunity as you're having fun – perhaps at a resort, or party or the sports field. Speculations are more favourable this month too – though you should only speculate under intuition – never blindly. Pisceans are very creative people. Thus, this aspect shows that your personal creativity is more marketable now. Children or children figures in your life seem financially supportive: sometimes this is in a physical way, sometimes they have good financial ideas and sometimes they inspire a person to earn more.

Health improves dramatically after the 21st. Good emotional health is still important, but it is also important to eat right. Abdominal massage is good.

July

Best Days Overall: 3, 4, 13, 14, 21, 22, 30, 31
Most Stressful Days Overall: 5, 6, 19, 20, 25, 26
Best Days for Love: 4, 10, 16, 19, 20, 25, 26, 28, 29
Best Days for Money: 1, 3, 4, 10, 11, 13, 14, 15, 16, 19, 20, 23, 28, 29, 30, 31
Best Days for Career: 1, 5, 6, 10, 11, 19, 20, 28, 29

Your cosmic holiday continues until the 22nd. Fun and joyful creativity are the order of the day. The wherewithal for this is there. Mars, your financial planet, is still in your 5th house until the 20th. Review our discussion of this last month.

Your financial planet in the sign of Cancer enhances the financial intuition, but also makes you more moody about financial matters. In a good mood you're richer than Bill Gates; in a bad mood you feel like a pauper. You tend to spend based on mood as well. If you're making important financial decisions or major purchases, sleep on things first. Make sure you're in a state of peace and harmony. Then the decision or purchase will tend to be good.

Your 6th house of health and work becomes strong after the 22nd. This is a wonderful financial period for the children or children figures in your life. They earn more and acquire big ticket items. It is also a wonderful transit for job seekers or those who hire others. There are many opportunities. Health is basically good, but you're focused here. You can be overly focused if you're not careful – there is a tendency to magnify little things into big things. (For example, is this pimple on my face cancer? Is this tightness in the chest a heart attack?) Many of these little things arise because of the Sun's transits and not because of any serious pathology. The best way to use this health focus is to set up constructive health regimes and diets. It is a good idea to get into a healthier kind of lifestyle now and to stick to it.

Your financial planet moves into your 6th house on the 20th. This shows earnings from work, from the job, from productive service to others. You might still be speculating this period – Mars will be in Leo – but your work will produce the good luck. You're spending more on health and health gadgetry too. You can also earn from the health field – opportunities will come.

The love planet Mercury moves very quickly this month – through three signs and houses of your chart. This increases your fickleness in love. The love needs and love attitudes change quickly. Someone who satisfied you early in the month might not satisfy you later on, as your needs have changed. A place that was conducive to love early in the month is not so conducive later on. On the other hand, it shows more dating and more social activity. There is greater social confidence.

Until the 6th love happens in 'fun' places – at resorts, the movies, the theatre or park. From the 6th to the 16th, love happens at the workplace or with people you work with. Health professionals are attractive. After the 16th love happens in the usual places – at parties, gatherings and social events.

August

Best Days Overall: 9, 10, 18, 26, 27
Most Stressful Days Overall: 1, 2, 3, 16, 22, 23, 29, 30
Best Days for Love: 4, 5, 9, 10, 13, 14, 18, 19, 22, 23, 28, 29, 31
Best Days for Money: 1, 2, 6, 7, 11, 12, 16, 20, 21, 24, 25, 29, 30
Best Days for Career: 1, 2, 3, 6, 7, 16, 24, 25, 29, 30

Retrograde activity increases this month. Events in the world slow down. Perhaps there is a feeling of malaise or a feeling of being directionless. In a way this is good. With so many planets in the Western, social half of your chart, it isn't necessary for you to be too self-directed. Go with the flow as they say. Let others have their way, so long as it isn't destructive. Others should come before you now, but you are finding that difficult. Your sense of your self – your self-interest – still seems very strong. But cultivate the social skills as much as possible.

The world is slowing down but things will not be boring. Two eclipses this month will see to that.

The Lunar Eclipse of the 7th occurs in your 12th house of spirituality Thus there are important changes happening here. Your attitudes change. Your spiritual practice will change. People often change teachers or teachings. Often this happens because of inner revelation – and this is a good thing. There are upheavals and shakeups in spiritual or charitable organizations you're involved with. There are life-changing dramas in the lives of gurus and guru figures. Friends have financial dramas and need to make changes. There are dramas in the lives of uncles and aunts (or those who play this role in your life). Your financial planet Mars is affected by this eclipse. So you are forced to make important financial changes – corrections in your strategy, thinking and planning. Every Lunar Eclipse affect your children or the children figures in your life and this one is no different. They should definitely reduce their schedules and stay out of harm's way during this period. (This eclipse occurs in their 8th house and can bring encounters with death – though not actual physical death.)

The Solar Eclipse of the 21st occurs on the cusp (border) of the 6th and 7th houses. Thus the affairs of both these houses are affected here. Job changes can happen – either within the same company or a different one. The conditions of work change. If you employ others there can be more employee turnover now. Since the eclipse planet, the Sun, is your health planet, there can be health scares. But your health is basically good, so it is not likely to be anything more than just scares. The health regime will change dramatically too. There are financial dramas in the lives of children and children figures and they will be forced to make important, dramatic changes (and they will be good). Since your 7th house is affected, love will get tested. Be more patient with the beloved at this time. Good relationships survive these things, but the flawed ones are in danger. Those of you born early in the sign of Pisces – from February 18 to February 21 – will feel this most strongly. If this applies to you, reduce your schedule and take it easy this period.

September

Best Days Overall: 5, 6, 14, 15, 23, 24
Most Stressful Days Overall: 12, 13, 18, 19, 25, 26
Best Days for Love: 7, 8, 9, 16, 17, 18, 19, 28, 29
Best Days for Money: 3, 4, 7, 8, 9, 10, 12, 13, 18, 19, 20, 21, 28, 29, 30
Best Days for Career: 3, 4, 12, 13, 20, 21, 25, 26, 30

Love and the social life are the main headlines in the month ahead. The Western, social sector of your chart is dominant and your 7th house of love is ultra-powerful. The month ahead is about other people, their needs and getting on with them. If there is harmony in your relationships, there will be money, health, work and emotional harmony. Your thought process – the mental faculties – will also be much improved. Problems here will negatively impact all these other areas.

The social life is very active this month. Opportunities for love are there for singles. They happen at the usual places – at parties, social gatherings, weddings, etc. Marriage may or may not happen, but you're meeting people whom you would consider marrying – people who are marriage material.

The only problem with love is the usual one – self-will. You and the beloved are distant from each other – especially from the 10th onwards. This distance is not necessarily physical. Generally it is psychological. Two people can be watching the same sunset and be universes apart psychologically. You want your way, the beloved wants his or her way. You see things from totally opposite perspectives. It will be hard work to bridge your differences – but somewhere in the middle is the place where it can happen. If you can bridge your differences, love will be happy. Romance will bloom. It is said that opposites attract, but they can also wound each other.

Health needs more attention this month, with five (and at times six) planets in stressful alignment with you. So, as always, make sure to get enough rest. Don't push yourself when you're tired. Rest and recuperate, and then go back to your activity. With more energy you'll be less grumpy with others and the love life should go better. Enhance the health by giving more attention to the small intestine (abdominal massage is good for this) until the 22nd. After the 22nd give more attention to the kidneys and hips. Hip and buttock massage will be beneficial. Detox regimes are effective after the22nd too.

If health problems arise this month, discords in the love life are probably the cause. Restore harmony here as quickly as you can.

Mars will be in your 7th house of love from the 5th onwards. Thus financial opportunities come through friends and social contacts. You're spending more on the social life too, but it seems a good investment. Who you know at this time is more important financially than how much you have.

October

Best Days Overall: 3, 4, 11, 12, 20, 21, 30, 31
Most Stressful Days Overall: 9, 10, 15, 16, 22, 23, 24
Best Days for Love: 1, 7, 8, 9, 10, 15, 16, 17, 18, 20, 27, 28, 30, 31
Best Days for Money: 1, 5, 6, 7, 8, 10, 11, 15, 16, 20, 27, 30
Best Days for Career: 1, 10, 11, 20, 22, 23, 24, 30

Jupiter has been in your 8th house of regeneration all year, and this house is extremely strong this month, thanks to the short-term planets – 60 per cent of the planets are either there or moving through there this month. So the themes of the 8th house are ultra-important.

In the 8th house we de-clutter our lives. This takes place on many levels – physical, emotional and mental – and also in your physical conditions and circumstances. Often we think we can attain our goals by 'getting, getting, getting'. In the 8th house we learn that goals are also achieved by 'cutting, eliminating and getting rid' of things. Your ability to do this helped the career this year. When a company is in trouble, the good executives start to cut – they cut useless stores or outlets, they cut posts that aren't necessary, they cut debt and expenses, they downsize. This is usually not pleasant, but there is cosmic logic to it. In order to grow, the useless must be eliminated. Death always precedes resurrection.

So you've been doing this in your career, and this month it is good to do it in your personal life too. Go through the home (it's easier if you do room by room and cupboard by cupboard). Put the things you find in a pile and go through each thing. Ask yourself, 'Is this something I use?' If the answer is no, get rid of it. If the answer is yes, keep it. You should do this in your finances too. 'Do I need three credit cards? Do I need those extra bank and savings accounts? Perhaps I can consolidate things.' There is great magic in this. The de-cluttering makes room for the new and better that wants to come in. You'll feel lighter and better after you've done this.

Jupiter makes a major move into your 9th house on the 11th. Your past experience in de-cluttering will be helpful in the year ahead too. (Jupiter will be in Scorpio, the sign that rules elimination.) But now you will see the expansiveness behind this. You prune a tree and it starts growing faster and better. Jupiter in your 9th house is a positive transit for the career. It shows expansion in the career. It is a very nice aspect for college students (and those bound for college) too. There is success in the coming year. There will be career-related travel happening now.

The career is improving this month, and will improve further in December and in 2018.

Your financial planet is still in your 7th house until the 22nd. So your social harmony and social contacts are still very important financially. When Mars moves into your 8th house on that date, it will be good to pay off, consolidate or restructure your debt. It is a good aspect for re-financing too. Tax efficiency is an important factor in the financial planning, and those of appropriate age should do estate planning.

November

Best Days Overall: 7, 8, 16, 17, 26, 27
Most Stressful Days Overall: 5, 6, 12, 13, 19, 20
Best Days for Love: 6, 7, 9, 12, 13, 16, 17, 19, 20, 26, 27, 29, 30
Best Days for Money: 1, 2, 5, 6, 7, 8, 14, 15, 16, 17, 24, 25, 26, 27, 29, 30
Best Days for Career: 7, 8, 16, 17, 19, 20, 26, 27

A happy and successful month ahead Pisces, enjoy.

Your 9th house is very strong this month, especially until the 22nd. So there is more travel happening – certainly the opportunities are there. College students are doing well in their studies, and applicants to college are hearing good news. If you are involved in legal issues there is good news on that front too.

When the 9th house is strong, interest in religion, theology and philosophy is strong. You have a natural interest in these things anyway, but now more so than usual. Your idea of fun these days is a juicy theological discussion or scripture study. In the philosophy of astrology, man's interest in religion is 'hard wired' in the psyche. Human attempts to abolish it are futile. It's like trying to abolish sex. People will follow it no matter how many laws are passed. This has been shown throughout the ages. Even people who profess to be atheists or non-religious are following (usually unconsciously) a certain religious path. This interest, intensified this month, generally brings religious and philosophical insights. The horizons are widened by these interests. More possibilities open to you.

Good health this month means more than just no physical symptoms; it means good philosophical health – the health of the upper mental body. It is a good month to examine your philosophical beliefs about health. It has been said that what we think is a health problem is really a theological problem – and this is certainly true for you this month. All the different healing modalities that we see – and there are hordes of them – are based on a certain philosophy of health and a certain metaphysical understanding of the body.

Health is good until the 22nd but you can enhance it further through detox regimes, practising safe sex and sexual moderation, and paying more attention to the colon and bladder.

On the 22nd the Sun moves into your 10th house of career and you begin a yearly career peak. A good work ethic brings success. Health becomes more delicate after the 22nd – probably due to overwork. Make sure you get enough rest.

Jupiter makes beautiful aspect to Neptune all month, but especially on the 29th and 30th. This brings money and career success (and opportunity). You have the favour of bosses and authority figures.

December

Best Days Overall: 5, 6, 14, 15, 24, 25
Most Stressful Days Overall: 3, 4, 9, 10, 16, 17, 30, 31
Best Days for Love: 7, 8, 9, 10, 16, 17, 26, 27, 28
Best Days for Money: 3, 5, 6, 14, 15, 24, 25, 26, 27
Best Days for Career: 5, 6, 14, 15, 16, 17, 24, 25

The career is still going strong and is still the main headline of the month. You're still in the midst of a yearly career peak. Jupiter is still making nice aspects to Neptune (from the 1st to the 5th), the ruler of your Horoscope. This brings money and career success. Like last month it indicates harmony with bosses and authority figures.

Perhaps the main headline in the career is not what's moving into your 10th house (the Sun and Venus) but what's leaving it. Saturn moves out of your career house on the 21st, and things will now get a lot easier career-wise. An over-controlling or over-exacting boss leaves the picture. You've earned your success by merit these past few years. You've proved your mettle. Now the career will become less intense. Later next year, Jupiter will move into your 10th house and success will skyrocket. And, because you have had to deal with so much resistance these past few years, you'll be strong enough to handle the success.

One of the main things you will feel when Saturn leaves your 10th house is an increase in your overall energy. Health is much improved after the 21st and for the next few years, although it will still need watching until the 21st. As always, make sure to get enough rest. The career is demanding and you're working hard, but you can maximize energy by delegating more, by dropping trivia from your life, and by scheduling in more 'down time'.

Your financial planet moves into your 9th house on the 9th and stays there for the rest of the month. This shows increased earnings. You've probably done some financial de-cluttering over the past few months. It is best when this is done consciously, but often the cosmos arranges this 'de-cluttering'. It happens seemingly by itself. A credit-card company cancels your account because of non-use. The same thing happens with a savings account. Perhaps a company in your portfolio goes under – it seems like a loss but, truth is, it needed to be gone anyway. The things you think you lost weren't needed in the first place. There are many, many stories to tell about this but space doesn't permit.

The financial planet in the 9th house shows good fortune in finances. In addition, Mars will make very nice aspects to Neptune from the 9th onwards. This also shows prosperity. Earnings can come from foreign countries or companies. Foreigners in general are important in the financial life. There is more business-related travel. Your financial judgement will be good and your intuition is super.

Love is complicated this month. Mercury, your love planet, is retrograde from the 3rd to the 23rd. Most of your socializing seems career-related.